KT-414-466
RKL
1905

EVERYMAN'S LIBRARY
EDITED BY ERNEST RHYS

HISTORY

TACITUS: THE HISTORY GERMANIA & AGRICOLA

EDITED BY E. H. BLAKENEY, M.A.

VOLUME II

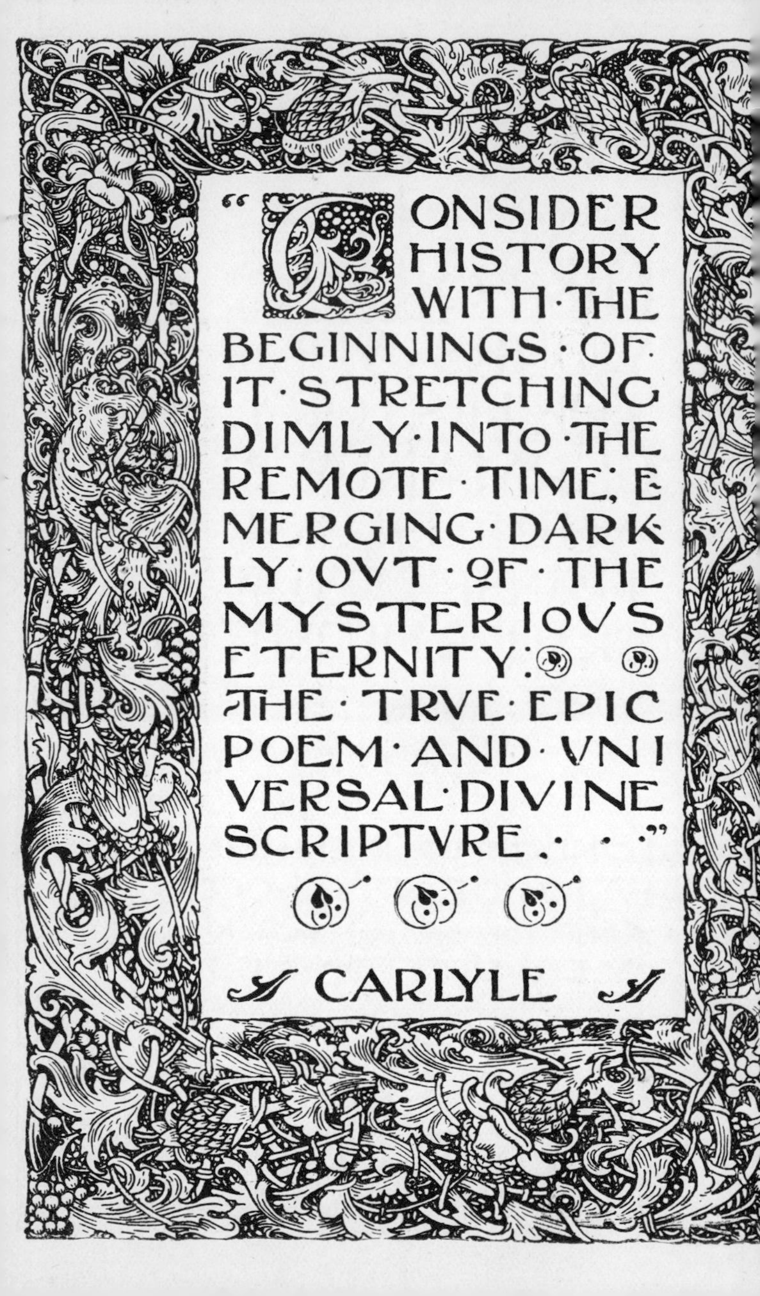
"CONSIDER HISTORY WITH·THE BEGINNINGS·OF IT·STRETCHING DIMLY·INTO·THE REMOTE·TIME; EMERGING·DARKLY·OUT·OF·THE MYSTERIOUS ETERNITY:
THE·TRUE·EPIC POEM·AND·UNIVERSAL·DIVINE SCRIPTURE . . ."
CARLYLE

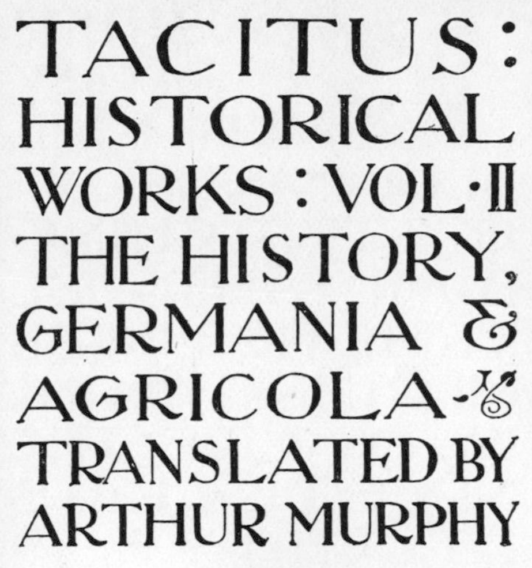

TACITUS: HISTORICAL WORKS: VOL·II THE HISTORY, GERMANIA & AGRICOLA

TRANSLATED BY ARTHUR MURPHY

LONDON: PUBLISHED by J·M·DENT·&·CO
AND IN NEW YORK BY E·P·DUTTON & CO

CONTENTS

THE HISTORY OF TACITUS

THE HISTORY OF TACITUS

BOOK I

CONTENTS

I. *Preface to the History.*—II. *Summary view of the whole work—State of the city, the armies, and the provinces.*—VI. *Galba's court, and the reigning vices.*—VIII. *Condition of Spain, Gaul, the Upper and Lower Germany, Syria, Egypt, and Africa.—The war against the Jews conducted by Vespasian.*—XII. *Revolt of the legions in Upper Germany—Galba consults about the choice of a successor—Different opinions among his ministers, Vinius, Laco, and Icelus, one of his freedmen. Otho has hopes of the nomination.*—XIV. *Choice of Piso for the succession.*—XV. *Galba's speech upon the occasion—He declares his adoption of Piso in the camp, and in the senate—Ill-timed severity of Galba—An embassy to the German legions.*—XXI. *Otho plans a revolution—He corrupts the prætorian guards—Two common soldiers undertake to dispose of the sovereignty—Otho proclaimed emperor.*—XXIX. *Galba, in the meantime, employed in a sacrifice in the capitol—Piso's speech to the soldiers.*—XXXVII. *Otho harangues the prætorians in the camp.*—XL. *The prætorians rush into the city—Galba murdered.*—XLII. *Death of Titus Vinius—The constancy of a centurion—Piso put to death—Otho received with adulation by the senate and the people.*—XLVI. *All things directed by the soldiers—Numbers executed—Marius Celsus saved by the artifice of Otho.*—XLVIII. *Characters of Piso and Titus Vinius.*—XLIX. *Character of Galba.*—L. *Vitellius, before Galba's death, aims at the sovereignty.*—LI. *Origin of the revolt among the German legions—Vitellius saluted emperor—He sends two armies to invade Italy, one under Fabius Valens, and the other under Cæcina—Vitellius follows with a third army—His excessive luxury and stupidity—The cruelty and rapine of Valens and Cæcina.*—LXIII. *The Gauls, partly through fear and partly from inclination, swear fidelity to Vitellius.*—LXIV. *Valens on his march hears of the death of Galba.*—LXVII. *Cæcina attacks the Helvetians, and lays waste the country—He passes over the Pennine mountains into Italy.*—LXXI. *Otho's conduct at Rome: he begins to act with vigour.*—LXXII. *Death of Tigellinus, and his character.*—LXXIV. *Letters between Otho and Vitellius: they endeavour to over-reach each other—Emissaries employed by both—The people of Sarmatia invade the province of Mæsia, and are put to the rout with great slaughter.*—LXXX. *An insurrection of the soldiers at*

Rome.—LXXXIII. *Otho's speech to the soldiers.*—LXXXVI. *Portents and prodigies spread a general alarm at Rome.*—LXXXVII. *Otho consults about the operations of the war: he appoints his generals, and sends his fleet to invade the Narbon Gaul.*—LXXXIX. *Melancholy condition of the people at Rome—Otho proceeds on his expedition against the Vitellian forces, and leaves his brother, Salvius Titianus, chief governor of Rome.*

These transactions passed in a few months.

Years of Rome.	Of Christ.	Consuls.
822	69	Servius Galba, 2nd time, Titus Vinius Rufinus.

I. The era, from which it is my intention to deduce the following narration, is the second consulship of Servius Galba, when Titus Vinius was his colleague in office.[1] Of the antecedent period, including a space of eight hundred and twenty years from the foundation of Rome,[1] the history has been composed by various authors, who, as long as they had before them the transactions of the Roman people, dignified their work with eloquence equal to the subject, and a spirit of freedom worthy of the old republic. After the battle of Actium, when, to close the scene of civil distraction, all power and authority were surrendered to a single ruler, the historic character disappeared, and genius died by the same blow that ended public liberty. Truth was reduced to the last gasp, and various circumstances conspired against her. A new constitution took place, undefined, and little understood. Men resigned their rights, and lived like aliens in their native country. Adulation began to spread her baneful influence, and a rooted hatred of their ambitious masters rankled in the breast of numbers. Between both parties, one paying their court, and the other brooding over public injuries, the care of transmitting due information to posterity was utterly lost. It is true, that against the seductions of the time-serving writer you may be upon your guard; but, on the other hand, spleen and calumny are devoured with a greedy ear. Flattery wears a badge of servitude, while malignity speaks the tone of independence, and is therefore well received. With regard to the writer of the following work, he can with truth aver, that Galba, Otho, and Vitellius, were neither known to him by marks of favour, nor by personal injury. The foundation of his fortune was laid by Vespasian, advanced by Titus,

[1] A.D. 69.
[2] Tacitus computes 820 years from the foundation of Rome to the end of Nero, when the following History begins.

and carried higher by Domitian. The fact must not be dissembled: but the historian who enters on his office with a profession of integrity, must not desert the cause of truth. No character should be touched with partiality; none should be disfigured by passion, or resentment. Of Nerva and Trajan,[1] if my health continues, it is my design to compose the history; it is a favourite plan, rich in materials, and every way safe. I have reserved it for the evening of my days; a glorious period! in which, through the rare felicity of the times, a man may think with freedom, and what he thinks he may publish to the world.

II. The subject now before me presents a series of great events, and battles fierce and bloody; a portion of time big with intestine divisions, and even the intervals of peace deformed with cruelty and horror: the whole a tragic volume, displaying, in succession, four princes[2] put to death; three civil wars;[3] with foreign enemies a greater number, and, in some conjunctures, both depending at once; prosperity in the east, disasters in the west; Illyricum thrown into convulsions; both the Gauls on the eve of a revolt; Britain[4] conquered, and, in the moment of conquest, lost again; the Sarmatians and the Suevians leagued against the Romans; the Dacian name ennobled by alternate victory and defeat; and, finally, the Parthians taking the field under the banners of a pretended Nero. In the course of the work, we shall see Italy overwhelmed with calamities; new wounds inflicted, and the old, which time had closed, opened again and bleeding afresh; cities sacked by the enemy, or swallowed up by earthquakes,[5] and the fertile country of Campania made a scene of desolation; Rome laid waste by fire; her ancient and most venerable temples smoking on the ground; the

[1] It is evident from this passage that Tacitus published his History in the reign of Trajan, since Nerva is called the deified Nerva, and the apotheosis of the emperors was always after their death.

[2] The history included the whole time from the first of Galba to the assassination of Domitian: and, for that reason, some of the commentators are of opinion that the four princes put to the sword are Galba, Otho, Vitellius, and Domitian. Others, observing that the whole of Domitian's reign is lost, adapt their notions to the present state of our author's work, and reckon Piso, who was adopted by Galba, one of the four murdered princes.

[3] The insurrection against Galba was an act of sudden violence; soon begun and ended. The three civil wars were as follows:—1. Otho and Vitellius; 2. Vitellius and Vespasian; 3. Lucius Antonius and Domitian.

[4] Britain was finally subdued in the reign of Domitian. See the life of Agricola. It was afterwards neglected and almost lost.

[5] The cities of Herculaneum and Pompeii were destroyed by an eruption of the lava of Mount Vesuvius, in the beginning of Titus's reign.

capitol wrapt in flames by the hands of frantic citizens; the holy ceremonies of religion violated; adultery reigning without control; the adjacent islands filled with exiles; rocks and desert places stained with clandestine murder, and Rome itself a theatre of horror; where nobility of descent, and splendour of fortune, marked men out for destruction; where the vigour of mind that aimed at civil dignities, and the modesty that declined them, were offences without distinction; where virtue was a crime that led to certain ruin; where the guilt of informers, and the wages of their iniquity, were alike detestable; where the sacerdotal order, the consular dignity, the government of the provinces,[1] and even the cabinet of the prince, were seized by that execrable race, as their lawful prey; where nothing was sacred, nothing safe, from the hand of rapacity; where slaves were suborned, or, by their own malevolence, excited against their masters; where freedmen betrayed their patrons; and he, who had lived without an enemy, died by the treachery of a friend.

III. And yet this melancholy period, barren as it was of public virtue, produced some examples of truth and honour. Mothers went with their sons into voluntary exile; wives followed the fortune of their husbands; relations stood forth in the cause of their unhappy kindred; sons appeared in defence of their fathers; slaves on the rack gave proofs of their fidelity; eminent citizens, under the hard hand of oppression, were reduced to want and misery, and, even in that distress, retained an unconquered spirit. We shall see others firm to the last, and, in their deaths, nothing inferior to the applauded characters of antiquity. In addition to the misfortunes usual in the course of human transactions, we shall see the earth teeming with prodigies, the sky overcast with omens, thunder rolling with dreadful denunciation, and a variety of prognostics, sometimes auspicious, often big with terror, occasionally uncertain, dark, equivocal, frequently direct and manifest. In a word, the gods never gave such terrible instructions, nor, by the slaughter of armies, made it so clear and evident, that, instead of extending protection to the empire, it was their awful pleasure to let fall their vengeance on the crimes of an offending people.

[1] Collectors of the imperial revenue were instituted by the emperors, in order to intrench on the power of the proconsuls, who were the proper officers in all the provinces that remained under the authority of the senate. Informers were raised to the office of imperial procurators, and obtained weight and influence in the cabinet.

IV. Before we take up the thread of our narrative, it will not be useless to inquire what, in that period, was the state of affairs at Rome, and what the spirit that went forth among her armies; how the provinces stood affected, and wherein consisted the strength or weakness of the empire. By proceeding in this manner, we shall not content ourselves with a bare recital of facts, which are often ascribed to chance: we shall see the spring of each transaction, and a regular chain of causes and effects will be laid open to our view.

The death of Nero, in the first tumult of emotion, was considered as a public blessing; but the senate, the people of Rome, the prætorian guards, and the legions, wherever stationed, were variously affected by that event. A new political secret was then for the first time discovered. It was perceived, that elsewhere than at Rome an emperor might be invested with the sovereign power. The fathers seized the opportunity, during the absence of a prince yet new to the reins of government, to exercise their ancient rights, pleased with the novelty of freedom, and the resumption of their legislative authority. The Roman knights caught the flame of liberty. Honest men began to entertain hopes of the constitution. Such as stood connected with families of credit, and the various clients and freedmen of illustrious men driven into exile, were all erect with expectation of better times. The inferior populace, who loitered away their time in the theatre and the circus; the slaves of abandoned characters, and the sycophant crew, who, without substance of their own, had been pampered by the vices of Nero; all of that description stood covered with astonishment, yet panting for news, and eagerly swallowing the rumour of the day.

V. The prætorian guards[1] had been, by habit and the obligation of their oath, always devoted to the imperial family. Their revolt from Nero was not so much their own inclination as the management of their leaders. Acting without principle, they now were ready for new commotions. The promise of a donative in the name of Galba was still to be performed. They knew that war is the soldier's harvest. Peace affords no opportunity to gain the recompense due to valour; and the favours of the new prince would be engrossed by the legions, to whom he owed his elevation. Fired by these

[1] The prætorian guards had shown themselves, at all times, firmly attached to the Cæsarian family.

reflections, and further instigated by the arts of Nymphidius Sabinus, their commanding officer, whose ambition aimed at the imperial dignity, they began to meditate a second revolution.

The conspiracy was crushed in the bud, and Nymphidius perished in the attempt. But the soldiers had thrown off the mask, and the sense of guilt served only to goad and spur their resolution. They talked of Galba with contempt and ridicule; they laughed at his advanced age; they inveighed against his avarice: and the rigorous discipline by which he had acquired his military character, inflamed the prejudices of men, who had been enervated by a long peace of fourteen years. During that time, the dissolute manners of Nero diffused a general corruption, insomuch that the virtues, which formerly gained the affection of the army, were fallen into contempt. Nero was endeared to the soldiers by his vices. Galba, on the contrary, was rendered unpopular by the austerity of his manners. He was used to say, that he chose his soldiers, but never bought them. The maxim was worthy of the old republic, but no man thought it an effusion from the heart. His conduct and his words were too much at variance.

VI. Galba, being now in the decline of life, resigned himself altogether to Titus Vinius and Cornelius Laco; the former the most profligate of men, and the latter despised for his sluggish inactivity. By those pernicious ministers he was involved in the popular hatred due to their own flagitious deeds. The wickedness of Vinius, and the incapacity of Laco, proved his ruin in the end. He made his approach to Rome by slow journeys, in his progress marking his way with blood and cruelty. Cingonius Varro, consul elect, and Petronius Turpilianus, of consular rank, were, by his orders, put to death; the former, as an accomplice in the enterprise of Nymphidius, and the latter, because he had been appointed to command the army under Nero. They were condemned unheard, and, for that reason, thought the innocent victims of a barbarous policy.

Galba's entry into the city of Rome, after the massacre of several thousands of unarmed and defenceless soldiers, struck a general panic. The people at large were thrown into consternation, and even the men who executed the orders of their general, stood astonished at the horrors of the scene. Rome, at that time, was filled with a prodigious body of troops, assembled from various parts of the empire. Besides the forces drawn from the fleet,[1] and left as a garrison by Nero, Galba, when he entered the city, brought with him a legion from Spain. To these must be added the several companies[2] from Germany, from Britain, and Illyricum, which had been sent forward towards the Caspian straits, to serve in the war then intended against the Albanians. In a short time afterwards, on the first notice of the revolt excited in Gaul by the turbulent genius of Vindex, they were all recalled; and the consequence was, that Rome saw within her walls the unusual spectacle of a vast military force. In so large a number of soldiers, not yet devoted to the interest of a single leader, the seed-plots of a new rebellion were prepared, and ready to break out on the first alarm.

VII. It happened, at this point of time, that an account arrived of two murders, committed at a distance from Rome; one of Clodius Macer in Africa, and the other of Fonteius Capito in Germany. Macer, beyond all doubt, was engaged in schemes of ambition, and, in the midst of his projects, was cut off by Trebonius Garrucianus, the procurator of the province, who had received his orders from Galba. Capito was put to death by Cornelius Aquinus and Fabius Valens, on a like suspicion of plotting innovations in the state. But the charge against him was by no means clear, nor had the emperor issued his orders. The general opinion was, that Capito, however branded with avarice, rapacity, and other vices, had not added to his crimes the guilt of rebellion; but that the authors of his destruction, having first endeavoured to draw him into their own designs, combined to execute on an innocent victim the vengeance due to their own iniquity.

Galba, with his usual facility, or, perhaps, wishing to avoid the danger of an inquiry into what could not be recalled, thought it prudent to give his sanction to the acts of his officers, however unjust and cruel. Both executions were, notwithstanding, the subject of public clamour: the usual fate of all unpopular princes: their actions, when the current of the times is set against them, are taken in the gross, and, whether good or evil, condemned without distinction. Venality and corruption were now fully established. The emperor's freedmen engrossed the whole power of the state,

[1] Nero had formed a new legion composed of men draughted from the marines.

[2] The forces from Britain and Germany, which Nero had sent forward on a wild expedition to the straits of the Caspian Sea, were all recalled to quell the insurrection of Vindex in Gaul.

and everything was put up to sale. Even the slaves, in haste to grow rich, and fearing the uncertainty of an old man's life, began to seize their share of the plunder. The new court opened with all the vices of Nero's reign, but without the same apology. The advanced age[1] of Galba was a subject of ridicule. Dissipation, at his time of life, excited laughter and contempt. Appearances are the reasons of the populace: they were accustomed to the youthful frolics of Nero, and in their comparison of princes, elegance of figure and the graces of deportment are decisive qualities.

VIII. Such was the posture of affairs at Rome, and such the sentiments that pervaded the mass of the people. With regard to the provinces, Spain was governed by Cluvius Rufus, a man distinguished by his eloquence, and well accomplished in the arts of peace, but of no reputation in war. In both the Gauls the name of Vindex was still held in veneration; and the people, pleased with their recent admission to the freedom[2] of Rome, and the diminution of their tribute, showed no symptoms of disaffection. In those parts, however, which lay contiguous to the German armies, the inhabitants of the several cities saw, with discontent, that they were not thought worthy of the like indulgence. Some of them complained that their territories were circumscribed within narrower limits; and, in vulgar minds, the good extended to others was an aggravation of the injury done to themselves.

The legions in Germany did not show a countenance that promised a perfect calm. The restless temper of the soldiers, by their late victory[3] flushed with pride, yet dreading the imputation of having conquered Galba's party, was thrown into violent agitations, by turns inflamed with rage, and overwhelmed with fear. From such a number of soldiers, who had the power of the sword in their own hands, nothing but danger was to be apprehended. They balanced for some time, before they detached themselves from Nero; nor did Verginius, their commanding officer, declare immediately for Galba. Whether that tardy movement was occasioned by his own ambitious projects, cannot now be known. The soldiers, it is certain, made him a tender of the imperial dignity. The

[1] Galba, at his elevation to the imperial dignity, was seventy-three years old.

[2] The people of Gaul, who stood for Vindex, were the Sequani, the Ædui, and the Arverni. The states that lay near the legions on the Upper and Lower Rhine, were the Lingones and the Remi.

[3] The German armies obtained a complete victory over Vindex at Vesontium.

death of Fonteius Capito was another cause of discontent. Even such as could not deny the justice of the measure, exclaimed against it with indignation. While the minds of men were thus distracted with contending passions, Galba thought fit, under a show of friendship, to recall Verginius from his post. The legions had now no chief at their head, and, if the conduct of their general was arraigned, they considered themselves as men involved in the same accusation.

IX. The legions on the Upper Rhine were ill retained in their duty by Hordeonius Flaccus, an officer far advanced in years, without vigour of mind, disabled in his limbs, and, by his infirmities, exposing himself and old age to scorn. Unequal to the command even in quiet times, he was now, in a camp full of bold and turbulent spirits, unable to support his authority. His endeavours to enforce obedience served only to irritate the minds of men disposed to mutiny. On the Lower Rhine, the army had been for some time without a general of consular rank, till Aulus Vitellius,[1] son of the person of that name who had been censor, and three times consul, was sent by Galba to take upon him the command. This to Galba seemed sufficient, and the Fates ordained it.

In Britain everything was quiet. The legions stationed in that island had no party divisions to distract them. During the civil wars that followed, they took no part in the contest. Situated at a distance, and divided by the ocean from the rest of the world, they did not catch the epidemic frenzy of the times. They knew no enemies but those of their country, and were not taught by civil discord to hate one another. Illyricum remained in a state of tranquillity, though the legions drawn by Nero from that country found the means, while they loitered in Italy, of tampering with Verginius. But the armies were at distant stations, separated by a long tract of sea or land; and that circumstance proved the best expedient to prevent a combination of the military. They could neither act with a spirit of union, nor, by communicating their vices, spread a general infection through the legions that lay remote from each other.

X. The east was hitherto free from commotion. Licinius Mucianus governed the province of Syria with four legions under his command. He was an officer of experience, distinguished, in the early parts of his life, by alternate vicissitudes of good and evil fortune. In his youth the favour of the

[1] This was Vitellius, whom in the sequel we shall see emperor of Rome.

great was the object of his ambition, and in that pursuit he wasted his fortune. His circumstances growing desperate, and a storm impending from the displeasure of Claudius, he retired into Asia, and there lived in obscurity, as little removed from the state and condition of a real exile, as he was afterwards from the splendour of imperial fortune. He united in his character a rare and wonderful mixture of repugnant qualities. He was affable and arrogant; addicted to pleasure, and by fits and starts a man of business. When at leisure from affairs, he gave a loose to his luxurious passions; if his interest required it, he came upon mankind with superior talents. The minister was praised, and the private man detested. The art of conciliating the good-will of others was his in an eminent degree. With his inferiors he knew how to soften authority; to his friends and equals his address was courtly; and yet, with these attractive arts, a man so various was fitter to raise others to the imperial dignity, than to obtain it for himself.

The war against the Jews had been committed by Nero to Flavius Vespasian, who was then in Judæa at the head of three legions. That commander had formed no design, nor even a wish, against the interest of Galba. He sent his son Titus to Rome, as will be seen hereafter, with congratulations to Galba, and assurances of fidelity. It was not then perceived that the sovereign power was destined, by the decrees of Heaven, for Vespasian and his two sons. After his accession, portents and prodigies, and the responses of oracles, were better understood.

XI. Egypt, and the forces stationed there to bridle the several provinces, were, according to the system established by Augustus, confided to the Roman knights, who exercised all the powers of the ancient kings. In order to keep in subjection a country difficult of access, and at the same time a granary of corn; where the genius of the people, deeply tinged with superstition, was ever wavering, and prone to change; where there was no plan of regular government, and, by consequence, no respect paid to the civil magistrate; it was the policy of Augustus to retain the administration, like a mystery of state, in his own hands, and under his own cabinet council. In the present juncture, Tiberius Alexander, a native of the country, was entrusted with the government of the province.

Africa, and the legions quartered there, were, since the murder of Clodius Macer, grown indifferent to all modes of government. Having experienced the authority of an inferior master, they were willing to submit to any prince. The two

Mauritanias, Rhætia, Noricum, and Thrace, with the places committed to the care of imperial procurators, had no fixed principle, no hatred, and no affection, but what was inspired by the force nearest at hand. They were always united in opinion with the strongest. The provinces, which were left naked and defenceless, and Italy in particular, were open to the first invader, the ready prey of any conqueror. Such was the situation of the Roman world, when Servius Galba, in his second consulship, and Titus Vinius, his colleague, began their year; a fatal year, which brought them both to a tragic catastrophe, and the commonwealth to the brink of ruin.

XII. In a few days after the calends of January, letters arrived at Rome from Pompeius Propinquus, the procurator of Belgic Gaul, with intelligence of a revolt in Upper Germany. The legions in that quarter, disregarding the obligation of their oath, shook off all obedience, and demanded another emperor; willing, however, to soften the violence of their proceedings, and, for that purpose, to leave the choice to the judgment of the senate, and the Roman people. The use that Galba made of this intelligence was, to hasten the adoption of a successor; a point which he had for some time revolved in his mind, and often discussed with his secret advisers. During the few months of his reign, no subject had so much engrossed the public conversation. The people, always politicians, and fond of settling state affairs, gave a loose to their usual freedom of speech; and, besides, an emperor on the verge of life made it natural to advert to the succession. Few were able to think with judgment, and fewer had the virtue to feel for the public good. Private views and party connections suggested various candidates. Different factions were formed, and all intrigued, caballed, and clamoured, as their hopes or fears directed. Titus Vinius did not escape the notice of the public. He grew in power every day, and the hatred of the people kept pace with his rising grandeur. In the sudden elevation of Galba, this man and his adherents, with all the creatures of the court, saw their opportunity to enrich themselves with the spoils of their country; and, encouraged as they were by the facility of a weak, a credulous, and superannuated prince, they were resolved to lose no time. In such a period the temptation was great, and guilt might hope to plunder with impunity.

XIII. The whole sovereign power was in the hands of Titus Vinius, the consul, and Cornelius Laco, the præfect of the prætorian guards. A third favourite soon appeared on the political stage, with a degree of influence not inferior to either of the former. The name of this man was Icelus, one of the emperor's freedmen, lately created a Roman knight, and, to suit his new dignity, honoured with the name of Martianus. The three confidential ministers were soon at variance. They clashed in interest, and, in all inferior transactions, drew different ways; but in the choice of a successor they were divided into factions. Vinius declared for Marcus Otho: Laco and Icelus joined in opposition to that measure, not so much to favour a friend of their own, as to thwart the designs of a rival. Galba was not to learn the close connection that subsisted between Vinius and Otho. The busy politicians, who loved to pry into everything, and divulge all they know, and all they think, had circulated a report that reached the ear of the emperor. Vinius had a daughter, at that time a widow; Otho was unmarried, and a match between them would make the minister the father-in-law of his future emperor.

Galba resolved to act with caution, and with due regard to the public welfare. He saw the sovereign power wrested out of the hands of Nero, but wrested in vain, if transferred to a man like Otho; a stranger, from his earliest days, to every fair pursuit, and in the prime of manhood distinguished by nothing but riot and debauchery. It was his taste for luxury and vicious pleasures, that first recommended him to the notice of Nero. He vied with his master in all kinds of dissipation, and, in consequence of that connection, became the worthy depositary to whom the prince entrusted the care of his dearly beloved Poppæa,[1] till such time as Octavia was, by a divorce, removed out of the way. But Otho's fidelity soon became suspected. Nero's jealousy could not bear a rival. He sent his favourite companion to govern the province of Lusitania, and, under that pretext, banished him from Rome. It is true that Otho, in the course of his administration, gained, by his mild and courtly manners, no small degree of popularity. In the late revolution, he was the first to espouse the interest of Galba. While the war lasted, he continued an active partisan, and, by his splendid appearance, did no small credit to the cause. Hence his hopes of being called to the succession. The soldiers favoured his pretensions; and the creatures of Nero's court promised themselves, under a sovereign so nearly resembling their master, a return of the same vices.

XIV. Galba saw, with deep anxiety, a storm gathering in Germany, and where it would burst he could not foresee. Of

[1] For Otho's connection with Poppæa, see *Annals*, xiii. 45 and 46.

Vitellius and his designs no certain account arrived. The revolt of the legions filled him with apprehensions, and he reposed no confidence in the prætorian guards. The nomination of a successor seemed, in such a crisis, to be the best expedient; and for that purpose he held a cabinet council. Besides Vinius and Laco, he thought proper to summon Marius Celsus, consul elect, and Ducennius Geminus, the præfect of the city. Having prefaced the business in a short speech concerning his age and infirmities, he sent for Piso Licinianus; whether of his own free choice, or at the instigation of Laco, remains uncertain. That minister had lived in friendship with Piso. He contracted an intimacy with him at the house of Rubellius Plautus, though he had now the address to conceal that connection, affecting, with public motives, to recommend a stranger. To this conduct, the fair esteem in which Piso was held, gave an appearance of sincerity. Piso was the son of Marcus Crassus and Scribonia, both of illustrious descent. His aspect was grave, and his deportment formal; such as gave an idea of primitive manners. By the candid and impartial he was called strict and severe; by his enemies, morose and sullen. With great excellences, he had a mixture of those qualities that are often the shades of eminent virtue; but those very shades, which seemed to others too dark and gloomy, in the eyes of Galba were the strokes of character, that gave Piso a cast of antiquity, and made him worthy to be the adopted heir to the empire.

XV. Galba, we are told, taking Piso by the hand, addressed him in the following manner: "If the adoption which I am now to make, were, like the act of a private citizen, to be acknowledged, as the law *Curiata*[1] directs, in the presence of the pontiffs, I should derive honour to myself from an alliance with a person descended from the great Pompey and Marcus Crassus: and, in return, you would add to the nobility of your own family the lustre of the Sulpician and Lutatian name. I now address you in a more exalted character. It is the emperor of Rome that speaks. Called by the consent of gods and men to that high station, I am now determined in my choice by your rare accomplishments, and the love I feel for my country. I invite you to the imperial dignity; that dignity for which our ancestors led armies to the field, and which I myself obtained in battle. Without your stir I now

[1] Romulus classed the citizens of Rome in thirty *curias*, and from that circumstance the *Lex Curiata* took its name. The law was enacted by the people assembled in their several curias.

make to you a voluntary offer. For this proceeding I have before me the example of Augustus, who associated to himself, first his sister's son Marcellus, and then Agrippa his son-in-law, his grandsons afterwards, and, finally, Tiberius, the son of his wife. Augustus, indeed, looked for an heir in his own family; I choose in the bosom of the commonwealth. If, upon such an occasion, I could listen to private affection, I have a numerous train of relations, and I have companions in war. But it was not from motives of pride that I accepted the sovereignty of the state: ambition had no share in my conduct. I brought with me to the seat of government an upright intention; and that I now act on the same principle may be fairly seen, when, in my present choice, I postpone not only my own relations, but even those of your own family. You have a brother, in point of nobility your equal; by priority of birth your superior; and, if your merit did not supersede him, a man worthy of the highest elevation.

"You are now at the time of life at which the passions subside. Your former conduct requires no apology. Fortune has hitherto frowned upon you: you must now beware of her smiles. Prosperity tries the human heart with the deepest probe, and draws forth the hidden character. We struggle with adversity, but success disarms us. I trust, however, that you will carry with you, to the highest station, the candour of your mind, your good faith, your independent spirit, and your constancy in friendship; virtues that exalt and dignify the human character; but the arts of insidious men will lay siege to your best qualities, and undermine them all. Dissimulation will deceive you; flattery will find admission to your heart; and self-interest, the bane of all true affection, will lay snares to seduce your integrity. To-day you and I converse without disguise, in terms of plain simplicity: how will others deal with us? Their respect will be paid to our fortunes, not to ourselves. To talk the language of sincerity to a prince, and guide him by honest counsels, is a laborious task: to play the hypocrite requires no more than to humour his inclinations, whatever they are. It is the grimace of friendship: the heart has no share in the business.

XVI. "If the mighty fabric of this great empire could subsist on any other foundation than that of a monarchy, the glory of restoring the old republic should this day be mine. But, at my age, all that remains for me is to bequeath to the people an able successor: your youth may give them a virtuous prince. Under Tiberius, Caligula, and Claudius, we were all the property of one family. By hereditary right the Roman world was theirs. The prince is now elective, and the freedom of choice is liberty. The Julian and the Claudian race are both extinct, and virtue may now succeed by adoption. To be born the son of a prince is the result of chance; mankind consider it in no higher light. The method of adoption allows time to deliberate, and the public voice will serve as a guide to direct the judgment of the emperor. Let Nero be for ever before your eyes: proud of his long line of ancestors, and warm with the blood of the Cæsars, he did not fall by the revolt of Vindex, at the head of a province naked and disarmed; nor was he deposed by me, who had only one legion under my command: his own vices, his own cruelty, hurled him from his throne, no more to trample on the necks of mankind. Of a prince condemned by a public sentence, there was till then no example.

"As to myself, raised as I was by the events of war, and called to the sovereignty by the voice of a willing people, I know what I have to expect: envy and malice may pursue me, but the glory of doing good shall still be mine. After the storm that lately shook the empire, you will not wonder that a perfect calm has not succeeded; and, if two legions waver in their duty, your courage must not be disconcerted. My reign did not begin in the halcyon days of peace. Old age, at present, is the objection urged against me: but when it is known whom I have adopted, I shall appear young in my successor. Nero is still regretted by the vile and profligate: that good men may not regret him, it will be ours to provide by our future conduct. More than I have said the time will not admit; if I have made a proper choice, I have discharged my duty. One rule, however, there is worthy of your consideration. In all questions of good and evil, ask yourself, when you were a subject, what did you expect from the prince, and what did you wish him to avoid? It is not at Rome as in despotic governments, where one family towers above mankind, and their subjects groan in bondage. You are to reign over the Roman people; a people whom no extreme will suit: when in full possession of liberty, enemies to their own happiness; when reduced to slavery, impatient of the yoke." To this effect Galba delivered himself, little doubting but that he was then creating a prince: the courtiers considered it as a complete legal act, and paid their homage to their future sovereign.

XVII. During the whole of this solemn transaction, Piso,

we are told, never lost the even tenor of his mind. From the first moment all eyes were fixed upon him; yet, on his part, no emotion was seen, no symptom of joy, no surprise, no confusion. He addressed the emperor, now his father, in terms of profound respect, and spoke of himself with reserve and modesty. His mien and countenance never betrayed the smallest inward alteration. He behaved with the apathy of a man who deserved to reign, but did not desire it. The next consideration was, in what place the adoption should be announced; in the forum before an assembly of the people, in the senate, or in the camp. The latter was thought most eligible: the army would feel the compliment; the affections of the soldiers, though of little value if purchased by bribery and low intrigue, are, notwithstanding, when they are gained by fair and honourable means, always of moment, and never to be neglected. Meanwhile, the populace, rushing in crowds from every quarter, surrounded the palace, burning with impatience for the important news, and growing still more eager in proportion to the delay of the profound politicians, who affected an air of mystery, when the secret had already transpired.

XVIII. On the fourth of the ides of January the weather was uncommonly tempestuous, accompanied with heavy rains, thunder and lightning, and all the uproar of the elements, which usually alarms the superstition of the multitude. In ancient times this phenomenon would have been sufficient to dissolve all public assemblies: but Galba was not to be deterred from his purpose. He proceeded to the camp, regardless of prodigies, which he considered as the effect of natural causes; or, it may be, that what is fixed by fate cannot by human prudence be avoided. A vast conflux of soldiers assembled in the camp. Galba addressed them in a short speech, such as becomes the imperial dignity. He told them that, in conformity to the example of Augustus, and the practice of the army, where each soldier chooses his companion in war, he had adopted Piso for his son. Fearing that his silence on the subject of the German revolt might tend to magnify the danger, he added, that the fourth and eighteenth legions were, by the artifice of a few factious leaders, incited to tumult and disorder; but their violence went no further than words, and he had no doubt but they would soon be sensible of their error. Such was his plain and manly language. He added no flattering expressions, no soothing hopes of a donative. The tribunes, notwithstanding, and the centurions and soldiers who stood nearest to his person, raised a shout of approbation. Through the rest of the lines a deep and sullen silence prevailed. The men saw, with discontent, that, on the eve of a war, they were deprived of those gratuities which had been granted in time of peace, and were now become the soldier's right. The emperor, beyond all doubt, had it in his power to secure the affections of the soldiers. From a parsimonious old man the smallest mark of liberality would have made an impression. But in an age that could no longer bear the virtues of the old republic, rigid economy was out of season, and, by consequence, the worst of policy.

XIX. From the camp Galba proceeded to the senate. His speech, like that to the soldiers, was short, unadorned, and simple. Piso delivered himself with grace and eloquence. The fathers heard him with attention; some with real affection, and others, who in their hearts opposed his interest, with overacted zeal; while the neutral and indifferent (by far the greatest number) made a tender of their services, all with private views, regardless of their country. This was the only public act in which Piso appeared. In the time that followed between his adoption and his death (an interval of four days), he neither said nor did anything that merits the attention of history.

Affairs in Germany began to wear a gloomy aspect. Messengers upon the heels of one another came posting to Rome; and in a city where men stood athirst for news, and swallowed the worst with avidity, nothing was seen but hurry and confusion. The fathers resolved to treat by their deputies with the German legions. In a secret council it was proposed that Piso should set out at the head of the embassy, that the army might have before their eyes the authority of the senate, and the majesty of the empire. It was further thought advisable that Laco, the præfect of the prætorian guards, should accompany the deputation; but he declined the office. Nor was the choice of the ambassadors easily arranged. The whole was left to Galba's judgment, and he executed it with caprice and shameful indecision. Men were appointed, and removed; others were substituted, and changed again; some excused themselves; numbers, as fear or ambition prompted, made interest for the preference, or for permission to remain at home.

XX. The means of raising money came next under consideration. Various expedients were proposed, but none appeared so just, as that of making reprisals on such as by their rapacity impoverished the commonwealth. Nero had lavished in pensions and donations above two and twenty millions of sesterces. The men who had enriched themselves by this wild profusion were allowed to retain a tenth part of the plunder, and condemned to refund the rest. But their tenth part was no longer in their possession. Prodigal no less of the public money than of their own, they had squandered all in riot and debauchery. They had neither lands nor funds of any kind. The wreck of their fortunes consisted of little more than the utensils of luxury, vice, and folly. To enforce a resumption of all enormous grants, a court of commissioners was established, consisting of thirty Roman knights. This tribunal, odious on account of its novelty, and still more so for its number of officers, and the spirit of cabal that prevailed in every part of the business, was found vexatious and oppressive. The auctioneer planted his staff in every street; the public crier was heard; sales and confiscations were seen; a general ferment spread through the city. And yet this scene of distress was beheld with pleasure. The men who had been pillaged by Nero, saw the minions of that emperor reduced to a level with themselves. About the same time several tribunes were discharged from the service. In that number were Antonius Taurus and Antonius Naso, both of the prætorian guards; Æmilius Pacensis, from the city cohorts, and Julius Fronto, from the night-watch. But this, so far from being a remedy, served only to alarm and irritate the rest of the officers. They concluded that all were equally suspected, and that a timid court, not daring at once to go the length of its resentment, would proceed to cull them out man by man.

XXI. Otho, in the meantime, felt every motive that could inflame ambition. In quiet times he had nothing before him but despair; trouble and confusion were his only source of hope. His luxury was too great for the revenue of a prince, and his fortune was sunk to the lowest ebb, below the condition of a private man. He hated Galba, and he saw Piso with an eye of envy. To these incentives he added real or imaginary fears for his own personal safety, and in those fears he found new motives for rebellion. "He had felt the weight of Nero's displeasure; and must he now wait for a second Lusitania? Was he to expect, under colour of friendship, another honourable banishment? The man whom the public voice has named for the succession, is sure to be suspected by the reigning prince. It was that jealousy that ruined his interest with a superannuated emperor; and the same narrow motive would act with greater force on the mind of a young man, by nature harsh, and in his exile grown fierce and savage. Otho was, perhaps, already doomed to destruction. But the authority of Galba was on the decline, and that of Piso not yet established. This was, therefore, the time to strike a sudden blow. The convulsion of states, and the change of masters, afford the true season for courage and vigorous enterprise. In such a period, when inactivity is certain ruin, and bold temerity may be crowned with success, to linger in doubt might be the ruin of his cause. To die is the common lot of humanity. In the grave, the only distinction lies between those who leave no trace behind, and the heroic spirits who transmit their names to posterity. And since the same end awaits alike the guilty and the innocent, the man of enterprise will provoke his fate, and close the scene with glory."

XXII. The mind of Otho was not, like his body,[1] soft and effeminate. His slaves and freedmen lived in a course of luxury, unknown to private families. They flattered their master's taste; they painted to him in lively colours the joys of Nero's court, and the perpetual round of gay delights in which he had passed his days; they represented to him adultery without control, the choice of wives and concubines, and scenes of revelry scarcely known to Asiatic princes. These, if he dared nobly, they represented to him as his own; if he remained inactive, as the prize of others. The judicial astrologers added a spur to inflame his ardour. They announced great events, and to Otho a year of glory. Society has, perhaps, never known a more dangerous pest than this race of impostors, who had been ever ready, with vile infusions, to poison the hearts of princes, and to stimulate ambition to its ruin; a set of perfidious men, proscribed by law, and yet, in defiance of all law, cherished in such a city as Rome.

It was with this crew of fortune-tellers that Poppæa held consultations when she aspired to the imperial bed. It happened that one of these pretenders to preternatural knowledge, a man of the name of Ptolemy, accompanied Otho into Spain. He had there foretold that Otho would survive the reign of

[1] The character of Otho, as here delineated by the unerring pencil of Tacitus, is finely copied by Corneille in his tragedy, entitled *Otho*. A review of the various passages, which are transplanted into the French play, would be an agreeable amusement to every reader of taste, but cannot be comprised within the limits of a note.

Nero; and the event giving credit to his art, he took upon him to promise greater things. He saw Galba on the verge of life, and Otho in the vigour of his days. From that circumstance, and the currents of popular rumour that filled the city of Rome, this man drew his conjectures, and ventured to announce Otho's elevation to the imperial dignity. These bodings were welcome to the ear of Otho: he considered them as the effect of science, and believed the whole, with that credulity, which, in a mind inflamed with ambition, stands ready to receive the marvellous for reality. From this time, Ptolemy was the chief actor in the dark scenes that followed. He inspired the plan of treason, and Otho embraced it with impetuous ardour. The heart that has formed the wish, and conceived the project, has seldom any scruple about the means.

XXIII. Whether this bold conspiracy was then first imagined, or prepared and settled long before, cannot now be known. It is, however, certain that Otho had been in the habit of courting the affections of the army, and this, either with a view of being called to the succession, or, if not, with a design to seize it by force. He omitted no opportunity to ingratiate himself with the common men; on their march, in the lines, at their quarters, he made it his business to converse freely with all; he accosted the veterans by name, and, remembering their service under Nero, called them his brother-soldiers; he renewed his acquaintance with some; he inquired after others, and with his interest and his purse was ready to be their friend. In these discourses he took care to mingle complaints, and, with half-hinted malignity, to glance at Galba. He omitted nothing that could fill the vulgar mind with discontent. The soldiers were prepared to receive the worst impressions. Fatiguing marches, provisions ill supplied, and a plan of rigorous discipline lately revived, turned their hearts against the reigning prince. They had known gentler times, when, at their ease, they traversed the lakes of Campania, and went on sailing-parties to the cities of Achaia; but now the scene was changed to the Alps, the Pyreneans, and long tracts of country, where they were to march under a load of armour scarce supportable.

XXIV. While the minds of the soldiers were, by these means, thrown into violent agitations, Mævius Pudens, a near relation of Tigellinus, added fuel to the flame. Whoever was known to be of a light and versatile disposition, in distress for money, or fond of public commotions, this man attracted to his party. He sapped his way with a degree of dexterity, as unperceived as it was successful. As often as Galba was entertained at Otho's house, he distributed to the cohort on duty a hundred sesterces for every man, under colour of an allowance for their usual convivial party. This generosity, which passed under the name of a largess, was increased by the secret, but well applied, bribery of Otho; who became at last a corrupter so bold and open, that, when Cocceius Proculus, a soldier of the body-guard, was engaged in a litigation with one of his neighbours about the boundaries of their respective grounds, Otho bought the whole estate of the adverse party, and conveyed it to the soldier as a present. And yet these practices gave no jealousy to the commander of the prætorian bands. To penetrate dark transactions was so far from being his talent, that he could not see what escaped no eye but his own.

XXV. Otho took into his councils one of his freedmen, by name Onomastus. This man was chosen to conduct the enterprise. He selected for his accomplices, Barbius Proculus, whose duty it was to bear the watch-word to the night-guard, and one Veturius, his chosen assistant. Otho sounded them apart; and finding them fit instruments for his purposes, subtle, dark, and resolute, he loaded them both with presents, and dismissed them with a sum of money, to be employed in bribing the rest of the guards. In this manner two soldiers undertook to dispose of the Roman empire, and what they undertook, they dared to execute. A few only were conscious of the plot. The rest, though held in suspense, were managed with such dexterity, that they stood in readiness, as soon as the blow was struck, to second the conspirators. The soldiers of note were told, that having been distinguished by Nymphidius, they lived in danger, suspected, and exposed to the resentment of Galba. The loss of the donative, so often promised, and still withheld, was the topic enforced, to irritate the minds of the common men. Numbers lamented the loss of Nero, and the agreeable vices of that dissolute reign. All were averse from the new plan of discipline, and the idea of a further reform diffused a general terror.

XXVI. The spirit of disaffection spread, as it were by contagion, to the legions and the auxiliary troops, all sufficiently agitated by the revolt in Germany. The vile and profligate were ready for any mischief, and among the few of sober conduct, inactivity was no better than treason in disguise. The conspirators saw their advantage, insomuch that, on the day ensuing the ides of January, they formed a resolution to take Otho under their care, as he returned from supper, and, without further delay, proclaim him emperor. This project, however, did not take effect. In the darkness of the night, and the confusion inseparable from it, no man could answer for the consequences. The city was full of soldiers; and among men inflamed with liquor, no union, no concerted measure, could be expected. The traitors desisted from their purpose, but with no public motive. The general welfare made no impression on men, who had conspired to imbrue their hand in the blood of their sovereign. What they chiefly feared was, that the first who offered himself to the troops from Germany and Pannonia, might by those strangers, and in the tumult of the dark, be mistaken for Otho, and saluted by the title of emperor. The plot, thus checked for the present, began to transpire, and must have been by various circumstances brought to light had not the chief conspirators laboured to suppress all appearances of lurking treason. Some facts, however, reached the ears of Galba; but the folly of Laco explained everything away, and, by consequence, the emperor was lulled into security. The præfect of the guards had no knowledge of the military character. Nothing could open the eyes of a man, who opposed every measure, however excellent, which did not originate with himself. By the perversity of his nature, he was always at variance with talents and superior judgment.

XXVII. On the eighteenth day before the kalends of February, Galba assisted at a sacrifice, in the temple of Apollo. In the midst of the ceremony, Umbricius the augur, after inspecting the entrails of the victims, announced impending treason, and a lurking enemy within the walls of Rome. Otho, who stood near the emperor, heard this prediction, but interpreted it in his own favour, pleased with omens that promised so well to his cause. In that moment, Onomastus came to inform him, that his builders and surveyors were waiting to talk with him on business. This, as had been concerted, was a signal, that the conspirators were ready to throw off the mask, and strike the decisive blow. Otho quitted the temple, having first told such as wondered at his sudden departure, that, being on the point of purchasing certain farm-houses, not in good repair, he had appointed workmen to examine the buildings before he concluded his bargain. Having made that feigned excuse, he walked off, arm in arm, with his freedman; and, passing through the palace formerly belonging to Tiberius, went directly to the great market-place, called the Velabrum, and thence to the golden mile-pillar near the temple of Saturn. At that place a small party of the prætorian soldiers, in number not exceeding three and twenty, saluted him emperor. The sight of such an insignificant handful of men struck him with dismay; but his partisans drew their swords, and, placing him in a litter, carried him off in triumph. They were joined in their way by an equal number, some of them accomplices in the treason: others, in wonder and astonishment, hurried along by the current. The conspirators, brandishing their swords, and rending the air with acclamations, pursued their course, while numbers followed in profound silence, determined to see the issue before they took a decided part.

XXVIII. Julius Martialis, a military tribune, was at that time commanding officer in the camp. Amazed at a treason so bold and daring, and perhaps imagining that it extended wider, he made no attempt to oppose the torrent. His inactivity had the appearance of a confederacy in guilt. The rest of the tribunes and centurions followed the same line of caution, in their solicitude for their own safety losing all sense of honour and of every public principle. Such, in that alarming crisis, was the disposition of the camp: a few seditious incendiaries dared to attempt a revolution; more wished to see it, and all were willing to acquiesce.

XXIX. Galba, in the meantime, ignorant of all that passed, continued in the temple, attentive to the sacred rites, and with his prayers fatiguing the gods of an empire now no longer his. Intelligence at length arrived, that a senator (who by name no man could tell) was carried in triumph to the camp. Otho was soon after announced. The people in crowds rushed forward from every quarter, some representing the danger greater than it was, others lessening it, and, even in ruin, still retaining their habitual flattery. A council was called. After due deliberation, it was thought advisable to sound the dispositions of the cohort then on duty before the palace, but without the interposition of Galba. His authority was to be preserved for the last extremity. Piso called the men together, and, from the steps of the palace, addressed them to the following purport: "It is now, my fellow-soldiers, the sixth day since I was made by adoption presumptive heir to this great empire. Whether I was called to a post of honour, or of danger, was more than I could then foresee. The offer was honourable, and I accepted it; with what advantage to my own family in particular, or to the commonwealth at large, it will be yours to determine. For myself, I have nothing to fear. Trained in the school of adversity, I now perceive that the smiles are no less dreadful than the frowns of fortune. But for myself I feel no concern: I feel for the situation of an aged father; I feel for the senate; I feel for my country. The lot of all three will be grievous, whether we fall this day by the hands of assassins, or, which to a generous mind is no less afflicting, find ourselves obliged to shed the blood of our fellow-citizens. In the late revolution, it was matter of joy to all good men, that the city was not discoloured with Roman blood, and that, without civil discord, the reins of government passed into other hands. To secure the same tranquillity was the object of the late adoption. By that measure, Galba had reason to think that he closed the scene of war and civil commotion.

XXX. "I will neither mention the nobility of my birth, nor claim the merit of moderation. I arrogate nothing to myself. In opposition to Otho there is no necessity to call our virtues to our aid. The vices of the man, even then, when he was the friend, or rather the pander, of Nero, were the ruin of his country. In those vices he places all his glory. And shall a life of debauchery, shall that effeminate air, and that soft solicitude for gay apparel, give an emperor to the Roman world? They, who suffer profusion to pass for liberality, will in time perceive their error. Otho may squander, but to bestow is not in his character. What think you are the objects that now engross his thoughts? What are his views? What does he aim at? Scenes of luxury, lawless gratifications, carousing festivals, and the embraces of lascivious women, are the imaginations of his heart. These with him are imperial pleasures, the rights of sovereignty. The joy will be his: it will be yours to blush for your new master. In the whole catalogue of those daring usurpers, who by their crimes have risen to power, is there an instance of one who made atonement by his virtues? Is there a man who gained an empire by iniquity, and governed it with moderation?

"Galba was raised by the voice of a willing people to his present situation: his inclination, and your consent, have added me to the line of the Cæsars. But after all, if the commonwealth, the senate, and the people, are no better than mere empty names, yet let me ask you, my fellow-soldiers, will you suffer a lawless crew to overturn the government?

From the worst and most abandoned of mankind, will you receive an emperor? The legions, it is true, have at different times mutinied against their generals; but your fidelity has never been questioned. Nero abdicated; you did not desert him. He fell without your treachery. And shall thirty ruffians—thirty did I say? their number is less—shall a wretched handful of vile conspirators, whom no man would suffer to vote in the choice of a tribune or centurion, dispose of the Roman empire at their will and pleasure? Will you establish such a precedent? and, by establishing it, will you become accomplices in the guilt? The example will pass into the provinces; confusion and anarchy will be the fatal consequence. Galba may fall, and I may perish with him; but the calamities of a civil war must remain for you. By murdering your prince you may earn the wages of iniquity; but the reward of virtue will not be less. Judge which is best, a donative for your innocence, or a largess for murder and rebellion."

XXXI. During this harangue, the soldiers belonging to the guard withdrew from the place. The rest of the cohort showed no sign of discontent. Without noise or tumult, the usual incidents of sedition, they displayed their colours according to the military custom, and not, as was imagined afterwards, with a design to cover, by false appearances, a settled plan of treachery and revolt. Celsus Marius was sent to use his influence with the forces from Illyricum, at that time encamped under the portico of Vipsanius.[1] Orders were likewise given to Amulius Serenus and Domitius Sabinus, two centurions of the first rank, to draw from the temple of Liberty the German soldiers quartered in that place. The legion, draughted from the marines, was not to be trusted. They had seen, on Galba's entry into Rome, a cruel massacre of their comrades, and the survivors, with minds exasperated, panted for revenge. At the same time, Cetrius Severus, Subrius Dexter, and Pompeius Longinus, three military tribunes, made the best of their way to the prætorian camp, with an intention, while the ferment was still recent, and before a general flame was kindled, to mould the minds of the men to a pacific temper. Subrius and Cetrius were repulsed with menaces. Longinus was roughly handled. The soldiers took away his weapons, unwilling to listen to a man, whom they considered as an officer promoted

[1] A portico built by Vipsanius Agrippa in the field of Mars. Horace says,

——Cum bene notum
Porticus Agrippæ, et Via te conspexerit Appi.

out of his turn, by the favour of Galba, and, for that reason, faithful to his prince. The marine legion, without hesitation, joined the prætorian malcontents. The detachment from the Illyrian army caught the infection, and obliged Celsus to retire under a shower of darts. The veterans from Germany remained for some time in suspense. They had been sent by Nero to Alexandria; but, being recalled in a short time afterwards, they returned to Rome, in a distressed condition, worn out with toil, and weakened by sickness during their voyage. Galba attended to their wants, and, in order to recruit their strength, administered seasonable relief. The soldiers felt the generosity of the prince, and gratitude was not yet effaced from their minds.

XXXII. The populace, in the meantime, with a crowd of slaves intermixed, rushed into the palace, demanding vengeance on the head of Otho, and his partisans. The clamour was loud and dissonant, like that of a rabble in the circus or amphitheatre, roaring for the public sports, or some new spectacle. The whole was conducted without principle, without judgment, or sincerity; and, before the close of day, the same mouths were open to bawl for the reverse of what they desired in the morning. To be ready with shouts and vociferation, let who will be the reigning prince, has been in all ages the zeal of the vulgar. Galba, in the meantime, balanced between two opposite opinions. Titus Vinius was for his remaining in the palace. "The slaves," he said, "might be armed, and all the avenues secured. The prince should by no means expose himself to a frantic mob. Due time should be allowed for the seditious to repent, and for good men to form a plan of union, and concert their measures. Crimes succeeded by hurry and sudden despatch: honest counsels gain vigour by delay. Should it be hereafter proper to sally forth, that expedient would be still in reserve; but if once hazarded, the error will be seen too late. The prince, in that case, would be in the power of his enemies."

XXXIII. It was argued on the other hand, "that the exigence called for vigorous measures. Before the conspiracy of a few traitors gained an accession of strength, one brave exertion might prove decisive. Confront the danger, and Otho will shrink back with terror and dismay. It is not long since he went forth by stealth. He has been joined by a few incendiaries, and hurried away to a camp, where no plan is settled; but now, while Galba's friends remain inactive, he assumes the sovereign, and has time to learn how to play his part. And shall we linger here in cold debate, till the usurper, having mastered the camp, comes forth to invade the forum, and, under the eye of a lawful prince, ascends the capitol? In the meantime, must our valiant emperor remain trembling in his palace, while his warlike friends barricade the doors, preparing, with heroic resolution, to stand a siege? But, it seems, the slaves are to be armed; and they, no doubt, will render effectual service, especially if we neglect the people, now ready to support our cause, and suffer their indignation to evaporate without striking a blow. What is dishonourable is always dangerous. If we must fall, let us bravely meet our fate. Mankind will applaud our valour, and Otho, the author of our ruin, will be the object of public detestation." Vinius maintained his former opinion. Laco opposed him with warmth, and even with violent menaces. In this Icelus was the secret prompter. That favourite hated the consul, and, in a moment big with danger, chose to gratify a little and a narrow spirit at the expense of the emperor and the public.

XXXIV. Galba adopted what appeared to him the most specious and most prudent advice. Piso, notwithstanding, was sent forward to the camp. The presence of a young man of high expectation, and lately called to the first honours of the state, might give a turn to the passions of the army. He was besides considered as the enemy of Vinius. If, in fact, he did not hate him, the enemies of the minister wished it; and malice, imputed to the mind of man, is easily believed to be a natural passion. Piso was hardly gone forth, when a rumour prevailed that Otho was slain in the camp. The report at first was vague and uncertain, but, like all important lies, gathered as it went, and grew into credit. It was confirmed by men who averred that they were eye-witnesses on the spot, and saw the blow given. The tale was welcome to a great many, and the credulous swallowed it without further inquiry. It was afterwards thought to be a political lie, framed by Otho's friends, who mingled in the crowd in order to entice Galba from his palace.

XXXV. The city resounded with acclamations. Not only the vulgar and ignorant multitude were transported beyond all bounds, but the knights and senators were hurried away with the torrent; they forgot their fears; they rushed to the emperor's presence; they complained that the punishment of treason was taken out of their hands. The men who, as it appeared soon after, were the most likely to shrink from danger, displayed their zeal with ostentation; lavish of words, yet cowards in their hearts. No man knew that Otho was slain, yet all averred it as a fact. In this situation, wanting certain intelligence, but deceived by his courtiers, Galba determined to go forth from his palace. He called for his armour. The weight was too much for his feeble frame; and, in the throng that gathered round him, finding himself overpowered, he desired to be placed in a litter. Before he left the palace, Julius Atticus, a soldier of the body-guard, accosted him with a bloody sword in his hand, crying aloud, "In me you see the slayer of Otho: it was I that killed him." Galba calmly answered, "Who gave you orders?" Such was the spirit of the man even in the last extremity, still determined to repress the licentiousness of the soldiers; by their insolence undismayed, by their flattery never softened.

XXXVI. Meanwhile, the prætorian guards threw off the mask, and with one voice declared for Otho. They ranged themselves in a body round his person, and, in the ardour of their zeal, placed him, amidst the standards and eagles, on the very tribunal where, a little before, stood the golden statue[1] of Galba. The tribunes and centurions were not suffered to approach. The common soldiers, having no kind of confidence in their officers, gave the word to watch the motions of all in any rank or command. The camp resounded with shouts and mutual exhortations, not with that faint-hearted zeal which draws from the mob of Rome their feeble acclamations, but with one mind, one general impulse, all concurred in support of their new emperor. The prætorians were almost frantic with joy. They embraced their comrades as they saw them advancing forward; they clasped their hands; they led them to the tribunal; they repeated the military oath, and administered it to all. They recommended the prince of their own choice to the affections of the men, and the men, in their turn, to the favour of the prince. Otho, on his part, omitted nothing that could conciliate the affections of the multitude. He paid his court to the rabble with his hands outstretched, bowing lowly down, and, in order to be emperor, crouching like a slave. The marine legion did not hesitate to take the oath of fidelity. By that event Otho felt himself inspired with uncommon ardour. Having hitherto tampered with the soldiers man by man, he judged right to address them in a body. He took his station on the rampart of the camp, and spoke to the following effect:

[1] In every Roman camp the statue of the emperor was placed in the tribunal, at the headquarters of the general.

XXXVII. "In what light, my fellow-soldiers, shall I now consider myself? In what character must I address you? A private man I cannot call myself, for you have bestowed upon me the title of prince: but can I assume that title, while another is still in possession of the sovereign power? In what description you yourselves are to be classed, is to me matter of doubt; and must remain so, till the question is decided, Whether you have in your camp the emperor of Rome, or a public enemy? You have heard the cry that has gone forth: the same voice that demands vengeance on me, calls aloud for your destruction. With my life your fate is interwoven. We must live or perish together. There is no alternative. The humanity of Galba is well known to us all. Perhaps, even while I speak, he has pronounced our doom. To yield to the advice of his friends, will be an easy task to him, who without a request, of his own free will, in cold blood, could give to the edge of the sword so many thousand innocent soldiers, all destroyed in one inhuman massacre. My heart recoils with horror, when I reflect on the disastrous day when he made his public entry into the city. After receiving the submission of the soldiers, with unheard-of treachery he ordered the whole body to be decimated; and, in the view of the people, exhibited a scene of blood and horror. These are the exploits of Galba, and this is his only victory. With these inauspicious omens he entered the city of Rome;—and what has been since the glory of his reign? Obultronius Sabinus and Cornelius Marcellus have been murdered in Spain; Betuus Chilo in Gaul; Fonteius Capito in Germany; and Clodius Macer in Africa. Add to these Cingonius Varro, butchered on his march, Turpilianus in the heart of the city, and Nymphidius in the camp. Is there a province, is there in any part of the empire a single camp, which he has not defiled with blood? This, he will tell you, is a reform of the army. In this language murder is a legal remedy: what all good men agree to call a deed of barbarity, passes with him for a correction of abuses. Under specious names he confounds the nature of things: cruelty is justice, avarice is economy, and massacre is military discipline. Since the death of Nero not more than seven months have elapsed; and, in that time, Icelus his freedman has amassed, by plunder, more enormous wealth than the Polycleti,[1] the Vatinii, the Elii, and the Haloti, were able to do in the whole course of that emperor's reign. Even Titus Vinius, if he

[1] Polycletus, Vatinius, Helius, and Halotus, were favourite freedmen, who rose to wealth and honours in the reign of Nero.

himself had seized the empire, would have had the grace to blush at such enormities; nor should we have groaned under such a load of oppression. Though no higher than a private citizen, he plunders without remorse; he seizes our property, as if we were his slaves; and he despises us as the servants of another master. His house alone contains wealth sufficient to discharge the donative every day promised, but promised merely to insult you.

XXXVIII. "That your hopes of better times may never succeed, Galba has taken care, by his choice of a successor, to entail upon you endless misery. He has adopted a man from whom you can have nothing to expect; a man recalled from banishment, in his temper dark and gloomy, hardened in avarice, the counterpart of the emperor himself. You remember, my fellow-soldiers, the day on which that adoption was made; a day deformed with storms and tempests, when the warring elements announced the awful displeasure of the gods. The senate and the people are now of one mind. They depend upon your valour. It is your generous ardour that must give vigour and energy to our present enterprise. Without your aid the best designs must prove abortive. It is not to a war, nor even to danger, that I am now to conduct you: the armies of Rome are on our side. The single cohort remaining with Galba is composed of citizens, not of soldiers; they are gowned, not armed: they do not stand forth in his defence; they detain him as their prisoner. When they see you advancing in firm array, and when my signal is given, the only struggle will be, who shall espouse my cause with the greatest ardour. The time forbids all dull delay: we have undertaken bravely; but it is the issue that must justify the measure, and crown us with applause." Having closed his harangue, he ordered the magazine of arms to be thrown open. The soldiers seized their weapons; they paid no regard to military rules; no distinction was observed; the prætorians, the legions, and the auxiliaries crowded together, and shields and helmets were snatched up in a tumultuary manner. No tribune, no centurion, was allowed to give orders. Each man was his own commanding officer. While the friends of discipline stood astonished at the scene of wild confusion, the evil-minded saw with pleasure that the regulars were offended, and in that sentiment found a new motive to increase the disorder.

XXXIX. The number of the rebels increased every moment, and their noise and clamour reached the city of Rome. Piso did not think it advisable to proceed to the camp. He met

Galba, who had left the palace, on his way to the forum. Marius Celsus had already brought alarming tidings. Some advised the emperor to return to his palace; others were for taking possession of the capitol, and the major part for proceeding directly to the tribunal of public harangues; numbers gave their advice, for no better reason than to clash with the opinions of others; and, in the distraction of jarring counsels, the misfortune was, that what ought to have occurred first, was seen too late. They decided when the opportunity was lost. We are told that Laco, without the privity of Galba, formed a design against the life of Vinius. The murder of that minister, he thought, would appease the fury of the soldiers, or it may be that he suspected treachery, and thought him joined in a secret league with Otho: perhaps his own malice was the motive. But for this dark purpose neither the time nor the place was convenient: the sword once drawn, there was no knowing where the scene of blood would end. Messengers arriving every moment increased the consternation; the spirit of Galba's friends began to droop; numbers deserted him; and of all that zeal which a little before blazed out with so much ardour, every spark was now extinguished.

XL. Galba, in the midst of a prodigious conflux of people, had not strength to support himself; and as the waving multitude was impelled different ways, he was hurried on by the torrent. The temples, the porticos, and great halls round the forum, were filled with crowds of gazing spectators. The whole presented an awful spectacle. A deep and sullen silence prevailed. The very rabble was hushed. Amazement sat on every face. Their eyes watched every motion, and their ears caught every sound. The interval was big with terror; it was neither a tumult, nor a settled calm, but rather the stillness of fear, or smothered rage, such as often precedes some dreadful calamity. Otho was still in the camp. He received intelligence that the populace had recourse to arms, and thereupon ordered his troops to push forward with rapidity, and prevent the impending danger. At his command the Roman soldiers, as if marching to dethrone an eastern monarch, a Vologeses, or a Pacorus, and not their own lawful sovereign, advanced with impetuous fury to imbrue their hands in the blood of an old man, naked and disarmed. They entered the city; they dispersed the common people; they spurred their horses at full speed, and, rushing into the forum sword in hand, trampled the senators under foot. The sight of the capitol made no impression; the temples sanctified by the religion of ages, could not restrain their fury; for the majesty of former princes they had no respect, and of those who were to succeed, no kind of dread. They rushed forward to commit a detestable parricide, forgetting, in their frantic rage, that crimes of that atrocious nature are sure to be punished by the prince that succeeds to the sovereign power.

XLI. The prætorians no sooner appeared in sight, than the standard-bearer of the cohort still remaining with Galba (his name, we are told, was Attilius Vergilio) tore from the colours the image of Galba, and dashed it on the ground. That signal given, the soldiers, with one voice, declared for Otho. The people fled in consternation. Such as lingered behind were attacked sword in hand. The men who carried Galba in a litter, were struck with terror. In their fright they let him fall to the ground near the Curtian lake.[1] His last words, according as men admired or hated him, have been variously reported. According to some, he asked, in a suppliant tone, What harm he had done? and prayed for a few days, that he might discharge the donative due to the soldiers. Others assure us, that he presented his neck to the assassin's stroke, and said with a firm tone of voice, "Strike, if the good of the commonwealth requires it." To ruffians thirsting for blood, no matter what he said. By what hand the blow was given, cannot now be known. Some impute it to Terentius, a resumed veteran; others, to a fellow of the name of Lecanius. A report still more general has transmitted down to us the name of Camurius, a common soldier of the fifteenth legion. This man, it is said, cut Galba's throat. The rest fell on with brutal rage, and finding his breast covered with armour, dissevered his legs and arms. Nor did the barbarians desist, till the emperor lay a headless trunk, deformed with wounds, and weltering in his blood.

XLII. Titus Vinius was the next victim. The manner in which he met his fate is likewise left uncertain. Whether on the first assault his utterance was suppressed by fear, or whether he had power to call out, that Otho had given no orders against his life, we have now no means of knowing. Those words, if really spoken, might be an effort of pusillanimity to save his life, or they were the confession of a man, who was actually an accomplice in the conspiracy. His life and manners leave no room to doubt but he was capable of

[1] This was in the forum near the Rostra.

joining in a parricide, of which his own administration was the principal cause. He fell by a wound that shattered the joint of his knee, and as he lay stretched in that condition, he was run through the body by Julius Carus, a legionary soldier. He expired before the temple of Julius Cæsar.

XLIII. While the rebels were acting their horrible tragedy, the age beheld, in the conduct of one man, a splendid example of courage and fidelity. Sempronius Densus was the person; a centurion of the prætorian cohort. Having been ordered by Galba to join the guard that escorted Piso, he no sooner saw a band of armed assassins, than he advanced to oppose their fury, brandishing his poniard, and exclaiming against the horrible deed. With his voice, with his hand, with every effort in the power of man, he made a brave resistance, and gave Piso, wounded as he was, an opportunity of making his escape. Piso reached the temple of Vesta, where a slave of the state, touched with compassion, conducted him to his own private apartment. Piso lay concealed for some time, not indebted to the sanctity of the temple, nor to the rites of religion, but sheltered by the obscurity of the place. At length, Sulpicius Florus, who belonged to a British cohort, and had been made by Galba a citizen of Rome, and Statius Marcus, a prætorian soldier, arrived in quest of him by Otho's special order. By these two men Piso was dragged to the vestibule of the temple, where, under repeated blows, he breathed his last.

XLIV. In the midst of a general massacre, no murder, we are told, gave so much satisfaction to Otho, nor was there, among the heads cut off, one, at which he gazed with such ardent eyes. By this event he felt himself relieved from all apprehensions. The fate of Galba and of Titus Vinius affected him in a different manner. The former brought to his mind an idea of majesty fallen from a state of elevation; and the death of the latter awakened the memory of an early friendship, and even into a heart like his, fierce, cruel, and ambitious, infused a tincture of melancholy. When Piso fell, an enemy expired. Feeling for him neither regret nor compunction, he gave a loose to joy. The three heads were fixed on poles, and carried, amidst the ensigns of the cohorts, with the eagle of the legion, through the streets of Rome. A band of soldiers followed, stretching forth their hands reeking with blood, and boasting aloud that they gave the mortal wounds, or that they were present aiding and abetting; all, with truth or falsehood, claiming the honour of an atrocious deed. No less than one hundred and twenty memorials, presented on this occasion, by persons who claimed the reward of crimes committed on that dreadful day, were afterwards found by Vitellius; and the several authors, after diligent search made by his orders, were punished with death, not from motives of regard for the memory of Galba, but with the usual policy of princes, who think, by punishing the malefactors of a former reign, that they establish a precedent, and, by the terrors of future vengeance, effectually secure themselves.

XLV. Another senate and another people seemed now to be in possession of Rome. All pressed forward to the camp. You would have thought it a race of servility, in which every man endeavoured to outstrip his fellow-citizens, and be the first to pay his court. They joined in reviling the name of Galba, and all applauded the conduct of the soldiers. They thronged round Otho, fawning to kiss his hand, and, in proportion to their want of sincerity, playing the farce with overacted zeal. Otho was not deficient in the mummery of thanks and gratitude. Attentive to all, and gracious to individuals, he took care at the same time, by his looks and actions, to restrain the soldiers, who, by the ferocity of their looks, seemed to threaten further mischief. Marius Celsus, the consul elect, was the object of their vengeance. He had been the friend of Galba, and, in the last extremity, continued faithful to that unhappy prince. His talents and integrity gave offence to a lawless crew, with whom every virtue was a crime. They demanded his immediate execution. But their views were too apparent. The best and ablest men in Rome were doomed to destruction by a set of men, who panted to let loose their rage, and lay a scene of blood, of plunder, and devastation. Otho was not yet in fulness of power. His authority was sufficient to command the perpetration of crimes; to prohibit them was still beyond him. The part he assumed was that of a man enraged, and bent on some atrocious deed. In that pretended fury, he ordered Celsus to be loaded with irons, as a man reserved for heavier punishment, and by that stratagem saved him from destruction.

XLVI. The prætorians, from this time, knew no control. They chose their own prefects; namely, Plotius Firmus, formerly a common soldier, raised afterwards to the command of the night-guard, and, even during the life of Galba, a partisan in favour of Otho. To him they added Licinius Proculus, a man who lived in intimacy with Otho, and was supposed to be an accomplice in all his dark designs. For the office of governor of Rome they named Flavius Sabinus,[1] influenced in their choice by their respect for the memory of Nero, who had committed to him the same important charge. The majority had another motive: by concurring in this nomination, they meant to pay a compliment to Vespasian, the brother of Sabinus. Their next object was, to abolish the fees exacted by the centurions for occasional exemptions from duty, and for leave of absence. These fees, in fact, were an annual tribute out of the pockets of the common men. In consequence of this abuse, a fourth part of every company was seen rambling about the country, or idly loitering in the very camp. The centurion received his perquisite, and had no other care. Nor was the soldier solicitous about the price; he purchased a right to be idle, and the means by which he enabled himself to defray the expense gave him no kind of scruple. By theft, by robbery, and by servile employments, he gained enough to enrich his officer; and the officer, in return, sold a dispensation from labour and the duties of the service. Whoever had hoarded up a little money, was, for that reason, harassed with discipline, and oppressed with labour, till he purchased the usual indulgence. By these extortions the soldier was impoverished, his stock was exhausted; and after a vagabond life, his industry relaxed, and his vigour wasted, he returned to the camp without courage, strength, or money. By these pernicious practices corruption grew into a system. The common men forgot all discipline; their morals went to ruin; and, in the natural progress of vice, all became ripe for tumult, insurrections, and civil war. To remedy the mischief, and, at the same time, not to alienate the minds of the centurions, Otho undertook to pay an annual equivalent to the officers out of his own revenue. This reform was, no doubt, both wise and just. Good princes adopted it afterwards, and it is now a settled rule in the military system. Laco, the late commander of the prætorians, was condemned to an island, there, as was given out, to pass the remainder of his days; but a veteran soldier, whom Otho had despatched for the purpose, put an end to his life. Martianus Icelus, being of no higher rank than that of a manumitted slave, died by the hand of the executioner.

XLVII. After the horrors of a day spent in guilt, and blood, and carnage, if anything could add to the public misery, it was the joy that succeeded to that dismal scene.

[1] The soldiers loved the vices of the former reign, and for that reason continued Sabinus in the same office.

The prætor of the city[1] summoned a meeting of the senate. The other magistrates strove to distinguish themselves by the vilest adulation. The fathers assembled without delay. The tribunitian power, the name of Augustus, and all imperial honours enjoyed by former princes, were by a decree granted to Otho. Several members of that assembly were conscious of having thrown odious colours on the name and character of their new emperor, and hoped to expiate, by present flattery, the bitterness of former invectives. Whether Otho despised those injurious reflections, or stored them in his memory for future occasions, is uncertain. The shortness of his reign has left that matter undecided. He was conveyed in triumph to the capitol, and thence to the imperial palace. In his way, he saw the forum discoloured with blood, and heaps of slaughtered citizens lying round him. He granted leave to remove the dead bodies, and to perform the rites of sepulture. The remains of Piso were buried by his wife Verania, and Scribonianus his brother. The last duty to Titus Vinius was performed by his daughter Crispina. Their heads, which the murderers had reserved for sale, were found, and redeemed at a stipulated price.

XLVIII. Piso had well-nigh completed the thirty-first year of his age; always high in the esteem of the public, yet never happy. Two of his brothers suffered a violent death; Magnus, by the command of Claudius, and Crassus, by the cruelty of Nero. He himself had passed a considerable part of his time in banishment; an outlaw for some years, and four days a prince by the adoption of Galba, he was raised above his elder brother; but, by that preference, all he gained was to be murdered first.

Titus Vinius had reached the age of fifty-seven; a man of unsettled principle, and various manners. His father was of a prætorian family; his grandfather by the maternal line was in the number proscribed by the triumvirate. His first campaign, under Calvisius Sabinus, began with disgrace. The wife of his commanding officer, prompted by wanton curiosity, went by night, in the disguise of a common soldier, to view the sight and disposition of the camp. In her frolic, she went round to visit the sentinels, and the posts and stations of the army. Arriving at length at the place where the eagles were deposited, she did not scruple to commit the act of adultery on that sacred spot. Vinius was charged as her

[1] The two consuls, Galba and Vinius, being cut off, the power of convening the senate devolved to the city prætor.

accomplice, and, by order of Caligula, loaded with irons. By the revolution which soon after happened, he regained his liberty, and from that time rose to honours. He discharged the office of prætor, and afterwards commanded a legion, free from reproach. His name, however, was soon after branded with a crime, which a common slave would have blushed to commit. Being a guest at the table of Claudius, he was charged with pilfering a golden goblet. On the following day that emperor, to distinguish Vinius from the rest of his company, gave orders that he should be trusted with nothing better than a cup of earthenware. Notwithstanding this disgrace, he became proconsul of Narbon Gaul, and acquitted himself in his administration with distinguished firmness and equal integrity. The friendship of Galba placed him on the brink of a precipice. Bold and prompt in action, of an enterprising genius and undaunted courage, he was at the same time dark, subtle, and deceitful. Qualified to succeed in whatever he undertook, and by nature ready for good or evil deeds, he practised vice and virtue with alternate success and equal ardour. His last will, on account of his immoderate wealth, was declared null and void. That of Piso was confirmed by his poverty.

XLIX. Galba's body, during the night that followed the murder, lay exposed to numberless indignities. It was at length conveyed by Argius, an ancient slave and steward of that unfortunate emperor, to the private gardens of his master, and there deposited in an humble manner without honour or distinction. His head, in a mangled condition, was fixed on a pole by the rabble of the camp, and set up to public view near the tomb of Patrobius, a slave manumitted by Nero, and by order of Galba put to death. In that situation it was found on the following day, and added to the ashes of the body, which had been already committed to the flames. Such was the end of Servius Galba, in the seventy-third year of his age. He had seen the reign of five princes, and enjoyed, during that whole period, a series of prosperity; happy as a private citizen, as a prince unfortunate. He was descended from a long line of ancestors. His wealth was great: his talents not above mediocrity. Free from vice, he cannot be celebrated for his virtues. He knew the value of fame, yet was neither arrogant nor vain-glorious. Having no rapacity, he was an economist of his own, and of the public treasure careful to a degree of avarice. To his friends and freedmen he was open, generous, and even resigned to their will. When his choice was happily made, his indulgence, however excessive, was at worst an amiable weakness; when bad men surrounded him, his good-nature bordered on folly. The splendour of his rank, and the felicity with which he steered through the dangers of a black and evil period, helped to raise the value of his character; his indolence passed for wisdom, and inactivity took the name of prudence. In the vigour of his days, he served with honour in Germany; as proconsul of Africa, he governed with moderation; and the Nethermost Spain, when he was advanced in years, felt the mildness of his administration. While no higher than a private citizen, his merit was thought superior to his rank; and the suffrages of mankind would have pronounced him worthy of empire, had he never made the experiment.

L. In this disastrous juncture, while Rome was shuddering with horror at the late dreadful carnage, and, from the well-known vices of Otho's nature, men were in dread of worse evils still to come, despatches from Germany brought an account of a new storm ready to burst in that quarter. The revolt of Vitellius, and the armies under his command, was no longer a secret. The intelligence arrived before the death of Galba, but was suppressed by that emperor, that the sedition on the Upper Rhine might be thought the only mischief that disturbed the tranquillity of the empire. At length the true state of affairs was known, and a general panic spread through the city. Not only the senators and Roman knights, who had still some shadow of authority, but the meaner populace, mourned over the distractions of their country. All were grieved to see two men of the most pernicious characters, enervated by luxury, and abandoned to every vice, chosen by some fatality to be the bane and ruin of the commonwealth. The crimes and miseries, which, under the late emperors, were one continued pestilence, were no longer the objects that employed the public mind. The civil wars were fresh in the memory of all; they talked of Rome besieged and taken by her own armies; they remembered Italy laid waste; the provinces plundered, the battles of Pharsalia and Philippi, and the siege of Modena and Perusia, two places well known in history, and each of them the scene of public calamity.

"In those tempestuous times, the struggle," it was observed, "lay between men of illustrious character, and by their contentions the state was brought to the brink of ruin. But, even then, under Julius Cæsar, the empire still survived and flourished. It survived under Augustus, and gained additional lustre. Under Pompey and Brutus, had their arms prevailed, the republic would have been once more established. But those men have passed away. Otho and Vitellius are now the competitors: and for them, or either of them, shall the people crowd to the temples? must they pray for a tyrant to reign over them? Vows, in such a cause, were impious, since, in a war between two detestable rivals, he, who conquers, will be armed with power to commit still greater crimes, and prove himself the worst." Such were the reasonings of the people. Some, who saw at a distance, fixed their eyes on Vespasian, and the armies in the east. They foresaw new commotions in that part of the world, and dreaded the calamities of another war. Vespasian, they agreed, was in every respect superior to the two chiefs, who now convulsed the state; but even his character was rather problematical. The truth is, of all the princes who to his time reigned at Rome, he was the only one, whom power reformed, and made a better man.

LI. That the revolt under Vitellius may be seen in its true light, it will be necessary to state the causes that produced it. I therefore go back to the origin of that event. After the defeat of Julius Vindex, and the total rout of his armies, the victorious legions, enriched with booty, grew wanton with success. To men, who without fatigue or danger had closed a lucrative war, the love of enterprise became a natural passion. They preferred hostilities to a state of inaction, and plunder to the soldier's pay. They had, till the late commotions called them forth, endured the hardships of a rigorous service, in a bleak climate and a desolate country, where, even in time of peace, discipline was enforced with strict severity. But discipline, they knew, would be relaxed by civil discord. In the distractions of parties, both sides encourage licentiousness; and, by consequence, fraud, corruption, and treachery, triumph with impunity. The mutinous soldiers were abundantly provided with arms and horses, both for parade and service. Before the late war in Gaul, they saw no more than the company, or the troop of horse, to which they belonged. Stationed at different quarters, they never went beyond their limits, and the boundaries of the provinces kept the armies distinct and separate. Being at length drawn together to make head against Vindex, they felt their own strength; and, having tasted the sweets of victory, they wanted to renew the troubles, by which their rapacity had been so amply gratified. They no longer treated the Gauls as their allies and friends; they considered them as enemies, and a vanquished people.

In these hostile sentiments they were confirmed by such of the Gallic nation as dwelt on the borders of the Rhine. The people, on that side of the country, had taken up arms against Vindex, and his allies, whom, since the death of that chief, they chose to call the GALBIAN FACTION; and now, by every artifice, by infusions of their own malice, they endeavoured to kindle a war between the Romans and their countrymen. The animosity of the legions was easily excited. The Sequanians, the Æduans, and other states, according to their opulence, were the chief objects of resentment. The soldiers thought of nothing but towns assaulted and carried by storm, the plunder of houses, and the desolation of the country. In the heat of imagination, every man anticipated the booty that was to fall to his share. To their arrogance and avarice, the never-failing vices of the strongest, they united the indignation of men, who felt themselves insulted by the vain-glory with which the Æduans and the rest of the obnoxious states made it their boast, that, in despite of the legions, they had extorted from Galba a remission of one-fourth of their tribute, and an extension of their territory. To these incentives was added a report, artfully thrown out and readily believed, that the legions were to be decimated, and the best and bravest of the centurions to be dismissed from the service. To increase the ferment, tidings of an alarming nature arrived from every quarter, and, in particular, a storm was said to be gathering over the city of Rome. The people of Lyons, still faithful to the memory of Nero, and the avowed enemies of Galba, took care to disseminate the worst reports. From that place, as from the centre of intelligence, rumours constantly issued: but the camp was the magazine of news, where invention framed the lie of the day, and credulity stood ready to receive it. The passions of the soldiers were in constant agitation: malice embittered their minds, and fear held them in suspense. But they viewed their numbers, and their courage revived. They found themselves in force, and in full security laughed at the idea of danger.

LII. It was near the calends of December in the preceding year, when Aulus Vitellius first appeared in the Lower Germany. He made it his business to review the legions in their winter quarters; he restored several officers who had been degraded, and relieved others from the disgrace of an ignominious sentence. In these proceedings he acted, in some instances, with justice, in others, with a view to his own ambition. He condemned the sordid avarice with which Fonteius Capito granted or refused rank in the army. He established a fair and regular system of military promotion, and in the eyes of the soldiers appeared to exceed the powers usually vested in consular generals. He seemed to be an officer of superior weight and grandeur. Reflecting men saw the baseness of his motives, while his creatures extolled every part of his conduct. The profusion, which, without judgment or economy, lavished away in bounties all his own property, and squandered that of others, was by his sycophants called benevolence and generosity. Even the vices, that sprung from lust of dominion, were by his creatures transformed into so many virtues.

In the two armies on the Upper and Lower Rhine, there were, no doubt, men well disposed, and of sober conduct; but, at the same time, both camps were infested by a set of desperate incendiaries. At the head of the factious and the turbulent stood Alienus Cæcina and Fabius Valens, each the commander of a legion, both remarkable for their avarice, and both of a daring spirit, ready for any desperate enterprise. Valens had served the interest of Galba, by detecting Verginius, as soon as the conduct of that officer seemed to be equivocal: he had also crushed the machinations of Capito, and for those services thought himself ill requited. Stung with resentment, he now endeavoured to rouse the ambition of Vitellius. "The soldiers," he said, "were zealous in his service, and the name of Vitellius stood in high esteem throughout the Roman world. From Hordeonius Flaccus no opposition was to be apprehended. Britain was ready to declare against Galba, and the German auxiliaries would follow their example. The provinces wavered in their duty, and, by consequence, the precarious authority of a feeble old man would be soon transferred to other hands. Fortune courted Vitellius: he had nothing to do but to open his arms, and receive her favours. Verginius, indeed, had everything to chill his hopes, and damp his resolution. He had no splendid line of ancestors to recommend him. He was of an equestrian family; but his father lived and died in obscurity. A man of his cast would have proved unequal to the weight of empire. A private station was to him a post of safety. The case of Vitellius was very different. Sprung from a father who had been three times consul, once in conjunction with the emperor Claudius, and who, moreover, had discharged the office of censor, he might well aspire to the highest elevation. The honours of his family marked him out for the imperial dignity. Too great for a private station, he must reach the summit of power, or be utterly lost." Notwithstanding this inflammatory speech, the phlegmatic temper of Vitellius was not to be roused. A few faint wishes fluttered at his heart, but hope could find no admission.

LIII. Meanwhile Cæcina, who served in the army on the Upper Rhine, had drawn to himself the affections of the army. Young, and of a comely figure, tall and well proportioned, with an air of dignity in his deportment, a flow of eloquence, and an aspiring genius, he had all the qualities that made an impression on the military mind. Though a young man, he discharged the office of quæstor in the province of Bætica in Spain, and was among the first that went over to Galba's interest. The emperor, to reward his zeal, gave him the command of a legion in Germany; but finding, afterwards, that he had been guilty of embezzling the public money, he ordered him to be called to a strict account. Cæcina was not of a temper to submit with patience. He resolved to embroil the state, and in the general confusion hoped to find a remedy for his own private afflictions. The seed-plots of rebellion were already laid in the army. In the war against Vindex they had taken the field, and, till they heard that Nero was no more, never declared in favour of Galba. Even in that act of submission, they showed no forward zeal, but suffered the legions on the Lower Rhine to take the lead. There was still another circumstance that helped to sharpen their discontent. The Treviri, the Lingones, and other states, which had felt the severity of Galba's edicts, or had seen their territory reduced to narrow limits, lay contiguous to the winter quarters of the legions. Hence frequent intercourse, cabals, and seditious meetings, in which the soldiers grew more corrupt, envenomed as they were by the politics of discontented peasants. Hence their zeal to promote the interest of Verginius, and, when that project failed, their readiness to list under any other chief.

LIV. The Lingones, in token of friendship, had sent presents to the legions, and, in conformity to their ancient usage, the symbolical figure of two right hands clasping one another. Their deputies appeared with the mien and garb of affliction. They went round the camp, and in every quarter disburthened their complaints. In the tents, and in the place for the standards and eagles, they painted forth their own private injuries, while other states enjoyed the favour and the protection of Galba. Finding that they made an impression, they represented to the soldiers the dangers that hung over their own heads, and the hardships under which they laboured. The Romans caught the infection. A general frenzy spread through the camp; the flame of sedition was ready to break out; and some dreadful mischief seemed to be impending, when Hordeonius Flaccus, in the dead of night, ordered the deputies to depart without further delay. A report soon prevailed that they were all treacherously murdered, and that, if the soldiers did not instantly provide for their own safety, the best and bravest of the army would be cruelly butchered, under covert of the night, far from their comrades, and without the knowledge of their friends. A secret combination was immediately formed. The soldiers joined in a bond of union. The auxiliary cohorts, at first suspected of a design to rise against the legions, and put the whole body to the sword, entered into the league with eager ardour. Such is the nature of profligate and abandoned minds; in peace and profound tranquillity, they seldom agree; but for seditious purposes a coalition is easily formed.

LV. The legions on the Lower Rhine, on the calends of January, went through the usual form of swearing fidelity to Galba; but the form only was observed. No man was seen to act with alacrity. In the foremost ranks a feeble sound was heard; the words of the oath were repeated with an unwilling murmur, while the rest remained in sullen silence; each man, as usual in dangerous enterprises, expecting the bold example of his comrades, ready to second the insurrection, yet not daring to begin it. A leaven of discordant humours pervaded the whole mass of the army. The first and fifth legions were the most outrageous: some of them pelted the images of Galba with a volley of stones. The fifteenth and sixteenth abstained from acts of violence, but were loud and clamorous; they bawled sedition, but waited for ringleaders to begin the fray.

In the Upper Germany the tumult was still more violent. On the same calends of January, the fourth and eighteenth legions, quartered together in one winter-camp, dashed the images of Galba into fragments. In this outrage the fourth legion led the way; and the eighteenth, after balancing for some time, followed their example. Unwilling, however, to incur the imputation of a rebellion against their country, they agreed to revive the antiquated names of the SENATE AND ROMAN PEOPLE, and in that republican form took the oath of fidelity. Not one commander of a legion, nor even so much as a tribune, appeared in favour of Galba; on the contrary, many of them, as often happens in cases of public confusion, not only connived, but helped to increase the tumult. The mutineers were still without a leader. No man took upon him to harangue the multitude; no orator ascended the tribunal; nor could the incendiaries tell in whose service their eloquence was to be employed.

LVI. Hordeonius Flaccus beheld this scene of confusion, and, though a consular commander, never once interposed with his authority to restrain the violent, to secure the wavering, or to animate the well-affected. He looked on, a calm spectator, tame and passive; it may be added, innocent, but innocent through sluggish indolence. Four centurions of the eighteenth legion, namely, Nonius Receptus, Donatius Valens, Romilius Marcellus, and Calpurnius Repentinus, attempted to defend the images of Galba. The soldiers attacked them with impetuous violence, and all four were loaded with fetters. From that moment all fidelity was at an end. The obligation of the former oath was no longer binding. It happened in this, as in all seditions: one set appeared to be the most numerous, the rest followed the leaders, and the whole herd was of one party. In the course of the night that followed the calends of January, the eagle-bearer of the fourth legion arrived at the Agrippinian colony, where Vitellius was engaged at a banquet, with intelligence, that the fourth and eighteenth legions, having destroyed the images of Galba, took a new form of oath to the SENATE AND ROMAN PEOPLE. As that government existed no longer, the oath was deemed a nullity. In this crisis it was judged proper to seize the opportunity that fortune offered, and, by the nomination of an emperor, fix the wavering temper of the legions. Despatches were accordingly sent to inform the army in the Lower Germany, that the soldiers on the Upper Rhine had revolted from Galba, and that, by consequence, it remained for them either to march against the rebels, or, for the sake of peace and mutual concord, to create another emperor. In choosing for themselves they would hazard little; but indecision might be dangerous.

LVII. The winter quarters of the first legion were nearest to the residence of Vitellius. Fabius Valens was the commanding officer; a prompt and daring leader of sedition. On the following day he put himself at the head of the cavalry belonging to his own legion, and, with a party of the auxiliaries, proceeded by a rapid march to the Agrippinian colony. He no sooner entered the city, than he saluted Vitellius by the title of emperor. The legions of the province, with zeal and ardour, followed his example; and three days before the nones of January, the legions in Upper Germany declared for Vitellius, losing all memory of the senate and the Roman people. Those specious words, which a few days before resounded with so much energy, were dropt at once; and the men, it now was plain, were never in their hearts the soldiers of a republic. The Agrippinian people, the Treveri, and Lingones, were determined not to be behindhand in demonstrations of zeal. They offered a supply of arms and horses, of men and money, in proportion to their respective abilities. The strong and valiant were willing to serve in person; the rich opened their treasure; and the skilful gave their advice. The leading chiefs, as well in the colonies as in the camp, who had already enriched themselves by the spoils of war, wished for another victory that might bring with it an accumulation of wealth. The zeal with which they entered into the league, was what might be expected; but the alacrity of the common men was beheld with wonder. Poor and destitute, they made a tender of their travelling subsistence, their belts, their accoutrements, and the silver ornaments of their armour; all excited by one general impulse, a sudden fit of blind enthusiasm. In their motives there was, no doubt, a mingle of avarice; and plunder, they hoped, would be the reward of valour.

LVIII. Vitellius, after bestowing the highest praise on the spirit with which the soldiers embraced his cause, proceeded to regulate the various departments of public business. He transferred the offices, hitherto granted to the imperial freedmen, to the Roman knights; and the fees claimed by the centurions for exemptions from duty, were, for the future, to be defrayed out of the revenue of the prince. The fury of the soldiers, demanding vengeance on particular persons, was not to be repressed. He yielded in some instances, and in others eluded their resentment under colour of reserving the obnoxious for heavier punishment. Pompeius Propinquus, the governor of Belgic Gaul, was put to death on the spot; but Julius Burdo, who commanded the German fleet, was saved by an artful stratagem. The army considered that officer as the accuser first, and afterwards as the murderer, of Fonteius Capito, whose memory was still held in respect. To pardon openly was not in the power of Vitellius: he could execute in open day; but to be merciful, he was obliged to deceive. Burdo remained in prison till the victory obtained by Vitellius appeased the wrath of the soldiers. He then was set at liberty. In the meantime, Centurio Crispinus, who with his own hand had shed the blood of Capito, suffered as a victim to expiate that atrocious deed. His guilt was manifest; the soldiers demanded his blood, and Vitellius thought a man of that description no kind of loss.

LIX. Julius Civilis was the next whom the army doomed to destruction; but being of high rank and consequence among the Batavians, fear of a rupture with that fierce and warlike people saved his life. There were, at that time, in the territory of the Lingones, no less than eight Batavian cohorts, annexed at first as auxiliaries to the fourteenth legion, but separated in the distraction of the times; a body of men, in that juncture, of the greatest moment. It was in their power to turn the scale in favour of whatever party they espoused. Nonius, Donatius, Romilius, and Calpurnius, the four centurions already mentioned, were, by order of Vitellius, hurried to execution. They had remained steady in their duty to their prince; and fidelity is a crime which men in open rebellion never pardon. Valerius Asiaticus, the governor of Belgic Gaul, to whom, in a short time after, Vitellius gave his daughter in marriage; and Junius Blæsus, who presided in the province of Lyons, and had under his command the Italic legion,[1] and the body of horse called the Taurinian cavalry,[2] went over to the party of the new emperor. The forces in Rhætia were not long in suspense, and the legions in Britain declared, without hesitation, in favour of Vitellius.

LX. Britain was, at that time, governed by Trebellius Maximus; a man, for his avarice and sordid practices, despised and hated by the army. Between him and Roscius Cælius, who commanded the twentieth legion, there had been a long-subsisting quarrel, renewed of late with keener

[1] For the legion called the Italic, see ii. 6, note.

[2] The Taurinian squadron was so called from the Taurini, or people of Turin.

acrimony, and embittered by the distractions of a civil war. Cælius was charged by his superior officer with being the fomenter of sedition, and an enemy to discipline and good order: in return, he recriminated, alleging that the commander-in-chief plundered the legions, and left the soldiers to languish in distress and poverty. From this dissension between their officers the common men caught the infection. All discipline was at an end. Licentiousness prevailed, and the tumult rose at length to such a height, that Trebellius, insulted openly by the auxiliaries, deserted by the cavalry, and betrayed by the cohorts, was obliged to fly for refuge to Vitellius. The province, however, notwithstanding the flight of a consular governor, remained in a perfect state of tranquillity. The commanders of the legions held the reins of government, by their commissions equal in authority, but eclipsed by the enterprising genius and the daring spirit of Cælius.

LXI. The arrival of the forces from Britain was an accession of strength; and thereupon Vitellius, flushed with hope, abounding in resources, and strong in numbers, resolved to carry the war into Italy by two different routes, under the conduct of two commanders. Fabius Valens was sent forward, with instructions to draw to his interest the people of Gaul, and, if he found them obstinate, to lay waste their country with fire and sword. He was afterwards to pass over the Cottian Alps, and make an irruption into Italy. Cæcina, the other general, was ordered to take a nearer way, over the Pennine mountains, and make his descent on that side. The flower of the army from the Lower Rhine, with the eagle of the fifth legion, and the cohorts and cavalry, amounting to forty thousand men, were put under the command of Valens. Cæcina advanced from the Upper Germany with no less than thirty thousand, of which the one and twentieth legion was the main strength. Each commander had a reinforcement of German auxiliaries. Vitellius followed them, with a third army, to crush whatever resisted, and bring up the whole weight of the war.

LXII. The new emperor and his army presented a striking contrast: the soldiers burned with impatience, and with one voice demanded to be led against the enemy. "It was time," they said, "to push on the war with vigour, while the two Gauls are in commotion, and Spain is yet undecided. The winter season is far from being an obstacle; nor were the men to be amused with idle negotiations to bring on a compromise. Italy, in all events, must be invaded, and Rome taken by storm. In civil dissensions, it is expedition that gives life and energy to all military operations. The crisis called for vigour, and debate was out of season." Vitellius, in the meantime, loitered away his time in dull repose, lifeless, torpid, drunk at noonday, and overwhelmed with gluttony. The imperial dignity, he thought, consisted in riot and profusion, and he resolved to enjoy the prerogative of a prince. The spirit of the soldiers supplied the defects of their prince. They neither wanted him in the ranks to animate the brave, nor to rouse the tardy and inactive. Each man was his own general. With one consent they formed the ranks, and demanded the signal for the march. They saluted Vitellius by the name of Germanicus; that of Cæsar he chose to decline, and even after his victory always rejected it. Valens began his march. On that very day his army beheld a joyful omen. An eagle appeared at the head of the lines, measuring his flight by the movement of the soldiers, as if to guide them on their way. The air resounded with shouts of joy, while the bird proceeded in the same regular course, undismayed by the uproar, and still seeming to direct their march. A phenomenon so unusual was considered as a sure prognostic of a signal victory.

LXIII. The army advanced in good order towards the state of the Treveri, whom they considered as their friends and allies. At Divodurum (a city of the Mediomatrici) they received every mark of kindness, but were seized unaccountably with a sudden panic, in its effect so extraordinary, that the soldiers grasped their arms, and fell upon the innocent inhabitants sword in hand. In this dreadful outrage the love of plunder had no share; a sudden frenzy possessed every mind; and, as the cause was unknown, no remedy could be applied. No less than four thousand men were massacred; and, if the entreaties of the general had not at length prevailed, the whole city had been laid in blood. The rest of Gaul was alarmed by this horrible catastrophe to such a degree, that, wherever the army approached, whole cities, with the magistrates at their head, went forth in a suppliant manner to sue for mercy. Mothers with their children lay prostrate on the ground, as if a conquering enemy advanced against them; and, though nothing like hostility subsisted, the wretched people were obliged, in profound peace, to deprecate all the horrors of war.

LXIV. Valens arrived with his army at the capital city of the Leucians. At that place he received intelligence of the murder of Galba, and the accession of Otho. The news made no impression on the soldiers. Unmoved by joy or fear, they thought of nothing but the spoils of war. The Gauls, released by this event from their attachment to Galba, were now at liberty to choose their party. Otho and Vitellius were objects of their detestation; but they feared the latter. The army proceeded on their march to the territory of the Lingones, a people well disposed towards Vitellius. They met with a friendly reception, and passed their time in acts of mutual kindness. But this amicable intercourse was interrupted by the intemperance of the cohort which had been separated, as already mentioned, from the fourteenth legion, and by Valens incorporated with his army. Being of the Batavian nation, and by nature fierce and warlike, they lived on bad terms with the legions. Opprobrious words passed between them; from words contention arose: the legionary soldiers entered into the dispute, and joined the different parties as judgment or inclination prompted. The quarrel arose to such a pitch, that, if Valens had not interposed, and, by making a few examples, recalled the Batavians to a sense of their duty, a bloody battle must have been the consequence.

A colourable pretext for falling on the Æduans was the ardent wish of the army; but that people not only complied with the demand of money and arms, but added a voluntary supply of provisions. What was thus done by the Æduans through motives of fear, the people of Lyons performed with inclination and zeal to serve the cause of Vitellius. From that city the Italic legion and the Taurinian cavalry were ordered to join the army. The eighteenth cohort,[1] which had been used to winter there, was left in garrison. Manlius Valens at that time commanded the Italic legion. This officer had rendered good service to the cause; but his services were repaid with ingratitude by Vitellius. The fact was, Fabius Valens, the commander-in-chief, had given a secret stab to his reputation, and, to cover his malice, played an artful game, with all the plausible appearance of sly hypocrisy. In public he praised the person whom he wounded in the dark.

LXV. The late war had kindled afresh the deadly feud,

[1] This cohort was usually quartered at Lyons.

which had long subsisted between the people of Lyons and the inhabitants of Vienne. In the various battles, which they had fought with alternate success, and prodigious slaughter, it was visible that so much animosity was not merely the effect of party rage in a contest between Nero and Galba. The people of Lyons had felt the weight of Galba's displeasure;[1] they saw their revenues wrested out of their hands, and confiscated to the imperial treasury, while their inveterate enemies enjoyed the favours of the emperor. Hence a new source of jealousy. The two cities were separated by a river;[2] but they were hostile neighbours, and they saw each other with inflamed resentment. Revenge and malice were not to be appeased. The citizens of Lyons omitted nothing that could excite the legions against their rivals; they talked with the soldiers, man by man, and nothing less than the utter destruction of Vienne could satisfy their indignation. "Lyons," they said, "had been besieged by their mortal enemies, who had taken up arms in the cause of Vindex, and lately raised recruits to complete the legions in the service of Galba." To these incentives they added the temptation of plunder in a rich and opulent city. Finding that they had infused their rancour into the minds of the soldiers, they no longer depended on secret practices, but openly, and in a body, preferred their petition, imploring the army to march forth the redressers of wrong, and raze to the ground a city, that had been the nursery of war, and a hive of enemies; a foreign race, who hated the Roman name. Lyons, they said, was a confederate colony,[3] a portion of the army, willing, at all times, to share in the good or evil fortune of the empire. The issue of the present war might be disastrous to their party. They therefore implored the legions not to leave them, in the event of a defeat, at the mercy of a furious and implacable enemy.

LXVI. These entreaties had their effect. The legions were roused to vengeance, and the flame rose to such a height, that the commanders and other officers despaired of being able to extinguish it. The inhabitants of Vienne had notice of their danger. They came forth in solemn procession, bearing in

[1] The people of Lyons waged war against Vindex, and on that account Galba made them feel his resentment.

[2] The cities of Lyons and Vienne were separated by the river Rhodanus, now the *Rhone*.

[3] The people of Vienne favoured the revolt of Vindex.

their hands the sacred vestments,[1] and all the usual tokens of peace and humble supplication. They met the Romans on their march, and, falling prostrate on the ground, clasped their knees, and in a pathetic strain deprecated the vengeance ready to burst upon them. Fabius Valens judged it expedient to order a distribution of three hundred sesterces to each man. The soldiers began to relent, and the colony was respected for its worth and ancient dignity. The general pleaded in behalf of the inhabitants, and was heard with attention. The state, however, was obliged to furnish a supply of arms and warlike stores. Individuals, with emulation, contributed from their private stock. The report however was, that the people, in good time, applied a large sum of money, and purchased the protection of the commander-in-chief. Thus much is certain, that, after being for a long time depressed with poverty, he grew suddenly rich, but took no pains to conceal his affluence. The art of rising in the world with moderation, was not the talent of Valens. His passions had been restrained by indigence, and now, when fortune smiled, the sudden taste of pleasure hurried him into excess. A beggar in his youth, he was, in old age, a voluptuous prodigal.

The army proceeded by slow marches through the territory of the Allobrogians, and thence to the Vocontians; the general, during the whole progress, making his market at every place, and selling his favours for a sum of money. For a bribe, he fixed the length of each day's march, and shifted his camp for a price agreed upon between him and the owners of the lands. In all these exactions Valens enforced his orders with unrelenting cruelty, nor did he blush to drive open bargains with the magistrates of the several cities. Torches and firebrands were prepared to fire the town of Lucus, situate in the territory of the Vocontians; and the place would infallibly have been burnt to the ground, if the people had not ransomed themselves with a considerable sum. Where pecuniary bribes were not to be had, women were obliged to resign their persons, and prostitution became the price of common humanity. In this manner, gratifying his avarice, or his brutal passions, Valens arrived at the foot of the Alps.

LXVII. Cæcina, who commanded the second army, marked his way with greater rapine and more horrible cruelty. He found in the territory of the Helvetians abundant cause to provoke a man of his ferocious temper. The people of that

[1] Olive branches and sacred vestments were usually displayed in cases of distress, when the conquered sued for mercy.

district, originally a Gallic nation,[1] were renowned in former times for their valour, and their exploits in war. Of late years the history of their ancestors was their only glory. Not having heard of the death of Galba, they were unwilling to acknowledge Vitellius. In this disposition of their minds, they had soon a cause of quarrel, occasioned by the rapacity of the twenty-first legion. That body of men fell in with a party, who were escorting a sum of money to a strong fort, where the Helvetians had immemorially maintained a garrison. The Romans seized the whole as lawful plunder. An act of violence so unwarranted, raised the indignation of the people. Determined to make reprisals, they intercepted a small party on their way to Pannonia, with letters from the German army to the legions stationed in that country. They seized the papers, and detained in custody a centurion with some of his soldiers. This, to such a man as Cæcina, was ample provocation. He wished for nothing so much as a pretence for open hostility. Whenever he took umbrage, he struck his blow without delay. To defer the punishment, were to leave time for repentance. He marched against the Helvetians, and, having laid waste the country, sacked a place, built, during the leisure of a long peace, in the form of a municipal town, remarkable for the beauty of the situation, and, by reason of its salubrious waters, much frequented. Not content with this act of revenge, he sent despatches into Rhætia, with orders to the auxiliaries of that country to hang upon the rear of the Helvetians, while he advanced to attack them in front.

LXVIII. The spirit of the Helvetians, fierce and intrepid while the danger was at a distance, began to droop as soon as the war drew nearer. In the beginning of these hostilities they had chosen Claudius Severus to command their forces, but terror and confusion followed. They neither knew the use of their arms, nor the advantage of discipline. To keep their ranks in battle was not their practice, nor were they able to act in concert with their united force. The contest, they now perceived, must be unequal with a veteran army; and, their fortifications being everywhere in decay, to stand a siege was not advisable. Cæcina advanced at the head of a numerous army; the cavalry and auxiliary forces from Rhætia, with the youth of that country, inured to arms, and trained to the art of war, were ready to attack them in the rear. The country

[1] The territory of the Helvetii was a part of Celtic Gaul, more extensive than what is now called Switzerland. The people are celebrated by Julius Cæsar for their military virtue, and constant warfare with the Germans.

was laid waste, and a dreadful carnage followed. The Helvetians betook themselves to flight; and, after wandering about in a general panic, wounded, maimed, and unable to resist, they threw down their arms, and fled for refuge to the mountain, known by the name of Vocetius.[1] A band of Thracians was sent to dislodge them. Driven from their fastness, they betook themselves to the woods, or fled to their lurking-places, while the Germans and Rhætians hung upon them in their flight. Several thousands were put to the sword, or sold to slavery. Having ravaged the country, and laid a scene of desolation, the army marched to the siege of Aventicum, the capital city of the Helvetians. The inhabitants sent their deputies, offering to surrender at discretion. Their submission was accepted. Julius Alpinus, one of the leading chiefs, charged with being the author of the war, was by order of Cæcina publicly executed. The rest were left to the mercy or resentment of Vitellius.

LXIX. The Helvetians sent their ambassadors to the new emperor; but which was most implacable, he or his army, it is difficult to decide. The soldiers clamoured for the utter destruction of the whole race. They brandished their arms in the face of the ambassadors, and threatened blows and brutal violence. Vitellius showed no less ferocity. He gave vent to a torrent of abuse, and threw out violent menaces. At length Claudius Cossus, one of the deputies, who possessed an uncommon share of eloquence, but had the skill, under an appearance of well-acted terror, to conceal his power over the passions of his audience, had the address to soothe the minds of the soldiers. Their rage subsided, and compassion took its turn. Such is the nature of the multitude; easily inflamed, and with a sudden transition shifting to the opposite extreme. They melted into tears, and never ceased their supplications till they prevailed on Vitellius, and saved the people from destruction.

LXX. Cæcina, wanting further instructions from Vitellius, and, at the same time, making all proper arrangements for his passage over the Alps, halted for a few days in the territory of the Helvetians. In that situation, he received intelligence that the squadron of horse called Sulla's squadron, at that time quartered on the banks of the Po, had sworn fidelity to Vitellius. They had formerly served under Vitellius, when he was the proconsular governor of Africa. Nero, when he

[1] Probably in the Jura.

projected an expedition into Egypt, ordered them to sail for that country; but, being soon after alarmed by the commotions stirred up by Vindex, he called them back to Italy, where they remained from that time. Their officers, unacquainted with Otho, and closely connected with Vitellius, espoused the interest of the latter. By representing to the men the strength of the legions then on their march to the invasion of Italy, and by extolling the valour of the German armies, they drew the whole squadron into their party. As a further proof of their zeal for their new prince, they attracted to his interest the chief municipal towns on the other side of the Po, namely, Mediolanum, Novaria, Eporedia, and Vercellus. Of this fact Cæcina was apprised by despatches from the officers. But a single squadron, he knew, was not sufficient to defend so large a tract of country. In order to reinforce them, he sent forward the cohorts of Gaul, Lusitania, and Britain, with the succours from Germany, and the squadron of horse called the *Ala Petrina*.[1] How he himself should pass into Italy was his next consideration. His first plan was to march over the Rhætian mountains, in order to make a descent into Noricum, where Petronius Urbicus, the governor of the province, supposed to be a partisan in Otho's service, was busy in collecting forces, and destroying the bridges over the rivers. But this enterprise was soon relinquished. The detachment already sent forward might be cut off, and, after all, the secure possession of Italy was the important object. The issue of the war, wherever decided, would draw after it all inferior places, and Noricum would fall, by consequence, into the hands of the conqueror. He resolved, therefore, to proceed by the shortest way into Italy. For this purpose, he ordered the troops lightly armed to proceed on their journey, and, with the legions heavily armed, he marched himself over the Pennine Alps, through a waste of snow, and all the rigours of the winter season.

LXXI. Otho, in the meantime, displayed a new and unexpected character. He renounced his love of pleasure, or, at least, dissembled for the present. Scorning to loiter in luxury and inglorious ease, he assumed a spirit becoming the majesty of empire. And yet the change diffused a general terror: men knew that his virtues were false, and they dreaded a return of his former vices. He ordered Marius Celsus, the consul elect, whom he had put in irons in order to rescue him

[1] The squadron of horse, called *Ala Petrina*, had been stationed in Cumberland.

from the hands of the soldiers, to appear before him in the capitol. To acquire the fame of clemency, by releasing a man of illustrious character, and well known to be an enemy to Otho and his party, was the object of his ambition. Celsus appeared with unshaken constancy. He confessed the crime of adhering faithfully to the unfortunate Galba, and, by that firmness, gave the emperor a fair opportunity to grace his character. Otho did not assume the tone of a sovereign granting pardon to a criminal; but, to show that he could think generously of an enemy, and to remove all doubt of the sincerity of his reconciliation, he received Celsus among his intimate friends, and, in a short time afterwards, appointed him one of his generals to conduct the war. Celsus accepted the commission, and remained steady to his trust. His fidelity was honourable, but unfortunate. The clemency of the prince gave great satisfaction to the leading men at Rome; the populace applauded, and even the soldiers admired the virtue which they had condemned.

LXXII. The joy excited on this occasion was followed by an event no less acceptable, but for reasons of a different nature. The public voice was loud against Sophonius Tigellinus,[1] and accordingly his doom was fixed. From low beginnings this man had raised himself to eminence in the state. His birth was obscure. Stained in his youth with the worst impurities, he retained, in his advanced years, all his early habits, and closed with disgrace a life begun in infamy. By his vices, the surest road to preferment, he obtained the command, first of the city cohorts, and afterwards of the prætorian guards. The rewards which were due to virtue only, he obtained by his crimes. To his effeminate qualities he united some of those rougher evils which may be called manly passions, such as avarice and cruelty. Having gained an entire ascendant over the affections of Nero, he was, in some instances, the adviser of the horrors committed by that prince, and in others the chief actor, without the knowledge of his master. He corrupted Nero at first, and in the end deserted him. Hence it was that the blood of a criminal was never demanded with such violent clamour. The men who detested the memory of Nero, and those who still regretted him, concurred in one opinion. They all joined in the cry for public justice. During the short reign of Galba, he lived secure under the protection of Titus Vinius. In fact,

1 Tigellinus has been often mentioned. See *Annals*, xiv. 57, xv. 37.

he had some merit with that minister, having saved the life of his daughter; but, in that very act, humanity was not his motive. A man who had shed so much innocent blood, could not be suspected of a single virtue. His design was, by a new connection, to screen himself from future danger.

Such at all times is the policy of the worst of men: they dread a reverse of fortune, and, in the hour of need, hope to shelter themselves under the protection of some pernicious favourite. Innocence is no part of their care; they know that the guilty are ever ready to defend each other. But the friendship of Vinius, who was still remembered with detestation, was an additional spur to the populace. They crowded together from all quarters; they surrounded the palace; they filled the forum; and in the circus and the theatre, where licentiousness is most apt to show itself, they clamoured, with a degree of violence little short of sedition, for the punishment of a vile malefactor. Tigellinus was then at the baths of Sinuessa. Orders were sent to him to put a period to his life. He received the fatal news in a circle of his concubines; he took leave with tenderness; and after mutual embraces and other trifling delays, he cut his throat with a razor; by the pusillanimity of his last moments disgracing even the infamy of his former life.

LXXIII. About the same time, the execution of Calvia Crispinilla was demanded by the public voice: but by various artifices, in which the duplicity of the prince covered him with dishonour, she was saved from danger. She had been, in the reign of Nero, the professed teacher of lascivious pleasures, and, in the various scenes of that emperor, the caterer for his appetite. She passed afterwards into Africa, and, having instigated Clodius Macer to revolt, became an accomplice in the plot to cause a famine in the city of Rome. She was married soon after to a man of consular rank, and, by that connection, gained a powerful interest, insomuch that, during the reigns of Galba, Otho, and Vitellius, she lived in perfect security. Even in the following reign she was high in credit. Her riches, and her want of children, placed her in a flourishing state; and those two circumstances, in good as well as evil times, are sure to be of weight.

LXXIV. Otho, in the meantime, endeavoured by frequent letters to divert Vitellius from his purpose. His proposals were in the soft style of female persuasion; he offered money, and a retreat for voluptuous enjoyments, with all that the prince's favour could bestow. Vitellius answered in the same delicate strain. Both parties corresponded in dainty terms, with dissembled hatred, and frivolous negotiation, till, exasperated by want of success, they changed their tone, and, with unguarded invective, charged each other with criminal pleasures and flagitious deeds. Both had truth on their sides. Weary of altercation, Otho recalled the deputies, who had been sent by Galba, and, in their room, despatched others to the German army, to the Italic legion, and the troops quartered at Lyons, with instructions to negotiate in the name of the senate. The men employed in this embassy tarried with Vitellius, and, by their cheerful compliance, left no room to think that they were detained by force. Under pretence of doing honour to the embassy, Otho had sent a detachment of the prætorian guards. Without suffering them to mix with the soldiers, Vitellius ordered them to return without delay. Fabius Valens took the opportunity to write, in the name of the German army, to the prætorian guards. His letters, in a style of magnificence, set forth the strength of the legions, and, at the same time, offered terms of mutual concord. He condemned the forward zeal, with which they presumed to transfer to Otho an empire which had been vested in Vitellius. He mingled promises with expressions of anger, and, after treating the prætorians as men unequal to an important war, gave them assurances that they would lose nothing by peace and unanimity. These letters, however, were without effect. The prætorians continued firm in their duty.

LXXV. The rival chiefs began to lay snares for each other. They waged a war of treachery. Emissaries were sent by Otho into Germany, and others by Vitellius to Rome. Both parties missed their aim. The agents of Vitellius passed undetected. Amidst a concourse of people, in so vast a city as Rome, they could lurk with impunity; while, on the other hand, in a camp where all were known to each other, the men employed by Otho were soon discovered by the novelty of their faces. Vitellius, anxious for his family, then residing at Rome, sent letters to Titianus, the brother of Otho, threatening, if any violence was offered to his mother or his children, to make reprisals, and put both him and his son to death. Both families remained unhurt. As long as Otho lived, fear might be the motive: Vitellius, after his victory, added to his laurels the palm of clemency.

LXXVI. The first occurrence that inspired Otho with confidence in his cause, was an account from Illyricum that the legions of Dalmatia, of Pannonia, and Mæsia, had declared in his favour. Advices from Spain brought the like intelligence; and in a public edict, honourable mention was made of Cluvius Rufus, the governor of the province. That compliment, however, was found to be premature. Spain went over to the interest of Vitellius. The people of Aquitaine, under the influence of Julius Cordus, had sworn obedience to Otho; but a little time showed, that the obligation of an oath was no longer binding. All principle, all affection, and all truth, were banished. Fear, and the necessity of the times, governed in every quarter. Narbon Gaul acceded to Vitellius. A party in force, and near at hand, found no difficulty in drawing their neighbours into a league with themselves. The distant provinces, and all places separated by the Mediterranean, adhered to Otho, not from motives of regard for him or his party, but because the name of Rome and the senate was still respected by foreign nations. Besides this, Otho, being the first announced in foreign parts, had already made his impression. The army in Judæa under the conduct of Vespasian, and that in Syria under Mucianus, swore fidelity to Otho. Egypt, and the provinces in the east, acknowledged his authority. The same disposition prevailed in Africa. The whole country was willing to follow the example set by the people of Carthage. In that city, without any order or authority from Vipsanius Apronianus, then proconsular governor of the province, a public treat was given by a pragmatical fellow, of the name of Crescens, one of Nero's freedmen, who had the ambition to distinguish himself as an active partisan in the interest of Otho. Such, in times of public distraction, is the presumption of the lowest men in the state. They think it time to emerge from their obscurity, and act their part, as if they had an interest in the commonwealth. The mob of Carthage expressed their zeal with all demonstrations of joy, and the rest of Africa followed their example.

LXXVII. In this posture of affairs, while the armies and the several provinces embraced opposite interests, it was evident that Vitellius, to secure his title, had nothing left but the decision of the sword. Otho, in the meantime, remained at Rome, discharging all the functions of the sovereign power, as if he was established in profound tranquillity. His conduct, in some instances, was such as became the dignity of the state; but his measures, for the most part, were hastily adopted, the mere expedients of the day. He named himself and his brother Titianus joint consuls,[1] to continue in office till the kalends of March. For the two following months, with a view to curry favour with the German army, he appointed Verginius, and gave him for his colleague Pompeius Vopiscus. For the nomination of the latter he pretended motives of friendship; but, as men of penetration thought, his real view was to pay court to the people of Vienne. With regard to future consuls, no alteration was made in the arrangement settled by Nero or by Galba. Cælius Sabinus and his brother Flavius were to succeed for the months of May and June. From the first of July to September, Arrius Antoninus[2] and Marius Celsus were to be in office. Nor did Vitellius, after his victory, disturb this order of succession. Otho, at the same time, thought proper to grant the augural and pontifical dignities, as the summit of civil honours, to such of the senators as were grown grey in public stations; nor was he unmindful of the young patricians lately recalled from banishment. To soothe the remembrance of their sufferings, he bestowed upon them the sacerdotal honours which had been enjoyed by their ancestors. Cadius Rufus, Pedius Blæsus, and Sævinus Pomtinus, who under Claudius or Nero had been charged with extortion, and expelled the senate, were restored to their rank. To varnish this proceeding, the real offence was suppressed, and what was, in fact, public rapine, in the style of the pardon took the name of violated majesty; a charge held in such general detestation, that, to elude it, the best and wisest laws were set aside.

LXXVIII. In order to extend his popularity, Otho, in the next place, turned his thoughts to the cities and provinces,

1 The number of consuls, in the course of this eventful year, was so great, that it will not be useless to place the list in one view before the eye of the reader.

A.D. 70.	Consuls.
On the Kalends of January, *Hist.* i. 1 . .	Galba, Vinius.
On the Kalends of March, *Hist.* i. 77 . .	Salvius Otho, Titianus Otho.
On the Kalends of May, *Hist.* i. 77 . . .	Verginius Rufus, Pompeius Vopiscus.
On the Kalends of July, *Hist.* i. 77 . . .	Cælius Sabinus, Flavius Sabinus.
On the Kalends of September, *Hist.* i. 77 .	Arrius Antoninus, Marius Celsus.
On the Kalends of November, *Hist.* ii. 1 .	Fabius Valens, Alienus Cæcina.

Cæcina being pronounced a traitor by the senate, on the day before the kalends of January, the consul for a single day, being the last of the year, was Rosius Regulus. *Hist.* iii. 37.

2 Arrius Antoninus, who appears in the foregoing list of the consuls, was grandfather to Antoninus Pius, the upright and virtuous emperor.

little doubting but by acts of munificence he should be able to strengthen his interest. To the colonies of Hispalis and Emerita,[1] then on the decline, he transplanted a number of families: the Lingones were honoured with the privileges of Roman citizens, and to the province of Bætica all the Moorish cities were annexed. He gave a new code of laws to Cappadocia, and another to Africa; all popular grants, and splendid for the present, but soon to fade away, and sink into oblivion. Amidst these innovations, all of them temporising acts, occasioned by the pressure of his affairs, and perhaps on that account excusable, he did not forget his tender passions. Even in the moment when the sovereign power was still at stake, his love of Poppæa was not extinguished. With fond remembrance of that connection, he caused her statues to be restored by a decree of the senate. There is reason to think, that, with a view to popularity, he intended to celebrate the memory of Nero with public honours. Many were for erecting the statues of that emperor, and even proposed it as a public measure. The populace and the soldiers, as if they meant to decorate their emperor with additional splendour, saluted him by the title of NERO OTHO. He heard their acclamations, but remained silent; perhaps unwilling to reject the compliment, perhaps ashamed to accept it.

LXXIX. The public mind being now intent on the great scene that began to open, no wonder if foreign affairs fell into neglect. Encouraged by the inattention that prevailed at Rome, the Rhoxolanians, a people of Sarmatia, who in the preceding winter had cut off two entire cohorts, made an irruption into the province of Mæsia, with nine thousand horse; a band of freebooters, determined to ravage the country. Plunder, and not war, was their passion. They prowled about in quest of prey, without order, or apprehension of an enemy, when, on a sudden, they found themselves hemmed in by the third legion and their auxiliaries. The Romans advanced in order of battle. The Sarmatians, overloaded with booty, were taken by surprise. On a damp and slippery soil, the swiftness of their horses was of no use. Unable to retreat, they were cut to pieces, more like men bound in fetters, than soldiers armed for the field of battle. It may seem strange, but it is not less true, that the courage of the Sarmatians has no inward principle, but depends altogether upon external circumstances; a kind of courage, that has no source in the mind, but may be said

[1] Seville and Merida.

to be out of the man. In an engagement with the infantry, nothing can be more dastardly; in an onset of the cavalry, they are impetuous, fierce, and irresistible. Their weapons are long spears or sabres of an enormous size, which they wield with both hands. The chiefs wear coats of mail, formed with plates of iron, or the tough hides of animals, impenetrable to the enemy, but to themselves an incumbrance so unwieldy, that he who falls in battle is never able to rise again.

In their encounter with the Romans, a heavy fall of rain and a sudden thaw deprived them of all advantage from the velocity of their horses; the consequence was, that they were overwhelmed in a deep waste of snow. The light breastplates of the Romans were no impediment. With their missive weapons, and their swords of a moderate length, they were able to rush into the thickest ranks; while the Sarmatians, who wear neither shield nor buckler, were a mark at a distance, or in close engagement cut to pieces. The few who escaped from the slaughter, fled for refuge to their fens and marshes, and there died of their wounds, or perished under the inclemency of the season. An account of this transaction being received at Rome, a triumphal statue was decreed to Marcus Aponius, then governor of Mæsia. Fulvius Aurelius, Julianus Titius, and Numisius Lupus, all three commanders of legions, obtained the consular ornaments. The joy expressed by Otho was beyond all bounds. He assumed the merit of the victory, boasting, with vain-glory, that, by his own auspicious fortune, and the valour of his officers and his armies, he had aggrandised the Roman name.

LXXX. From a cause altogether contemptible, and in its origin threatening no kind of danger, a violent sedition well-nigh involved the city in ruin. The seventeenth cohort, then quartered at Ostia, had orders to remove to Rome. The care of providing them with arms was committed to Varius Crispinus, a tribune of the prætorian bands. That officer, intending to execute his orders without noise or bustle, chose his time towards the close of day, when the camp was quiet. He opened the magazine of arms, and ordered the waggons to be loaded. The lateness of the hour filled the men with suspicion; the intention seemed dark and dangerous, and the affectation of secrecy produced a general tumult. The soldiers were in liquor, and, at the sight of their arms, reasoning like drunken men, they thought it their business to seize them without delay. They murmured, they complained; they charged the tribunes and centurions with treachery, declaring aloud, that a dark conspiracy was formed, with intention to arm the slaves and domestics of the senators against the life of Otho. A scene of uproar and confusion followed. Some were stupefied with liquor, and comprehended nothing: the profligate liked the opportunity to commit midnight plunder; and the multitude, as usual, were ready to mix in any sudden commotion. Those who regarded discipline and good order were undistinguished in the dark. The tribune who attempted to restrain their fury, was murdered on the spot. The centurions, who exerted themselves on the occasion, suffered in like manner. The soldiers seized their arms: they mounted their horses, and, entering the city sword in hand, rushed in a body to the imperial palace.

LXXXI. Otho was engaged at a grand entertainment, to which he had invited the most distinguished of both sexes. A sudden terror seized the whole company. The cause was unknown. Was it an accidental fray among the soldiers, or the perfidy of the emperor? What was to be done? should they stay and perish together? or was it more advisable to disperse, and fly different ways? In the hurry and agitation no one could decide. They made a show of resolution: their courage failed; they stood covered with consternation, and, with their eyes fixed on Otho, endeavoured to peruse his countenance. The usual fate of suspicious minds attended them all. They were afraid of Otho, and he stood trembling for himself. He trembled also for the senate, and thought of their danger no less than of his own. He ordered the two prætorian commanders to go forth, in order to appease the tumult, and, in the meantime, advised his company to depart. They fled with precipitation. The magistrates threw aside the ensigns of their office, and dispersed without their friends, without their train of attendants. Old men and women of distinction wandered about in the dark, they knew not whither. Few dared to venture towards their own habitations. The greatest part took shelter with their friends; and where the meanest of their dependants lived, that place they thought the safest refuge.

LXXXII. The madness of the soldiers was not to be controlled. They burst the palace gates, and rushed forward to the banqueting-room, with outrageous clamour demanding a sight of Otho. Julius Martialis, one of the tribunes, and Vitellius Saturninus, the prefect of the legion, endeavoured to oppose the torrent, and were both wounded in the fray. Nothing was to be seen but the flash of arms, and nothing heard but threats and denunciations of vengeance, now against the centurions, and, at times, against the whole body of the senate. The soldiers neither knew the cause nor the object of their frenzy, and, having no particular victim in view, they resolved to lay a scene of general slaughter. They forced their way into the apartment of the prince. Otho, forgetting his own rank and the majesty of empire, stood up on his couch, with tears and supplications imploring the soldiers to desist. He prevailed at length. The men retired to the camp, with a sullen spirit, and guilt at their hearts. On the following day Rome had the appearance of a city taken by assault. The houses were shut, the streets deserted, the populace in a general panic. The soldiers wandered about in a sullen mood, with looks of discontent, rather than repentance. The two prefects, Licinius Proculus and Plotius Firmus, went round to the several companies, and harangued the men, each according to his own peculiar temper, in soothing terms, or in a style of reproach. A distribution of five thousand sesterces to each man concluded the business. The tumult over, Otho ventured to enter the camp. The tribunes and centurions gathered round him, but without the military ornaments of their rank, praying to be dismissed from the service, that they might retire to live in ease and safety. The soldiers felt the request as a reproach for their own conduct. Remorse and sorrow took possession of every mind. They expressed their willingness to return to their duty, and, of their own motion, desired to see the authors of the insurrection brought to punishment.

LXXXIII. In this delicate conjuncture, when the times were big with danger, and a discordant soldiery heightened the distraction, Otho felt that he had a difficult game to play. All who wished well to the service, called for an immediate reform of the army: while on the other hand, the loose and profligate, always the greatest number, liked nothing so well as tumult and insurrections, under the conduct of an ambitious leader. To such minds, Otho knew that the strongest motives to a civil war are the hopes of growing rich by the spoils of the public; nor was he to learn, that power obtained by guilt, is incompatible with a new system of laws and the rigour of ancient manners. But still the danger that hung over the city and the Roman senate filled him with anxiety. In this alarming situation, he spoke to the following effect:

"I come not now, my fellow-soldiers, to excite your zeal for me and the cause in which we are engaged; much less do I come to add new ardour to your courage. Both are too well known: they need no incentive. Perhaps some restraint may be necessary; perhaps the zeal, that pervades you all, requires a degree of moderation. In the late tumult, it was not the love of plunder, nor ill-will to any man, or any set of men, that urged you on. From those motives, discord and mutiny have often broke out in various armies; but upon your conduct they had no effect. Nor was there in that transaction any fear of danger, or so much as a wish to renounce your duty. It was your regard for me, sincere indeed, but generous to excess, that hurried you on to acts of intemperance, and even violence. You listened to your passions, but not to your judgment; and where judgment does not direct and guide, the best counsels and the best cause are often ruined. We are going forth to a great and important war. And must all intelligence be communicated to the army? Must every secret be disclosed? And must councils of war be held in a public assembly of the soldiers? The reason of things, and the opportunity, which must be seized at once or lost for ever, will not allow a mode of proceeding so slow and dangerous to the service. To know some things is the duty of the soldier; in others, not to be informed is his happiness, and submission is his virtue. Even the tribunes and centurions must often receive their orders, without a reason assigned: to know the motives that weigh with the general, is not their province; to obey is the duty of the inferior officer. If every subaltern may discuss the operations of war, and cavil with the commander-in-chief, subordination ceases, discipline is at an end, and the best-concerted enterprise may be defeated. And are we now to imagine, that the soldier, when the enemy is at hand, may seize his arms, and, as caprice or fancy prompts, sally forth in the dead of night? Shall two or three drunken men (in the last night's fray, I do not believe there were more) imbrue their hands in the blood of their officers? Shall they murder the centurions, and, in a fit of frenzy, rush to the pavilion of their general?

LXXXIV. "You, my fellow-soldiers, have transgressed the bounds of your duty; the fact must be admitted; but your zeal for me was the cause. And yet, reflect for a moment, what might have been the consequence. Amidst that general uproar, in the gloom of midnight darkness, the assassin's blow might have been aimed at me, whom you wished to defend. Give Vitellius his option; let him and his rebel soldiers have the power of choosing, and what greater curse could they invoke? what calamity could they call down upon us, so much to be dreaded, as a turbulent and factious spirit, and all the evils of discord and sedition? Let the soldier refuse to obey his centurion; let the centurion shake off the authority of the tribune; let the cavalry and the foot soldiers be intermixed, without order or distinction; and let us all, in one promiscuous body, go forward to the war. Need our enemies wish for more? We should rush on sure destruction. It is obedience, my fellow-soldiers, implicit, prompt obedience, without pausing to wrangle with our superior officer, that gives to military operations all their energy. The army that shows itself, in time of peace, attentive to discipline and good order, is sure to be the most formidable in the day of battle. It is yours to arm in the cause of your country, and to face the enemy with heroic valour: be it mine to form the plan of operations, and, in the execution, to direct and guide the courage of the army. The guilt of last night extends to a few only; and of those few, two only shall expiate the offence. That done, let us bury in oblivion the horrors of that shameful tumult; and may no other army hear those dreadful imprecations uttered against a Roman senate, against that venerable body, the head of the empire, and the fountain, from which justice flows through the provinces, not even Vitellius, nor his rash-levied crew of Germans, would dare to meditate so vile a deed.

"And can there be in Italy a race of men, the genuine offspring of Roman citizens, who are capable of so foul a parricide? who can lift their impious hands against the sacred order, from whom our cause derives so much lustre, to the confusion of Vitellius and the scum of nations that follows him to the field? Some states, it is true, have been induced to join his standard; he has the appearance of an army; but the senate is on our side. The commonwealth is with us; our enemies are the enemies of Rome. And when I mention Rome, when you yourselves behold that magnificent city, do you imagine that it consists in walls, and buildings, and a pile of stones? Inanimate structures and mute and senseless edifices may moulder away, and rise again out of their ruins; but the stability of empire depends upon the senate: upon the safety of that august assembly, the welfare of the community, the peace of nations, your fate and mine, are grafted. It was Romulus, the founder of the city, and the father of the Roman state, who instituted, with solemn auspices, that sacred order. It has subsisted in vigour from that time; from the expulsion of Tarquin, to the establishment of the Cæsars, it has been preserved inviolate. We received it from our ancestors; let us transmit it to our posterity, unshaken, unimpaired, immortal. From your order, from the people at large, the senate is supplied with its brightest ornaments: and from the senate you derive a succession of princes."

LXXXV. This speech, seasoned with reproof, yet tempered with conciliating language, was favourably received; and the moderation of the prince, who punished only two of the mutineers, gave general satisfaction. By that lenient measure, the soldiers, too fierce to be controlled, were quieted for the present. Rome, however, was not in a state of tranquillity. A constant din of arms was heard, and warlike preparations were seen in every quarter. The soldiers did not, as before, riot in tumultuous bodies; but, being dispersed throughout the city, they found means, in various shapes, to insinuate themselves into houses, where they watched, with sufficient malignity, the motions and words of all who, by their nobility, their wealth, or their talents, were eminent enough to be objects of calumny. A report prevailed at the same time, that Vitellius had a number of emissaries dispersed among the populace, to act as spies, and watch the state of parties. Hence jealousy, mistrust, and fear. No man thought himself safe under his own roof. Abroad and under the eye of the public the alarm was still greater. Whatever was the rumour of the day, all degrees and ranks were obliged to set their faces for the occasion: if bad, they were afraid of seeming to despond; and, if propitious, unwilling to be thought backward in demonstrations of joy. With events of either kind, their features were taught to comply.

The fathers had the hardest task. Silence in the senate might be thought sullen discontent, and liberty of speech might be deemed a crime. Adulation itself was at a stand. Who could deceive a prince, who was but lately a private man, and, in that station, practised flattery till he became a perfect master of that insidious art? The fathers were driven to little stratagems; they tortured every sentence into a thousand forms, and, to diversify one and the same thought, all the colours of rhetoric were exhausted. All agreed to call Vitellius A PUBLIC ENEMY AND A PARRICIDE. This was the burden of every speech. Cautious men, who looked forward to their own security, avoided entering into particulars, content with hackneyed declamation: others, without reserve or management, poured out a torrent of virulent invective, but generally chose to rise in the midst of noise and clamour, when nothing could be distinctly heard, and the speaker could mouth and bellow, without the danger of being understood or remembered.

LXXXVI. A number of prodigies, announced from different quarters, diffused a general panic. The goddess of victory, in the vestibule of the capitol, let the reins of two horses, harnessed to her chariot, fall from her hand. A form of more than human size was seen to issue from the chapel of Juno. In an island in the Tiber,[1] the statue of Julius Cæsar, without any apparent cause, on a day perfectly serene and calm, turned round from the west to the east. In Etruria an ox was said to have spoken; animals brought forth monstrous births; and to these was added a variety of preternatural appearances, such as in rude and barbarous ages were the coinage of superstition; and, even in profound peace, made an impression on vulgar credulity, though of late years they have so far lost their effect, that, unless it be a time of public distress, they pass away unheeded and forgotten. Amidst the omens, which seemed to threaten impending danger, an inundation of the Tiber was the most alarming. The waters swelled above their banks, and overflowed the adjacent country. The Sublician bridge was carried away by the flood; and the ruins that fell in, obstructing the course of the river, the torrent was driven back with such impetuous violence, that not only the level parts of the city, but even the higher grounds, were covered with a general deluge.[2] The people in the streets were swallowed up, and numbers were drowned in their shops, and in their beds. The corn in the public granaries was destroyed; a famine ensued, and the common people were reduced to the last distress. The waters, that lay for some time in the streets of Rome, sapped the foundation of several insulated houses; and when the flood fell back into its channel, the superstructure tumbled to the ground. This disaster was no sooner over than a new occurrence spread a general terror. Otho was preparing to set out on his expedition. His way was over the field of Mars, and the Flaminian road; but both places were impassable. This circumstance, though accidental, or the effect of natural causes, was magni-

[1] The isle in the Tiber, now called *Isola di St. Bartolomeo.*

[2] The Sublician bridge, so called, because built with wood. A foundation of solid marble was laid afterwards.

fied into a prodigy, by which the gods denounced the slaughter of armies and a train of public calamities.

LXXXVII. The emperor ordered a lustration,[1] and, having purified the city, turned his thoughts to the conduct of the war. The Pennine and the Cottian Alps, with all the passes into Italy, were in the possession of Vitellius and his armies. Otho resolved, therefore, to make a descent on the coast of Narbon Gaul, with a fleet well manned; and in force to keep the command of those seas. All who survived the massacre at the Milvian bridge, and had been, by Galba's orders, thrown into prison, were released by Otho, and incorporated with the legions. He depended on the fidelity of those men, and by giving to others the like hopes of preferment, he inspired the whole body with zeal and ardour. In order to strengthen his fleet, he embarked the city cohorts, and a considerable detachment from the prætorian guards; a body of men capable of defending their generals by their courage, and of assisting with their advice. The conduct of the marine was committed to three officers; namely, Antonius Novellus and Suedius Clemens, both centurions of principal rank, and Æmilius Pacensis, a tribune degraded by Galba, but, since the death of that emperor, restored to his rank. A freedman of the name of Oscus was appointed to direct the operations of the fleet, and act as a spy on better men than himself. The land forces, both horse and infantry, were put under the command of Suetonius Paulinus, Marius Celsus, and Annius Gallus. To them was added Licinius Proculus, the prefect of the prætorians, and in him Otho reposed his whole confidence. This officer, in time of peace, discharged the functions of his station with sufficient ability; but he had seen no service, and had therefore no skill in military affairs. He had talents for mischief, and knew how to obstruct the authority of Paulinus, to check the ardour of Celsus, and to thwart the judgment of Gallus. An enemy to every excellence of those three officers, he found, as usually happens, that worth and modest merit were no match for malice and left-handed policy.

LXXXVIII. Before Otho set out from Rome, Cornelius Dolabella was, by his order, conveyed under a guard to the Aquinian colony, there to be kept out of the way, but not in close confinement. His only crime was the antiquity of his family, and his affinity to Galba. Several magistrates, and others of consular rank, had it in command to attend Otho on

[1] See *Annals*, xiii. 24.

his expedition, not to assist in the war by their counsels or their valour, but to swell the pomp of the emperor's retinue. In the number was Lucius Vitellius, who was suffered to mix with the rest of the train, undistinguished either as the brother of one emperor, or the enemy of another. During these preparations, Rome presented a scene of hurry and confusion. No order of men was exempt from fear or danger. The principal senators, enfeebled by age, or softened by a long peace; the nobility, sunk in sloth; and the Roman knights, who had lost their warlike spirit; were all obliged to put themselves in readiness. They assumed an air of courage, but their fears were seen through the vain disguise. Some affected to make a display of their alacrity. They bought with vain ostentation the most splendid armour, horses for parade, and all the conveniences of a luxurious table, as if such implements were a necessary part of their camp-equipage. The wise and moderate thought of nothing but their own safety and the public welfare; while the vain and senseless, whose views did not extend to remote consequences, filled their minds with chimerical expectations; and all who were bankrupts both in fame and fortune, hoped to find in the distractions of their country that security, which in quiet times they had never known.

LXXXIX. The people at large, unacquainted with the secrets of state, and of course free from solicitude, began, however, to feel the ill effects of the impending war. They saw the public revenue exhausted in the service of the army; they laboured under a scarcity of provisions, and the price was rising every day; whereas in the troubles stirred up by Vindex, none of those inconveniences affected the city of Rome. That commotion was at a distance, a war in the remote parts of Gaul, decided between the legions and the provincial insurgents. The Roman citizens looked on in perfect tranquillity, as if it were no more than a foreign quarrel. From the reign of Augustus, when that emperor established the power of the Cæsars, this had constantly been the case. The issue of every war affected the sovereign only. Under Tiberius and Caligula, the evils of peace were the worst calamities. The attempt of Scribonianus to shake the authority of Claudius was crushed as soon as discovered. Nero was undone by rumours and vague intelligence, not by force of arms. In the present juncture, the face of things was changed. The pressure was felt at home. The fleets and legions were in motion, and beyond all example, the prætorian bands and city cohorts were obliged to take the field. The east and west were engaged in the contest; the several provinces, which the leading chiefs left behind them, were up in arms; and, under better generals, there were ample materials for a long and difficult war. Otho was now on the point of beginning his march. A scruple was started to deter him from proceeding, till the ceremony of depositing the sacred shields called the *Ancilia*[1] was performed with due rites and ceremonies. He rejected the advice. Delay had been the ruin of Nero, and Cæcina by this time had passed the Alps. The time called for vigour and expedition.

XC. On the day preceding the ides of March, Otho called a meeting of the senate. He recommended the care of the commonwealth to the wisdom of that assembly, and ordered the property of such as had been recalled from banishment, since the death of Nero, to be restored to the respective owners. To this liberality nothing could be objected: it was an act of justice, in appearance magnificent, but of little use, as the public officers had already seized the whole into their own hands. From the senate Otho proceeded to harangue the people; he talked in a pompous style of the fathers, and the majesty of the Roman citizens. He mentioned the adverse party in managed terms, imputing to the legions error in judgment rather than a turbulent and factious spirit. Of Vitellius he made no mention; perhaps from motives of delicacy, or, more probably, because the writer of the speech, looking forward to his own safety, thought it prudent to exclude all personal invective. For the last opinion there seems to be some foundation. In all military operations, Suetonius Paulinus and Marius Celsus were Otho's confidential advisers; but in matters that concerned the civil administration, Galerius Trachalus was the person on whose talents he relied. That minister had gained reputation at the bar; and those who were best acquainted with his mode of eloquence, and the harmony of his copious periods, discovered, in the composition of the speech, the style and manner of that celebrated orator. Otho was received with acclamations: the populace, according to custom, yielded to the impulse of the moment, full of sound and servile adulation, but nothing from the heart. You

[1] Numa, the founder of religious ceremonies, made the Romans believe, that as long as they preserved the celestial arms, called *Ancilia*, which, he said, were sent down by the gods, Rome would prove invincible, and triumph over all her enemies. Accordingly we read in Livy the procession of the Salian priests, on stated days, attending the *Ancilia* with song and dance through the streets of Rome. This institution was neglected by Otho.

would have thought that it was Cæsar the dictator, or Augustus the emperor, for whom they contended with so much emulation. And yet, in all this show of zeal, there was at the bottom neither love nor fear; servility was the motive; all courted the yoke, and all rushed headlong into slavery. The public, at this time, presented no better spectacle than what is seen every day in a family of domestic slaves; each individual had his own private views; and for the public interest, or the honour of the state, no care remained. Otho was now ready to depart; he left the government of Rome, and the whole weight of empire, to his brother Salvius Titianus, and proceeded on his expedition.

BOOK II

CONTENTS

I. *Titus, sent by his father Vespasian to congratulate Galba, hears of that emperor's death, and stops at Corinth—He resolves to return to Syria, and sails to Rhodes and Cyprus—At the last place he visits the temple of the Paphian Venus—Some account of the goddess, and the rites of worship—He lands in Syria.*—V. *Character of Vespasian, and of Mucianus—They lay aside their mutual animosities, and act in concert—The legions of the East resolve to have a share in the making of emperors.*—VIII. *A counterfeit Nero detected and seized.*—X. *From trivial matters great discord at Rome—Vibius Crispus accuses Annius Faustus, an informer, and procures his condemnation, though hated himself for the same practices.*—XI. *An account of Otho's forces.*—XII. *His fleets command the sea extending to the maritime Alps—The city of Intemelium sacked and plundered by the Othonians—The exemplary courage of a mother in the protection of her son.*—XIV. *Otho's fleet infests the coast of Narbon Gaul—An engagement with the Vitellians in that quarter, in which the Othonians had the advantage.*—XVI. *Pacarius, the governor of Corsica, favours the cause of Vitellius, and is murdered.*—XVII. *Cæcina, with the Vitellian forces, enters Italy, and besieges Placentia—Spurinna, one of Otho's officers, defends the place—Cæcina raises the siege, and retires with his army to Cremona—A battle at that place, and the Othonians prove victorious—Valens enters Italy—Cæcina resolves to strike a blow before the arrival of that general—He lays a snare for the Othonians, but is defeated by Suetonius Paulinus at a place called Castorum—King Epiphanes, on Otho's side, is wounded.*—XXVII. *Valens arrives at Ticinum—A violent sedition occasioned by the Batavians—Valens joins the army under Cæcina.*—XXXI. *Comparison of Otho and Vitellius—Otho holds a council to deliberate on the plan of the war—Some are for delay; others for an immediate action—Otho is for a decisive blow, and, by advice, retires to Brixellum.*—XXXIV. *Cæcina and Valens wait for the motions of the enemy—A bridge thrown over the Po to amuse Otho's forces, who are worsted in a skirmish.*—XXXVII. *A report that both armies were inclined to peace, shown to be highly improbable.*—XXXIX. *Titianus, Otho's brother, and Proculus, the prefect of the prætorian bands, entrusted with the chief command—They encamp within four miles of Bedriacum—Otho, by despatches from Brixellum, hurries them on to an engagement.*—XLI. *The battle of Bedriacum—The Othonians defeated, and on the next day lay down their arms—The Vitellians enter the camp, and both armies embrace with tears of joy.*—XLV. *Otho is weary of civil war, and, though the soldiers are still devoted to his cause, resolves to prevent further effusion of blood—He falls on his own sword—His funeral immediately performed—Some of the men slay themselves near the funeral pile.*—L. *Otho's origin and character.*—LI. *A mutiny among his soldiers—Verginius in danger from their fury.*—LII. *A great part of the senate, who had followed Otho, involved in danger.*—LV. *Tranquillity prevails at Rome—The games in honour of Ceres celebrated according to custom—Otho's death made known in the theatre—The people declare for Vitellius with shouts of applause.*—LVI. *Italy ravaged by the Vitellians.*—LVII. *Vitellius advances towards Italy, and hears of the victory gained by his officers—The two Mauritanias declare in his favour—Albinus their governor cut off by the emissaries of Cluvius Rufus, who had passed over from Spain into Africa.*—LX. *Vitellius orders the bravest of Otho's centurions to be put to death—The wild attempt of Maricus in Gaul—In a fit of enthusiasm he calls himself a god—He is taken, and put to death.*—LXII. *The gluttony of Vitellius—Italy exhausted to supply his voracious appetite—In his despatches to Rome he declines for the present the name of Augustus, and wholly rejects that of Cæsar—The judicial astrologers banished out of Italy—Laws for restraining the Roman knights from appearing on the stage, or in the games of the circus.*—LXIII. *Dolabella put to death with treachery by Vitellius—The furious temper of Triaria, the wife of L. Vitellius, and the amiable character of his mother Sextilia.*—LXV. *Cluvius Rufus arrives from Spain, and is pardoned by Vitellius—The vanquished troops still retain their ferocity—A quarrel between the Batavians and the soldiers of the fourteenth legion.*—LXVIII. *A violent sedition at Ticinum, while Vitellius carouses at a feast.*—LXX. *Vitellius proceeds to Cremona, and views the field of battle at Bedriacum, which was still covered with a dreadful carnage—He vies with the luxury of Nero, and marches to Bononia, still plunging into deeper debauchery as he draws near to Rome.*—LXXII. *A slave of the name of Geta assumes the name of Scribonianus—He is detected, and put to death by order of Vitellius.*—LXXIV. *Deliberations held in the East by Vespasian and Mucianus—The speech of Mucianus on the occasion.*—LXXVII. *Vespasian encouraged by the responses of oracles—His consultation on Mount Carmel.*—LXXIX. *Vespasian is declared emperor, first in Egypt, and afterwards by the army in Syria.*—LXXXI. *The kings Sohemus, Antiochus, and Agrippa, as also queen Berenice, enter into the league.*—LXXXII. *Plan of the war—Vespasian holds Egypt in his possession—His son Titus carries on the war against the Jews—Mucianus sets out on his march towards Italy.*—LXXXV. *The legions in Mœsia, Pannonia, and Dalmatia, revolt to Vespasian, at the instigation of Antonius Primus and Cornelius Fuscus.*—LXXXVII. *Vitellius, at the head of a prodigious multitude, all debauched by luxury, enters the city of Rome.*—XC. *He makes a speech, in pompous terms, celebrating his own praise—His conduct there.*—XCII. *Cæcina and Valens carry on the administration—Sloth, riot, and mortality among the soldiers—Vitellius in want of money, and yet prodigal beyond all measure—Asiaticus, his freedman, amasses enormous wealth.*—XCV. *The people distressed, and yet the birthday of Vitellius celebrated with pomp and profusion—The emperor performs the funeral obsequies of Nero—Rumours of a revolt in the East ineffectually suppressed—Vitellius sends for succours into Spain, Germany, and Britain, but endeavours to disguise the necessity.* —XCIX. *Parties of the enemy advance into Italy—Cæcina and Valens ordered to take the field—Cæcina's treachery—He combines with Lucilius Bassus, the commander of the fleets at Ravenna and Misenum.*

These transactions passed in a few months after the death of Galba, and Vinius his colleague in the consulship.

Years of Rome.	Of Christ.	Consuls.
822	69	M. Salvius Otho, Salvius Otho Titianus.
		L. Verginius Rufus, Pompeius Vopiscus.
		Cælius Sabinus, T. Flavius Sabinus.
		T. Arrius Antoninus, P. Marius Celsus.

I. FORTUNE was already preparing, in another quarter of the world, to open an important scene, and to produce to mankind a new imperial family, destined, at first, to flourish in prosperity, and, in the end, after a disastrous reign, to fall by a dreadful catastrophe. While Galba still possessed the sovereign power, Titus, by order of Vespasian, his father, set out from Judæa, with congratulations to that emperor, and, as was natural, with the ambition of a young man eager to begin the career[1] of public honours. The common people, according to their custom, found deeper reasons for the journey. Titus, they believed, was to be adopted heir to the empire, and what they believed they took care to circulate. The advanced age of Galba, and his want of issue, gave colour to the story; and the busy spirit of the populace relied on vain conjecture, impatient to decide what still remained in suspense. The character and personal accomplishments of Titus added weight to the report. He had talents for the highest station, and to the dignity of his stature united a graceful mien and amiable countenance. The success that attended the exploits of the father, threw a lustre round the son: oracular responses foretold the grandeur of the family; and, while the minds of men stood ready for the reception of every rumour, even trifling incidents, the mere result of chance, confirmed the popular opinion. At Corinth in Achaia, Titus received intelligence of the death of Galba, and, at the same time, undoubted assurances, that Vitellius, at the head of powerful armies, was in

[1] Titus, at this time, was in his twenty-eighth year. By the favour of Narcissus, to whom Vespasian paid his court, Titus was educated in the palace with Britannicus, the son of Claudius. The prince, then destined by his father to succeed to the empire, was cut off by the villainy of Nero; and Titus, whose elevation was not then foreseen, lived to be the delight of the Roman people.

motion to claim the empire. In this posture of affairs, he called a council of select friends. The conjuncture was alarming, and to choose among difficulties was all that was left. "If he proceeded on his way to Rome, the homage intended for a prince now no more, would have no merit with his successor; and to remain a hostage in the custody of Otho, or Vitellius, would most probably be his lot. On the other hand, if he returned to Judæa, that cold indifference would give umbrage to the conqueror; and yet, while the issue of the war was still uncertain, the conduct of a young man would admit of alleviating circumstances in the opinion of the prince whom Vespasian should think proper to join. Above all, it was possible that Vespasian might declare himself a candidate: in that case, petty offences would be of little consequence, when all were to be involved in a general war."

II. After balancing the motives on every side, and fluctuating for some time between opposite passions, hope, at length, prevailed, and Titus returned to Judæa. A change so sudden was by some imputed to his love of queen Berenice.[1] It is true, that princess had engaged his affections; but the business of his heart never interfered with the duties of his station. Youth being the season of pleasure, Titus gave a loose to those desires, which he afterwards so well knew how to regulate. In his own reign he was remarkable for that self-control, which he never practised under his father. He set sail from Corinth, and after steering along the coast of Achaia and Asia, which lay to the left, he directed his course towards Rhodes and Cyprus. From those islands he went, by a more bold navigation, across the open sea to the coast of Syria. At Cyprus curiosity led him to visit the temple of the Paphian Venus, famous for the worship paid by the inhabitants, and the conflux of strangers who resorted thither from all parts. If we take this opportunity to trace the origin of that singular worship,[2] and to describe the situation of the temple, and the form of the goddess, differing entirely from what is seen in any other place, the digression will, perhaps, be neither tedious, nor unacceptable to the reader.

III. The founder of the temple, if we believe ancient tradition, was King Ærias; a name ascribed by some writers to the goddess herself. According to a more recent opinion, the

[1] Berenice was sister to Agrippa II. and wife of Herod, king of Chalcis, in Syria.

[2] At the town of Paphos, which stood on the western side of the isle of Cyprus, a temple was dedicated to Venus, thence called the Paphian Venus.

temple was built and dedicated by King Cinyras, on the spot where the goddess, after emerging from her native waves, was gently wafted to the shore. The science of divination, we are told, was of foreign growth, imported by Thamyras, the Cicilian, and by him established with mysterious rites and ceremonies. In consequence of this institution, it was settled by mutual compact, between the priest and Cinyras, the king of the island, that the sacerdotal function should be hereditary in the descendants of their respective families. In process of time, the race of Thamyras, willing that the sovereign should be distinguished by a superior prerogative, resigned into the hands of Cinyras the whole conduct of the mysteries, of which their ancestors were the original founders. A priest of the royal line is, at present, the only person consulted. For victims, to be offered as a sacrifice, animals of every species are allowed, at the option of the votarist, provided he chooses from the male kind only. Discoveries made in the fibres of kids are deemed the best prognostics. The altar is never stained with blood, and, though exposed to the open air, never moistened by a drop of rain. Supplications and the pure flame of fire are the only offerings. The statue of the goddess bears no resemblance to the human form. You see a round figure, broad at the base, but growing fine by degrees, till, like a cone, it lessens to a point. The reason, whatever it be, is not explained.

IV. Titus viewed the wealth of the temple, the presents of eastern kings, and the collection of rarities, which the genius of the Greeks, fond of tradition and the decorations of fabulous narrative, affected to trace from remote antiquity. He then consulted the oracle about his future voyage. A calm sea and a safe passage were promised. He slew a number of victims, and, in terms properly guarded, attempted to pry into his own destiny. The priest, whose name was Sostratus, explored the entrails of various animals, and, finding that the goddess was propitious, answered, for the present, in the usual style, but afterwards, at a secret interview, laid open a scene of glory. Titus, with a mind enlarged, and swelling with vast ideas, proceeded on his voyage, and joined his father. The armies and provinces of the East were at that time wavering; but the presence of Titus inspired them with vigour and alacrity. Vespasian had almost brought the Jewish war to a conclusion. Nothing remained but the siege of Jerusalem; an arduous enterprise, which threatened great toil and difficulty, not on account of the strength or resources of the enemy, but by reason of a hill almost inaccessible, and, what was still more hard to conquer, the stubborn genius of superstition. Vespasian, as already mentioned, had three legions under his command, all inured to the service, and eager against the enemy. Mucianus, in a province where profound tranquillity was established, was at the head of four legions, not, as usual in time of peace, relaxed in indolence, but animated by the gallant exertions of the army under Vespasian, and fired with a spirit of emulation. Having no enemy to oppose, they were not made soldiers in the field; but their spirit was roused, and, being unimpaired by fatigue, they were ready for a vigorous campaign. The two commanders had an additional force of auxiliary horse and foot, besides a naval armament on the coast, and the support of all the neighbouring kings. Add to this, their own military character was a tower of strength. Both stood high in reputation, but for different reasons, and for qualities peculiar to each.

V. Vespasian possessed all the requisites that form a soldier and an officer. Prompt and zealous in the service, he was often seen at the head of a march; he went in person to mark out the ground of his camp, and, by night as well as day, he kept the enemy in a constant alarm, planning his measures with judgment, and executing with vigour. To his diet he paid no regard, content with whatever came before him. In his apparel, plain and simple, he was scarce distinguished from the common men. With all this he had a leaven of avarice. Forgive that vice, and he was equal to the best generals of antiquity.

Mucianus was of a different cast. Rich and magnificent, he appeared with an air of elevation above the rank of a private citizen. An able orator, and versed in civil business, he laid his schemes with judgment: the politician appeared in all his measures. In the two men was seen a rare assemblage of extraordinary qualities. By weeding out the vices of each, and uniting their virtues, the commonwealth would have had an accomplished prince. Situated as they were in contiguous provinces, Vespasian in Judæa, and Mucianus in Syria, they beheld each other, for some time, with the jealousy of rivals. The death of Nero put an end to their dissensions. From that time they began to act in concert. Their mutual friends made the first advances towards a reconciliation, and, by the address of Titus, a mere cessation of animosities was turned into a lasting peace. The power of winning the affections of men was in an eminent degree the talent of that young officer. Nature and art conspired to render him acceptable to all; and even Mucianus could not resist his influence. The tribunes, the centurions, and the common men were, by various artifices, fixed in the interest of the two commanders. The diligent met with encouragement, the licentious with indulgence, and, according to the bent of each man's disposition, all were secured by their virtues or their vices.

VI. Before the arrival of Titus, both armies had sworn fidelity to Otho, with the precipitation of men who had quick intelligence of all that passed at Rome. They were not, in that juncture, ripe for a revolt. Preparations for a civil war are in their nature slow and difficult. The East had been composed by a long peace, and now, for the first time, began to think of mixing in the feuds that shook the empire. They had hitherto seen the convulsions of the state at a distance only. The quarrel always broke out in Gaul or Italy, and was there decided by the forces of the West. It is true, that Pompey, Cassius, Brutus, and Antony, carried the war across the Mediterranean, and had reason to repent. Syria and Judæa heard of the Cæsars, but seldom saw them. The legions, undisturbed by sedition, had no war upon their hands. Embroiled at different times with the Parthians,[1] they had a few slight conflicts, with doubtful success, and passed the rest of the year in profound tranquillity. In the late civil war,[2] when every part of the empire was in motion, the East was perfectly quiet. Galba obtained the sovereignty, and the oriental legions acquiesced; but it was no sooner known that Otho and Vitellius were engaged in an impious war against their country, than they began to shake off their pacific temper. They saw the supreme authority in the hands of other armies, who granted it away at their own pleasure, and reaped the profits of every revolution, while the soldiers of the East had nothing but a change of servitude, condemned, at the will of others, to submit to new masters.

Discontent and loud complaints were heard throughout the army. The common men began to survey their strength and numbers. They reckoned seven legions, besides a large body of auxiliaries. Syria and Judæa were in their possession. Egypt had two legions at their service. Cappadocia and

[1] The Parthians were originally a people from Scythia: in process of time, when their empire grew in strength, they became the grand rivals of the Romans. The overthrow of Crassus is well known.

[2] The last civil war was that between Vindex and Nero.

Pontus afforded ample resources; and the forces that lined the frontier of Armenia stood ready at their beck. Asia, and the rest of the provinces, were provided with men and money. In a word, the islands, and the sea that surrounds them, were under their command; and the Mediterranean, while it separated them from the rest of the empire, left them at leisure to prepare for war.

VII. The zeal of the soldiers was no secret to the commanders-in-chief; but they judged it best to wait the issue of the war in Europe; aware that, between the victor and the vanquished, a sincere coalition never can succeed, and whether fortune favoured the arms of Otho or Vitellius, the consequence in either event would be the same. And if the pride of victory is apt to corrupt the ablest generals, from the present chiefs what was to be expected? Their own vices would destroy them. Discord, sloth, and luxury would be the ruin of both: one would be undone by the fate of war, and the other by success. For these reasons it was agreed to suspend all military operations. Vespasian and Mucianus, lately reconciled to each other, concurred in this opinion, which had been beforehand adopted by their friends. Men of principle gave their advice with a view to the public good; others looked for their own private advantage; and public confusion was the only resource of such as, in their domestic affairs, saw nothing but distress and ruin. One mind, one spirit pervaded the whole army. Good and evil motives conspired, and, for different reasons, war became the passion of all.

VIII. About this period of time, a report that Nero was still alive, and actually on his way to the provinces of the east, excited a general alarm through Achaia and Asia. The accounts of that emperor's death[1] had been so various, that conjecture had ample materials. Hence numbers asserted that Nero survived the fury of his enemies, and they found credulity ready to believe them. In the course of this work the reader will hear of various pretenders, and the fate that attended them. The impostor who now took upon him to personate that emperor, was a slave from Pontus, or, according to some writers, a freedman from Italy, who played with skill on the harp, and had a musical voice. With those talents, and a countenance that resembled Nero, he was able to impose on vulgar minds. By the force of promises he drew to his party a number of deserters,

[1] A number of impostors, at different times, assumed the name of Nero.

whom their poverty induced to lead a vagrant life. With this crew he put to sea, but was thrown by adverse winds on the isle of Cythnus. At that place he fell in with a party of soldiers on their return from the east. Some of these he listed; and such as refused, he ordered to be put to death. Having plundered the merchants, and armed the stoutest of their slaves, he endeavoured to seduce Sisenna, a centurion from Syria, who happened to land on the island of Cythnus, on his way to greet the prætorian bands in the name of the Syrian army, and, in token of friendship, to present two right hands clasping each other. Apprehending danger from so bold an adventurer, Sisenna made his escape from the island. A general panic seized the inhabitants. Numbers rejoiced to find the name of Nero once more revived, and, hating the new system, wished for nothing so much as another revolution.

IX. The fame of this pretended Nero gained credit every day, when by a sudden accident the illusion vanished. It happened that Calpurnius Asprenas, whom Galba had appointed governor of Galatia and Pamphylia, arrived, on his way to those provinces, at the isle of Cythnus, with two galleys from the fleet that lay at Misenum. The commanders of the ships were summoned, in the name of Nero, to attend their lawful prince. The impostor continued to act his part. He received the naval officers with an air of dejection, and, by the duty which they owed him, implored their assistance, and safe conduct either to Syria, or to Egypt. The masters of the galleys, alarmed at the proposal, or intending to deceive, desired time to prepare the minds of their sailors, faithfully promising to return without delay. Asprenas, duly informed of all that passed, gave orders to attack the impostor and his crew of adherents. The ship was seized, and the pretended emperor, whoever he was, suffered death. The air of the man, his eyes, his hair, and the ferocity of his countenance, bore a strong resemblance to Nero. His body was conveyed to Asia, and afterwards sent to Rome.

X. In a city, distracted by internal discord, and, after so many revolutions, fierce with a spirit of liberty that led to the wildest anarchy, no transaction, however trifling in itself, could pass, without exciting violent commotions. Vibius Crispus, a man, for his wealth, his power, and his talents, always ranked among the most eminent citizens, but never for his virtues numbered with the good, cited to the bar of the senate Annius Faustus, a Roman knight, and in the reign of Nero an informer by profession. In the beginning of Galba's reign, it was ordained by a decree, that all causes against the race of public accusers should be fairly heard. This law, however salutary, was forced to yield to the temper of the times; it was enforced, or relaxed, as the person accused happened to be of weight and consequence, or poor and friendless: it was, notwithstanding, still in force; and Crispus, availing himself of it, exerted all his influence to ruin the man who had been the prosecutor of his brother. In the senate his party was strong and powerful. Without hearing the criminal, the fathers were for condemning him to immediate execution. The violence of this proceeding stirred up an opposition. A party was formed against the overgrown power of the prosecutor. They insisted that the specific charge should be exhibited, and a day fixed, when the delinquent, however guilty, should be allowed the common right of being heard in his defence. This motion was carried, and the hearing of the cause was adjourned for a few days. The trial at length came on, and Faustus was condemned, but not with that universal assent of the people which a life of iniquity might have warranted. The accuser, it was well known, had been concerned in the conduct of prosecutions, and received the profits of his trade. Men rejoiced to see the punishment of a crime so dangerous and detestable; but the triumph of a notorious offender gave disgust.

XI. Meanwhile the affairs of Otho wore a favourable aspect. The armies in Dalmatia and Pannonia were on their march to join him. A detachment of two thousand advanced by rapid marches, while the main body followed at moderate distances. The legions that composed this force were the seventh, which had been raised by Galba; the eleventh, the thirteenth, and fourteenth, all veterans in the service, and the last in great renown for the vigour with which they quelled the insurrection in Britain, and still more famous for the choice made by Nero, who had selected that corps as the best in the empire. They remained to the last faithful to that emperor, and, after his death, declared with equal zeal in favour of Otho. Knowing their own strength, they were inspired with confidence, but a confidence that made them judge for themselves, and proceed on their march by slow journeys, as their humour prompted. The cavalry and auxiliary cohorts came forward with more alacrity.

The troops that marched from Rome were a formidable body. They consisted of five prætorian cohorts, several squadrons of horse, and the first legion. To these were added two thousand gladiators; a resource altogether ignoble, but in civil commotions often employed by generals of the first reputation. Annius Gallus and Vestricius Spurinna were sent at the head of this whole force, with orders to take post on the banks of the Po. The first intention was to keep the enemy locked up in Gaul; but that project proved abortive, Cæcina having already passed the Alps. Otho followed with a select body of the prætorian guards, and all the veterans of that corps, with the city cohorts, and a prodigious number drafted from the marines. On the march he betrayed no symptom of sloth, no passion for luxury: he advanced on foot, at the head of the colours, covered with an iron breastplate, rough and soldier-like, exhibiting a striking contrast to his former character.

XII. In this posture of affairs, fortune seemed to open a flattering prospect. Otho was master of the greatest part of Italy, and his fleets had the command of the sea. To the foot of the maritime Alps the country was in his possession. To pass over those mountains, and make a descent on Narbon Gaul, was the measure which he had projected. To conduct that expedition he appointed Suedius Clemens, Antonius Novellus, and Æmilius Pacencis. The last was loaded with irons by his own soldiers. Antonius Novellus lost all authority; and Suedius Clemens, proud of his rank, but not knowing how to maintain it, yielded too much to the humours of the men. He preserved no discipline, and yet was eager for action. His army presented no appearance of men marching through their own country. They forgot that Italy was their native soil, and that the lands and houses belonged to their fellow-citizens. Regardless of the Roman name, they laid waste the country with fire and sword; they pillaged, destroyed, and plundered, as if the war had been in a foreign realm, against the enemies of their country. The wretched inhabitants were oppressed by men, against whom, having entertained no fear, they had prepared no defence. The fields were covered with grain and cattle; the houses were open; and the owners, with their wives and children, went forth, in the simplicity of their hearts, to meet the army. In the midst of peace, they were surrounded with all the horrors of war. Marius Maturus was, at that time, governor of the maritime Alps. He resolved to dispute the passage with Otho's troops, and, for that purpose, armed the youth of the country. In the first encounter, the mountaineers were either cut to pieces or put to the rout. A band of rustics, suddenly levied, and ignorant of military discipline, could not make head against a regular army. Expecting no fame from victory, they feared no disgrace from an ignominious flight.

XIII. An opposition so rash and feeble served only to exasperate the Othonian soldiers. They fell with fury upon Albium Intemelium, a municipal town. The late victory was a fruitless advantage, affording neither spoil nor plunder. The peasants had no property, and their arms were of no value. Even prisoners of war could not be made. The fugitives knew the course of the country, and were too swift of foot. Enraged at the disappointment, the soldiers wreaked their vengeance on the innocent inhabitants of Intemelium, and glutted their avarice with the effects of innocent men. Amidst the barbarities committed on this occasion, a Ligurian woman gave a noble example of courage and maternal affection. She had concealed her child from the fury of the slaughtering sword. The soldiers, fully persuaded that she had deposited her treasure in the same place, stretched her on the rack, and pressed the unhappy mother to tell where she had secured her son. She laid her hand on her womb, and, "here," she said, "here my child is sheltered." From that moment, unmoved by menaces, and unsubdued by torture, she never changed her tone. Nothing could conquer that generous obstinacy. She died a bright example of undaunted virtue.

XIV. Meanwhile, Fabius Valens received intelligence that Otho's fleet was hovering on the coast of Narbon Gaul, with intent to invade that province, which had already embraced the interest of Vitellius. The adjacent colonies, by their deputies, sued for protection. Valens despatched two Tungrian cohorts, four squadrons of horse, with the whole cavalry of the Treviri, under the command of Julius Classicus; reserving, however, a sufficient detachment from those forces to garrison the port of Forojulium, that the colony might not, while the troops marched up the country, lie exposed to sudden incursions from the fleet. This arrangement being made, Classicus marched in quest of the enemy, at the head of twelve troops of horse, and a select body from the cohorts. To these were added the Ligurian cohort, which had been usually quartered at Forojulium, and five hundred men from Pannonia, not yet ranged in companies under distinct and regular colours. Neither side declined an engagement. The disposition made by Otho's officers was as follows: A body of marines, intermixed with the peasantry, took post on the heights near the sea. The level space between the hills and the coast was occupied by the prætorian soldiers; and, to support them, the fleet stood in close to the shore, drawn up in order of battle, and presenting a formidable line. The strength of the Vitellians, consisting of cavalry, was stationed in front; the infantry close embodied in their rear, and their Alpine mountaineers on the ridge of the neighbouring hills. The Trevirian squadrons began the attack with less skill than courage. The veterans of Otho's army received the attack in front, while their peasants, from the high grounds, discharged a volley of stones, and, being expert slingers, annoyed the enemy in flank. They mixed in the lines with the regular soldiers, and performed feats of valour. In the moment of victory, there was no distinction between the coward and brave; all pursued their advantage with equal ardour. The Vitellians were thrown into disorder; and being driven towards the margin of the sea, they were there attacked in the rear by the soldiers belonging to the fleet. This was a danger unforeseen. Hemmed in on every side, they must have been to a man cut off, if the night had not come on in time to favour their retreat, and restrain the victorious army from pursuing them in their flight.

XV. The Vitellians, though defeated, still retained their warlike spirit. With a reinforcement drawn together in haste they returned to the charge; and, finding the enemy elate with joy, and by success lulled into security, they assaulted the outposts, put the advance guard to the sword, and forced their way into the camp. The Othonians were struck with terror, and near the fleet all was tumult and disorder. The surprise, however, soon began to subside. The Othonians betook themselves to an adjacent hill, and, having there collected their strength, rushed down with impetuous fury. A dreadful slaughter followed. The Tungrian cohorts stood the brunt of the action, till their commanding officers fell under a shower of darts. The Othonians conquered, but their victory was dearly bought. They pursued the flying enemy with more rage than prudence, when the Trevirian cavalry, wheeling round, attacked them in the rear, and put a large party to the sword. From this time the two armies remained inactive. As if a truce had taken place, and both sides had agreed by compact to suspend hostilities, and no more molest each other by sudden incursions, the Vitellians retired to Antipolis, a municipal town of Narbon Gaul, and the Othonians to Albingaunum, in the inland part of Liguria.

XVI. Corsica, Sardinia, and the rest of the islands in those seas, were overawed by the victorious fleet, and kept in subjection to Otho. Corsica, indeed, suffered a sudden convulsion from the temerity of the governor. The name of this officer was Decimus Pacarius. Though the island, in a war carried on by such powerful adversaries, was of no importance, he endeavoured to seduce the inhabitants to the interest of Vitellius. The project, which would have decided nothing, ended in his own ruin. He summoned a council of the leading men, and communicated his design. Claudius Phirricus, who commanded the galleys on that station, and Quinctius Certus, a Roman knight, objected to the measure, and were put to instant death. The rest of the assembly, terrified by this act of violence, swore fidelity to Vitellius. The populace, as usual, blind and ignorant, but by contagion catching the fears of others, followed the example of the leading chiefs. Pacarius began to muster his men, and train them to the use of arms. A race of rude and vulgar peasants, who had no relish for the fatigue of military discipline, began to consider the nature of their situation, and their inability to support a war. "They were islanders, remote from Germany, and out of the reach of the legions. The fleets of Otho commanded the seas, and had lately ravaged the maritime countries, though defended by the cohorts and cavalry of Vitellius." This reflection produced a sudden change in every mind. They resolved to assert their independence, not with open force, but by covert stratagem; and, for that purpose, to lie in wait for their opportunity. Pacarius, as soon as his train of visitors left him, retired to his bath. In that moment the conspirators fell upon him naked and disarmed. He was put to instant death, and his attendants suffered the same fate. Their heads, like those of traitors, were conveyed to Otho. And yet the assassins were neither rewarded by that prince, nor punished by Vitellius. In the mass of atrocious deeds that disgraced the times, petty villainies were suffered to pass with impunity.

XVII. The cavalry, called the Sullanian Squadron, had, as already mentioned,[1] forced their way into Italy, and there

[1] *Hist.* i. 70.

fixed the seat of war. In the conduct of these men nothing proceeded from principle. They had no regard for Otho, nor so much as a wish to serve Vitellius; but their vigour being relaxed by a long peace, and their minds debased and prepared for slavery, they stood ready to stretch their necks to the yoke, whatever hand imposed it, in their choice of a master wholly indifferent. The fairest portion of Italy, extending from the Po to the Alps, with all its fertile plains and flourishing cities, was in the possession of Vitellius: the forces sent forward by Cæcina having already penetrated into that quarter. At Cremona a Pannonian cohort laid down their arms; and between Placentia and Ticinum a party of a hundred horse, with a thousand marines, were made prisoners. In this tide of success nothing could withstand the vigour of the Vitellians. The Po opposed its stream and its banks in vain. To the Batavians, and the troops from beyond the Rhine, the river was no more than a new motive to inflame their ardour. They passed over with their usual rapidity under the walls of Placentia, and in sight of the enemy. Having gained a footing on the land, they intercepted the enemy's scouts, and spread such a general panic, that all who escaped their fury fled with precipitation, announcing the arrival of Cæcina and his whole army.

XVIII. Spurinna, who commanded at Placentia, was well informed of Cæcina's motions. He knew him to be still at a distance; and, if at any time he should show himself before the place, he had taken his measures. Three prætorian cohorts, and no more than a thousand vexillaries, with a small body of horse, would be ill opposed to a veteran army. He resolved, therefore, to remain within his fortifications. But an unruly soldiery, fierce and unskilled in military operations, was not to be restrained. They seized the colours, and sallied forth in a body. The general endeavoured in vain to check their violence; the men pointed their weapons at his breast; they spurned at the tribunes and centurions, who extolled the wisdom of their superior officer; they rejected all advice, declaring aloud that treason was at work; they were betrayed: and Cæcina was invited to take possession of the place. Spurinna was obliged to yield to this sudden frenzy, and even to proceed on the march. He went forth against his will, but with a show of approbation, in hopes, if the sedition died away, that he might then resume his former authority.

XIX. The soldiers pushed on with spirit, till the Po appearing in sight, and night coming on, they halted for the first time. It was now judged necessary to fortify a camp. Labour and castrametation were new to men who had only served within the walls of Rome. Their ferocity abated, and they began to see their error. The veterans in the service condemned their own credulity, and pointed out to their comrades the common danger of all, if Cæcina with a numerous army had come up in time to surround them in a wide champaign country. Throughout the ranks nothing was heard but penitence and submission. The tribunes and centurions regained their influence, and all were loud in praise of their general, who had, with judgment, chosen a strong and powerful colony for the seat of war. Spurinna seized his opportunity, choosing rather to convince by reason, than to irritate by reproof. Having quelled the sedition, he left some flying parties to watch the motions of the enemy, and, with an army now disposed to obey his orders, marched back to Placentia. The fortifications of the place were repaired; new works were added; towers were constructed; the soldiers were provided with arms; and, what was of greater moment, a spirit of discipline and prompt obedience was diffused through the army. This was, no doubt, an essential service. Want of courage could not be imputed to Otho's party. Inattention to their superior officers was the disadvantage under which they laboured.

XX. Cæcina advanced into Italy with a well-conducted army, observing in his march the strictest discipline, as if on the other side of the Alps he had left his cruelty and love of plunder. His dress gave offence to the colonies through which he passed. His mantle, decorated with various colours, passed for a mark of arrogance; and his drawers,[1] used only by savage nations, did not agree with the ideas of a Roman citizen. Besides this, the splendid appearance of his wife, Salonina, mounted on a superb horse, adorned with purple ornaments, though in itself a matter of no importance, and certainly injurious to no person whatever, was held to be a public insult. Such is the nature of the human mind, disposed at all times to behold with jealousy the sudden elevation of new men, and to demand, that he, who has been known in an humble station, should know how to rise in the world with temper and modest dignity. Cæcina passed the Po, and by negotiation and artful promises endeavoured to seduce the

[1] Cæcina wore the *sagum*, which was the German dress, and the *braccæ*, or breeches, which distinguished the *Gauls*. The southern part of Gaul was called *Gallia Narbonensis* and also *Braccata*.

leaders of Otho's party. The like insidious game was played against himself. Both sides talked of peace and concord, but they amused each other with words of specious sound importing nothing. Tired of fruitless artifices, Cæcina began to concert his measures for the reduction of Placentia. He determined to invest the place; and knowing how much the fame of the general, and, by consequence, the events of war, depend on the first exploit, he made every preparation to carry on the siege with vigour.

XXI. The first approach to the town displayed the bravery, but nothing of the skill, which might be expected from a veteran army. The soldiers, intoxicated with liquor, advanced to the foot of the walls, without shelter, or due precaution. In this attack, a magnificent amphitheatre, which stood on the outside of the fortifications, was set on fire, and levelled to the ground. Whether this was occasioned by the flaming brands and other combustibles thrown in by the besiegers, or by the like missive weapons discharged from the works, cannot now be ascertained. The vulgar herd of the city, apt and willing, like the populace in every quarter, to believe whatever malignity can invent, imputed the disaster to the neighbouring colonists, who saw with envy a spacious and magnificent structure, that surpassed every monument of art and labour throughout Italy. The sense of this misfortune, however begun, was lost in the pressure of immediate danger; but the enemy was no sooner withdrawn from the walls, than the inhabitants, in the moment of security, lamented the loss of their amphitheatre, as the worst calamity that could befall them. Cæcina was repulsed with considerable loss. The night, on both sides, was employed in necessary preparations. The Vitellians provided themselves with moving penthouses, and other warlike machines, under which the men might advance to sap the foundation of the walls. The besieged were busy in preparing stakes and rafts of timber, with huge heaps of stone and lead and brass, in order to crush the assailants under their own works. Both armies felt every motive that could rouse their valour. The love of glory, and the fear of shame, throbbed in every breast. In the camp of the Vitellians, nothing was heard but the vigour of the legions, and the fame of the German armies; within the town, the honour of the city cohorts, and the dignity of the prætorian bands, were the topics that inflamed their minds with heroic ardour. They considered the Vitellians as a set of desperate adventurers, and despised them as

Barbarians, foreigners, and aliens in Italy; while, in their turn, they were held in contempt by the besiegers, as a weak enervate band, who had lost every warlike principle in the circus and the theatres of Rome. Otho and Vitellius were the subject of alternate praise and calumny; but praise was soon exhausted, and for abuse each party found abundant materials.

XXII. At the return of the day, the city and the country round displayed a scene of warlike preparation: the walls and ramparts were covered with Othonian soldiers, and the fields glittered with the blaze of hostile arms. The legions in close array advanced to the assault, and the auxiliaries in separate divisions. The attack began with a volley of stones and darts aimed at the highest part of the fortifications; and where the works were either impaired by time, or thinly manned, the Vitellians attempted a scalade. The German auxiliaries, rending the air with their savage war-songs, and, according to the custom of their country, waving their shields over their shoulders, advanced with impetuous fury; while the garrison, with deliberate aim, discharged a volley of stones and darts. In the meantime, the legionary soldiers, under their covered way, battered the foundation of the walls, and, having thrown up mounds of earth, attempted to force the gates. A pile of massy stones which had been prepared by the besieged, was instantly rolled down with prodigious ruin; the Vitellians, crushed under the weight, or transfixed with darts, lay wounded, maimed, and mangled at the foot of the ramparts. Horror and confusion followed. The Othonians were inspired with fresh courage. The slaughter increased; and the assailants, finding all their efforts defeated, with great precipitation, and no less dishonour, sounded a retreat. Cæcina saw the folly of an enterprise rashly undertaken. To avoid further disgrace, he resolved to raise the siege, and leave a camp, where he had nothing to expect but reproach and shame. He repassed the Po, and bent his march towards Cremona. He had not proceeded far, when he was joined by Turullius Cerealis, a centurion of principal rank, who had served under him in Germany, and also by Julius Briganticus, a Batavian by birth: the former deserted with a strong body of marine soldiers, and the latter, with a small party of horse.

XXIII. Spurinna, as soon as he was informed of the movements of the enemy, sent despatches to Annius Gallus, with the particulars of the siege, the gallant defence of Placentia, and the measures concerted by Cæcina. Gallus was then on his march, at the head of the first legion, to the relief of the place, little imagining that a few cohorts would be able to hold out against the strength and valour of the German army. It was, however, no sooner known that Cæcina had abandoned his enterprise, and was then proceeding to Cremona, than the spirit of the legion blazed out at once. They desired to be led against the enemy. Their impatience rose to a pitch little short of sedition. It was with difficulty that Gallus appeased the tumult. He made halt at Bedriacum,[1] a village situated between Verona and Cremona, and unhappily famous for the slaughter of two Roman armies. About the same time the Othonians gained a second advantage over the enemy. Martius Macer fought with success near Cremona. That officer, with the spirit of enterprise that distinguished him, embarked the gladiators on the Po, and, making a sudden descent on the opposite bank, fell with fury on the auxiliaries of Vitellius. All who attempted to make head against him were put to the sword; the rest fled with precipitation to Cremona. Macer was not willing to lose by rashness the fruit of his victory. He knew that, by the arrival of fresh forces, the fortune of the day might be changed, and, for that reason, recalled his men from pursuit. This measure spread a general discontent amongst the soldiers. It was the misfortune of Otho's party to be on all occasions infected with suspicion, and, with a strange perversity, to put the worst construction on the conduct of their officers. The base of heart and petulant of tongue combined together, and with virulent invective defamed and blackened every character without distinction. Even Annius Gallus, Suetonius Paulinus, and Marius Celsus, three eminent generals, did not escape the shafts of calumny. They were charged with various crimes. But the murderers of Galba were the worst incendiaries. Conscious of their guilt, and finding no respite from remorse and fear, these miscreants made it their business to embroil, to distract, and throw everything into confusion. They gave vent to their seditious designs with open insolence, and by clandestine letters infused their venom into the mind of Otho; a mind too susceptible, always hearkening to every malignant whisper, and only guarded against men of worth and honour: in prosperity

[1] This village, which stood at the distance of twenty miles from Cremona, and is now called *Caneto*, has been rendered famous by the defeat of Otho, and afterwards, as will be seen in the third book of this History, by that of Vitellius.

weak and irresolute; in distress collected, firm, determined; misfortune made him a better man. In his present situation, easily alarmed, and suspecting all his officers, he sent to Rome for his brother Titianus, and committed to him the whole conduct of the war. The interval was filled by Celsus and Paulinus with active enterprise and brilliant success.

XXIV. Cæcina felt the disgrace of his late defeat, and saw with anxiety the fame of his army mouldering away. He had been roughly handled at Placentia, his auxiliaries were cut to pieces, and in every skirmish, not worthy of a particular detail, the enemy had the advantage. He likewise knew by sure intelligence that Valens was advancing with his army, and that commander might reap the laurels of the war. To prevent a circumstance so humiliating, he resolved, with more courage than judgment, to redeem his glory. With this intent he marched to a village called Castorum, distant about twelve miles from Cremona. At that place, in a wood that overhangs the road, he stationed the flower of his auxiliaries in ambuscade. His cavalry had orders to take an advanced post, and, after provoking an engagement, to give ground at once, and draw the enemy forward, till an unexpected sally could be made from the woods. The stratagem was betrayed to the generals of Otho's army. Paulinus took the command of the infantry, while Celsus led on the cavalry. Their men were ranged in order of battle. In the left wing were placed the vexillaries of the thirteenth legion, four auxiliary cohorts, and five hundred horse. The high road was occupied by three prætorian cohorts, who formed the centre. The left wing consisted of the first legion, two auxiliary cohorts, and five hundred horse. Besides these, a thousand of the cavalry, selected from the prætorian and auxiliary bands, were kept as a body of reserve to support the broken ranks, or, if the enemy gave way, to rush on at once and complete the victory.

XXV. Before the two armies came to action, the Vitellians feigned a flight. Aware of the stratagem, Celsus checked the ardour of his men, and in his turn pretended to give ground. The adverse party, as they lay in ambush, thought they saw their opportunity, and, rushing forward inconsiderately, fell into a snare. The legions flanked them from both wings; the cohorts attacked in front; and the cavalry, wheeling round with rapidity, charged in the rear. Suetonius Paulinus still kept his infantry out of the engagement. By his natural temper slow and deliberate, he chose to take his measures with precaution, rather than hazard a sudden conflict, and owe his success to the chance of war. He ordered the hollows to be filled up, the ground to be cleared, and his ranks to be extended; wisely judging that it would then be time to think of victory, when he had taken care not to be conquered. During this delay the Vitellians seized the opportunity to shift their ground. They betook themselves to the adjacent vineyards, thick with interwoven branches, and, by consequence, difficult of access. Having there, and in a wood that lay contiguous, found a safe retreat, they recovered their courage, and sallied out to attack the prætorian cavalry. The best and bravest officers of that corps were cut to pieces. Epiphanes, the eastern king, who in support of Otho's cause faced every danger, was wounded in the engagement.

XXVI. At length the infantry, under the command of Paulinus, entered into the action. The front line of the enemy gave way at once, and the parties that came to support them were in like manner put to the rout. Cæcina had not the judgment to act with his whole strength at once. He brought up his men in detachments; and the consequence was, that, coming forward in succession, and nowhere strong enough, they soon gave way and fled with the ranks already broken. During this confusion, a violent tumult broke out in Cæcina's camp. The soldiers were enraged that the whole army was not drawn out. They seized Julius Gratus, the prefect of the camp, and loaded him with irons, on a suspicion that he held secret intelligence with his brother Julius Fronto, at that time a tribune in Otho's army, and under a similar accusation, then confined in prison by the adverse party. Nothing now could equal the disorder and consternation that covered the whole Vitellian army. In the camp, in the field of battle, in the flight, and amongst the parties that came to support the fugitives, the confusion was such, that, if Paulinus had not sounded a retreat, it was the general opinion that Cæcina, with his whole army, might have been cut to pieces. In defence of his conduct, Paulinus answered, that, seeing how much toil and labour still remained, he was not willing to expose his men, already spent with the fatigue of the day, to fresh forces kept in reserve, and ready to issue from the adverse camp. An exhausted soldiery might, in that case, be overpowered; and, if once broken, no post, no station remained behind. With this reasoning the judicious few were satisfied, but in the lower ranks of the army discontent and murmuring still prevailed.

XXVII. The loss sustained in this engagement had no

other effect on the vanquished Vitellians, than to reduce their turbulent spirit to a sense of military duty. Cæcina threw the whole blame of his defeat upon the ungovernable temper of the army, at all times more disposed to mutiny than to face the enemy. The men now saw their error, and began to submit to authority. Nor was this the case with regard to Cæcina only: the same reformation showed itself in the camp of Fabius Valens, who was now advanced as far as Ticinum. The soldiers under his command were taught, by the late event, no longer to despise the enemy. To retrieve the honour of the army, they now were willing to behave with due submission to their general. They had been, not long before, guilty of a bold and dangerous tumult, of which, at the exact point of time, no notice could be taken, without breaking the thread of the narrative, and departing too much from the transactions under Cæcina.

It may now be proper to give an account of that insurrection. The reader will remember, that, in the war between Nero and Vindex, the cohorts of the Batavian nation separated from the fourteenth legion, then on its way to Britain; and having heard, in the city of the Lingones, of commotions in favour of Vitellius, went over to the standard of Fabius Valens. Their arrogance, from that time, knew no bounds. They paraded the camp in every quarter, and in the tents of the legions, making it their boast, "that by them the fourteenth legion had been overawed: by them Italy was wrested out of the hands of Nero; and upon their swords the issue of war depended." The Roman soldiers heard these speeches with indignation; disputes and quarrels filled the camp, and discipline was at an end. Valens saw his authority lessened, and knew too well, that from clamour to actual mutiny the transition is short and sudden.

XXVIII. In this posture of affairs, Valens received advice that the Tungrians and Treverians had met with a defeat, and that Otho's fleet was hovering on the coast of Narbon Gaul. He took that opportunity to order a detachment of the Batavians to march to the relief of the province; intending, at the same time, by a stroke of policy, to divide the mutinous troops, whom, in their collective body, he found impatient of control. This measure gave umbrage to the rest of his army. The auxiliaries murmured, and the legions complained aloud, "that they were now to lose the bravest troops in the service. The enemy was near at hand, and was that a time to withdraw a body of gallant soldiers, who had so often fought with undaunted courage, and so often returned crowned with victory? If a single province is of more moment than the city of Rome, and the empire is but a secondary consideration, why not march with the united strength of the whole army? On the other hand, if Italy must be the theatre of war—if there, and there only, a decisive victory can be obtained—why separate from the army those gallant veterans, like the soundest limbs cut off from the body?"

XXIX. To allay this ferment, Valens went forth, preceded by his lictors. The men paid no regard to their general; they pelted him with stones; they forced him to fly before them; they pursued him with opprobrious language, accusing him of having embezzled, to his own private use, the spoils of Gaul, the gold of Vienne, and the recompense due to the soldiers for all their toil and labour. They rushed to his pavilion, pillaged his camp-equipage, and, in hopes of finding hidden treasure, pierced the ground with their spears and javelins. Valens in the meantime, disguised like a slave, lay concealed in the tent of an officer of the cavalry. Alphenus Varus, the prefect of the camp, saw the frenzy subsiding, and, in the ebb of their passions, thought it best to let repentance take possession of them by degrees. With that intent, he gave orders to the centurions neither to visit the night watch, nor suffer the usual signals to be given by sound of trumpet. A dead silence followed. The mutineers stood covered with astonishment, wondering that no one assumed the command; they gazed at each other, and trembled at being left to themselves. By silence and resignation they hoped to give a proof of returning virtue. In the end they burst into tears, and with humble supplications implored forgiveness. Valens ventured to appear. As soon as the soldiers saw him, beyond expectation, safe, unhurt, in a sordid dress, with tears starting from his eyes, a mingled tumult of joy and sorrow and affection swelled in every breast. With the quick transition of passions common with the multitude, they poured forth their congratulations; and with shouts of applause placed their general amidst the eagles and standards, on his tribunal. Valens acted with well-timed moderation. No man was singled out for punishment. Afraid, however, that, by too much coolness, he might make them suspect some deep design, he thought fit to reprimand a few by name, and his resentment went no further. In the distractions of a civil war, he knew that the power of the general is never equal to the liberty claimed by his soldiers.

XXX. While Valens employed his army in throwing up

intrenchments at Ticinum, an account of Cæcina's defeat reached the camp. The flame of sedition was ready to break out a second time. All agreed, that by the treachery of Valens they were detained from the field of battle. They resolved to linger no longer; they scorned to wait the motions of an inactive commander: they marched before the colours, and, ordering the standard-bearers to push on with alacrity, never halted, till, by a rapid march, they joined Cæcina's army. In that camp Valens was in no kind of credit. The vanquished soldiers complained, that with an inferior force they were left exposed to the enemy; and, by extolling the strength and valour of their new friends, they hoped to conciliate esteem, and throw from themselves the imputation of cowardice. Valens was at the head of an army which exceeded that of Cæcina by almost double the number, and yet the latter was the favourite of the men. His liberal spirit gained him friends, and his generosity was praised by all. To the vigour of youth he united a graceful figure, and he possessed those nameless qualities, which, though of no solid value, conciliate favour, men know not why. Hence a spirit of emulation between the two commanders. Cæcina objected to his rival the sordid vices that disgraced his character; and, in return, Valens laughed at a man elate with pride and vain ostentation. And yet the two chiefs acted towards each other with disguised hostility. In their zeal for the common cause, their mutual animosities were suppressed, though not extinguished. In their letters, they treated Otho and his licentious practices in a style that showed they scorned all terms of future reconciliation. The conduct of the officers in the opposite army was very different. They spoke of Vitellius with reserve; and though his manners afforded ample materials for invective, they chose to contain themselves within the bounds of prudence.

XXXI. It may be here observed, that, whatever were the shades of vice in the opposite characters of the contending chiefs, death in the end made the true distinction between them: Otho fell with glory, and Vitellius with disgrace and infamy. During their lives, men dreaded greater mischief from the unbridled passions of Otho, than from the sluggish debauchery of Vitellius. The murder of Galba made the former an object of detestation; while the latter was never charged with being the author of the war. Vitellius, by his gluttony and sensual appetites, was his own enemy; Otho, by his profusion, his cruelty, and his daring spirit, was the enemy of his country. As soon as the forces under Cæcina and Valens had formed a junction, the Vitellian party wished for nothing so much as a decisive action. Otho was not determined which was most for his interest, a speedy engagement or a lingering war. In this state of irresolution, he called a council, when Suetonius Paulinus, an officer surpassed by no man of that age, judged it consistent with his high military character, to weigh all circumstances, and upon the whole to give a decided opinion. He contended, that to bring the dispute to an immediate issue, was the business of Vitellius; and, on the contrary, to draw the war into length was the game that Otho ought to play. He argued as follows:

XXXII. "The whole collected force of Vitellius is now in Italy: the resources which he has left behind him are inconsiderable. From Gaul he has nothing to expect. The spirit of that fierce and turbulent people is still in agitation; and while Germany, with hostile numbers, is ever ready to invade the Roman provinces, the banks of the Rhine cannot be left naked and defenceless. The legions in Britain have the natives on their hands, and they are divided by the sea. Spain cannot boast of resources. The province of Narbon Gaul has been harassed by Otho's fleet, and is still covered with consternation. The part of Italy which lies beyond the Po is shut in by the Alps, deprived of all relief by sea, and the armies that passed that way have made the whole country a scene of desolation. There is no place from which Vitellius can hope to be supplied with grain; and he who wants provisions, in a short time will want an army. The Germans, a brave and warlike people, constitute the strength and bulwark of the Vitellian party: protract the war, and will they be able to go through a summer campaign? The change of soil, and the heat of the climate, will relax their vigour. The war, that by strenuous efforts may be pushed to a prosperous issue, grows languid when drawn into length, and in a state of tedious suspense whole armies have mouldered away.

"On the other hand, Otho's party is in no want of supplies; their friends are firm, and great resources are still in reserve. Pannonia, Mæsia, Dalmatia, and the eastern provinces, are able to send numerous armies into the field. All Italy declares for Otho: Rome, the capital of the empire, is still in his possession; and, above all, he has on his side the senate and the Roman people; illustrious names, and always of the first importance, though their glory in some conjunctures has been eclipsed. There is still in reserve a store of wealth, both public and private; and riches at all times are the sinews of war, in public dissensions more powerful than the sword. The soldiers in the service of Otho are in good condition, inured to Italy, or seasoned to the heat in warmer climates. In their front the river Po is a barrier, and there are fortified cities, strongly garrisoned, all determined to hold out to the last. Of this the gallant defence of Placentia is a sufficient proof. For these reasons, a slow and lingering war is the best expedient. Pass but a few days, and the fourteenth legion, famous for its bravery, will arrive with a strong reinforcement of auxiliaries from Mæsia. A council of war may then be called; and should it be thought advisable to hazard a battle, Otho, in that event, may take the field with a superior army."

XXXIII. Marius Celsus concurred in this opinion. Annius Gallus was not present. He had been hurt by a fall from his horse a few days before, and was not yet recovered; but being consulted by persons sent for the purpose, he acceded to the counsels of Paulinus. Otho was for trying the issue of a battle. His brother Titianus, and Proculus, the prefect of the prætorian guards, though neither of them had any military experience, did what in them lay to incite a temper of itself rash and precipitate. The gods, they said, and the tutelar genius of Otho, were present in council, and would not fail to guide and animate the battle. Such was the language of flattery. They made their poison palatable, and no man presumed to administer an antidote.

To offer battle was the result of the debate; but whether the emperor should command in person, or withdraw to a place of safety, was a question still to be discussed. Celsus and Paulinus gave no opinion. To expose the prince to the dangers of the field, was more than they chose to hazard. That point was left to the authors of the pernicious counsel already given. By their advice Otho retired to Brixellum, there to reserve himself for the good of the people and the majesty of empire. From this day the ruin of Otho may be dated. He took with him a considerable detachment of the prætorian cohorts, the body-guard, and a strong party of horse. After their departure, the spirit of the army began to droop. They suspected their officers. The prince, to whom the soldiers were faithfully attached, and who, in return, confided in them, and them only, abandoned his cause, without having a head to direct, or a general to whose authority the men were willing to submit.

XXXIV. During these transactions, nothing of all that passed was a secret in the camp of Vitellius. From the deserters, who in civil wars are always numerous, and also from the spies, whose genius it is, while they pry into the secrets of others, to betray their own, everything transpired. Cæcina and Valens lay in wait for the motions of an enemy, whom they saw contriving their own destruction. To plan an enterprise was unnecessary, where the best wisdom was to succeed by the folly of others. In order, however, to give jealousy to the gladiators [1] on the opposite bank of the Po, and at the same time to keep their own soldiers employed, they began to throw a bridge over the river. As a foundation for the work, they ranged in proper order a number of boats, made fast at equal distances by strong timbers, with their prows turned against the current, and by their anchors secured from driving from the spot. The cables were of a length to play in the water, in order, when the stream increased, that the vessels might be gently lifted up and down without danger or confusion. In the boat at the further extremity of the bridge, they caused a tower to be erected, which served at once to close the passage, and give the men a station, where they might, with their battering engines, prevent the approach of the enemy.

XXXV. The Othonians also raised a tower on the opposite bank, and thence were able to annoy the enemy with massy stones and flaming brands. A small island stood in the middle of the water. The gladiators attempted to pass over in boats; but the Germans, expert in swimming, dashed into the stream, and took possession of the place. In order to dislodge them, Macer put off with a strong party of gladiators on board his galleys: but the gladiators were not able to cope with regular soldiers; and the motion of the vessels not allowing them a firm footing, they fought at a disadvantage with men who from the land were able to discharge their missive weapons with surer aim and more certain effect. On board the vessels all was hurry and confusion. The rowers and combatants obstructed each other. The Germans plunged into the river, and, seizing hold of the boats, boarded several, and sunk others to the bottom. The whole passed under the eye of both armies. The Vitellians looked on with joy, while the adverse party, stung with indignation, railed at Macer, whom they called the author of their disgrace.

[1] It has been already mentioned, that Otho had in his army two thousand gladiators; a disgraceful expedient, says Tacitus, but in civil wars adopted by the ablest generals.

XXXVI. The gladiators, in such vessels as they could save, retreated from the island, and by their flight put an end to the engagement. Macer was devoted to destruction. The soldiers clamoured for his blood. One of them darted his lance, and actually wounded him; while the rest rushed on sword in hand, and would have killed him on the spot, if the tribunes and centurions had not interposed to save him from their fury. In a short time after, Vestricius Spurinna, having, by order of Otho, left a moderate garrison at Placentia, came up to the main body with the cohorts under his command. Macer was superseded, and in his place Flavius Sabinus, consul elect, was appointed; to the great joy of the common men, who saw with pleasure every change of their officers. The commanders, in their turn, saw the unruly spirit of the army, and, with reluctance, accepted a service so often disturbed by tumult and sedition.

XXXVII. I find it asserted as a fact, and by authors of credit, that the two armies, dreading the calamities of war, and at the same time detesting the two rival princes, whose flagitious deeds grew every day more notorious, were disposed to lay down their arms, and either to name a person worthy of the succession, or to refer that matter to the choice of the senate. This, we are told, was the consideration that weighed with Otho's generals, when they proposed to draw the war into length, and, in particular, that Paulinus acted with that motive. He was the first and most distinguished of the consular rank, the highest in military reputation, and his conduct in Britain[1] had given superior lustre to his name. But though it may be reasonable to admit, that a few, in that juncture, had the public good at heart, and wished to see two vile competitors, the most abandoned of mankind, postponed to a virtuous prince; it is, notwithstanding, highly improbable that Paulinus, a man of experience and consummate understanding, should, in an age so corrupt and profligate, amuse himself with hopes of finding one spark of virtue. He knew the madness of the times; and could he expect, that the same infatuated multitude, whose wickedness had kindled the flame of war, would on a sudden prefer the blessings of peace, and consent, for the repose of the world, to sheathe the destructive sword? Can it be imagined, that the armies then in the field, dissonant in language, and in their manners still more discordant, could ever be brought to coalesce in one opinion? Above

[1] For the conduct of Suetonius Paulinus, and the brilliant success of his arms in Britain, see *Annals*, xiv. 29-40.

all, can it be supposed that the leading chiefs, a set of men immersed in luxury, overwhelmed with debts, and conscious of their crimes, would submit to any master who was not, like themselves, plunged in vice, and by gratitude for his elevation obliged to be the patron of the most pernicious citizens?

XXXVIII. The love of power and domination seems to be an instinct of the human heart, implanted by the hand of nature. Coeval with the foundation of Rome, it grew with the growth of the empire, and, in the hour of pride and grandeur, broke out with resistless violence. Before that period, while the republic was in its infancy, the equality of conditions was easily preserved. In process of time, when the pride of foreign kings was humbled, and rival nations submitted to the Roman arms, avarice began to accumulate riches, and contentions arose between the senate and the people. Factious tribunes prevailed at one time, and ambitious consuls at another. In the heart of the city, and even in the forum, the sword of discord was drawn, and those dissensions were a prelude to the rage of civil war. Caius Marius, a man sprung from the dregs of the populace, and Lucius Sulla, fierce and cruel beyond the rest of the nobility, overturned the constitution of their country, and on the ruins of public liberty established a system of tyranny and lawless power. Pompey came soon after, with passions more disguised, but no way better. From that time, the struggle has been for supreme dominion. The legions that filled the plains of Pharsalia, and afterwards met at Philippi, though composed of Roman citizens, never once thought of laying down their arms. And are we to believe that the armies of Otho and Vitellius were of a more pacific temper? They had instigations equally powerful; the same wrath of the gods pursued them; the same popular frenzy kindled the flame of discord; and the same vices conspired to urge them on to mutual slaughter. Their war, it is true, was ended by a single battle; but for that speedy issue the world was indebted, not to the virtue of the armies, but to the abject spirit of the contending princes. But these reflections on the spirit of ancient and modern times have betrayed me into a long digression. I resume the thread of my narrative.

XXXIX. From the time when Otho withdrew to Brixellum, his brother Titianus assumed all the pride and pomp of commander-in-chief, but the power and real authority remained in the hands of Proculus. Celsus and Paulinus were no more than mere nominal generals. No man sought their advice.

They were, in fact, superseded; serving no purpose but that of screening the folly of others, and bearing the blame of blunders not their own. The tribunes and centurions could render no effectual service, while ignorance and insufficiency were preferred, and real talents lay neglected. The common men appeared with an air of alacrity, but more disposed to cavil with their generals, than to execute their orders. A sudden resolution was taken to shift their ground, and encamp within four miles of Bedriacum. They conducted their march, and chose their station, with such want of skill, that, though it was then the spring of the year, and the country round abounded with rivers, the army was distressed for want of water. The expediency of hazarding a battle became again the subject of debate. Otho, by frequent despatches, insisted on the most vigorous measures: the soldiers called for their emperor, and with clamour demanded his presence on the day of battle. Many were of opinion, that the forces beyond the Po should be called in to reinforce the army. History has not materials to decide what would have been the most prudent measure; but it is certain, that of all possible evils they chose the worst.

XL. They resolved to march to the conflux of the Po[1] and the Addua, at the distance of sixteen miles. In this movement the soldiers presented no appearance of an army going to offer battle. They marched as if going to open a campaign, not to decide it. The measure was in direct opposition to the advice of Celsus and Paulinus. Those officers represented the danger of exposing the soldiers, fatigued by their march, and bending under the weight of their baggage, to the attack of an enemy unincumbered, and fresh from a march of four miles only. An army in that condition would seize their opportunity, and begin a general assault before Otho's men could form the line of battle; perhaps they were dispersed in small parties, or employed at the intrenchments. Titianus and Proculus were not to be convinced. When overcome by argument, they resorted to their orders, and the will of the prince was a decisive answer. About the same time a Numidian horseman, posting at full speed, arrived with letters from Otho, in a style of sharp reproof condemning the tedious operations of the army, and in a peremptory tone commanding his generals to bring on a decisive action. To a mind like his the interval of suspense was dreadful. Delay

[1] The Addua falls into the Po, about six miles to the west of Cremona.

kept him in restless anxiety, and hope and fear distracted him.

XLI. On the same day, while Cæcina was employed in throwing a bridge over the Po, two prætorian tribunes arrived to demand an interview. They were admitted to an audience, when a sudden alarm from the scouts announced the enemy at hand. The business broke off abruptly, and the intention of the tribunes was left in the dark. What their design was, whether to betray their own party, to lay a snare for the Vitellians, or to make a fair and honourable proposal, cannot now be known. Cæcina dismissed the tribunes, and made the best of his way to the camp. He found that Valens had lost no time: the signal for battle was already given, and the men were drawn out under arms. While the legions were eagerly employed in settling by lot the order in which they were to take their stations in the field, the cavalry advanced to charge the enemy, and, contrary to all expectations, were put to the rout by an inferior number. The Othonians pursued with vigour, and would have forced them to fly for shelter to their intrenchments, had not the Italic legion opposed the runaways, and sword in hand compelled them to return to the charge. Meanwhile, the rest of the army, without hurry or confusion, drew up in order of battle, unmolested by the enemy, and, in fact, without being seen: as a thick coppice, that stood between both parties, intercepted their view.

In Otho's army nothing was seen but tumult and distraction; the chiefs without courage, or authority; the men mistrusting the officers; the ground not cleared of the baggage, and the followers of the camp mixing in the ranks. The road which they occupied was rendered so narrow, by a ditch on each side, that, even though no enemy were at hand, a march over the causey would have been performed with difficulty. Their whole army was in confusion; some crowding about their colours; others at a loss and running to and fro to find their proper post; all in a confused clamour, roaring for their comrades, answering to their names, and confounding one another with noise and uproar. Some, still shifting their ground, advanced to the front line; others fell into the rear; none remaining in one spot, but shifting their ground, as fear or courage happened to prompt them.

XLII. The Othonians had scarce recovered from their surprise, when a sudden incident diffused a general joy; but a joy that tended to lull them into security, and relax their courage into languor and stupid amazement. A report was spread, that the forces of Vitellius had abandoned his cause: but from what quarter it took its origin; whether by design or chance; from the emissaries of the Vitellians, or the adverse party, has never been explained. The effect on the minds of the Othonians was altogether extraordinary. Laying aside all thoughts of coming to action, they saluted the opposite army, who stood astonished, and returned a deep and hollow murmur. Those in Otho's ranks who did not know the cause of the civility shown by their friends, thought themselves betrayed. In that moment the Vitellians began the attack. Their army was in regular order, and their numbers were superior. The Othonians, still in disorder, and fatigued by their march, received the first impression with undaunted firmness. The place where the action grew warm being thick with trees and interwoven vine-branches, the combat varied according to the nature of the ground. They fought man to man; they engaged at a distance; they discharged their darts and missive weapons; they brought forward separate battalions, or advanced in the form of a wedge. On the high road the engagement was close and obstinate. Darts and lances were of no use. They fought hand to hand, foot to foot, and buckler against buckler. With their swords and axes they cut through helmets and breastplates. They knew one another; each individual was conspicuous to his friends and enemies; his exploits were seen by all; and every man fought, as if the issue of the war depended upon his single arm.

XLIII. Upon an open plain of considerable extent, that lay between the Po and the high road, two legions met in fierce encounter; on the part of Vitellius, the one-and-twentieth, famed for its valour, and commonly known by the name of RAPAX; on the side of Otho, the first legion, entitled ADJUTRIX, which had never been in action, and now panted for an opportunity to flesh their maiden swords. Their first attack was not to be resisted. They broke through the ranks of the one-and-twentieth, and carried off their eagle. Roused by this disgrace, the Vitellians added rage to bravery, and bore down all before them. Orphidius Benignus, who commanded Otho's legion, fell in the conflict. His men were driven back with great slaughter, and the loss of several standards. In another part of the field the thirteenth legion was routed by the fifth, and the fourteenth was hemmed in by superior numbers. Otho's generals had long since fled the field, while Cæcina and Valens continued to exert themselves, watching every turn of the battle, and supporting the ranks in every quarter. Fresh forces came to their assistance. The Batavians, under Varus Alphenus, having cut to pieces the gladiators attempting in boats to cross the Po, came into the field, flushed with success, and charged the enemy in flank.

XLIV. The centre of Otho's army gave way, and fled with precipitation towards Bedriacum. A long space lay before them; the road was obstructed with heaps of slain, and the enemy hung upon their rear. In civil wars no prisoners are reserved for sale: the slaughter, for that reason, was the more dreadful. Suetonius Paulinus and Licinius Proculus fled different ways, both resolved not to return to the camp. Vedius Aquila, who commanded the thirteenth legion, by his own indiscretion exposed himself to the fury of the soldiers. He entered the camp, while it was yet broad daylight; and the very men, who were the first to turn their backs on the enemy, were now the foremost in sedition. They crowded round their superior officer with a torrent of abusive language, and offered violence to his person. They charged him with treachery and desertion, in the true spirit of vulgar minds, transferring to others their own guilt and infamy. Titianus and Celsus owed their safety to the darkness of the night. They did not venture into the camp, till the sentinels were stationed at their posts, and the tumult was appeased by the entreaties, the advice, and authority of Annius Gallus, who had the address to make the men sensible of the folly and madness of adding to the havoc of the field by their own destructive fury. Whether the war was at end, or to be once more renewed with vigour, he represented, in either case, the necessity of union among themselves. A face of sorrow and dejection covered the camp. All were hushed in silence; all but the prætorians, who still grumbled discontent, asserting that they were defeated by treachery, not by the valour of the enemy. "The Vitellians," they said, "could not boast of a cheap victory. Their cavalry was routed, and one of their legions lost their eagle. Otho still survived, and the troops beyond the Po were ready to advance; the legions from Mæsia were on their march; and a considerable part of the army, detained at Bedriacum, had no share in the action. These were still in reserve; they were not conquered; and if a total overthrow was to be their lot, they might fall with glory in the field of battle." With these and such-like reflections the prætorians kept their minds in agitation, by turns inflamed with anger, or depressed with fear. They saw their ruined condition; despair succeeded, and from despair they derived courage and a spirit of revenge.

XLV. The victorious army halted at the distance of five miles from Bedriacum. The generals did not think it advisable on the same day to attempt the enemy's camp. Expecting a voluntary surrender, they were willing to give their men some time to repose. To encamp was not in their power. The soldiers took the field, prepared for battle, unincumbered, and of course without the means of throwing up intrenchments. Their arms and their victory were their only fortification. On the following day the Othonians showed a pacific disposition; and even those, who the night before breathed nothing but war and vengeance, with one consent agreed to send a deputation to the enemy. The Vitellian leaders were willing to hearken to terms of accommodation. The deputies not returning immediately, the suspense occasioned an awful interval in Otho's camp. Peace was at length announced, and the intrenchments were thrown open. A tender scene ensued. The conquerors and the conquered embraced each other, and with mingled joy and sorrow lamented the horrors of civil war. In the same tents, relations, friends, and brothers, dressed each other's wounds. They now perceived that their hopes were a mere delusion, and that slaughter, sorrow, and repentance, were their certain lot. Nor was there in the two armies a single person who had not the death of a friend or a relation to lament. The body of Orphidius, the commander of a legion, after diligent search, was found among the slain, and burned with the usual solemnities. A few of the common men were buried by their friends: the rest were left to welter on the bare earth.

XLVI. Otho, in the meantime, having taken his resolution, waited, without fear or dejection of mind, for an account of the event. Vague and uncertain rumours reached his ear. At length the fugitives, who escaped from the field, brought sure intelligence that all was lost. The soldiers, who stood near his person, did not stay to hear the sentiments of the emperor, but broke out with impatient ardour, exhorting him to summon up his best resolution. There were forces still in reserve, and, in their prince's cause, they were ready to brave every danger. In this declaration there was no flattery; they spoke from the heart. In a fit of instinctive fury they desired to be led against the enemy; by their example the drooping spirit of their friends would be once more excited to deeds of valour. The men who stood at a distance stretched forth their hands in token of their assent, while such as gathered round the prince fell at his feet, and clasped his knees. Plotius Firmus distinguished himself by his zeal. This officer commanded the prætorian guards. He implored his master not to abandon an army devoted to his interest, nor to renounce a brave and generous soldiery, who had undergone so much, and were still ready to face every danger. "The noble mind," he said, "stands a siege against adversity, while the little spirit capitulates at once. True courage grapples with misfortune, and, in the last distress, still makes head against every difficulty. The mean and abject sink down in despair, and yield without a struggle." The soldiers fixed their eyes on the prince, and with every symptom in his countenance their passions varied. If he assented, they thundered forth their applause; if he seemed inflexible, a groan expressed the anguish of their hearts. Nor was the spirit confined to the prætorians, who were properly the soldiers of Otho: it extended to the detachment sent forward by the Mæsian legions. These men with one voice declared for Otho; they assured him, that the same zeal pervaded their comrades, who were coming forward by rapid marches, and even then had entered Aquileia. Hence it is evident, that great resources still remained, and that a fierce and obstinate war, uncertain in the event, and big with danger to all parties, might have been renewed, and carried on with vigour.

XLVII. Otho had weighed all circumstances: ambition was at an end, and he prepared to close the scene. He addressed the soldiers to the following effect: "When I behold the ardour that glows in every breast; when I consider the virtue that inspires so many gallant friends, I cannot think of exposing you again to the destructive sword; nor do I value my life at such a price. The views which you display to me, were I disposed to live, are bright and tempting; by renouncing them, I fall with greater glory. I have made acquaintance with fortune; we have tried each other, for what length of time is not material; but the felicity, which does not promise to last, cannot be enjoyed with moderation. Vitellius began the war; he claimed the empire, and, by consequence, I was obliged to have recourse to arms. That we fought once, his ambition was the cause; to end the dispute by the event of one battle, and stop the effusion of Roman blood, shall be my glory. By this conduct let posterity judge of Otho. I restore to Vitellius his brother, his wife and children. I want no revenge, I seek no lenitives to soothe calamity. Others have held the sovereign power longer than I have done; with equal calmness no man has resigned it. Can I give to the edge of the sword so many gallant soldiers? Can I see the armies of Rome devoted to mutual slaughter, and for ever cut off from their country. It is enough for me, that in my cause you are ready to shed your blood. Let that generous zeal attend me to my grave. I thank you for it: but you must still survive to serve the commonwealth. For this great end, let us agree to remove all obstacles; I will be no bar to your preservation; nor will you attempt to frustrate my resolution. When death approaches, to linger in vain discourse is the design of a little spirit. The temper, with which I meet my fate, will be seen and known by this circumstance: I complain of no man. He who, in his last moments, can look back to arraign either gods or men, still clings to life, and quits it with regret."

XLVIII. Having thus declared his sentiments he talked apart with his friends, addressing each of them in gracious terms, according to his rank, his age, or dignity, and advising all to depart without loss of time, and make their terms with the conqueror. He entreated the old men, and with the young exerted his authority. Calm and undisturbed, serenity in his countenance, and firmness in his voice, he saw his friends weep, and endeavoured to repress their tears. He ordered boats or carriages for those who were willing to depart. He selected all such papers and letters as happened to contain expressions of duty towards himself, or ill-will to Vitellius, and committed them to the flames. He distributed money in presents, but not with the profusion of a man quitting the world. Observing that his brother's son, Salvius Cocceianus, a youth in the flower of his age, was dissolved in tears, he endeavoured to assuage his sorrows. He commended the goodness of his heart, but his fears, he said, were out of season. "Could it be supposed that Vitellius, finding his own family safe, would refuse, with brutal inhumanity, to return the generosity shown to himself? My death will leave him without a rival, and that very act will be a demand upon his clemency; especially, since it is not an act of despair, but a voluntary resignation, made at a time when a brave and generous army calls aloud for another battle. For the good of the commonwealth I am a willing victim. For myself I have gained ample renown, and I leave to my family an illustrious name. After the Julian race,[1] the Claudian, and the Servian, I am the first who transferred the sovereignty to a new family. It becomes you, young man, to act with courage; you must dare to live. Remember that Otho was your uncle, but remember it with modesty, and without resentment."

XLIX. After this, he desired his friends to withdraw. Being left alone, he composed himself to rest, and in a short time began to prepare for the last act of his life. In that moment he was interrupted by a sudden uproar. The soldiers, he was told, threatened destruction to all who offered to depart, and in particular to Verginius,[2] whom they kept besieged in his house. Otho went forth to appease the tumult. Having reproved the authors of the disturbance, he returned to his apartment, and received the visits of all that came to bid the last farewell: he conversed with them freely and cheerfully, and saw them depart without let or molestation. Towards the close of day, he called for a draught of cold water, and, having quenched his thirst, ordered two poniards to be brought to him. He tried the points of both, and laid one under his pillow. Being informed that his friends were safe on their way, he passed the night in quiet. We are assured, that he even slept. At the dawn of day, he applied the weapon to his breast, and fell upon the point. His dying groans alarmed his freedmen and slaves. They rushed into the chamber, and with them Plotius Firmus, the prætorian prefect. They found that with one wound he had despatched himself. His body was burned without delay. This had been his earnest request, lest his head should fall into the hands of his enemies, and be made a public spectacle. He was borne on the shoulders of the prætorian soldiers to the funeral pile. The men, during the procession, paid all marks of respect to his remains. They printed kisses on his hands, and on the mortal wound, and, in a flood of tears, poured forth their warmest praise. At the funeral pile some of the soldiers put an end to their lives; not from any consciousness of guilt, nor yet impelled by fear; but to emulate the example of the prince, and to show themselves faithful to the last. At Bedriacum, Placentia, and other camps,

[1] Augustus, Tiberius, and Caligula, were of the Julian line; Claudius, and Nero (by adoption), were of the Claudian; Galba was of the house of Servius; Otho, of the Salvian family.

[2] This was Verginius Rufus, who conquered Vindex in Gaul, and had the moderation to decline the imperial dignity offered to him by the legions.

numbers followed the example. A sepulchre was raised to the memory of Otho, but of an ordinary structure, protected by its meanness, and therefore likely to last.

L. Such was the end of Otho, in the thirty-seventh year of his age. He was born in the municipal city of Ferentum. His father was of consular rank; his grandfather had discharged the office of prætor. By the maternal line his descent was respectable, though not illustrious. The features of his character, as well in his earliest days as in the progress of his youth, have been already delineated. By two actions of his life he stands distinguished; one, atrocious and detestable; the other, great and magnanimous: the former has consigned his name to eternal infamy, and the last will do honour to his memory. History cannot descend to the frivolous task of collecting vague reports, in order to amuse the reader with a fabulous detail; but there are traditions, which have been handed down with an air of authenticity, and these I shall not take upon me to suppress or to refute. On the day when the battle was fought at Bedriacum, a bird of unusual appearance was observed to perch in a grove near Regium Lepidum, and, notwithstanding the great concourse of people, and a numerous flight of other birds, never to move from its place till Otho put an end to his life. That event no sooner happened, than it waved its wings, and vanished out of sight. The people of the village aver the fact; and according to curious observers, who made an exact computation of the time, this extraordinary phenomenon tallied exactly with the beginning of the battle and the prince's death.

LI. The grief of the soldiers, at the funeral ceremony, drove them, in a fit of distraction, to another mutiny. No officer assumed the command; no one interfered to allay the ferment. The men demanded a sight of Verginius; one moment calling upon him to accept the sovereignty, and the next, with mingled prayers and menaces, pressing him to undertake an embassy on their behalf to Valens and Cæcina. Verginius, seeing them determined to enter his house by force, made his escape at the back door. The cohorts that lay encamped at Brixellum, deputed Rubrius Gallus with terms of submission. That officer obtained their pardon. At the same time Flavius Sabinus made terms for himself, and, with the troops under his command, submitted to the conqueror.

LII. Though the war was now at an end, a great part of the senate, who accompanied Otho from Rome, and by him were left at Mutina, found themselves involved in the utmost danger. They received an account of the defeat at Bedriacum, but the soldiers treated it as a false alarm. Suspecting the integrity of the fathers, and fully persuaded that they were, in secret, enemies to Otho and his cause, they watched their motions, listened to their words, and, with their usual malignity, gave to everything that passed the worst construction. They proceeded to reproach and every kind of insult, hoping to find a pretence for an insurrection and a general massacre. The senators saw another cloud gathering over their heads: they knew that the Vitellian party triumphed; and, if they were tardy with their congratulations, the delay might be thought a spirit of disaffection. In this dilemma they called a meeting of the whole order. No man dared to act alone. In the conduct of all, each individual hoped to find his own personal safety. At the same time an ill-judged compliment from the people of Mutina increased the apprehensions of the senators. The magistrates of the city made a tender of arms and money for the public service, and, in the style of their address, gave to a small party of senators the appellation of conscript fathers; a title always applied to the collective body.

LIII. In the debate that followed in a thin meeting of the fathers, a violent dispute broke out between Licinius Cæcina and Eprius Marcellus; the former, with warmth and vehemence, charging it as a crime against Marcellus, that he spoke in ambiguous terms and with studied obscurity. The case was by no means singular; all were equally dark and mysterious: but the name of Marcellus, who had conducted so many prosecutions, was universally detested; and Cæcina, a new man lately admitted into the senate, thought to rise by encountering powerful enmities. The dispute was ended by the interposition of wiser men. The senate adjourned to Bononia, intending there to meet again, when they hoped to have more certain intelligence. They stationed messengers on all the public roads to interrogate every man that passed. One of Otho's freedmen came in their way. Being asked why he had left his master, he made answer, "I have with me the directions and last will of the prince, who is still alive: but he renounces all the joys of life; his thoughts are fixed upon posterity, and he has now no other care." This account made an impression on every mind: all stood astonished, and soon after, without asking any further questions, went over to Vitellius.

LIV. Lucius Vitellius, brother of the new emperor, attended the meeting of the senate. The fathers began to address him in a flattering strain, and he was willing to receive their incense. His joy was soon interrupted. One Cænus, a freedman of Nero's, by a bold and impudent falsehood, threw the assembly into consternation. He affirmed it as a fact, that the fourteenth legion, with the forces from Brixellum, attacked the victorious party, and gained a complete victory. The motive of this man for framing a story so false and groundless, was because he saw Otho's orders for road-horses[1] and carriages no longer in force, and he wished to revive their former authority. By this stratagem he gained a quick conveyance to Rome, and in a few days was put to death by order of Vitellius. In the meantime, the Othonian soldiers gave credit to the fiction, and even believed that the fathers, who had departed from Mutina to deliberate at Bononia, were gone over to the enemy. From this time the senate was convened no more. Every man acted with his own private views, till letters arrived from Fabius Valens, and put an end to all their fears. Besides this, the death of Otho was universally known. The velocity of fame was equal to the glory of that heroic action.

LV. Meanwhile, at Rome a general calm prevailed. The games sacred to Ceres[2] were celebrated according to annual custom. In the midst of the public spectacle, intelligence arrived that Otho was no more, and that all the military then in the city had, at the requisition of Flavius Sabinus, sworn fidelity to Vitellius: the people heard the news with transport, and the theatre shook with applause. The audience, crowned with laurel wreaths, and strewing the way with flowers, went forth in procession, and, with the images of Galba displayed in a triumphant manner, visited the several temples, and afterwards with their chaplets raised a fancied tomb to his memory, on the spot, near the lake of Curtius, where that emperor breathed his last. The various honours which flattery at different times had lavished on former princes, were decreed by the senate to the new sovereign. They passed a vote of thanks to the German armies, and despatched special messengers to congratulate Vitellius on his accession to the imperial dignity. A letter from Fabius

1 The passports, called *Diplomata Othonis*, were granted for the protection of travellers and messengers.
2 The festival of Ceres began on the 19th of April.

Valens to the consuls was read in the senate; and though there was nothing of arrogance in the style, the respectful modesty of Cæcina, who remained silent, gave greater satisfaction.

LVI. Peace was now established throughout Italy; but it was a peace more destructive than the calamities of war. The Vitellian soldiers, quartered in the colonies and municipal cities, were still bent on spoil and rapine. They committed the most horrible outrages, deflowering the women, and trampling on all laws human and divine. Where they refrained from injury, they received a bribe for their forbearance. Nothing sacred or profane was spared. Innocent men were marked out as soldiers of Otho's party, and under that pretence, murdered by their private enemies. The soldiers who best knew the country, fixed upon the opulent farmers as their devoted prey. Where the lands were rich, they laid waste and plundered without control. All who resisted were put to the sword. The general officers had no power to check the mischief. What they had done themselves, they could not oppose in others. Cæcina had not the avarice of his colleague; popularity was his passion. Valens, on the contrary, had made himself infamous by his rapacity, and was therefore obliged to connive, when he saw his own vices practised by others. Italy was long since exhausted, and, in that impoverished state, obliged to maintain numerous armies, and to bear the superadded grievances of riot, insult, and devastation.

LVII. Vitellius, in the meantime, advanced towards Italy with the remainder of the German armies, ignorant of his victory, and still conceiving that he was to meet the whole weight of the war. A few of the veteran soldiers were left behind in winter quarters; and to recruit the legions, which retained little more than their name, hasty levies were made in Gaul. On the frontiers bordering on the Rhine the command was given to Hordeonius Flaccus. To his own army Vitellius added eight thousand men from Britain. Having marched a few days, he received intelligence of the victory at Bedriacum, and the conclusion of the war by the death of Otho. He called an assembly of the soldiers, and, in a public harangue, extolled the valour of the troops that conquered in his service. He had with him a freedman of the name of Asiaticus. The army wished to see him raised to the dignity of a Roman knight. Vitellius knew that the request was a flight of adulation, and had the spirit to reject it: but such was his natural levity, that what he refused in public, he granted in private over his bottle. And thus a despicable slave, who was goaded on by ambition, and had nothing to recommend him but his vices, was honoured with the equestrian ring.

LVIII. About the same time Vitellius received advices that the two Mauritanias had acceded to his party. This event was occasioned by the murder of Lucceius Albinus, the governor of that country. The province which was called Cæsariensis had been by Nero committed to Albinus; and the other, called Tingitana, was afterwards added by Galba. In consequence of his extensive command, the governor was master of a considerable force; not less than nineteen cohorts, five squadrons of horse, and a numerous body of Moors, accustomed to live by depredation, and by their hardy course of life prepared for the fatigues of war. Albinus, on the death of Galba, declared in favour of Otho, and, not content with his power in Africa, began to form an enterprise against Spain, which was separated by a narrow channel.[1] Cluvius Rufus presided in Spain. Alarmed at the projects of the commander in Africa, he ordered the tenth legion to march to the sea-coast, with a design, as he gave out, to cross the sea. In the meantime, he despatched a few chosen centurions to tamper with the Moors, and draw them over to the interest of Vitellius. This was not a difficult task. The fame of the German armies resounded through all the provinces. A report prevailed, at the same time, that Albinus, disdaining the title of procurator, had usurped the regal diadem, and the name of Juba.

LIX. The currents of popular opinion were by these circumstances entirely changed in Africa. Asinius Pollio, who commanded a squadron of horse in that country, and professed himself devoted to Albinus, was immediately murdered. Festus and Scipio, each the prefect of a cohort, shared the same fate. Albinus himself, after a short voyage from the province of Tingitana to that of Cæsariensis, was put to death as soon as he landed. His wife, attempting to oppose the assassins, perished with her husband. These transactions passed without the notice of Vitellius. Nothing awakened his curiosity. Even in matters of the highest importance, the attention of a moment was all that could be expected from a man who had neither talents nor application to business.

[1] The straits of Gibraltar.

He ordered his army to pursue their march into Itaiy, while he himself sailed down the Arar;[1] not with the pomp and grandeur of a prince, but still exposing to public view the distress and poverty of his former condition. At length Junius Blæsus, at that time governor of the Lyonese Gaul, a man of a large and liberal mind, by his birth illustrious, and of a spirit equal to his vast possessions, supplied Vitellius with a train suited to the imperial dignity, and attended in person to do honour to the new emperor. Vitellius saw this display of magnificence with an evil eye, but under specious and even servile caresses took care to hide his jealousy. At Lyons the general officers of both parties, as well the vanquished as the victorious, attended to do homage to the prince. Vitellius in a public speech pronounced the panegyric of Valens and Cæcina, whom he placed on each side of his curule chair. He then ordered out the whole army to receive his son, then an infant of tender years. The soldiers obeyed. The father took the child in his arms, and, having adorned him with a purple robe, and other marks of princely grandeur, saluted him by the title of GERMANICUS; in this manner bestowing extravagant honours, even in the tide of prosperity ill-judged and out of season; but, perhaps, in the reverse of fortune that happened afterwards, some source of consolation.

LX. The centurions who had signalised themselves in Otho's service, were by order of Vitellius put to death. By this act of cruelty he lost the affections of the forces from Illyricum. The rest of the legions caught the infection, and, being already on bad terms with the German soldiery, began to meditate a revolt. Suetonius Paulinus and Licinius Proculus were kept for some time in a wretched state of suspense. Being at length admitted to an audience, they made a defence, which nothing but the necessity of the times could excuse. They charged themselves with treachery to Otho, and to their own sinister designs ascribed the march of the army on the day of battle, the fatigue of the troops, and the confusion in the ranks, occasioned by not removing the baggage, with many other incidents, from which, though accidental, they derived to themselves the merit of fraud and perfidy. Vitellius gave them credit for their guilt, and pardoned, though they had been in arms against himself, their attachment to his enemy. Salvius Titianus was exempt from danger. Natural affection made him join his brother, and his despicable char-

[1] The Arar, now the Soane.

acter sheltered him from resentment. Marius Celsus, consul elect, was suffered to succeed to his honours, though Cæcilius Simplex, as was generally believed, endeavoured by bribery to supplant him. His ambition aimed at the consulship, and would fain have risen on the ruins of an Othonian officer. The attempt was afterwards objected to him in open senate. The emperor, however, withstood his solicitations, but, in time, raised him to that high office, without the guilt of bribery or murder. Trachalus was attacked by his enemies, but owed his safety to the protection of Galeria, the wife of Vitellius.

LXI. Amidst the dangers that involved the first men of the age, it may be thought beneath the dignity of history to relate the wild adventure of one Mariccus, a Boian by birth, and sprung from the dregs of the people. This man, however mean his condition, had the presumption to mix his name with men who fought for the empire of the world. In a fit of enthusiasm, pretending to have preternatural lights, he called himself the tutelar deity of Gaul, and, in the character of a god, dared to defy the Roman arms. He played the impostor so well, that he was able to muster eight thousand men. At the head of that deluded multitude, he made an attempt on the adjacent villages of the Æduans. The people of that nation were not to be deluded. They armed the flower of their youth, and, with a reinforcement from the Roman cohorts, attacked the fanatics, and put the whole body to the rout. Mariccus was taken prisoner, and soon after given to the wild beasts. The populace, astonished to see that he was not immediately torn to pieces, believed him to be sacred and inviolable. Vitellius ordered him to be executed under his own eye; and that catastrophe cured the people of their bigotry.

LXII. From this time the partisans of Otho were no longer persecuted. Their persons and their effects remained inviolable. The last wills of such as fell in that unfortunate cause were allowed to be valid, and, where no will was made, the law in cases of intestacy took its course. In fact, it was the luxury of Vitellius that oppressed mankind: from his avarice there was nothing to fear. His gluttony knew no bounds. To administer to his appetite, Rome and Italy were ransacked for rarities. The roads from both the seas rung with a din of carriages, loaded with whatever was exquisite to the palate. To entertain him on his march, the principal men of every city were obliged to lavish all their wealth, and the country was exhausted. The soldiers, degenerating into a band of epicures, lost all regard for military duty. They despised their prince, yet followed his example. Vitellius, by an edict sent forward to Rome, signified his pleasure to postpone for the present the title of Augustus; and for that of Cæsar, he declined it altogether. The prerogative of the prince was sufficient for his ambition. He ordered the mathematicians to be banished out of Italy, and, under heavy penalties, restrained the Roman knights from disgracing themselves by fighting for prizes like common gladiators, and by exhibiting their persons on the public stage. That infamous practice was introduced by former princes, who did not scruple to allure men to the theatre by donations of money, and, when bribery failed, to drive them to it by force and violence. The contagion reached the municipal towns and colonies, where it became the general practice to lie in wait for the young and profligate, in order, by the temptation of money, to invite them to disgrace and infamy.

LXIII. The character of Vitellius, soon after the arrival of his brother and other courtiers from Rome, came forth in the blackest colours. That pernicious crew began to teach their maxims of despotism, and the prince displayed his cruelty and his arrogance. He gave orders for the execution of Dolabella, who, as already stated, on the first breaking out of the war, was banished by Otho to the colony of Aquinum. Being there informed of that emperor's death, he ventured to return to Rome. That step was objected to him as a crime by his intimate friend, Plancius Varus, a man of prætorian rank. He preferred his accusation, in form, before Flavius Sabinus, the prefect of the city. The specific charges were, that Dolabella broke from his place of confinement, to offer himself as a leader to the vanquished party, and with that view, had endeavoured to seduce to his interest the cohort stationed at Ostia. In the course of the trial, Dolabella heard the whole of the evidence with undaunted firmness, never showing the smallest symptom of anxiety: but sentence of condemnation was pronounced, and he then found it too late to sue for mercy. The business, however, seemed to Flavius Sabinus of such importance, that he began to hesitate, till Triaria, the wife of Lucius Vitellius, a woman fierce and cruel beyond her sex, advised him not to seek the fame of clemency by sacrificing the interest of the prince. Sabinus did not want humanity; but, when danger threatened himself, his resolution failed. With a sudden change of mind he began to temporise, and in order to secure his own personal safety, lent his aid to precipitate the fall of a man whom he did not dare to protect.

LXIV. By this business Vitellius was alarmed for himself, and he had motives of inveterate hatred. Petronia, his former wife, was no sooner divorced, than Dolabella married her. Hence that unhappy man was an object of the emperor's fixed resentment. By letters despatched to Rome, he invited him to his presence, advising him, at the same time, to shun the Flaminian road, and come more privately by the way of Interamnium. At that place, he ordered him to be put to death. The assassin thought he should lose too much time. Impatient to do his work, he attacked Dolabella at an inn on the road, and, having stretched him on the ground, cut his throat. Such was the beginning of the new reign, a prelude to scenes of blood that were still to follow. The furious spirit of Triaria, who took so active a part in this affair, was the more detested, as it stood in contrast to the mild character of Galeria, the emperor's wife, and also to that of Sextilia, his mother; a woman of virtue and benevolence, formed on the model of ancient manners. On receipt of the first letters from the emperor, wherein he assumed the title of Germanicus, she is said to have declared, that she had no son of that name, but was the mother of Vitellius. She persevered with the same equal temper, never elated by the splendour of her family, nor deceived by the voice of flattery. In the prosperity of her sons she took no part; in their distress, she grieved for their misfortunes.

LXV. Vitellius set out from Lyons, but had not proceeded far, when he was met by Marcus Cluvius Rufus, who came from his government in Spain to congratulate the emperor on his accession. That officer appeared with joy in his countenance, and anxiety in his heart. He knew that an accusation had been prepared against him by Hilarius, one of the emperor's freedmen, importing that, during the war between Otho and Vitellius, Rufus intended to set up for himself, and convert both the Spains into an independent state; and that, with this view, he had issued various edicts, without inserting the name of any prince whatever, and also made public harangues, to blacken the character of Vitellius, and recommend himself to popular favour. The interest of Rufus was too powerful. He triumphed over his adversary, and the freedman was condemned to punishment. Rufus, from that time, ranked among the emperor's intimate friends. He continued in favour at court, and, at the same time, retained his government of Spain; during his absence carrying on the administration of the province by his deputies, according to the precedent left by Lucius Arruntius, whom Tiberius, from suspicion and the jealousy of his nature, never suffered to depart from Rome. Trebellius Maximus had not the good fortune to meet with equal favour. He had been the governor of Britain, but by a mutiny among the soldiers was obliged to escape out of the island. Vettius Bolanus, then a follower of the court, succeeded to the command.

LXVI. Vitellius heard, with deep anxiety, that the vanquished legions still retained a fierce and unconquered spirit. Dispersed through Italy, and in every quarter intermixed with the victorious troops, they talked in a style of disaffection, breathing vengeance and new commotions. The fourteenth legion took the lead, denying, with ferocity, that they were ever conquered. It was true, they said, that at Bedriacum a vexillary detachment from their body was defeated, but the legion had no share in the action. To remove such turbulent spirits, it was judged proper to order them back into Britain, where they had been stationed till recalled by Nero. The Batavian cohorts were ordered to march at the same time; and, as an old animosity subsisted between them and the soldiers of the fourteenth legion, orders were given that they should all be quietly quartered together. Between men inflamed with mutual hatred a quarrel soon broke out. It happened, at the capital of the Turinians, that a Batavian soldier had words with a tradesman, whom he charged with fraud and imposition. A man belonging to the legion took the part of his landlord. A dispute ensued; their comrades joined them; from abusive language they proceeded to blows; and, if two prætorian cohorts had not overawed the Batavians, a bloody conflict must have been the consequence. Vitellius, satisfied with the fidelity of the Batavians, incorporated them with his army. The legion had orders to proceed over the Graian Alps, and by no means to approach the city of Vienne, where the inhabitants were suspected of disaffection. The legion marched in the night, and left their fires burning. The consequence was a conflagration, by which a great part of the Turinian city was destroyed. The loss sustained by the inhabitants, like many other calamities of war, was soon obliterated by the ruin of other cities. The soldiers had scarce descended from the Alps, when they ordered the standard-bearers to march towards the colony of Vienne. The attempt, however, was prevented by the good sense of such as were observers of discipline, and the whole legion passed over into Britain.

LXVII. The prætorian cohorts gave no less disquietude to

Vitellius. To break their force, he separated them first into small parties, and soon after discharged them from the service; professing, however, in order to soften resentment, that they were, by their length of service, entitled to an honourable dismission. They delivered up their arms to the tribunes; but, being informed that Vespasian was in motion, they assembled again, and proved the best support of the Flavian cause. The first legion of marines was ordered into Spain, that in repose and indolence their spirit might evaporate. The seventh and eleventh returned to their old winter quarters. For the thirteenth employment was found in the building of two amphitheatres; one at Cremona, and the other at Bononia. In the former Cæcina was preparing to exhibit a spectacle of gladiators, and Valens in the latter; both wishing to gratify the taste of their master, whom, in the midst of arduous affairs, nothing could wean from his habitual pleasures.

LXVIII. By these measures the vanquished party was sufficiently weakened; but the spirit of the conquerors could not long endure a state of tranquillity. A quarrel broke out, in its origin slight and ridiculous, but attended with consequences that kindled the flame of war with redoubled fury The occasion was as follows:—Vitellius gave a banquet at Ticinum, and Verginius was of the party. The manners of the chiefs are ever sure to set the fashion for the tribunes and centurions. From the example of the officers, vice or virtue descends to the soldiers. In the army of Vitellius, all was disorder and confusion; a scene of drunken jollity, resembling a bacchanalian rout, rather than a camp, or a disciplined army. It happened that two soldiers, one belonging to the fifth legion, the other a native of Gaul, serving among the auxiliaries of that nation, challenged each other to a trial of skill in wrestling. The Roman was thrown; his antagonist exulted with an air of triumph; and the spectators, who had gathered round them, were soon divided into parties.

The legions, provoked by the insolence of the Gaul, attacked the auxiliaries sword in hand. Two cohorts were cut to pieces. The sudden danger of another tumult put an end to the fray. A cloud of dust was seen at a distance, and, at intervals, the glittering of arms. A report was instantly spread, that the fourteenth legion was returning to offer battle; but the mistake was soon discovered. It was found, that the men who brought up the rear of the army were approaching. That circumstance being known, the tumult subsided, till one of the slaves of

Verginius was observed by the soldiers. They seized the man, and, in their fury, charged him with a design to assassinate Vitellius. With this notion in their heads, they rushed directly to the banqueting-room, and with rage and clamour demanded the immediate execution of Verginius. The emperor, though by nature addicted to suspicion, entertained no doubt of Verginius. He interposed to save his life, and with difficulty restrained the men, who thirsted for the blood of a consular commander, at one time their own general. It had ever been the fate of Verginius, more than of any other officer, to encounter the seditious spirit of the army. His character, notwithstanding, was held in great esteem; his brilliant talents extorted admiration even from his enemies; but the moderation with which he rejected the imperial dignity, was considered as an affront. The soldiers thought themselves despised, and from that moment resented the injury.

LXIX. On the following day, the deputies from the senate, who according to order attended at Ticinum, were admitted to an audience. That business over, Vitellius visited the camp, and, in a public harangue, expressed a lively sense of the zeal which the soldiers had exerted in his service. This proceeding roused the jealousy of the auxiliaries. They saw the insolence of the legionary soldiers, and the impunity with which they committed the most outrageous actions. It was to prevent the consequences of this dangerous jealousy, that the Batavian cohorts had been ordered back to Germany, the Fates even then preparing the seeds of a foreign[1] and a civil war. The allies from Gaul were also dismissed to their respective states; a vast unwieldy multitude, drawn together in the beginning of the revolt, not for actual service, but chiefly for vain parade, and to swell the pomp of a numerous army. The imperial revenues being well-nigh exhausted, there was reason to apprehend a want of funds to answer the largesses of the prince. To prevent that distress, Vitellius ordered the complement of the legions and auxiliaries to be reduced, and no new levies to be made. Dismissions from the service were granted indiscriminately to all who applied. The policy was of the worst consequence to the commonwealth, and, at the same time, a grievance to the soldiers, who felt themselves oppressed by returns of military duty, too frequent for the scanty numbers that remained. Their fatigue increased, while their manners were debauched, and

[1] The foreign war was with the Batavians, under Civilis; the domestic, with Vespasian.

their vigour wasted, by the vices of a luxurious life, so different from the institutions of the old republic, when money was despised, and virtue was the energy of the state.

LXX. Vitellius proceeded to Cremona. Having there attended a spectacle of gladiators exhibited by Cæcina, he was led by curiosity to the field of Bedriacum, in order to see on the spot the vestiges of his recent victory. The fields around presented a mournful spectacle. Forty days[1] had elapsed, and the plain was still covered with bodies, gashed and mangled; with broken limbs, and men and horses in one promiscuous carnage; clotted gore, and filth, and putrefaction; the trees cut down, and the fruits of the earth trampled under foot; the whole a dreary waste, the desolation of nature. The view of the high road was no less shocking to humanity. The people of Cremona, amidst the horrors that covered the face of the country, had strewed the way with roses and laurels, and had even raised altars, where victims were slain, as if a nation of slaves had been employed to adorn the triumph of a despotic prince. But these servile acts, with which an abject people rejoiced over human misery, in a short time after brought on their own destruction. Valens and Cæcina attended the emperor to the field. They pointed to the particular spots, where the stress of the battle lay: "Here the legions rushed on to the attack; there the cavalry bore down all before them; from that quarter the auxiliaries wheeled about, and surrounded the enemy." The tribunes and prefects of cohorts talked of their own exploits: and the truth, if they mingled any, was warped and disfigured by exaggeration. The common soldiers quitted the road, to mark the places where they had fought, and to survey the arms and dead bodies of the vanquished piled up in heaps. They viewed the scene with brutal joy, and wondered at the destruction they had made. Some, with generous sympathy, felt the lot of humanity, and tears gushed from every eye. Vitellius showed no symptom of compassion. He saw, without emotion, the bodies of Roman citizens unburied on the naked ground, and, with fell delight, offered a sacrifice to the deities of the place, little then suspecting the reverse of fortune which was soon to overtake himself.

LXXI. At Bononia, Fabius Valens exhibited a show of gladiators, with a pompous display of decorations, which he had ordered to be brought from Rome. In proportion as the

[1] This was the 24th of May.

emperor advanced towards the capital, riot and licentiousness grew still more outrageous. Players of interludes and a band of eunuchs mixed with the soldiers, and revived all the vices of Nero's court. Vitellius admired the manners of that shameful period; and wherever Nero went to display his voice and minstrelsy, he was sure to be one of his followers, not by compulsion, as was the case with men of integrity, but of his own motion, a willing sycophant, allured by his palate, and bribed by gluttony. In order to open the way for Valens and Cæcina to the honours of the consulship, the time of those in office[1] was abridged. Martius Macer, who had been a general in Otho's party, was passed over in silence; and Valerius Marinus, who had been put in nomination by Galba, was also set aside, not for any charge alleged against him, but because, being a man of a passive temper, he was willing to acquiesce under every injury without a murmur. Pedanius Costa shared the same fate. He had taken an active part against Nero, and even endeavoured to excite the ambition of Verginius. He was, in fact, rejected for that offence, though other reasons were pretended. For this proceeding, Vitellius received public thanks: to acts of oppression, the servility of the times gave the name of wisdom.

LXXII. About this time a daring fraud was attempted, at first with rapid success, but in a short time totally defeated. A man of low condition thought he might emerge from obscurity, by taking upon him the name of Scribonianus Camerinus. His story was that, during the reign of Nero, to elude the fury of the times, he had lain concealed in Istria, where the followers of the ancient Crassi still occupied the lands of their former masters, and retained the veneration for that illustrious house. To carry on this ridiculous farce, the impostor engaged the vile and profligate in his interest. The vulgar, with their usual credulity, and the soldiers, either led into an error, or excited by their love of innovation, joined in the plot. Their leader was seized, and brought into the presence of Vitellius. Being interrogated who and what he was, he was found to be a fugitive slave, of the name of Geta, recognised, as soon as seen, by his master. He was condemned to suffer the death of a slave,[2] in the manner inflicted by the law.

LXXIII. Advice was at length received from Syria and

[1] Valens and Cæcina entered on their joint consulship on the kalends of November.

[2] The slaves were condemned to suffer death on a cross.

Judæa, that the east submitted to the new emperor. The pride with which Vitellius was bloated on this occasion, is scarcely credible. Intelligence from that part of the world had been hitherto vague and uncertain; but Vespasian was in the mouths of men, and the rumour of the day filled the world with reports, that sometimes roused Vitellius from his lethargy. He started at the name of Vespasian. At length the cloud was blown over, and a rival was no longer dreaded. The emperor and his army plunged into every excess of cruelty, lust, and rapine, as if a foreign tyranny and foreign manners had overturned the empire.

LXXIV. Meanwhile Vespasian took a view of his own situation, and weighed with care all possible events. He considered the importance of the war, and made an estimate of his strength, the resource in his power, and the forces at a distance, as well as those that lay near at hand. The legions were devoted to his interest, insomuch that, when he showed himself the first to swear fidelity to Vitellius, and offer up vows for the prosperity of his reign, the soldiers marked their displeasure by a sullen silence. Mucianus was the friend of Titus, and by no means averse from the father. The prefect of Egypt, whose name was Alexander, was ready to promote the enterprise. The third legion, which had been removed from Syria to Mæsia, Vespasian considered as his own, and had, besides, good reason to hope, that the forces in Illyricum would enter into the confederacy. In fact, the armies, wherever stationed, were every day more and more incensed against the soldiers that came amongst them from the Vitellian party; a set of men, rough and horrid in their appearance, savage in their manners, and in their brutal discourse affecting to treat the legions of the east with contempt and derision. But, in an enterprise of such importance, it was natural to doubt and hesitate. Vespasian remained for some time in a state of suspense, now elate with hope, and soon depressed with fear. "What an awful day must that be, when he should unsheathe the sword, and commit himself, at the age of sixty, with his two sons[1] in the prime season of life, to the danger of a civil war! In undertakings of a private nature, men may advance or retreat, as they see occasion; but when the contest is for sovereign power, there is no middle course. You must conquer, or perish in the attempt."

LXXV. An officer of his experience was no stranger to the

[1] Titus and Domitian.

strength and valour of the German armies. "The legions under his command had not been tried in a war against their fellow-citizens, while, on the other hand, the Vitellians added to their experience all the pride of victory. The vanquished would, undoubtedly, be dissatisfied; but to murmur discontent was all that fortune left in their power. In the rage of civil war the common soldier renounces every honest principle; treachery becomes habitual; and every man who sets no value on his own life, holds the chief in his power. Cohorts of foot, and squadrons of horse, make a vain parade, if one intrepid villain, for the reward promised by the adverse party, may strike a sudden blow, and by a murder terminate the war. Such was the fate of Scribonianus in the reign of Claudius: he was murdered by Volaginius, a common soldier, and the highest posts in the service were the wages of that desperate assassin. An army may be drawn up in order of battle, and to animate them to deeds of valour is not a difficult task: but the private ruffian is not easily avoided."

LXXVI. Such were the reflections that presented themselves to the mind of Vespasian. His friends and the principal officers endeavoured to fix his resolution. Mucianus lent his aid, and, not content with private conferences, took a public opportunity to declare his sentiments, in effect as follows: "In all great and arduous undertakings, the questions of importance are, Is the enterprise for the good of the commonwealth? Will it do honour to the man who conducted it? And are the difficulties such as wisdom and valour may surmount? Nor is this all: the character of the man who advises the measure should be duly weighed: is he willing to second the counsel which he gives, at the hazard of his life? What are his views? And who is to reap the reward of victory? It is Mucianus who now calls upon Vespasian; Mucianus invites you to imperial dignity; for the good of the commonwealth he invites you; for your own glory he exhorts you to undertake the enterprise. The gods are with you, and under them the rest depends upon yourself. The advice which I give is honest: there is no flattery in it. For let me ask, can it be flattery to prefer you to Vitellius? To be elected after such an emperor is rather a disgrace. With whom are we to contend? Not with the active mind of Augustus, nor with the craft of the politic Tiberius. Nor is it against Caligula, Claudius, or Nero, that we propose to rise in arms. They had a kind of hereditary right: their families were in possession of the sovereignty.

"Even Galba could boast of an illustrious line of ancestors, and for that reason you were willing to acknowledge his title. But in the present juncture, to remain inactive, and leave the commonwealth a prey to vice and infamy, were a desertion of the public, which nothing can excuse. Do you imagine that in a state of servitude you can find your own personal safety? Even in that case, submission would be attended with disgrace and infamy. But ambition is not now imputed to you for the first time: you have been long suspected, and nothing remains but vigorous enterprise. The sovereign power is your only refuge. Have we forgot the fate of Corbulo?[1] It may be said that the nobility of his birth (superior, it must be confessed, to you as well as myself) exposed him to danger. It may be so; but let it be remembered, that Nero towered above Vitellius: and remember besides, that, in the eyes of the person who lives in fear, the man who makes himself dreaded is illustrious. Do we doubt whether the armies can create an emperor? Vitellius furnishes the proof; a man without military fame, who never served a campaign, but owes his elevation, not to his own merit, but to Galba's want of popularity. His victory was not obtained by the ability of his generals, or the valour of his troops: Otho was conquered by his own hand: that precipitate action made Vitellius master of the Roman world, and, in return, the infamy of Vitellius gives a lustre to the name of Otho, insomuch that men regret that unfortunate prince.

"At present what is the conduct of our new emperor? He disbands the legions; he disarms the cohorts, and every day furnishes arms against himself. The ferocity of his soldiers, whatever it may have been, has long since evaporated in victualling-houses and drunken revelry. After the example of their master, the soldiers are dissolved in sloth and luxury. On the other hand, you have in Syria, Judæa, and Egypt, no less than nine legions, all high in spirit, unimpaired by war, and not yet taught by sedition to renounce all regard for discipline. You have an army inured to the operations of war, and crowned with victory over the enemies of their country. You have a body of cavalry, auxiliary cohorts, a naval armament, and powerful kings, all devoted to your cause. Above all, you have your own talents and your renown in arms.

[1] Corbulo was put to death by Nero.

LXXVII. "To myself I arrogate nothing: yet let me not be thought inferior to Valens or Cæcina. If Mucianus does not aspire to be your rival, you will not therefore think meanly of him. Willing to yield to Vespasian, I claim precedence of Vitellius. Your house has been distinguished by triumphal honours; you have two sons, and one of them[1] is already equal to the weight of empire. The German armies saw him give an earnest of his future character. Were I this very moment possessed of the sovereign power, I should call Titus my son by adoption; with propriety, therefore, I yield to his father. The enterprise, to which I exhort you, will not, in its consequences, be the same to us both. If we succeed, the honours which I may receive must flow from you: in toil and danger I am willing to be your rival; or, if you will (and it is the best expedient), remain here to issue your orders, and leave me to conduct the war.

"The troops that lately conquered are by no means formidable. In the vanquished party there is more order and better discipline. The latter, stung with shame and indignation, are burning for revenge. All motives conspire to inflame their ardour. The Vitellians, on the contrary, intoxicated with success, and elate with pride, disdain all rules of subordination. They are undone by luxury. Their wounds, as yet scarcely closed, will open in a new war and bleed afresh. My dependence, it is true, must be upon your vigilance, your economy, your wisdom; but I expect no less advantage from the ignorance, the stupidity, and cruel disposition of Vitellius. In a word, war must be our choice: to us it is safer than peace, for we have already deliberated; and he who deliberates, has rebelled."

LXXVIII. By this animating speech, all who assisted at the council were inspired with new confidence. They pressed round Vespasian, exhorting him to undertake the enterprise; they recalled to his memory the responses of oracles, and the predictions of men skilled in judicial astrology. Nor was Vespasian untinctured with that superstition. Even afterwards, when possessed of the supreme authority, he retained a mathematician named Seleucus, to assist his councils with his insight into future events. A number of prognostics, that occurred to him in his youth, came fresh in his mind. He recollected a cypress-tree of prodigious

[1] Titus had served in the rank of military tribune in Britain as well as Germany, and gave early proofs of the modest merit that distinguished his character.

size, on his own estate, that fell suddenly to the ground, and, on the following day, rose on the same spot, and flourished in new strength and verdure. This was considered by the interpreters of prodigies as an early prelude to future grandeur. At length, having obtained triumphal honours, together with the consular rank, when he had conducted the war against the Jews with such rapid success, the prediction seemed to be verified; and, thus encouraged, he looked from that eminence to higher elevation, and even to the imperial dignity. Between Syria and Judæa stands a mountain, known by the name of MOUNT CARMEL, on the top of which a god is worshipped, under no other title than that of the place, and, according to ancient usage, without a temple, or even a statue. An altar is erected in the open air, and there adoration is paid to the presiding deity. On this spot Vespasian offered a sacrifice. In the midst of the ceremony, while his mind expanded with vast ideas, Basilides, the officiating priest, examined the entrails of the victims, and, in his prophetic manner addressing himself to Vespasian, "Whatever," he said, "are your designs, whether to build a mansion, to enlarge your estate, or increase the number of your slaves, the Fates prepare for you a vast and magnificent seat, with an immense territory, and a prodigious multitude of men." This prediction, though involved in mysterious language, was spread abroad at the time, and now received a favourable interpretation. The story gathered strength among the populace, and in conversation with Vespasian was the favourite topic of his friends, who thought they could not enlarge too much on the subject, while the passions of the hearer stood ready to receive their advice.

LXXIX. Mucianus and Vespasian settled their plan, and took leave of each other: the former went to Antioch, the capital of Syria, and the latter to Cæsarea, the metropolis of Judæa. The first public step towards creating Vespasian emperor of Rome, was taken at Alexandria in Egypt: Tiberius Alexander, the prefect of the province, eager to show his zeal, administered the oath to the legions under his command. The ceremony was performed on the calends of July, and that day was ever after celebrated as the first of Vespasian's reign, though the army in Judæa swore fidelity on the fifth before the nones of the same month, in the presence of Vespasian himself. Titus was then on his way from Syria with despatches from Mucianus, but the impatience of the men could not brook the delay of waiting for the emperor's son. The whole transaction originated with the soldiers, and was hurried on with such violent impetuosity, that the business was finished without any public harangue, and even without a previous assembly of the legions.

LXXX. For this great revolution no arrangement was made; no time, no place was fixed; nor was it known who was to be the author of the measure. In this state of uncertainty, while every bosom panted with hope and fear, and the motives of the revolt, with all the dangers that might ensue, kept the army in agitation, a small number of soldiers, who mounted guard near the apartment of the general, no sooner saw him coming forth from his chamber, than with one voice they saluted him by the title of Emperor. The whole body followed their example. They pressed forward in crowds, calling him by the name of Cæsar, styling him Augustus, and conferring every other title of imperial grandeur. Vespasian balanced no longer. His fears subsided, and he now resolved to pursue the road of ambition. Even in this tide of his affairs he still preserved the equal tenour of his mind, free from arrogance, and such in his manners as he had always been. The new man never appeared. The change, as was natural, dazzled his imagination; but he took time to allay the hurry of his spirits, and then calmly addressed the men in the language of a soldier. He was heard with shouts of applause. Mucianus waited for this event. On the first intelligence, he declared for Vespasian, and the soldiers with alacrity took the oath of fidelity to the new emperor. That business over, Mucianus went to the theatre of Antioch, where the inhabitants were used to hold their public debates. He found a crowded meeting, and was received with acclamations.

He harangued the multitude, and his speech, though in Greek, was eloquent. In that language he had acquired sufficient facility, and he possessed, besides, the happy art of giving grace and dignity to whatever he uttered. He inflamed the passions not only of the army, but also of the province, by asserting roundly, "that it was a fixed point with Vitellius, to quarter the German troops in the delightful region of Syria, that, in a rich and plentiful province, they might grow wanton in ease and luxury; while, in exchange, the legions of Syria were to be removed to cold encampments in Germany, there to endure the inclemency of the weather, and the rigours of the service." The natives of the province have lived in habits of friendship with the legions, and, by intermarriages, had formed family connections. The soldiers, on their part, were naturalised in the country, and the stations to which they were accustomed, were, by long residence, grown as dear to them as their native home.

LXXXI. Before the ides of July, the whole province of Syria acceded to Vespasian. His party was further strengthened by Sohemus, who joined the league with the whole weight of his kingdom, and also by Antiochus, who inherited immense treasures from his ancestors, and was, of all the kings who submitted to the authority of Rome, the most rich and powerful. Agrippa, who was then at Rome, received private expresses from the east, requesting his presence in his own country. He departed, before Vitellius had any intelligence, and by a quick navigation passed over into Asia. Queen Berenice, at that time flourishing in the bloom of youth, and no less distinguished by the graces of her person, espoused the interest of Vespasian, to whom, notwithstanding his advanced age, she had made herself agreeable by magnificent presents. The several maritime provinces, with Asia and Achaia, and the whole inland country between Pontus and the two Armenias, entered into the general confederacy; but from the governors of those provinces no forces could be expected, as they were not, at that time, strengthened by the legions stationed in Cappadocia. To settle the plan of operation, a grand council was held at Berytus. Mucianus attended. He was accompanied by a train of officers, tribunes, and centurions, and a considerable body of soldiers, selected to swell the pomp and grandeur of the scene. From Judæa the most distinguished officers went to the meeting, with the flower of their troops. An assembly, consisting of such a numerous train of horse and foot, and of eastern kings, who vied with each other in splendour and magnificence, presented a spectacle worthy of the imperial dignity.

LXXXII. The first and most important object was to raise recruits, and recall the veterans to the service. In all the strong and fortified cities, workmen were appointed for the forging of arms, and a mint for gold and silver coin was established at Antioch. The whole was carried on with diligence, under the direction of proper inspectors. Vespasian visited every quarter, by his presence giving spirit and animation to the cause. He encouraged the industrious by the warmth of his commendations; he roused the inactive by his example, and succeeded more by gentle methods than by the rigour of authority. To the failings of his friends he was often blind, but never to their virtues. He advanced some to the administration of provinces, and others to the rank of senators; all men of distinguished character, who rose afterwards to eminence in the state. There were others who owed their success more to their good fortune, than to their merit. Mucianus in his first harangue made incidental mention of a donative, but in guarded terms; nor did Vespasian, though engaged in a civil war, grant at any time a larger bounty than had been usual in times of profound peace. He chose that his soldiers should act on principles of honour, not from motives of bribery and corruption. To that firmness he owed the good order and regular discipline of his army. Ambassadors were sent to the courts of Parthia and Armenia in order to settle a mutual good understanding, that, when the legions marched forward to open the campaign, the back settlements should not be exposed to sudden incursions of the enemy. Titus was to remain in Judæa to complete the conquest of that country, while Vespasian made himself master of the passes into Egypt. To make head against Vitellius, part of the army was deemed sufficient, under the conduct of such a general as Mucianus, with the additional terror of Vespasian's name, and the Fates on his side superior to every difficulty. Letters were despatched to the several armies, and the officers in command, with instructions to conciliate the prætorian soldiers, who had been disbanded by Vitellius, and, by a promise that all should be restored to their rank, to invite them once more into the service.

LXXXIII. Mucianus, with the appearance rather of an associate in the sovereign power, than of a general officer, advanced at the head of a light-armed detachment, never lingering in the course of his progress, that delay might not be thought a symptom of irresolution; and, on the other hand, not proceeding by rapid marches, that fame might fly before him, and spread the terror of his approach. He knew the weakness of his numbers, and that danger at a distance is always magnified. He was followed by the sixth legion, and thirteen thousand veterans, forming together a considerable army. The fleet at Pontus had orders to assemble at Byzantium. That station was thought convenient, as Mucianus had not yet determined, whether he should not avoid the territory of Mæsia, and proceed in force to Dyrrhachium; while his naval armament commanded the seas of Italy, and, by consequence, protected the coasts of Achaia and Asia against the attempts of Vitellius, who, in that case, would not only see Brundisium and Tarentum in danger, but also the whole coast of Calabria and Lucania kept in a constant alarm.

LXXXIV. Throughout the provinces nothing was heard but the din and bustle of warlike preparations. Soldiers were assembling, ships were preparing for sea, and the clink of armourers resounded in every quarter. How to raise supplies of money was the chief difficulty. Pecuniary funds, Mucianus used to say, were the sinews of war. For this purpose, in all questions touching the sum demanded, he regarded neither the truth nor the justice of the case. To be rich was to be liable to taxation, and money was to be raised in all events. Informations followed without number, and confiscations without mercy. Oppressive as these proceedings were, the necessity of the times gave a colourable excuse; but the misfortune was, the practice did not cease with the war, but continued, in the season of profound peace, to harass and oppress mankind. Vespasian, in the beginning of his reign, showed no disposition to enrich his coffers by acts of injustice; but, being corrupted afterwards by the smiles of fortune, and listening to pernicious counsels, he learned the arts of rapacity, and dared to practise them.[1] Mucianus, from his own funds, contributed to the exigencies of the war, generous from his private purse, that he might afterwards indemnify himself at the expense of the public. The rest of the officers, following his example, advanced sums of money, but were not, in like manner, repaid with usury.

LXXXV. Vespasian, in the meantime, saw his affairs assume a promising aspect. The army in Illyricum went over to his interest. In Mæsia the third legion revolted, and drew after them the eighth, and also the seventh, called the Claudian; both devoted to Otho, though not engaged in the action at Bedriacum. Before the battle, they had advanced as far as Aquileia; and being at that place informed of a total overthrow, they assaulted the messengers who brought the news; broke to shivers the standards that displayed the name of Vitellius; plundered the military chests; and, having divided the spoil, proceeded to every act of outrage and sedition. Conscious of that offence, and dreading the punishment that might follow, they consulted together, and clearly saw, that what they had done required a pardon from Vitellius, but with

[1] Vespasian, in the height of his power, did not scruple to raise large sums of money by severe exactions; but the apology for his avarice was the liberal spirit with which he adorned Rome and Italy with grand and useful works.

Vespasian stood in the light of real merit. To strengthen their cause, they sent despatches to the army in Pannonia, inviting them to join the league; determined, if they did not comply, to compel them by force of arms. In this juncture, Apronius Saturninus, governor of Mæsia, conceived the design of perpetrating a barbarous murder. Under colour of public zeal, but with malice festering at his heart, he despatched a centurion to murder Tertius Julianus, who commanded the seventh legion. That officer had timely notice. He provided himself with guides, who knew the course of the country, and escaped through devious tracts as far as Mount Hæmus. From that time, he took no part in the civil war. He affected often to be on the point of setting out to join Vespasian; but delayed his journey, at times seeming eager to depart, then doubting, hesitating, waiting for intelligence, and, during the whole war, resolving without decision.

LXXXVI. In Pannonia, the thirteenth legion, and the seventh, called the Galbian, embraced the interest of Vespasian. They still remembered, with indignation, their defeat at Bedriacum, and the influence of Antonius Primus proved a powerful instigation. That officer, convicted of forgery in the reign of Nero, remained obnoxious to the laws, till, among the evils that spring from civil dissension, he rose from infamy to his senatorian rank. He was advanced by Galba to the command of the seventh legion, and, according to report, offered himself to Otho, desiring, by letters, the rank of general against his benefactor. Otho paid no attention to the proposal, and, by consequence, Antonius remained inactive. In the present juncture, seeing a storm ready to burst upon Vitellius, he veered round to Vespasian, and became the grand support of the party. To his vices he united great and useful qualities: brave and valiant, he possessed uncommon eloquence; an artful and insidious enemy, he had the art of involving others in danger; in popular insurrections, a bold and turbulent leader; at once a plunderer and a prodigal, what he gained by rapine he squandered in corruption; during the calm season of peace, a pernicious citizen; in war, an officer not to be neglected.

The armies of Mæsia and Pannonia formed a junction, and drew the forces of Dalmatia into the revolt. The consular governors of those provinces were neutral on the occasion; they took no share in the business, nor did the soldiers wait for their direction. Titus Ampius Flavianus ruled in Pannonia, and Poppæus Silvanus in Dalmatia; both rich, and advanced in years. Cornelius Fuscus, descended from illustrious ancestors, and then in the vigour of life, was, at the same time, imperial procurator. In his youth he had resigned his senatorian rank, to seek in solitude a retreat from public business. Joining afterwards with Galba, he drew forth, in support of that emperor, the strength of his own colony, and for his services obtained the post of procurator. In the present commotions, he declared for Vespasian; and, by his ardent spirit, gave life and vigour to the cause. Self-interest did not mix with the motives that determined his conduct. His pride was in the field of action. He gloried in facing danger, and despised the reward of merit. War was his passion; and, though possessed of an ample fortune, he preferred a life of enterprise to indolence and his own personal safety. He acted in concert with Antonius Primus, and both exerted themselves to kindle the flame of war in every quarter. Where they saw a discontented spirit, they were sure to increase it by infusions of their own venom. They sent despatches to the fourteenth legion in Britain, and to the first in Spain, knowing that both had favoured the cause of Otho against Vitellius. Their letters were spread all over Gaul, and, by their joint efforts, the Roman world was roused to arms. The forces in Illyricum declared for Vespasian; and in other parts, as soon as the first blow was struck, the troops stood ready to take the field.

LXXXVII. While Vespasian and the leaders of his party were thus employed in concerting measures throughout the provinces, Vitellius, sunk in sloth, and growing every day more contemptible, advanced by slow marches towards the city of Rome. In all the villas and municipal towns through which he passed, carousing festivals were sufficient to retard a man abandoned to his pleasures. He was followed by an unwieldy multitude, not less than sixty thousand men in arms, all corrupted by a life of debauchery. The number of retainers and followers of the army was still greater, all disposed to riot and insolence, even beyond the natural bent of the vilest slaves. To these must be added a train of officers and servile courtiers, too haughty to be restrained within due bounds, even though the chief had practised the strictest discipline. The crowd was still increased by a conflux of senators and Roman knights who came from Rome to greet the prince on his way; some impelled by fear, others to pay their court, and numbers, not to be thought sullen or disaffected. All went with the current. The populace rushed forth in crowds, accompanied by an infamous band of pimps, of players, buffoons, and charioteers, by their utility in vicious pleasures all well-known and dear to Vitellius. Such were the disgraceful connections of the emperor, and he enjoyed them without a blush. To supply so vast a body with provisions, the colonies and municipal cities were exhausted; the fruits of the earth, then ripe and fit for use, were carried off; the husbandman was plundered; and his land, as if it were an enemy's country, was laid waste and ruined.

LXXXVIII. The fierce animosity that broke out at Ticinum between the legions and the auxiliaries, was not yet extinguished. Frequent quarrels occurred, and ended always in mutual slaughter. Against the peasants and farmers they were sure to be unanimous, but agreed in nothing else. The most dreadful carnage happened within seven miles of Rome. At that place Vitellius ordered victuals, ready dressed, to be distributed among the soldiers, as if he had prepared a feast to pamper a band of gladiators. The common people, who had come in crowds from Rome, were dispersed through the camp. To divert themselves with what they thought an arch and pleasant trick, they cut away the belts of the soldiers, and with an air of humour asked, whether they were properly accoutred. The soldiers had no taste for raillery. They retaliated with their weapons, and fell with fury on the defenceless multitude. Among the slain was the father of one of the soldiers, killed as he stood engaged in conversation with his son. The unhappy victim was soon known; and, by that incident, the further effusion of blood was prevented. Rome, in the meantime, was thrown into consternation. A number of soldiers entered the city in a tumultuous manner, and rushed forward to the forum, impatient to see the spot where Galba perished. Covered with the skins of savage beasts, and wielding large and massy spears, the spectacle which they exhibited to the Roman citizens was fierce and hideous. Unused to crowded streets, they had not the skill to conduct themselves amidst a vast concourse of people, but with rude force pushed against the passengers; and sometimes slipping down, or, as might happen, thrown by the pressure of the throng, they rose hastily to resent what was no more than an accident, and from abusive language proceeded sword in hand to the most violent outrage. The tribunes and centurions, at the head of their troops of cavalry, paraded the streets in a warlike manner, and spread a general panic through the city.

LXXXIX. Vitellius himself, in his military apparel, mounted on a superb horse, advanced from the Milvian bridge, while the senate and the people pressed on before him to make way for their new master. His friends, however, remonstrated against his making a public entry in a military style, like a conqueror marching into a city taken by storm. He conformed to their advice, and, having put on his senatorian robe, made his entry in a pacific manner. His troops followed in regular order. The eagles of four legions led the way, with an equal number of standards on each side. The colours of twelve squadrons of horse were displayed with great pomp. The infantry followed, and after them the cavalry. The procession was closed by four and thirty cohorts, distinguished by the arms and habits of their respective nations. The prefects of the camp, the tribunes, and principal centurions, arrayed in white, preceded their several eagles. The rest of the officers marched at the head of their companies. The blaze of arms and rich apparel added splendour to the scene. The burnished collars of the common men, and the trappings of the horses, glittered to the eye, while the whole presented a magnificent spectacle, worthy of a better emperor. In this manner Vitellius proceeded to the capitol, and there, embracing his mother, saluted her by the name of Augusta.

XC. On the following day, Vitellius delivered a public harangue, and spoke of himself in magnificent terms, as if he had for his audience the senate and people of a foreign city. He assumed the virtues of industry and temperance; never considering, that he was in the hearing of men who had seen his vices, and that every part of Italy, through which he had passed, had known and felt his abandoned profligacy. The populace, as usual, knowing neither truth nor falsehood, and indifferent about both, paid their tribute of flattery with noise and uproar. They pressed him to accept the title of Augustus; he declined it for some time, but the voice of the rabble prevailed. He yielded to their importunity; but his compliance was useless, and the honour was of short duration.

XCI. In a city where superstition interpreted everything, the first act of Vitellius, in the character of sovereign pontiff, was considered as an omen that portended mischief. He issued an edict concerning the rites and ceremonies of religion, dated the fifteenth before the calends of August, a day rendered inauspicious by two victories formerly obtained over the armies of Rome; one at Cremera, and the other at Allia.[1] But

[1] At Allia (now *Torrenti di Catino*) the Roman army was put to the sword by the Gauls, under Brennus. The slaughter was so great, that the day on which it happened (*Dies Alliensis*) was marked as unlucky in the calendar, and, according to Cicero, thought more fatal than that on which the city of Rome was taken.

Vitellius was unacquainted with the antiquities of his country. He knew nothing of laws, either human or divine. The same stupidity possessed his friends and his band of freedmen. The whole court seemed to be in a state of intoxication. In the assemblies held for the election of consuls, Vitellius assumed nothing above the rights of a citizen. He behaved to the candidates on a footing of equality. He attended in the theatre, giving his applause as a common spectator, and in the circus mixing with the factions of the populace. By those arts he tried to gain the suffrages of the electors; arts, it must be acknowledged, often practised, and, when subservient to honest purposes, not to be condemned. But in a man like Vitellius, whose former life was too well known, the artifice served only to sink him into contempt.

He went frequently to the senate, even on frivolous occasions, when the subject of debate was altogether uninteresting. In that assembly Helvidius Priscus,[1] prætor elect, happened to differ from the opinion of the emperor. Vitellius took fire in the moment, but checking himself in time, called upon the tribunes of the people to support his authority. His friends, apprehending the consequences of a deep and smothered resentment, interposed with their good offices to soften prejudice. His answer was, "Nothing new has happened: two senators have differed in opinion; and is not that a common occurrence? I have myself often opposed the sentiments of Thrasea."[2] The allusion to a character so truly eminent provoked a smile of contempt. Some, however, were glad to find, that, instead of the men who glittered in the sunshine of a court, he chose Thrasea for the model of true greatness.

XCII. Publius Sabinus, the prefect of a cohort, and Julius Priscus, a centurion, were advanced from those inferior stations to the command of the prætorian guards. The former owed his elevation to the friendship of Valens, and the latter to that of Cæcina. By those two ministers, though always at variance with each other, the whole power of the state was usurped and exercised. The authority of the emperor was merely nominal: Valens and Cæcina transacted everything. Their mutual animosity, which had been suppressed during the war, but not extinguished, broke out at Rome with redoubled violence. Their friends, with officious care, envenomed the minds of the rival statesmen, and the various factions that for ever distract

[1] Helvidius Priscus: often mentioned, *Annals*, xii., xiii., xvi.; and *Life of Agricola*, 2.
[2] Pætus Thrasea, *Annals*, xiv. 12; xvi. 21.

the city of Rome, furnished every day new materials to inflame their jealousy. They vied with each other for pre-eminence, and by intrigue, by cabal, by their train of followers and their crowded levees, endeavoured to manifest their superiority; while Vitellius wavered between both, and, as his inclinations shifted, the balance changed alternately from one to the other. Their authority exceeded all bounds, and was therefore, like all ill-gotten power, uncertain and precarious. They saw the caprice that marked the character of Vitellius, one moment inflamed with anger, and the next lavish of his favours. Neither of the ministers could be sure of fixing the affections of his master, and both despised and feared him.

Nothing, however, could satisfy their rapacity; they seized houses, gardens, and the whole wealth of the empire; while a number of illustrious men, whom Galba had recalled from banishment, were left to languish in distress and poverty. Their situation awakened no compassion in the breast of the emperor. He restored them, it is true, to their rights over their freedmen; and, by that act of justice, not only gratified the senators and other grandees of the city, but also gained the applause of the populace. But even this show of benignity was rendered useless by the low cunning that marks the genius of slavery. To evade the claims of their patrons, the freedmen concealed their wealth in obscure places, or else deposited it in the custody of the great. Some of them contrived to insinuate themselves into the imperial family, and there growing into favour, looked down with pride and insolence on their disappointed masters.

XCIII. The multitude of soldiers was so enormous, that the camp overflowed, and poured the redundant numbers into the city; a wild disorderly band, who fixed their station in the public porticos, and even in the temples. The men wandered about the streets of Rome, so utterly careless, that they forgot where they were quartered. Having no regular place of rendezvous, and performing no kind of duty, they gave themselves up to the dissolute manners of the city, and the practice of vices too foul to be named. In this course of life, their bodily strength decayed; the vigour of their minds was sunk in sloth, and their health entirely neglected. They chose for their abode the most vile and infamous places in the neighbourhood of the Vatican,[1] where they contracted diseases,

[1] The lands round the Vatican were covered with stagnated water, and the air, of course, was unwholesome. St. Peter's church stands there at present.

till an epidemic distemper began to rage amongst them. A dreadful mortality followed. The Gauls and Germans suffered most by their own imprudence. Infected with disorders, inflamed with fevers, and being naturally impatient of heat, they plunged into the Tiber, which unluckily was near at hand, and took delight in cooling their limbs; which proved a remedy as bad as the disease. The confusion introduced by another circumstance, proved the bane of the army. It was thought advisable to raise sixteen cohorts [1] for the prætorian camp, and four for the city, each to consist of a thousand men. This measure, by cabals among the soldiers, and the jealousy subsisting between the two commanding officers, was the ruin of all discipline. Valens arrogated to himself the chief direction of the business. He had relieved Cæcina and his army, and on that account claimed pre-eminence. The Vitellian party had certainly gained no advantage over the enemy, till the arrival of Valens gave life and vigour to the cause. If the slowness of his march was at first liable to censure, the victory that followed made ample atonement, and redeemed the character of the general. The soldiers from the Lower Germany were to a man devoted to his interest. It was upon this occasion, according to the general opinion, that Cæcina first began to meditate the treachery, which he afterwards carried into execution.

XCIV. The indulgence shown by Vitellius to his principal officers was exceeded by nothing but the licentiousness of the common soldiers. Each man enrolled himself in what company he thought proper, and chose his own station in the service. Some preferred the city cohorts; and without considering merit or fitness for that employment, their wish was gratified. Others, who ought to have been selected, were suffered, at their own will and pleasure, to continue in the legions or the cavalry. This was the choice of numbers, who had impaired their constitutions, and were therefore willing to remove from the sultry heats of Italy to a more temperate climate. By these arrangements, the main strength of the legions and the cavalry was drafted away. A motley body of twenty thousand men was formed out of the whole army, without choice or judgment. The consequence was, that the camp retained neither the strength nor the beauty of military system.

[1] Before the augmentation, the prætorian cohorts (that is, those that were encamped near Rome) were only nine; the city guard consisted of three, called *Cohortes Urbanæ*.

Vitellius thought fit to harangue the soldiers. In the midst of his speech, a clamour broke out, demanding the execution of Asiaticus, and of Flavius and Rufinus, who had been commanders in Gaul, and listed on the side of Vindex. Nor did Vitellius endeavour to appease the tumult. From his sluggish temper nothing like firmness or authority could be expected. He knew that the time for discharging the promised donative was drawing near; and having no funds to answer the expectation of the soldiers, he thought it his best policy to atone by mean compliances for that deficiency. In order, however, to raise supplies, a tax was imposed on all the freedmen of former emperors, to be collected in proportion to the number of their slaves. To squander with wild profusion, was the only use of money known to Vitellius. He built a set of stables for the charioteers, and kept in the circus a constant spectacle of gladiators and wild beasts; in this manner dissipating with prodigality, as if his treasury overflowed with riches.

XCV. Cæcina and Valens resolved to celebrate the birthday of their master with all demonstrations of joy. They gave a show of gladiators in every quarter of the city, with a display of pomp and magnificence beyond all example. Vitellius resolved to solemnise the obsequies of Nero. He erected altars to that emperor in the field of Mars. The sight was highly pleasing to the vile and profligate, but gave disgust to all who had any principle, or a spark of remaining virtue. Victims were slain, fires were kindled, and the torch was carried by the Augustan priests; an order dedicated by Tiberius to the Julian family, in imitation of that consecrated by Romulus to Tatius the Sabine king. From the victory at Bedriacum four months had not elapsed; and yet, in that short time, Asiaticus, the manumitted slave of the emperor, had already accumulated riches nothing short of the Polycleti, the Patrobii, and others of the servile race, whose names have been given up to the execration of mankind. The court of Vitellius was not the scene of honest emulation. No man endeavoured to rise by his virtue or his talents. The road to preferment was open to vice and luxury. He who entertained the prince in the gayest manner, and with sumptuous banquets glutted that craving appetite, was sure to be in favour. To enjoy the present hour, and seize with avidity the pleasures near at hand, was the whole occupation of Vitellius. Future events and distant consequences gave him no solicitude. He is said to have dissipated in a few months no less than nine millions of sesterces. Such was the sad condition of Rome; a great yet miserable city, obliged, in the space of one year, to groan under the yoke of an Otho and a Vitellius; and still worse, to suffer the depredations of Vinius, Valens, Icelus, and Asiaticus, till the people were at length transferred, like a herd of slaves, to Mucianus and Marcellus.[1] New men succeeded, but the measures were still the same.

XCVI. The first intelligence of a revolt that reached the ear of Vitellius, was that of the third legion in Illyricum. The account was sent by Aponius Saturninus, before that officer had formed his resolution to join Vespasian. His despatches, made up in the first tumult of surprise, did not state the whole of the mischief. The creatures of the court, to soothe their master, endeavoured to palliate every circumstance. They called it the seditious spirit of one legion only, while every other army preserved unshaken fidelity, and there was, therefore, no danger to be apprehended. Vitellius addressed the soldiers to the same effect. He added that the prætorians, lately disbanded, were the authors of false reports, fabricated with a seditious intent to disturb the public peace: but still there was no reason to fear a civil war. He made no mention of Vespasian; and, to suppress all talk among the populace, a band of soldiers had orders to parade the streets. The policy, however, did not answer the end. Silence was commanded, and the people talked with greater freedom.

XCVII. Despatches were, notwithstanding, sent to Germany, to Spain, and Britain, for a supply of men; but, as Vitellius wished to conceal the urgency of his affairs, his orders were not decisive, and, by consequence, the governors of the provinces were in no haste to obey. Hordeonius Flaccus, who commanded on the banks of the Rhine, having reason to fear the designs of the Batavians, expected to have a war upon his hands, and therefore thought it prudent not to diminish his force. In Britain, Vectius Bolanus was kept in a constant alarm by the restless genius of the natives. At the same time, those two officers began to balance between Vitellius and Vespasian. Spain showed no alacrity. That country, left without a governor of proconsular authority, was under the direction of three commanders of legions, all equal in rank, and all willing, as long as Vitellius flourished in prosperity, to hold their employments under him, but in the day of

[1] Mucianus was the active partisan of Vespasian. Eprius Marcellus, a man who raised himself by his flagitious deeds (*Annals*, xvi. 28), was the favourite minister of Vespasian.

distress ready to abandon his cause. Affairs in Africa wore a better aspect. The legion and the cohorts which had been raised in that country by Clodius Macer, and disbanded by Galba, were again embodied by order of Vitellius, and the young men of the nation went in crowds to be enrolled in the service. The fact was, Vitellius and Vespasian had been proconsuls in Africa: the former governed with moderation, and was remembered with gratitude; the latter incurred the hatred of the people. From past transactions, the province and the allies in the neighbourhood formed their idea of what they had to expect under the reign of either of them; but the event convinced them of their error.

XCVIII. The exertions in Africa were at first carried on with vigour. Valerius Festus, the governor of the province, co-operated with the zeal of the people, but in a short time began to waver between the contending parties. In his letters and public edicts he stood firm for Vitellius; his secret correspondence favoured Vespasian; and, by this duplicity, he hoped, in the end, to make terms for himself with the conqueror. In Rhætia and the adjacent parts of Gaul, certain emissaries, employed by Vespasian's friends, were seized with letters and proclamations in their possession. They were sent to Vitellius, and by his order put to death. Others, by their own address, or the protection of their friends, escaped detection. The consequence was, that the measures adopted by Vitellius were known to the opposite party, while those of Vespasian remained an impenetrable secret. The stupidity of Vitellius gave the enemy this advantage in the outset. Afterwards, when the passes over the Pannonian Alps were secured by a chain of posts, all intelligence by land was entirely cut off; and by sea, the Etesian winds, that favoured the navigation to the east, were adverse to the homeward voyage.

XCIX. Vitellius, finding that the advanced parties of the enemy had made an irruption into Italy, and news big with danger arriving from every quarter, gave orders to his generals to take the field without delay. Cæcina undertook the command, while Valens, who was just risen from a sick bed, remained at Rome for the recovery of his health. The German forces, marching out of the city, exhibited an appearance very different from the ferocity of their first approach. Their strength wasted, their vigour of mind depressed; their numbers thin; their horses slow and lifeless; their arms an incumbrance; and the men drooping under the heat of the season, overpowered by the dust, and unable to endure the weather, presented to all who beheld their march, a languid, spiritless, and dejected army; averse from labour, and, for that reason, ready to revolt.

The character of Cæcina must be taken into the account. Ambition was his ruling passion: sloth and indolence, the effect of success and luxury, were vices newly contracted; or perhaps meditating even then a stroke of perfidy, it was part of his plan to countenance whatever tended to impair the vigour of the army. The revolt of this commander has been ascribed by various writers to Flavius Sabinus, who had the address, by means of Rubrius Gallus, his intermediate agent, to seduce Cæcina to the interest of his brother, under positive assurances that the terms stipulated between them would be ratified by Vespasian. The jealousy subsisting between Cæcina and Valens had its effect on the mind of an aspiring chief, who saw his rival in the highest credit with Vitellius, and was, therefore, easily persuaded to merit the protection of a new prince.

C. Cæcina took leave of Vitellius, and received at parting the highest marks of distinction. He sent forward a detachment of the cavalry to take possession of Cremona. The veterans of the fourteenth and sixteenth legions followed, and after them the fifth and twenty-second. The rear was closed by the twenty-first, distinguished by the name of RAPAX, and the first legion called the ITALIC, with the vexillaries of three British legions, and the flower of the auxiliary forces. Cæcina was no sooner set out on his expedition, than Valens sent directions to the army, which he had conducted into Italy, to wait for his arrival, according to the plan which, he said, was settled between himself and Cæcina. But the latter, being on the spot, and by consequence, having greater weight and influence, assured the men that, upon mature deliberation, that whole plan had been altered, to the end that they might meet the first impression of the enemy with the united vigour of the army. Having thus secured in his own hands the whole command, he ordered the legions to proceed by rapid marches to Cremona, while a large detachment went forward to Hostilia. He himself turned off towards Ravenna, under a pretence of conferring with the officers of the fleet, but, in fact, with a design to make the best of his way to the city of Pavia, judging that place the fittest for a treasonable convention. He there met Lucilius Bassus, a man who, from a squadron of horse, had been raised by Vitellius to the command of two fleets, one at Ravenna, and the other at Misenum. Not content with that sudden rise, he thought himself entitled to be made prefect of the prætorian guards. That disappointment he considered as an injury, and therefore resolved to gratify his unjust resentment by a stroke of perfidy. For this purpose he joined Cæcina. Which seduced the other, cannot now be known. Two evil minds might form the same black design, and, having formed it, they would find in congenial qualities a secret impulse to each other.

CI. In the memoirs of various authors who composed their work during the reign of the Flavian family,[1] we are told that Cæcina acted on the most upright principles, with a view to the public tranquillity, and the good of his country. But this seems to be the language of flattery to the reigning prince. The conduct of Cæcina may be fairly traced to other motives. The natural inconstancy of the man, and, after his treachery to Galba, the confirmed habit of betraying without a blush, would be sufficient to remove all doubt, if we had not to add to the account his disappointed ambition, and the corrosions of envy, with which he saw himself eclipsed by the superior genius of his rival. Rather than be supplanted by others in the esteem of Vitellius, the ruin of that emperor was his remedy.

Having settled his plan of operations with Bassus, Cæcina once more put himself at the head of the legions, and by various artifices began to undermine the interest of Vitellius, and wean the centurions and soldiers from all affection for his person. Bassus, on his part, was equally active, and met with little difficulty. The officers and men belonging to the fleet remembered that they had lately distinguished themselves in the cause of Otho, and were therefore ready to declare against the enemy who had triumphed over him.

[1] That is, during the reigns of Vespasian, Titus, and Domitian, the last of the Flavian line.

BOOK III

CONTENTS

with a view to reduce Rome by famine.—XLIX. *Antonius leaves part of his army at Verona, and marches forward in quest of the Vitellians.*—LI. *A soldier demands a reward for having killed his brother in battle—Reflections on that unnatural conduct.*—LII. *Mucianus, in his letters to Vespasian, charges Antonius with too much precipitation.*—LIII. *Antonius complains against Mucianus in a style of pride and resentment—The two generals become inveterate enemies.*—LIV. *Vitellius endeavours to conceal the defeat at Cremona from the people at Rome—Remarkable firmness of Julius Agrestis, a centurion.*—LV. *Vitellius orders the passes over the Apennine to be secured, and goes in person to the camp.*—LVI. *Portents and prodigies—Vitellius himself the greatest prodigy—He returns to Rome.*—LVII. *Revolt of the fleet at Misenum—The people of Puteoli declare for Vespasian—Capua firm for Vitellius—Claudius Julianus goes over to Vespasian, and makes himself master of Terracina.*—LVIII. *Lucius Vitellius, the emperor's brother, sent to conduct the war in Campania—An army raised at Rome, but the senators and Roman knights relinquish the undertaking.*—LIX. *Vespasian's forces begin their march over the Apennine—Petelius Cerealis, disguised like a peasant, joins the army, and is received as a general officer.*—LX. *The soldiers eager for action—Antonius make an harangue, and restrains their violence.*—LXI. *A spirit of defection prevails among the Vitellians—Priscus and Alphenus leave the camp, and return to Vitellius*—LXII. *Fabius Valens put to death at Urbinum—His character.*—LXIII. *The Vitellian forces at Narnia lay down their arms—Proposals from the enemy to Vitellius—He inclines to accept the offer, and talks of a pleasant retreat.*—LXIV. *The leading men at Rome endeavour to animate Flavius Sabinus, Vespasian's brother—He pleads his advanced age, and enters into a treaty with Vitellius.*—LXV. *The treaty concluded in the temple of Apollo.*—LXVI. *The friends of Vitellius endeavour to inspire him with courage, but in vain—He comes forth from the palace, and makes a voluntary abdication—He is forced by the soldiers and the populace to return to the palace.*—LXIX. *Sabinus takes upon himself the government of Rome—The German soldiers declare against him—A skirmish ensues—The Vitellians have the advantage—Sabinus shuts himself up in the capitol.*—LXXI. *The capitol besieged, and burnt to the ground—Reflections on that disaster.*—LXXIII. *Sabinus, and Quinctius Atticus the consul, taken prisoners.*—LXXIV. *Domitian concealed and saved by the address of a freedman—Sabinus dragged into the presence of Vitellius, and by him well received, but murdered by the soldiers—His body thrown into the common charnel of malefactors.*—LXXV. *The character of Sabinus—Quinctius Atticus, the consul, takes upon himself the guilt of setting fire to the capitol, and is saved by Vitellius.*—LXXVI. *Tarracina taken by Lucius Vitellius—Claudius Julianus put to death.*—LXXVIII. *Vespasian's forces halt for several days amidst the Apennine mountains—But, roused at length by the destruction of the capitol, they pursue their march towards Rome.*—LXXIX. *The Vitellians gain the advantage over Petelius Cerealis in a battle at a small distance from Rome.* LXXX. *Ambassadors sent to treat with Antonius—The soldiers attack the ambassadors—Arulenus Rusticus wounded—A procession of the vestal virgins—They are dismissed with respect, and Vitellius receives for answer, that the firing of the capitol has precluded all terms of accommodation.*—LXXXI. *Vespasian's forces advance in three divisions to the city—Various engagements on the outside of the walls—The Vitellians routed—They rally in the city, and again face the enemy.*—LXXXIII. *A dreadful slaughter ensues—Rome a scene of murder and debauchery—The people behold the combatants, and applaud as at a public spectacle of gladiators.*—LXXXIV. *The prætorian camp besieged and taken by Vespasian's soldiers.*—LXXXV. *Vitellius detected in his lurking-place, and, after various insults from the populace, put to death.*—LXXXVI. *The character of Vitellius—Domitian saluted by the name of Cæsar.*

These transactions passed in a few months.

Year of Rome.	Of Christ.	Consuls for a short time.
822	69	Fabius Valens, Alienus Cæcina.
		Rosius Regulus, Cæcilius Simplex,
		Quinctius Atticus.

I. MEANWHILE, the leaders of Vespasian's party, acting in concert, and with strict fidelity, laid the plan of their operations with better success. They met at Pætovio, the winter quarters of the thirteenth legion, and there held a council of war. The question on which they deliberated was, which was most advisable, to secure the passes over the Pannonian Alps, and there make halt till the forces behind came up to their support, or to push forward with vigour, and penetrate at once into Italy. Some proposed dilatory measures, in order to pursue the campaign with their united force. They founded their opinion on the following reason: "The fame and valour of the German legions were greatly to be dreaded. Vitellius had been reinforced by the flower of the army in Britain. The legions on the side of Vespasian were inferior in number, and had been lately conquered. They talked, indeed, with ferocity; but the minds of the vanquished are always depressed. If the Alps were guarded by a chain of posts, Mucianus would have time to come up with the strength of the east, and Vespasian, in the meantime, would remain master of the seas. He had powerful fleets, and the provinces espoused his cause. With these resources he might, if necessary, prepare his measures for a second war. The advantages, therefore, which might arise from delay, were sufficiently evident; new succours would arrive, and their present force, in the meantime, would not be exposed to the chance of war."

II. This reason was opposed by Antonius Primus, the

grand promoter of the confederacy. "Activity," he said, "will give every advantage to Vespasian, and prove the ruin of Vitellius and his party. The conquerors have gained nothing by their victory; on the contrary, their vigour is melted down in sloth and luxury. They are neither inured to a regular camp, nor trained to arms, nor kept in exercise by military duty. Dispersed through the municipal towns of Italy, they have lost their martial spirit, and now are soldiers to their landlords only. Their taste of pleasure is a new acquirement, and they enjoy it with the same spirit that formerly incited them to the most ferocious deeds. The circus, the theatre, and the delights of Rome, have sunk their vigour, and disease has rendered them unfit for military duty. Allow them time, and they will recruit their strength. The very idea of war will animate their drooping courage. Their resources are great; Germany is near at hand, and from that hive new swarms may issue forth; Britain is separated by a narrow channel; Spain and Gaul lie contiguous, and from both they may draw supplies of men, and horses, and money. All Italy is theirs, and the wealth of Rome is at their mercy. Should they resolve to wage a distant war, they have two fleets, and the Illyrian sea lies open to their operations. In that case, what will be the use of posts and stations on the Pannonian Alps? and what the advantage of drawing the war into length? Wait for another campaign; and where, in the meantime, are we to find supplies of money and provisions? To act with vigour is our best, our only expedient. The legions of Pannonia were surprised, not conquered: they are now breathing revenge; they wish for nothing so much as an opportunity to signalise their valour in the field. The forces of Mæsia have neither wasted their strength, nor have they been humbled by defeat. If the strength on both sides is to be estimated by the number of men, and not of the legions, the superiority is on the side of Vespasian. In his army no corruption, no licentiousness. Even former misfortunes are now of use; the men have seen their error, and the sense of shame has established discipline and good order. In the last action the cavalry suffered no disgrace: on the contrary, though the event of the day was adverse, they broke through the ranks of the enemy. And if two squadrons of horse, one from Pannonia, and the other from Mæsia, could bear down all before them, what may not be expected from the joint force of sixteen squadrons, whose banners glitter in the service of Vespasian? Their impetuosity in the first onset, their uproar, the clangour of their arms, and the clouds of dust raised by their horses' hoofs, will confound, distract, and overwhelm a feeble enemy, who have lost their warlike spirit. What I advise, I am willing to execute. Those who have not taken a decided resolution, may, if they will, remain behind. Let them detain their legions. Give me the light-armed cohorts: I ask no more. With those gallant soldiers my intention is, to force a passage into Italy. The Vitellians will shrink from the attack; and when you hear the tidings, you will then pursue the footsteps of Antonius, glad to follow where victory leads the way."

III. Such was the reasoning of this active partisan. He delivered the whole with a spirit that convinced the prudent, and roused the timorous. His eyes flashed fire; his voice expanded, that the centurions and soldiers, who had pressed into the council-room, might hear the sentiments of a brave and experienced officer. All were carried away by a torrent of eloquence. The crowd extolled his courage, and despised the other officers for their want of spirit. He, and he alone, was the man of enterprise, the general worthy of the command. In a former council of war, where Vespasian's letters were read to the whole meeting, Antonius had announced his character, and made a deep impression on the minds of the soldiers. Upon that occasion, he entered with warmth into the debate, disdaining the little policy of using equivocal terms, which might afterwards receive the construction that suited the views of the speaker. Intrepid and decisive, he laid himself open at once. He spoke with that frank and generous ardour, which is always sure to captivate the affections of the army. The soldiers admired a general, whom they saw ready to share every danger, and to be their partner in the rashness or the glory of the enterprise.

IV. The person who, in the opinion of the common men, filled the second place, was Cornelius Fuscus, the procurator of the province. That officer, by his freedom of speech, had already pledged himself to the cause: if it miscarried, his bold and forward censure of Vitellius left him no room to retreat. Titus Ampius Flavianius stood in a very different light. His natural slowness, rendered still more languid by the increase of years, drew upon him the suspicion of the soldiers, who knew that he was allied to Vitellius. In the beginning of the present commotions, he fled from his post, to avoid the storm then gathering round him, and, shortly afterwards, returned to the province, with intent, as was generally imagined, to execute some treacherous design. He had made his escape into Italy; but, when he heard that the legions were in motion, he returned to Pannonia, and resumed his authority, fond of innovation, and willing to hazard himself in the troubles of a civil war. To this last step he was incited by the advice of Cornelius Fuscus, who wished to see him in Pannonia; not with a view of deriving advantage from his talents, but because the name of a consular officer was of moment, and, in the first efforts of a party not yet established, a person of that rank might give credit and lustre to the cause.

V. The march into Italy being the measure adopted, in order to secure the passes over the mountains, letters were sent to Aponius Saturninus, ordering him to advance, by rapid marches, with his army from Mæsia. At the same time, that the provinces thus evacuated might not lie open to the incursions of Barbarians on the borders, the chiefs of the Jazyges, a people of Sarmatia, were engaged to co-operate with the Roman army. The new allies offered to bring into the field a body of the natives, and also their cavalry, in which consists the strength of the country. Their service, however, was not accepted, lest a number of foreign mercenaries should take advantage of the distractions that convulsed the empire, or for better pay desert to the opposite party. The Suevian nation had, at all times, given proofs of their steady attachment to the interest of Rome; and no doubt being entertained of their fidelity, their two kings, Sido and Italicus, were admitted into the league. On the confines of Rhætia, where Portius Septimius, the procurator of the province, remained firm to Vitellius, a range of posts were stationed to bridle that part of the country. With this view Sextilius Felix was sent forward, at the head of a squadron of horse called AURIANA, eight cohorts, and the militia of Noricum, with orders to line the banks of the river Ænus, which divides Rhætia from Noricum. Those two commanders were content to act on the defensive, and no engagement followed. The fate of empire was elsewhere decided.

VI. Antonius Primus began his march at the head of a body of vexillaries drafted from the cohorts, and a detachment of the cavalry. He pushed forward with eager speed to the invasion of Italy, accompanied by Arius Varus, an officer of distinguished valour, who had served under Corbulo in Armenia, and from the talents and brilliant success of that applauded commander derived all his reputation. In secret cabals with Nero he is said to have whispered away the character of his general, converting into crimes the eminent virtues of that great officer. He rose to the rank of principal centurion; but his sudden advancement, obtained as it was by treacherous arts, proved his ruin in the end. Antonius, in conjunction with this commander, took possession of Aquileia. The adjacent towns submitted with alacrity. At Opitergium and Altinum they were received with demonstrations of joy. At the last of those places a garrison was left to check the operations of the fleet stationed at Ravenna, which was not then known to have revolted. The cities of Patavium and Ateste made a voluntary surrender. The generals received intelligence that three Vitellian cohorts, with the squadron of horse called Scriboniana, had taken post at Forum Allienum, and, after throwing up a bridge, loitered away the time in careless security. The opportunity seemed fair to attack them by surprise. At the dawn of day the place was taken by storm, before the enemy had time to get under arms. It had been previously issued out in orders, that, after a moderate slaughter, the assailants should give quarter to the rest, and by the terror of their arms force them to join Vespasian's party. Numbers surrendered at discretion: but the greater part broke down the bridge, and saved themselves by flight.

VII. The fame of a victory, obtained in the beginning of the war, made an impression favourable to Vespasian's cause. In a short time after, two legions, namely, the seventh, called GALBIANA, and the thirteenth, named GEMINA, under the command of Vedius Aquila, arrived at Padua. A few days were spent at that place to refresh the men. In that interval, Minucius Justus, prefect of the camp to the seventh legion, enforcing his orders with more severity than was consistent with the nature of a civil war, provoked the fury of the soldiers. He was ordered to join Vespasian, and by that artifice he saved his life. Antonius, at that time, had the judgment to do a public act, which had been long desired, and, by consequence, gave universal satisfaction. He ordered the statues of Galba, which the rage of civil discord had levelled to the ground, to be again set up in all the municipal towns. By doing honour to the memory of Galba, and reviving the hopes of a ruined party, Antonius had no doubt but he should greatly serve the cause in which he was embarked.

VIII. Where to fix the seat of war was now a question of moment. Verona was thought the most eligible spot. In that open champaign country, the cavalry, in which the strength of the army consisted, would have ample space; and the glory of wresting out of the hands of Vitellius a colony so strong and flourishing, would draw after it the greatest advantages. The army pushed forward with rapidity, and, in their march, became masters of Vicetia;[1] a city in itself of small importance, but, being the birthplace of Cæcina, the acquisition was deemed a triumph over the adverse general. The reduction of Verona brought an accession of wealth, and gave an example to other cities. Moreover, as it lies between Rhætia and the Julian Alps, it was a post of importance, where an army in force might command the pass into Italy, and render it impervious to the German armies. Of these operations Vespasian had no knowledge; on the contrary, his orders were, that the troops should halt at Aquileia, and push the war no further till Mucianus arrived with all his force. Vespasian explained the motives that determined his counsels. While he was master of Egypt, the granary of Italy, and commanded, besides, the revenues of the most opulent provinces, the Vitellian army, for want of pay and provisions, might be forced to capitulate. Mucianus, in all his letters, recommended the same measure; adding, that a victory obtained without blood, and without causing a tear to be shed, would be the truest glory. But those reasons were specious and ostensible only: avarice of fame was his motive; he wished to engross the whole honour of the war. But the fact was, Vespasian and his general planned their operations in a distant part of the world, and before their orders could arrive the blow was struck.

IX. Antonius was not of a temper to remain inactive. He resolved to attempt the stations of the enemy. His attack was sudden; and, after trying in a slight engagement the strength and disposition of the Vitellians, he thought proper to desist. Both parties retired wlth equal success. In a short time afterwards Cæcina pitched his camp in the neighbourhood of Verona, between the village of Hostilia, and the morass on the banks of the river Tartarus. This post afforded him every advantage: he had the river in his rear, and the fens on each flank. He wanted nothing but fidelity. Beyond all question he had it in his power, with the whole strength of his army, to crush two legions under Antonius, who had not yet been joined by the Mæsian army, or, at least, he might have forced

[1] Vicetia, now *Vicenza*.

them by a shameful flight to evacuate Italy. But he trifled away the time with specious delays, and, losing all opportunities, treacherously sacrificed the most precious moments of the war. He carried on a correspondence with Antonius, content by his letters to debate with a man whom he ought to have conquered. He continued to temporise, till by secret negotiations he settled the price of perfidy.

During this suspense, Aponius Saturninus arrived at Verona with the seventh legion, called the CLAUDIAN, under the command of Vipsanius Messala, then in the rank of tribune; a man of illustrious birth, and of character worthy of his ancestors: of all who entered into that war, the only person who carried with him fair and honourable motives. With this reinforcement the army amounted to no more than three legions; and yet to that inferior force Cæcina thought proper to despatch a letter, condemning the rashness of men, who, after their late defeat, presumed again to try the fortune of the field. He extolled the bravery of the German soldiers, making the slightest mention of Vitellius, but with regard to Vespasian not hazarding one disrespectful word. Nor was there in the whole tenor of his letter a single expression that tended either to impress the enemy with fear, or to induce them to revolt. Vespasian's generals returned an answer in a style of magnanimity They entered into no defence of their former conduct; they bestowed the highest praise on Vespasian: relying on the goodness of their cause, they spoke with confidence of the event, and without reserve declaimed against Vitellius in the style of men who had nothing to fear. To the tribunes and centurions who had been rewarded by Vitellius, they promised a continuance of the same favours, and in explicit terms invited Cæcina to join their party. The letters of that officer, and the several answers, were read, by order of Antonius, in the hearing of the army. The soldiers observed the caution with which Cæcina spoke of Vespasian, and the undisguised contempt of Vitellius expressed by the Flavian generals. From that circumstance they derived new alacrity, and thorough confidence in their cause.

X. Antonius, reinforced by the arrival of two legions, namely, the third, commanded by Dillius Aponianus, and the eighth, by Numisius Lupus, resolved to make a display of his strength, and enclose Verona with lines of circumvallation. An accident interrupted the progress of the works. It happened that the Galbian legion was employed in an advanced part of the trenches, fronting the enemy. They perceived at a distance a body of cavalry, and, though in fact they were friends, mistook them for a party of the Vitellians. Thinking themselves betrayed they seized their arms, and, in the hurry of surprise, charged Ampius Flavianus as the author of the plot. They had no kind of proof; but they hated the man, and hatred was sufficient evidence of his guilt. They roared and clamoured for his blood; and nothing less, they said, would satisfy their indignation. He was the kinsman of Vitellius, the betrayer of Otho, and he had embezzled the donative intended for the soldiers. These reproaches were loud and violent. Flavianus endeavoured to obtain a hearing; he stretched forth his hands; he prostrated himself before them; rent his garments, beat his breast, and with tears and groans endeavoured to mitigate resentment. The men despised him in that abject condition, and from his distress inferred a confession of guilt.

Aponius Saturninus attempted to speak, but was overpowered by a general clamour. The rest of the officers were silenced in like manner. Antonius was the only person who could make himself heard. To his authority and eloquence he united the art of managing the temper of the soldiers. Their rage, however, did not subside; from foul abuse they proceeded to violence, and even began to brandish their weapons. The general ordered Flavianius to be seized, and loaded with irons. This was understood to be no more than a subterfuge to elude the vengeance of the soldiers, who rushed to the tribunal, and, having dispersed the guards, threatened immediate execution. Antonius opposed his bosom to their fury, and, drawing his sword, declared aloud that he would fall by their weapons or his own. He looked around, invoking the assistance of all, whom he either knew, or saw distinguished by any kind of military decoration; he directed his eyes to the eagles and standards, those gods of the camp, and in a pathetic strain implored them to transfuse that frantic spirit into the breasts of the enemy. At length the sedition began to abate, and day closing apace, the men withdrew to their tents. In the course of the night, Flavianus left the camp. He had not travelled far, when he received letters from Vespasian, in a style that left him no room to fear the displeasure of the prince.

XI. The frenzy of the soldiers did not stop here. It spread as it were by contagion, and fell with violence on Aponius Saturninus, who had brought with him the Mæsian forces. A letter to Vitellius had been intercepted, and he was supposed to be the author. The story was believed, and all were fired with resentment. The tumult did not, as before, begin when the soldiers were fatigued with the labours of the day; it broke out at noon, when they were in full vigour, and for that reason more to be dreaded. How unlike the spirit of ancient times! Under the old republic, a generous emulation in virtue and heroic valour was the only struggle in a Roman camp: but now to be the foremost in sedition was the grand effort of a depraved and licentious soldiery. The fury that showed itself against Flavianus was inflamed to madness against Saturninus. The Mæsian legions made it a merit with the Pannonian army, that, in the late insurrection, they had lent their assistance; and, in return, the Pannonians joined their friends, willing to encourage a mutiny, by which they hoped that their own guilt would be justified, or at least excused. With this spirit all were ready to repeat their crime. They rushed to the gardens, where Saturninus was walking for recreation. Antonius opposed the mutineers; Messala and Aponianus exerted their best endeavours, but without effect. If Saturninus had not luckily found a lurking-place, in the furnace of a bath not then in use, there is no doubt but he must have fallen a sacrifice. As soon as an opportunity offered, he dismissed his lictors, and made the best of his way to Padua. There being now no officer of consular rank left with the army, the whole command devolved upon Antonius. The soldiers were willing to submit to his authority. The other officers declined all competition. But if the general did not, by secret practices, excite the two seditions, that he alone might gain the honour of the war without a rival, the suspicion, which numbers entertained, was injurious to his character.

XII. During these transactions, the camp of Vitellius was not free from disturbance. The discord there did not originate from suspicions entertained by the soldiers, but had its source in the perfidy of the general officers. Lucilius Bassus, who commanded the fleet at Ravenna, had already drawn over to his party a number of the marines, all natives of Dalmatia and Pannonia, and, those provinces having all already declared for Vespasian, ready to follow the example of their countrymen. The dead of night was chosen as the fit time for carrying their treasonable designs into execution. At that hour, when all was hushed in sleep, the conspirators agreed to meet in the quarter where the colours were deposited. Bassus remained in his own house, conscious of his treachery, or, perhaps, alarmed for himself, and willing to wait the issue. The masters of the galleys began the revolt. They seized the images of Vitellius, and put to the sword all who attempted to resist. The common herd, with their usual love of innovation, went over to Vespasian. Bassus, in that moment, ventured to appear, avowing himself the author of the treason. The fleet immediately chose another commander. Cornelius Fuscus was the person appointed. That officer soon appeared at Ravenna, and took upon him his new commission. By his order, Bassus, under a proper guard, but honourably treated, was obliged to embark for Atria.[1] At that place he was thrown into fetters by Mennius Rufinus, who commanded the garrison; but he was soon released at the desire of Hormus, one of Vespasian's freedmen, who, it seems, had the presumption to figure away among the general officers.

XIII. The defection of the fleet was no sooner known, than Cæcina, having removed out of the way the best part of his army under various pretexts of military duty, called a meeting of the principal centurions, and a select party of soldiers, in the place assigned for the eagles, the most private part of the camp. He there opened his mind without reserve. He expatiated in praise of Vespasian, and painted forth in glaring colours the strength of the combination formed in his favour. The fleet, he said, had revolted, and, by consequence, Italy would be distressed for provisions. Spain and both the Gauls were up in arms: at Rome the minds of men were wavering, and a storm was ready to burst upon Vitellius. The men whom Antonius had engaged in the plot threw off the mask, and the rest, incited by their example, took the oath of fidelity to Vespasian. The images of Vitellius were torn from the ensigns, and despatches were sent off with intelligence to the adverse army. This transaction was no sooner known in Cæcina's camp, than the rest of the soldiers rushed in a body to the quarter of the eagles and standards. They saw the name of Vespasian displayed to view, and the images of Vitellius scattered about in fragments. A deep and sullen silence followed. A general uproar soon broke out, and with one voice the men exclaimed, "Where is now the glory of the German armies? Without hazarding a battle, and without a wound,

[1] A town situated between the Po and the Adige.

we must lay down our arms, and deliver ourselves to the enemy bound in chains. And to what enemy? To the legions lately vanquished by superior valour: nay, to a part of those legions: for the strength and bulwark of Otho's forces, the first and fourteenth, are not with the army. And is this the issue of our fame in arms, and of our late glorious victory? Did so many brave and gallant soldiers distinguish themselves by their bravery in the field, that they might now, like a drove of slaves, be delivered up to Antonius, a man formerly banished for his crimes? The fleet, we are told, has revolted: and shall eight legions be transferred as an appendage to their treachery? Bassus, it seems, will have it so; and such is the pleasure of Cæcina. They have despoiled the prince of his houses, his gardens, and his treasure; and they want now to rob him of his soldiers; of soldiers, who, with swords in their hands, and in full possession of their strength and vigour, are to yield without an engagement, and bear the scorn and mockery of Vespasian and his party. To such as may hereafter desire an account of the battles we have fought, and the dangers which we have encountered, what answer shall we make?"

XIV. Such were the complaints, and such the language, not of individuals only, but of the whole body. Each man spoke his feelings, and all concurred in one general uproar. The fifth legion took the lead: they restored the images of Vitellius; they seized Cæcina, and loaded him with fetters. Fabius Fabullus, commander of the fifth legion, and Cassius Longus, the prefect of the camp, were declared commanders-in-chief. A party of marines belonging to three light galleys fell into the hands of the enraged soldiery, and though ignorant of all that passed, and innocent of the late defection, were to a man put to the sword. After this exploit, the discontented troops broke up their camp, and, having demolished the bridge, marched back to Hostilia, and thence to Cremona, where the first legion, called ITALICA, and the one-and-twentieth, known by the name of RAPAX, had been stationed by Cæcina.

XV. Apprised of these transactions, Antonius resolved, while the enemy was still distracted, and dispersed at different stations, not to let the war languish till the Vitellians began to act with unanimity, and the generals recovered their authority. He knew that Valens had set out from Rome, and Cæcina's treachery, he had reason to think, would make him push forward with expedition to join the army. The zeal of Valens for the cause in which he embarked, was sufficiently distinguished, and he was known to be an officer of experience. Besides this, a large body of Germans was expected to force their way through Rhætia into Italy, and Vitellius had sent for succours into Britain, Gaul, and Spain; a formidable preparation, if Antonius had not determined to strike a decisive blow. He moved with his whole army from Verona, and in two days arrived at Bedriacum. On the following morning he set the legions to work at the intrenchments, and, under colour of foraging, but in truth to give the men a relish for plunder, sent the auxiliary cohort to ravage the plains near Cremona. To support them in this expedition, he himself, at the head of four thousand horse, advanced eight miles beyond Bedriacum; while his scouts took a wider range, to discover the motions of the enemy.

XVI. About the fifth hour of the day, a soldier at full speed brought intelligence that the enemy was approaching. He had seen their advanced parties, and distinctly heard the bustle of the whole army. Antonius began to prepare for action. While he was deliberating, Arrius Varus, eager to distinguish himself, advanced at the head of a party of horse, and put the front line of the Vitellians to the rout. The slaughter was inconsiderable. A party of the enemy advanced to support the broken ranks, and changed the fortune of the field. Varus and his men were obliged to give ground, and they, who had pursued with eagerness, were now in the rear of the retreat. In this rash action Antonius had no share. He foresaw the consequence, and now exerted himself to prevent further mischief. Having exhorted his men, he ordered the cavalry to open their ranks, and draw off in two divisions towards the flanks of the army, in order to leave a void space for the reception of Varus and his routed party. The legions were called out, and, in the country round, the signal was given to the foraging cohorts to abandon their booty, and repair forthwith to the field of battle. Varus, in the meantime, returned to the main body, covered with dismay, and by his appearance diffusing terror through the ranks. He and his men had retreated with precipitation; the able and the wounded in one promiscuous panic fled before the enemy, all in wild confusion, and, on a narrow causey, obstructing one another.

XVII. Antonius, in this pressing exigence, omitted

nothing that could be expected from a commander of experience and undaunted valour. He rallied the broken ranks: where the men were giving way, by his presence he revived their drooping courage; wherever there was either danger, or an advantage to be taken, he was ready on the spot, with his directions, with his voice, with his sword, inspiring courage, conspicuous in every part of the field, and manifest to the enemy. His courage rose to the highest pitch, and transported him beyond himself. In a noble fit of martial ardour, he transfixed with his spear a standard-bearer in the act of flying, and instantly seizing the colours, advanced against the enemy. This bold exertion had its effect. A party of the cavalry, in number about a hundred, felt the disgrace of deserting their general, and returned to the charge. The nature of the ground favoured Antonius. The causey was narrowest in that part, and the bridge over the river that flowed in the rear being broken down, the men could not pursue their flight where the banks were steep, and the fordable places were unknown. By this restraint, or by some turn of fortune, the battle was restored. The soldiers made a stand, and, having recovered their ranks, received the Vitellians, who rushed on with eagerness, but without order, and in a short time were put to the rout. Antonius pressed on the rear of such as fled, and all who resisted died on the spot. The rest of Vespasian's army acted as the impulse of individuals prompted; they secured their prisoners, they seized the arms and horses of the slain, and made the field resound with shouts of victory. The runaways, who had dispersed themselves in various quarters, heard the joyful acclamations of their comrades, and, to claim part of the glory, hurried back to the scene of action.

XVIII. At the distance of four miles from Cremona, the banners of the two legions called RAPAX and ITALICA appeared in view. The advantage gained by the Vitellian cavalry, in the beginning of the day, was their motive for advancing so far: but, seeing a reverse of fortune, they neither opened their ranks to receive their flying friends, nor dared to attack an enemy at that time well-nigh exhausted by the labours of the day. In the hour of prosperity they despised their general officers, and in their distress began to feel that they wanted an able commander. While they stood at gaze, irresolute, and covered with consternation, the cavalry of Antonius attacked them with impetuous fury. Vipsanius Messala followed to support the ranks, at the head of the Mæsian auxiliaries, who, though they had made a long march, were so well inured to discipline, that they were deemed nothing inferior to the legionary soldiers. The foot and cavalry, acting with united vigour, bore down all opposition. The Vitellians hoped to find within the walls of Cremona a safe shelter from the rage of a pursuing enemy, and for that reason were less inclined to maintain the conflict.

XIX. Antonius did not think it prudent to pursue his advantage: he was content to remain master of the field. The victory, he knew, was dearly bought; and it behoved him to spare both men and horses, fatigued with toil, and fainting under their wounds. Towards the close of day, the whole force of Vespasian's army arrived and joined Antonius. Having seen, on their march, the plains covered with dead bodies, and the ground still reeking with blood, they concluded, from so vast a scene of slaughter, that the war was nearly over, and, to give the finishing blow, desired to be led on to Cremona, either to receive a voluntary surrender, or to carry the place by storm. This demand sounded like courage and public spirit: but other motives were at the bottom. In their hearts the men argued for their own personal advantage. "Cremona," they said, "was situated in an open plain, and might be taken by assault. The darkness of the night would not abate their courage, and for spoil and plunder that was the proper season. If they waited for the return of day, terms of peace might arrive; a capitulation would be proposed; and, in that case, what reward was the soldier to expect for all his labour, and his blood spilt in the service? The cold, the useless praise of moderation and humanity would be his only recompense, and the wealth of the place would fall to the principal officers. By the laws of war, when a town is carried by storm, the booty belongs to the soldiers; but a surrender transfers the whole to the generals." Inflamed by these considerations, they disdained to listen to the tribunes and centurions; with the clangour of their arms they suppressed the voice of reason, determined, if not led on to the attack, to shake off all authority.

XX. Antonius made his way through the ranks, and, by his presence having commanded silence, spoke as follows: "It is neither in my temper nor my intention to deprive a set of gallant soldiers of the glory, or the recompense, due to their valour: but the general, and the men under his command, have their distinct provinces. Courage and ardour for the conflict are the soldier's virtues: to foresee events, to provide against disasters, and to plan with deliberation, and even with delay, is the duty of the commander-in-chief. By suspending the operations of war, success is often ensured: by temerity all is put to the hazard. In the last battle I exposed my person, I fought in the ranks, I strained every nerve to gain the victory: let me now by my experience, by advice, and by prudent counsels, the true arts of a general, endeavour to terminate the war with glory. The question at present does not admit of a doubt. We have the night before us; the town, its entrance, and the condition of the works, are unknown to us: the enemy is within the walls, and may try various stratagems. And if the gates were thrown open, even then, without the best intelligence, without broad daylight, and without a view of the fortifications, it would be madness to venture. And will you hazard an assault, without knowing the approaches to the place, the height of the walls, and without being able to judge whether we ought to batter a breach, or by missive weapons drive the enemy from the works? Which of you has been provident enough to bring his hatchet, his pickaxe, and the various tools which a siege requires? With those instruments you are unprovided: and what arm among you is strong enough with a sword and spear to sap the walls of Cremona? How are we to throw up ramparts, and how prepare hurdles and penthouses to cover our approach? In the moment of need, must we all stand at gaze, wondering at our folly, and the strength of the fortifications? Pass but one night, and with our battering engines, and our warlike machines, we shall advance in force, and carry victory along with us at the point of our swords." At the close of this harangue he ordered the followers of the camp, escorted by a select party of the cavalry, to set out for Bedriacum, in order to bring a supply of provisions, and all necessaries for the use of the army.

XXI. The soldiers were still dissatisfied, and a mutiny was ready to break out, when a party of horse that went out to scour the country, and advanced as far as the walls of Cremona, returned with intelligence, obtained from the stragglers who had fallen into their hands, that the whole Vitellian army encamped at Hostilia, having heard of that day's defeat, made a forced march of thirty miles, and, with a reinforcement of six legions, were near at hand, breathing vengeance, and determined to offer battle. In this alarming crisis the soldiers were willing to listen to their superior officer. Antonius prepared to receive the enemy. He ordered the thirteenth legion to take post on the Posthumian causey; on the open plain, towards their left, he stationed the seventh, called the GALBIAN; and at a small distance the seventh, named the Claudian, on a spot defended by a mere country ditch. On the right he placed the eighth legion, on a wide-extended plain, and the third in a thick copse, that stood near at hand. Such was the arrangement of the eagles and standards: the soldiers took their posts as chance directed them in the dark. The prætorian banner stood near the third legion; the auxiliary cohorts were in the wings: the cavalry covered the flanks and the rear. The two Suevian kings, Sido and Italicus, with the best troops of their nation, took their post in the front of the lines.

XXII. The Vitellian army had every advantage, without the skill to profit by their situation. Had they halted that night at Cremona, as prudence dictated, to refresh their men by food and sleep, the engagement, on the next morning, would have been with an enemy chilled by the damps of the night, and faint for want of provisions. A complete victory would, most probably, have been the consequence. But they had no commander. Without conduct or judgment, about the third hour of the night, they made a forward movement, and attacked an army drawn up in order of battle. Of the disposition made by the Vitellians in the gloom of night, without any guide but their own impetuous fury, it will not be expected that I should give an accurate account: we are told, however, that it was as follows; the fourth legion, called MACEDONICA, was stationed in the right wing; the fifth and fifteenth, supported by the vexillaries of three British legions, the ninth, the second, and the twentieth, formed the centre: in the left wing stood the first, the sixteenth, and two-and-twentieth. The soldiers of the two legions called RAPAX and ITALICA were mixed at random throughout the lines. The cavalry and anxiliaries chose their station. The battle lasted through the night with great slaughter on both sides, and alternate success. In the dark, courage gave no superiority; the ardent eye and the vigorous arm were of no avail. All distinction was lost. The weapons on both sides were the same. The watchword, frequently asked and repeated, was known to both armies. The colours, taken and retaken by different parties, were mixed in wild confusion. The seventh legion, lately raised by Galba, suffered the most. Six of their principal centurions were killed on the spot, and some of their colours taken. The eagle itself was in danger, had not Attilius Verus, the principal centurion,[1] enacted

[1] It appears from this, that the first centurion, *Primipili Centurio*, was the eagle-bearer.

wonders to prevent that disgrace. He made a dreadful carnage, and died, at last, fighting with undaunted bravery.

XXIII. Vespasian's army was giving way, when Antonius brought the prætorian cohorts into the heat of the action. They routed the enemy, and in their turn were forced to retreat. The Vitellians, at this time, changed the position of their battering-engines, which, in the beginning, were placed in different parts of the field, and could only play at random against the woods and hedges that sheltered the enemy. They were now removed to the Posthumian way, and thence, having an open space before them, could discharge their missive weapons with good effect. The fifteenth legion had an engine of enormous size, which was played off with dreadful execution, and discharged massy stones, of weight to crush whole ranks at once. Inevitable ruin must have followed, if two soldiers had not signalised themselves by a brave exploit. Covering themselves with the shields of the enemy which they found among the slain, they advanced undiscovered to the battering-engine, and cut the ropes and springs. In this bold adventure they both perished, and with them two names that deserved to be made immortal. The glory of the action is all that can be now recorded.

The battle was hitherto fought with doubtful success, when, night being far advanced, the moon rose, and discovered the face of things with great advantage to Vespasian's army. The light shone on their backs, and the shadows of men and horses projected forward to such a length, that the Vitellians, deceived by appearances, aimed at the wrong mark. Their darts, by consequence, fell short of their aim. The moonbeams, in the meantime, played on the front of their lines, and gave their bodies in full view to the adverse army, who fought behind their shadows, as if concealed in obscurity.

XXIV. Antonius, at length, was happy that he could see, and be seen. He did everything to rouse the courage of his men; he upbraided some; he applauded others; he made ample promises, and gave hopes to all. He asked the Pannonian legions, what was their motive for taking up arms? "Here," he said, "here is the spot where you may efface the memory of your former defeat: in this field you may redeem your honour." He called aloud to the Mæsians, "You were the first movers of the war; you talked in high-sounding words: but you talked in vain, if you can neither oppose the swords nor bear the eye of the enemy." He was busy in every quarter, and had apt words for all. To the third legion he spoke more at large: he called to mind their former and their recent exploits. "They," he said, "were the men, who under Mark Antony defeated the Parthians; and the Armenians, under Corbulo. In a late campaign the Sarmatians fled before them." The prætorians called forth his indignation: "Now," he said, "now is your time to conquer, or renounce the name of soldiers. If you give way, you will be deemed no better than a band of peasants. What general, or what camp, will receive you? Your ensigns and your colours are in the hands of the enemy. You may there regain them; you now must conquer, or be put to the sword; after your late disgrace there is no alternative." A general shout resounded through the field; and in that moment the third legion, according to the custom observed in Syria, paid their adoration to the rising sun.

XXV. This eastern form of worship, either by chance, or by the contrivance of Antonius, gave rise to a sudden report that Mucianus was arrived, and that the two confederate armies exchanged mutual salutations. Animated by this incident, Vespasian's soldiers, as if actually reinforced, charged with redoubled fury. The Vitellian ranks began to give way. Left to their own impulse, without a chief to conduct the battle, they extended or condensed their lines as fear or courage prompted. Antonius saw their confusion. He ordered his men to advance in a close compacted body. The loose and scattered numbers of the enemy gave way at once. The carriages and engines, that lay at random in various parts of the field, made it impossible to restore the order of the battle. The victors, eager to pursue their advantage, pushed forward to the causey, and having gained a sure footing, made a dreadful carnage.

An accident, that happened in the heat of the action, gave a shock to humanity. A father was killed by his own son. The fact and the names of the men are recorded by Vipstanius Messala: upon his authority I shall state the particulars. Julius Mansuetus, a native of Spain, enrolled himself in the legion already mentioned by the name of RAPAX. He left behind him a son, then of tender years. The youth, grown up to manhood, enlisted in the seventh legion raised by Galba. In the hurry and tumult of the fight, he met his father, and with a mortal wound stretched him on the ground. He stooped to examine and rifle the body. The unhappy father raised his eyes, and knew his son. The son, in return, acknowledged his dying parent; he burst into tears; he clasped his father in his arms, and, in the anguish of his heart, with earnest supplications entreated him not to impute to his unhappy son the detestable crime of parricide. "The deed," he said, "is horrible, but it is not mine; it is the guilt of civil war. In the general madness of the state, the act of one poor wretched soldier is a small portion of the public misery." He then opened a grave, embraced the body, and, with filial affection raising it in his arms, discharged the last melancholy duty to his murdered father.

This pathetic scene did not escape observation. A few drew near, others were attracted, and in a short time the fatal deed was known throughout the army. The soldiers heaved a sigh, and with curses execrated the frantic rage of civil discord. And yet, with those sentiments, they went the next moment to plunder their slaughtered friends, their relations, and brothers. They called it a crime, and yet repeated what their hearts condemned.

XXVI. The conquerors pushed on to Cremona, and no sooner drew near the place, than they saw a new difficulty still to be surmounted. In the war with Otho, the German legions had formed a camp round the walls of the town, and fortified it with lines of circumvallation. New works were added afterwards. The victors stood astonished at the sight, and even the generals were at a stand, undecided what plan to pursue. With troops harassed and worn-out by continual exertions through the night and day, an attempt to carry the place by storm was not advisable, and, without succours at hand, might be dangerous; and yet the march to Bedriacum would be a laborious undertaking, and to retreat were to give up the fruit of a victory dearly earned. In their present situation it would be necessary to throw up intrenchments; and that work, in the face of an enemy on the watch to sally out, might put everything to the hazard. A difficulty still greater than all arose from the temper of the men, who showed themselves, at all times, insensible of danger, and impatient of delay. A state of security was a state of listless indolence, and daring enterprise was the proper occupation of a soldier. Wounds, and blood, and slaughter, were nothing to men who thought that plunder can never be too dearly bought.

XXVII. Antonius judged it best to yield to the disposition of his men. He invested the works, determined to risk a general assault. The attack began at a distance, with a volley of stones and darts. The advantage was on the side of the besieged. They possessed the heights, and with surer aim annoyed the enemy at the foot of the ramparts. Antonius saw the necessity of dividing his operations: to some of the legions he assigned distinct parts of the works, and ordered others to advance against the gates. By this mode of attack in different quarters, he knew that valour as well as cowardice would be conspicuous, and a spirit of emulation would animate the whole army. The third and seventh legions took their station opposite to the road that leads to Bedriacum; the seventh and eighth Claudian legions carried on the siege on the right hand of the town; and the thirteenth invested the gate that looked towards Brixia.[1] In this position the troops rested on their arms, till they were supplied from the neighbouring villages with pickaxes, spades and hooks, and scaling-ladders. Being, at length, provided with proper weapons, they formed a military shell with their shields, and, under that cover, advanced to the ramparts. The Roman art of war was seen on both sides. The Vitellians rolled down massy stones, and, wherever they saw an opening, inserting their long poles and spears, rent asunder the whole frame and texture of the shields, while the assailants, deprived of shelter, suffered a terrible slaughter.

XXVIII. The assault was no longer pushed on with vigour. The generals saw that their exhortations had no effect, and that mere praise was a barren recompense. To inspire the men with courage, they pointed to Cremona as the reward of victory. Whether this expedient was, as Messala informs us, suggested by Hormus, or, on the authority of Caius Plinius, must be laid to the account of Antonius, we have now no means of knowing. Whoever was the author of a deed so cruel and flagitious, neither of these two officers can be said to have degenerated from his former principles. The place being thus devoted to plunder, nothing could restrain the ardour of the soldiers. Braving wounds and danger, and death itself, they began to sap the foundation of the walls; they battered the gates; they braced their shields over their heads; and, mounting on the shoulders of their comrades, they grappled with the besieged, and dragged them headlong from the ramparts. A dreadful havoc followed. The unhurt, the wounded, the maimed and the dying, fell in one promiscuous heap; and death, in all its forms, represented a spectacle of horror.

XXIX. The most vigorous assault was made by the

[1] The modern *Brescia*.

third and the seventh legions. To support them, Antonius in person led on a select body of auxiliaries. The Vitellians were no longer able to sustain the shock. They saw their darts fall on the military shell, and glide off without effect. Enraged at their disappointment, in a fit of despair they rolled their battering-engine on the heads of the besiegers. Numbers were crushed by the fall of such a ponderous mass. It happened, however, that the machine drew after it the parapet and part of the rampart. An adjoining tower, which had been incessantly battered, fell at the same time, and left a breach for the troops to enter. The seventh legion, in the form of a wedge, endeavoured to force their way, while the third hewed down the gate. The first man that entered, according to all historians, was Caius Volusius, a common soldier of the third legion. He gained the summit of the rampart, and, bearing down all resistance, with his voice, with his sword, made himself conspicuous to his comrades, crying aloud, "The camp is taken." The rest of the legion followed him with resistless fury. The Vitellians, in despair, threw themselves headlong from the works. The conquerors pursued their advantage with dreadful slaughter. The whole space between the camp and the walls of Cremona was one continued scene of blood.[1]

XXX. The town itself presented new difficulties, high walls, and towers of stone, the gates secured by iron bars, and the works well manned with troops, that showed themselves on the ramparts, in force, and brandishing their arms. The inhabitants, a large and numerous body, were all devoted to Vitellius; and the annual fair, which was then held, had drawn together a prodigious conflux from all parts of Italy. This appeared to the garrison in the nature of a reinforcement; but it was, at the same time, an accession of wealth that inflamed the ardour of the besiegers. Antonius ordered his men to advance with missive combustibles, and set fire to the pleasant villas that lay round the city, in hopes that the inhabitants, seeing their mansions destroyed, would more readily submit to a capitulation. In the houses that stood near the walls, of a height to overlook the works, he placed the bravest of his troops; and, from those stations, long rafts of timber, stones, and firebrands, were thrown in upon the garrison. The Vitellians were no longer able to maintain their post.

[1] Josephus says, that above thirty thousand of the Vitellians were put to the sword, and of Vespasian's army about four thousand five hundred.

XXXI. The legions under Antonius were now preparing for a general assault. They formed their military shell, and advanced to the works, while the rest of the army poured in a volley of stones and darts. The besieged began to despair; their spirit died away by degrees, and the men high in rank were willing to make terms for themselves. If Cremona was taken by storm, they expected no quarter. The conquerors, in that case, disdaining vulgar lives, would fall on the tribunes and centurions, from whom the largest booty was to be expected. The common men, as usual, careless about future events, and safe in indigence and obscurity, were still for making head against the enemy. They roamed about the streets in sullen obstinacy, or loitered in private houses, neither making war nor thinking of peace. The principal officers took down the name and images of Vitellius. Cæcina was still in confinement. They released him from his fetters, and desired his good offices with the conqueror. He heard their petition with disdain, swelling with pride and insolence in proportion to the meanness with which they implored his aid. The last stage of human misery! when so many brave and gallant men were obliged to sue to a traitor for protection. As a signal of submission, they hung out from the walls the sacerdotal scarfs [1] and sacred vestments. Antonius ordered a cessation of hostilities. The garrison marched out with the eagles and standards. The procession was slow and melancholy; the soldiers without their arms, dejection in their countenance, and their eyes riveted to the ground. The conquerors gathered round them, with taunts and ribaldry insulting their misfortunes, and even threatening violence to their persons. But the humility of the vanquished, and the passive temper with which they bore every indignity, without a trace remaining of their former ferocity, awakened compassion in every breast. It was now remembered, that these very men conquered at Bedriacum, and used their victory with moderation. At length Cæcina came forth in his ornamental robes, with all the pomp of a consular magistrate, the lictors preceding him, and opening a way for him through the crowd. The indignation due to a traitor broke forth at once. The soldiers treated him with every mark of contempt; they reproached him for his pride, his cruelty, and even for his treachery: so true it is, that villainy is sure to be detested by the very people who have

[1] The display of clothes and sacerdotal vestments in the act of suing for peace has been mentioned, *Hist.* i. 66.

profited by it. Antonius snatched him from the fury of the men, and soon after sent him, properly escorted, to Vespasian.

XXXII. The common people of Cremona, in the midst of so many soldiers flushed with the pride of victory, were in danger of being all put to the sword, if the general officers had not interfered to prevent the effusion of blood. Antonius called an assembly of the army. He spoke of the conquerors in magnificent terms, and of the vanquished with humanity. He mentioned Cremona with reserve and cold indifference. But the men were bent on the ruin of the colony. To their love of plunder they added an implacable aversion to the people, and various motives conspired to work the destruction of the place. In the war against Otho, the inhabitants were deemed the secret abettors of Vitellius; and afterwards, when the thirteenth legion was left among them to build an amphitheatre, the populace, in their usual strain of vulgar humour, made the soldiers an object of derision. In addition to this, the spectacle of gladiators exhibited by Cæcina was turned into a crime against the people. Their city was now for the second time the seat of war; and, in the heat of the last engagement, the Vitellians were thence supplied with refreshments; and some of their women, who had been led into the field of battle by their zeal for the cause, were slain among the ranks. But above all, the well-known opulence of the colony, increased, in that juncture, by the vast concourse attracted to the fair with their goods and merchandise, was a decisive argument for the demolition of the place. Antonius by his fame and brilliant success eclipsed all the other commanders. The attention of the men was fixed on him alone. Determined, however, to be neutral on the occasion, he retired to a bath to refresh himself after the fatigue of the day. Finding the water not sufficiently warm, he said in a careless manner, "It will be hot enough in a little time." That trifling expression, dropt by accident amongst his slaves, was afterwards caught up, and propagated to his prejudice, as if it were the intended signal for setting fire to Cremona. At that moment the city was in a blaze.

XXXIII. Forty thousand men had entered sword in hand. The number of slaves and mean attendants of the camp was still greater, all bent on mischief, and more inclined to acts of barbarity than even the soldiers. Neither sex, nor age, nor dignity of rank, was spared. A scene of blood was laid, and amidst the horrors of a general massacre, lust and violation triumphed. Old men and ancient matrons, who had no wealth to satisfy avarice, were dragged forth with scorn, and butchered with derision. The young and comely of either sex were sure to suffer the brutal passions of abandoned men, or to be torn piecemeal in the struggle for the possession of their persons. In those conflicts the contending rivals, in the rage of disappointed lust, turned their swords against each other. The men, who were seen carrying off the wealth of houses, or massy gold from the temples, were attacked and butchered by others as rapacious as themselves. Not content with the treasures that lay open to their view, they put several to the rack, in order to extort a confession of concealed riches. The ground was dug up, to gratify the rage of avarice. Numbers carried flaming torches, and, as soon as they had brought forth their booty, made it their sport to set the houses and temples on fire. In so vast a multitude, as dissonant in their language as their manners, composed of Roman citizens, allies, and foreign auxiliaries, all the fell passions of mankind were crowded together. Each soldier had his peculiar notions of right and wrong; and what one scrupled, another dared to execute. Nothing was unlawful, nothing sacred. Four days were spent in the destruction of this unfortunate city. Things profane and holy perished in the flames. The temple of Mephitis,[1] which stood on the outside of the walls, was the only structure left entire. It was saved by its situation, or perhaps, by the goddess to whom it was dedicated.

XXXIV. Such was the fate of Cremona, two hundred and eighty-six years from its foundation. The first stone was laid during the consulship of Tiberius Sempronius and Publius Cornelius, at the time when Hannibal threatened an irruption into Italy. The design was to have a frontier town, to bridle the Gauls inhabiting beyond the Po, or any power on the other side of the Alps. The colony, from that time, grew into celebrity; their numbers multiplied, and their wealth increased; the country round was intersected with rivers; the soil was fertile, and by intermarriages the inhabitants formed alliances with the neighbouring towns of Italy. The city continued to flourish in the worst of times, safe from foreign enemies, till ruined at last by the rage of civil war. Antonius felt that the whole disgrace of this horrible transac-

[1] Mephitis was the goddess worshipped in all places that sent forth noxious exhalations. Hence we read in Virgil,

"——Sævamque exhalat opaca Mephitim."

tion pressed hard upon himself. To soften resentment, he issued an edict, forbidding all manner of persons to detain the citizens of Cremona as prisoners of war. At the same time, all Italy entered into a resolution not to purchase the captives taken on that melancholy occasion. The soldiers, finding that their prey was rendered useless, began to murder the wretches whom they could not sell. This barbarity, however, was checked as soon as known. The prisoners were ransomed by their friends and relations. The survivors in a short time returned to Cremona. The temples and public places were rebuilt, at the recommendation of Vespasian, by munificence of the colony.

XXXV. A city buried in its own ruins, the country round polluted with gore, and the air infected by the exhalation of putrid bodies, afforded no place where the army could remain. They encamped at the distance of three miles. The Vitellian soldiers, who in their panic had fled different ways, were brought back, as fast as they were found, and once more enrolled in their proper companies; and, lest the legions to which they belonged should meditate hostile designs, they were sent into Illyricum, and there stationed, at a distance from the seat of war. To spread the fame of Vespasian's arms, messengers were despatched into Britain and both the Spains. Julius Calenus, one of the tribunes, was sent into Gaul, and Alpinus Montanus, the prefect of a cohort, into Germany. The former was by birth an Æduan, and the latter a native of Treves, both warmly attached to Vitellius, and for that reason chosen, with an air of triumph, to bear the news of his defeat. Care was also taken to secure by a chain of posts the passes over the Alps, to prevent an irruption from Germany, supposed, at that time, to be in arms in favour of the vanquished party.

XXXVI. Vitellius, in a few days after Cæcina set out from Rome, prevailed on Fabius Valens to take upon him the conduct of the war. From that moment he gave himself up to his usual gratifications, in wine and gluttony losing all sense of danger. He made no preparation for the field, and showed no attention to the soldiers. He neither reviewed, nor exercised, nor harangued them: never once appeared before the people. Hid in the recesses of his gardens, he indulged his appetite, forgetting the past, the present, and all solicitude about future events; like those nauseous animals that know no care, and, while they are supplied with food, remain in one spot, torpid and insensible. In this state of stupidity he passed his time in the grove of Aricia,[1] when the treachery of Lucilius Bassus, and the revolt of the fleet at Ravenna, roused him from his lethargy. In a short time after arrived other despatches, by which he learned, with mixed emotions of grief and joy, the perfidy of Cæcina, and his imprisonment by the soldiers. In a mind like his, incapable of reflection, joy prevailed over every other passion, and absorbed all ideas of danger. He returned to Rome in the highest exultation; and having extolled, before an assembly of the people, the zeal and ardour of the army, he ordered Publius Sabinus, the prefect of the prætorian guards, and the intimate friend of Cæcina, to be taken into custody. Alphenus Varus succeeded to the command.

XXXVII. Vitellius went next to the senate, and, in a speech of prepared eloquence, talked highly of the posture of affairs. The fathers answered him in a strain of flattery. The case of Cæcina was brought into debate by Lucius Vitellius. He moved that immediate judgment should be pronounced against him. The rest of the senate concurred; and, with well-acted indignation, launched out against the complicated perfidy of a man, who in the character of consul abandoned the commonwealth, as a general officer betrayed his prince, and, as a friend loaded with honours, gave an example of base ingratitude. In this specious manner they affected to lament the lot of Vitellius, but, in fact, felt only for themselves and the commonwealth. Through the whole debate, not a word was uttered against the leaders of Vespasian's party; the revolt of the several armies was called, in qualifying terms, an error in judgment; and, with studied circuity, the name of Vespasian was wholly avoided. They alluded to him, they hesitated, and yet passed him by in silence. To complete the consulship of Cæcina, one day remained. To fill that little interval, a man was found willing to be invested with the short-lived pageantry; and accordingly, on the day preceding the calends of November, Rosius Regulus entered on the office, and on the same day finished his career. The public saw with derision a farce of state altogether ridiculous, as well on the part of the prince who granted the mock dignity, as on that of the sycophant who had the pitiful ambition to accept it. It was observed by men versed in the history of their country, that no instance had ever occurred of a new consul, before the office was declared vacant in due

[1] In Latium.

course of law. Caninius Rebulus, it is true, had been the consul of a day;[1] but that was in the time of Julius Cæsar, when that emperor, in haste to reward his friends for their services in the civil wars, thought fit, by an act of power, to shorten the duration of the consulship.

XXXVIII. The death of Junius Blæsus became at this time publicly known, and engrossed the conversation of all ranks of men. The particulars of this tragic event, as far as they have come to my knowledge, are as follows: It happened that Vitellius, confined by illness in the gardens of Servilius, saw, in the night-time, a tower in the neighbourhood gaily illuminated. He desired to know the reason of that splendid appearance, and was told, that Cæcina Tuscus gave a grand entertainment to a party of his friends, amongst whom Junius Blæsus was the most distinguished. The sumptuous preparations, and the mirth of the company, were described with every circumstance of exaggeration. The creatures of the court did not fail to impute it as a crime to Tuscus and his guests, that they chose their time for revelling in an unseasonable juncture, when the prince was indisposed. Their malice chiefly glanced at Blæsus. The men who made it their business to pry into the secret thoughts of the emperor, soon perceived that they had infused their venom with success, and that the ruin of Blæsus might be easily accomplished. To make sure of their blow, they applied to Lucius Vitellius, who readily undertook to manage the accusation. Being himself stained with every vice, and for his life and morals universally decried, he saw with envy the fair reputation and the popular esteem that attended Blæsus. With this jealousy rankling in his heart, he clasped the emperor's infant son in his arms, and, entering the prince's chamber, went down on his knees. Vitellius asked him, Why that sudden alarm? "It is not for myself," replied the brother, "that I am thus distressed: it is for you I shed these tears; for you and your children I come to offer up my prayers and supplications. From Vespasian we have nothing to fear: the German legions are in arms to hinder his approach; the provinces declare against him, and vast tracts of sea and land detain him at a distance from the seat of war. The enemy to be dreaded is near at hand; he is in the city of Rome; he is even now lurking in your bosom. Proud of his descent from Mark Antony and the

[1] The consulship, in the time of the republic, was an annual office; but Julius Cæsar, in haste to reward his friends, shortened the duration of the office, and advanced several to that dignity within the year.

Junian family, he affects to be connected with the imperial line, and, by caresses and a style of magnificence, endeavours to conciliate to himself the affections of the soldiers. Upon this man all eyes are fixed. Vitellius, in the meantime, passes away his hours in unsuspecting security, neglecting at once his enemies and his friends; he cherishes in his bosom a treacherous rival, who from the banqueting-table, and his scene of midnight revelry, beheld with joy the languid condition of his sovereign. But for joy and riot let him be repaid with vengeance, and a night of mourning; let him know that Vitellius lives; that he is master of the Roman world, and, whenever the lot of humanity shall call him hence, that he has a son to follow in the order of succession."

XXXIX. Vitellius balanced, for some time, between the horror of the deed proposed and his apprehensions for himself. By deferring the fate of Blæsus he might accelerate his own ruin, and to give public orders for his execution were a dangerous expedient. A measure so bold and open would excite the indignation of the people. To despatch him by poison seemed to be the safest method. That he was guilty of that execrable villainy, the visit which he paid to Blæsus leaves no room to doubt. He was seen transported with savage joy, and was heard to say, "I have feasted my eyes with the pangs of an expiring enemy." Those were his words. The character of Blæsus was without a blemish. To the dignity of his birth, and the elegance of his manners, he united the strictest honour, and unshaken fidelity to the emperor. While Vitellius was still flourishing in prosperity, Cæcina, and other chiefs of the party, endeavoured to draw him into a league with themselves: but he was proof against all temptation; firm, upright, void of ambition. He sought no sudden honours, and to a mind like his the imperial dignity had no allurement. And yet his modesty threw such a lustre round his virtues, that he narrowly escaped being deemed worthy of the succession.

XL. During these transactions, Fabius Valens, with a number of concubines and eunuchs in his train, proceeded by slow and tedious marches, unlike a general going to a great and important war. On the road he received intelligence of the treachery of Lucilius Bassus, and the defection of the fleet at Ravenna. Had he then pushed on with vigour, he might have joined Cæcina, who was still wavering and undecided; at the worst, he might have put himself at the head of the legions before they came to a decisive action.

His friends were of opinion, that, with a few faithful attendants, avoiding the road that led to Ravenna, he ought to proceed with expedition, through private ways, to Hostilia or Cremona. Others pressed him to bring into the field the prætorian bands from Rome, and force his way to the Vitellian army. But the time was lost in fruitless deliberation. The posture of affairs called for vigour, and Valens remained irresolute and inactive. In the end, rejecting all advice, he chose the middle course, in pressing exigencies always the most pernicious. He neither acted with the courage nor the prudence of an able general.

XLI. He sent despatches to Vitellius for a reinforcement, and was soon after joined by three cohorts and a squadron of horse from Britain; a number too great to steal a march, and too weak to open a passage through an enemy's country. Even in this arduous juncture, amidst the dangers that pressed on every side, Valens was not to be weaned from his favourite vices. Riot, lust, and adultery, marked his way. He had power and money; and, even in his ruin, his libidinous passions did not desert him. He was no sooner joined by the foot and cavalry sent by Vitellius, than he saw, too late, the folly of his measures. With his whole force, supposing the men true to Vitellius, he could not hope to penetrate through the adverse army; much less could he expect it, when their fidelity was already suspected. Shame, and respect for their general, still left some impression on the minds of the men; but those were feeble restraints, when the love of enterprise was the ruling passion, and all principle was extinguished. Valens felt the difficulty of his situation. Having ordered the cohorts to march forward to Ariminum, and the cavalry to follow in the rear, he himself, with a few adherents whom adversity had not yet seduced, directed his course towards Umbria, and thence to Etruria, where he first heard of the defeat at Cremona. In that disastrous moment he conceived a bold design, in its extent vast and magnificent, and, had it been carried into execution, big with fatal consequences. He proposed to seize the ships on the coast, and bear away to Narbon Gaul, in order to land somewhere in that country, and rouse the provinces of Gaul, with the armies stationed there, and the various German nations. The project was worthy of a great officer, and, by its consequences, must have involved the world in a new war.

XLII. The departure of Valens threw the garrison of Ariminum into consternation. Cornelius Fuscus advanced, at the head of his army, to lay siege to the place, and, having ordered the fleet to sail round the coast, invested it by sea and land. His forces spread themselves over the plains of Umbria, and stretched into the territory of Picenum as far as the Adriatic Gulf. Italy was now divided between Vespasian and Vitellius by the Apennine mountains. Valens embarked at the port of Pisa, but being becalmed, or meeting with contrary winds, was forced to land at Monaco. Marius Maturus, the governor of the maritime Alps, was then in the neighbourhood; a man attached to Vitellius, and, though the country round espoused the opposite interest, still firm in his duty. This officer received Valens with open arms; but the design of making an attempt on the coast of Narbon Gaul appeared to him rash and impracticable. By his advice the project was laid aside. The few followers, who had hitherto adhered to Valens, began to think of shifting for themselves. They saw the adjacent cities going over to Valerius Paulinus, who commanded in the neighbourhood; an officer of distinguished merit, and, long before the war broke out, devoted to Vespasian. Under his influence the people declared for the new emperor.

XLIII. Paulinus was master of Forojulium, a place of importance, that gave him the command of those seas. He had there stationed a garrison, consisting of men disbanded by Vitellius, and therefore willing to take up arms against him. Paulinus was a native of the colony, and had, by consequence, great weight with his countrymen. He had also been a tribune of the prætorian guards, and was held in high esteem by the soldiers of that description. The people were willing to second the views of their fellow-citizen, and the hope of future advantages from his elevation was a spur to their zeal. In this posture of affairs, while everything was swelled by the voice of fame to greater magnitude, Valens saw the spirit of the Vitellian party depressed and broken. To return to his ships was now his only refuge. He took with him four prætorians, three faithful friends, and as many centurions. With those attendants he once more embarked, leaving Maturus, and such as were willing to submit to Vespasian, to pursue their own inclination. As to himself, the open sea was the safest place: on shore he saw no security, and in the adjacent cities no prospect of relief. Without a resource left, and rather seeing what was to be avoided than what he ought to pursue, he put to sea, and was thrown by adverse winds on the islands called the Stæchades, near Marseilles. Paulinus, without loss of time, sent out his light-armed galleys, and Valens was taken prisoner.

XLIV. The Vitellian general being now in the hands of the enemy, the whole force of the empire was transferred to Vespasian. In Spain, the first legion, called ADJUTRIX, still respecting the memory of Otho, and by consequence hostile to Vitellius, gave an example of revolt to the rest of the army. The tenth and sixth legions followed. The provinces of Gaul acceded without hesitation. In Britain the same spirit prevailed. During the reign of Claudius, Vespasian headed the second legion; and the men, still remembering the heroic ardour with which he led them on to victory, were soon decided in his favour. They met, however, some opposition from the other legions, in which a considerable number of centurions and soldiers, who had been promoted by Vitellius, were unwilling to desert a prince to whom they felt themselves bound by ties of gratitude. It was with reluctance that they were brought to acknowledge a new master.

XLV. Encouraged by the dissension among the legions, and also by the civil wars that distracted the empire, the Britons renewed their ancient animosity. Venusius headed the malcontents. To his own natural ferocity that chieftain added a rooted antipathy to the Roman name. He was, besides, the avowed enemy of Cartismandua,[1] queen of the Brigantes; a woman of high descent, and flourishing in all the splendour of wealth and power. In the reign of Claudius, she had treacherously delivered up Caractacus, to swell the pomp of that emperor's triumph. From that time riches flowed in upon her; but riches drew after them their usual appendages, luxury and dissipation. She banished from her presence Venusius her husband, and raised Vellocatus, his armour-bearer, to her throne and bed. By that criminal act she lost all authority. Convulsions shook her kingdom. The discarded husband had the people on his side, while the adulterer had nothing to protect him but the libidinous passions of the queen, and the cruelty of her reign. Venusius was in a short time at the head of a powerful army. The subjects of the queen flocked to his standard, and a body of auxiliaries joined him. Cartismandua was reduced to the last extremity. She invoked the protection of the Romans, who sent some cohorts and squadrons of horse to her relief. Several battles ensued, with various success. The queen,

[1] For Caractacus, and Cartismandua, queen of the Brigantes, see *Annals*, xii. 32-36.

however, was rescued from impending danger, though she lost her kingdom. Venusius wrested the sceptre out of her hands, and the Romans were involved in a war.

XLVI. About the same time, Germany was up in arms. The seditious spirit of the legions, and the sluggish inactivity of the commanders, encouraged the Barbarians to invade the Roman frontiers. By the treachery of the states in alliance, and the strength of the enemy, the interest of the empire was brought to the brink of ruin. Of this war, and the causes that produced it, with the various events that followed, I shall hereafter give a regular account: it would lead at present to a long digression. Commotions, about the same time, broke out in Dacia. Fidelity never was the character of that nation; and, since the legions were withdrawn from Mæsia, there remained no force to hold the people in subjection. They had the policy, however, to watch in silence the first movements of civil discord among the Romans. Seeing, at length, that Italy was in a blaze, they seized their opportunity, and stormed the winter quarters of the cohorts and the cavalry. Having made themselves masters of both banks of the Danube, they were preparing to raze to the ground the camp of the legions, when Mucianus, apprised of the victory at Cremona, sent the sixth legion to check the incursions of the enemy. The good fortune that had often favoured the Roman arms, brought Mucianus in the moment of distress, with the forces of the east, to quell the insurrection, before the people of that country, backed by the German nations, could make an irruption into Italy. In that juncture, Fonteius Agrippa arrived from Asia, where he had governed for a year with proconsular authority, and was now appointed to command in Mæsia. He undertook the charge, at the head of an army composed of Vitellian soldiers, whom it was then the policy to disperse through the provinces, and employ their arms against the foreign enemies of the empire.

XLVII. The rest of the provinces were by no means free from commotion. A man who had been originally a slave, and afterwards commanded a royal fleet, kindled the flame of war in Pontus, and drew together a body of men in arms. His name was Anicetus, the freedman and favourite minister of Polemon, high in power while that monarchy lasted, but now enraged to see the kingdom turned into a Roman province. In the name of Vitellius he roused the nations bordering on the Pontic sea. The hope of plunder attracted to his standard all the freebooters of the country. Finding himself in a short time at the head of a force not to be despised, he attacked and carried by assault the city of Trapezund,[1] founded in ancient times by a colony from Greece, at the extremity of the Pontic sea. An entire cohort, formerly a royal garrison, was put to the sword. The men had received the privilege of Roman citizens,[2] and, from that time, used the arms and banners of Rome, still retaining their native indolence, and the dissolute manners of the Greeks. This adventurer, after his first exploit, set fire to Vespasian's fleet, and put out to sea safe from pursuit, as the best of the light galleys, by order of Mucianus, were stationed at Byzantium. Encouraged by his example, the Barbarians on the coast began a piratical war. They roamed about in boats of a particular structure, the sides broad at the bottom, and growing narrow by degrees, in the form of a curve, and neither bound with hoops of iron nor of brass. In a tempestuous sea, they raise the sides with additional planks in proportion to the swell of the waves, till the vessel is covered over with an arched roof, and thence is called the floating CAMERA.[3] At either end they have a sharp-pointed prow; their oars are readily shifted to work backward or forward, moving with facility in either direction, and thus their mariners advance or retreat with ease and security.

XLVIII. Vespasian thought it of moment to chase this band of pirates from the seas, and, for this purpose, sent a detachment of the legions under the command of Virdius Geminus, an officer of known experience. He came up with the Barbarians as they were roaming on the shore in quest of prey, and forced them to fly with precipitation to their boats. Having, in a short time after, constructed a number of galleys fit for the service, he gave chase to Anicetus, and drove him up the mouth of the river Cohibus; a station where the freebooter thought himself safe under the protection of the king of the Sedochezan nation. By money and various presents he had purchased the friendship of that prince, and for a short time enjoyed the advantage of his alliance. The king threatened to take up arms in his defence; but finding that he was to choose between bribery or an impending war, he preferred his interest, and, with the usual treachery of the

[1] Now *Trebizond*.

[2] By granting the freedom of the city, the Romans drew distant colonies into a close alliance.

[3] These canoes were so light, that the Barbarians could carry them on their shoulders, and traverse woods and forests without being fatigued with their load.

Barbarians, having struck a bargain for the life of his friend, surrendered the whole party to the Romans. In this manner ended the servile war.

The issue of this piratical war gave the highest satisfaction to Vespasian; and to fill the measure of his joy, an account of the victory at Cremona reached him in Egypt. Without loss of time, he set out for Alexandria, with intent, since Vitellius could no longer keep the field, to reduce the people of Rome by famine; a project easily accomplished, as that city, for its subsistence, always depends on foreign supplies. It was also part of his plan to secure the coast of Africa both by land and sea, little doubting, when all resources were cut off, he should involve the Vitellian party in all the miseries of want, and, by consequence, in dissensions among themselves.

XLIX. While things in every quarter of the world tended with rapidity to a revolution, and the imperial dignity was passing into the hands of a new sovereign, Antonius, flushed with his success at Cremona, no longer preserved the moderation that marked his conduct before that important event. The war he thought so far decided, that everything would be speedily settled; or, perhaps, the sunshine of prosperity called forth the seeds of pride, of avarice, and the other vices of his nature. He considered Italy as a conquered country; he caressed the soldiers, as if he intended to secure them to himself; by his words and actions he seemed resolved to establish his own power; he encouraged the licentious spirit of the army, and left to the legions the nomination of centurions to fill the vacant posts of such as were slain in battle. The consequence was, that the most bold and turbulent were chosen, and discipline went to ruin. The officers lost all authority, and the soldiers commanded. The army being wholly corrupted by these popular but seditious arts, Antonius thought he might safely give the reins to his avarice, and began by public rapine to enrich himself. The approach of Mucianus was no restraint, though to incur the displeasure of that commander was more dangerous than to offend Vespasian himself.

L. The winter being now at hand, and the country laid under water by the overflowing of the Po, the army was obliged to march lightly equipped. The eagles and banners of the victorious legions, with the old, the wounded, and even numbers in full vigour, were left at Verona. The cohorts and cavalry, with a select detachment from the legions, were thought sufficient against the enemy already vanquished.

The eleventh legion, at first unwilling to enter into the war, but since the turn of affairs regretting that they had no share in the victory, had lately joined the army, accompanied by six thousand Dalmatians, newly levied. The whole body was, in appearance, led by Poppæus Silvanus, a man of consular rank: but, in fact, Annius Bassus governed their motions by his skill and advice. Silvanus had no military talents; in the moment that called for enterprise, he was more inclined to waste the time in words than to act with vigour. Bassus assisted him with his best counsels, appearing to obey, but in truth commanding. To this body of forces was added the flower of the marines from the fleet at Ravenna, who had desired to be considered as legionary soldiers. The fleet, in the meantime, was manned by the Dalmatians. The army proceeded as far as the temple of Fortune,[1] and there made halt by order of the chiefs, who had not yet settled their plan of operations. They had received intelligence that the prætorian cohorts were on their march from Rome, and the passes over the Apennine were supposed to be in the possession of the enemy. In a country laid waste by war, they dreaded the danger of wanting provisions; and the clamours of the soldiers demanding the donative, by the army called CLAVARIUM,[2] were loud, and tending to sedition. The generals had no money in their military chest; and their provisions were exhausted by the rapacity of the soldiers who seized the stores, which ought to have been distributed with frugal management.

LI. A fact extraordinary in its nature, and yet vouched by writers of good authority, will serve to show how little of moral rectitude and natural sentiment remained in the minds of the victorious army. A common soldier belonging to the cavalry averred that, in the late engagement, he killed his brother, and for that deed of horror he had the hardiness to demand a recompense. The laws of nature would not allow the superior officers to reward an action that shocked humanity; and to punish it was inconsistent with the policy of war. Under a plausible pretence of not being able, in that juncture, to proportion their bounty to the extent of the merit, they adjourned the business, and thought of it no more. In former civil wars, we have upon record a similar tragic incident, but with a different issue. In the battle with Cinna at Janiculum,[1] a

[1] *Fanum Fortunæ*, now *Fano.*

[2] *Clavarium* was a donative granted to the soldiers to enable them to purchase nails for their shoes. In like manner the donative for shoes was called *Calcearium.*

[3] *Janiculum*, a hill at Rome, but not one of the seven.

man of Pompey's party (as Sisenna relates the story) slew his brother, and soon after, finding his mistake, despatched himself; so true it is, that in ancient times men not only had a quick sense of glory, but also felt a just abhorrence of evil deeds. For the insertion of this anecdote no apology will be deemed necessary: on the contrary, it may be proper to revive the memory of past transactions, in order, whenever the occasion requires it, to exhibit a bright example of eminent virtue, or to soothe the mind under the pressure of recent calamity.

LII. Antonius, in concert with the principal officers, judged it prudent to send forward the cavalry, with orders to explore, in some part of the Umbria, a place of moderate acclivity over the Apennine mountains. In the meantime, the troops left behind at Verona were ordered to advance with the eagles and standards. Measures were also taken to procure a supply of provisions by sea, and also by the navigation of the Po. But delay was what some of the chiefs had much at heart. They knew the pride and growing ambition of Antonius, and thought it more for their interest to curry favour with Mucianus, who saw with a jealous eye the rapid success with which Antonius pushed on his conquest. If the general of the east did not arrive in time to enter Rome with the victorious army, it was evident that the whole glory of the war would fall to the lot of others. His letters to Varus and Antonius were dark, ambiguous, and contradictory; sometimes recommending despatch, and afterwards stating the advantages of caution and dilatory measures. By this duplicity he hoped to assume the merit of whatever succeeded, and, if any misfortune happened, to throw the blame on others. With his intimate friends, and in particular with Plotius Griphus, lately raised by Vespasian to the rank of senator, and the command of a legion, his correspondence was more open and direct. The answers which he received were in a style agreeable to his wishes, full of compliments to himself, and malignant reflections on the rashness of Varus and Antonius. These letters Mucianus took care to forward to Vespasian. The impression which they made was unfavourable to Antonius, who knew the value of his services, and yet found himself supplanted in the opinion of the future emperor.

LIII. Antonius, with the spirit of an injured man, complained of the insidious arts with which Mucianus undermined his character. Above disguising his passions, and scorning to temporise, he spoke his mind with freedom. His letters to Vespasian were in a tone more lofty than is usually addressed to princes. He talked of himself with an air of confidence, and with asperity of Mucianus, the assassin of his reputation. "It was by Antonius that the legions in Pannonia were excited to a revolt; by him the leaders in Mæsia were inspired with courage; by him the Alps were forced, Italy was subdued, and by him all succours from Germany and Rhætia were entirely cut off. By him the cavalry was led on to attack the legions of Vitellius, in the moment of disunion among themselves; and the complete victory obtained by the infantry, after an obstinate engagement that lasted night and day, was an exploit of which envy itself could not deny him the merit. The destruction of Cremona was a calamity incident to the rage of civil war; and yet that calamity, dreadful as it was, could not be compared to the disasters of former times, when the republic saw her cities razed to the ground, and the land deluged with blood. In the war which he had conducted, his sword, and not his pen, was the weapon which he employed. Instead of writing secret despatches, he sought the enemy in the field. Nor did he mean to detract from those who commanded in Asia: they had the mighty glory of preserving tranquillity in the distant territory of Mæsia, while he routed the Vitellian armies, and made himself master of Italy. Spain and Gaul, the two bulwarks of the empire, were by his influence drawn over to Vespasian. But his best efforts had been in vain exerted, if his laurels, so dearly earned, were to be transferred to men, who neither shared in the victory nor the danger." These remonstrances did not remain a secret to Mucianus. The consequence was, a deadly feud between the two commanders; on the part of Antonius, carried on with open and avowed hostility; on that of Mucianus, with close disguise, and, for that reason, the more implacable.

LIV. Vitellius, after the overthrow of his army at Cremona, thought it good policy to suppress the news. By that shallow artifice, he made everything worse. Dissimulation could only postpone the remedy, but not ward off the consequences of that dreadful defeat. Had the event been fairly told, a council might have been called, and there were resources still in reserve. In the midst of ruin, he pretended to be in a flourishing condition, and by that fallacy was undone. The war was not so much as mentioned in his presence. The citizens of Rome were forbid to talk of the news of the day, and for that reason they talked the more. Since liberty of speech was no longer allowed, instead of the plain truth they gave out fictitious accounts, and, because they were restrained, took their revenge by making everything worse. The chiefs of the adverse party omitted nothing that could extend the fame of their victory. The spies that fell into their hands were industriously led round the camp, and, after seeing the strength and spirit of the conquerors, dismissed to make their report at Rome. Vitellius examined them in private, and, that nothing might transpire, ordered them to be put to death. A singular proof of fidelity and generous courage was, at this time, given by a centurion; his name Julius Agrestis. This man, in several interviews with Vitellius, tried in vain to rouse his master to a spirit of enterprise. All he could obtain was leave to go in person to view the strength of the enemy, and see the real condition of Cremona. Scorning to approach Antonius in the character of a spy, he avowed the emperor's orders, and his own resolution. A guard was appointed to conduct him. He was led to the field of battle; he surveyed the ruins of Cremona, and saw the legions that had laid down their arms.

With that intelligence he returned to Vitellius. The emperor, deaf to the voice of truth, and unwilling to be convinced, charged the centurion with treachery and corruption. "I perceive," said Agrestis, "that some great and signal proof is necessary; and, since neither my life nor death can now be of any use, I will give you that evidence which cannot deceive." He retired, and fell on his sword. According to some historians, he was slain by order of Vitellius. Be that as it may, the fidelity of the generous centurion deserves to be transmitted to posterity.

LV. At length Vitellius was roused from his state of stupefaction. He ordered Julius Priscus and Alphenus Varus, at the head of fourteen prætorian cohorts, and the whole of the cavalry, to take possession of the Apennine mountains. A legion of marines was sent after them. A force so considerable, consisting of several thousand horse and foot, under any other general, would have been sufficient not only to withstand the enemy, but even to wage an offensive war. The cohorts that remained for the defence of the city, were put under the command of Lucius Vitellius, the emperor's brother. The emperor, in the meantime, abated nothing from his habitual luxury. He began, however, with a precipitation that sprang from fear, to grant away whatever the state had to bestow. He hurried on the election of public magistrates, and appointed a succession of consuls for several years; he concluded treaties with the allies of Rome; he invested foreign cities with the privileges of Latium: he granted to some nations an exemption from all kinds of tribute, and to others immunities unheard of before; regardless of posterity, and, in all events, determined to exhaust the commonwealth. The populace applauded the liberality of the emperor. Some were weak enough to purchase favours, which, it was evident, could not last; while men of reflection saw, that lavish grants, which could neither be made nor accepted without distressing the public, must be declared null and void. At length Vitellius, urged by the importunity of the army, which lay encamped at Mevania,[1] marched out of the city, attended by a numerous train of senators, all following with different motives; some to pay their court, and the greater part afraid of giving jealousy to a prince who joined his army without any settled plan, in himself no resource, no decision, the ready dupe of every treacherous adviser.

LVI. Having reached the camp, Vitellius called an assembly of the soldiers. During his speech, a wonderful phenomenon engaged the attention of all. A flight of ill-omened birds hovered over his head, forming a cloud that obscured the day. This was followed by another prognostic of an alarming nature. A bull broke loose from the altar, and, trampling under foot all the preparations for the sacrifice, fled to a distant place, and there, on a spot where victims were never slain, was felled to the ground. But Vitellius, in his own person, presented a sight that exceeded every prodigy: a chief void of military knowledge, without judgment to plan, or courage to execute. He had not skill enough to explore the motions of the enemy, and to the art of avoiding or bringing on a general engagement he was an utter stranger. Every incident betrayed his ignorance or his pusillanimity. When messengers arrived, he turned pale, faltered in his gait, asked questions, trembled, and returned to his bottle. Weary at length of the camp, and terrified by the revolt of the fleet at Misenum, he went back to Rome, alarmed at every new event, yet never looking forward to the issue of the war. All opportunities were utterly lost by his folly. The true and obvious measure would have been, to pass over the Apennine with his whole force, and seek an enemy distressed by the rigour of the winter season and a dearth of provisions. Instead of this, Vitellius suffered his army to be dispersed in different places, and, by that conduct, gave to the slaughtering sword a set of brave and gallant soldiers, whose valour and fidelity nothing

[1] In Umbria.

could shake. The centurions saw the blunder, and the best amongst them, had they been consulted, were ready with honest advice. But the creatures of the court banished every faithful counsellor. The ear of Vitellius was open to flattery only: useful advice was harsh and grating; and nothing was welcome but what soothed his passions, while it led to sure destruction.

LVII. The revolt of the fleet at Misenum was occasioned altogether by the fraud of Claudius Faventinus; so much in civil commotions depends on the boldness of a single traitor. This man had been a centurion under Galba, and was by that emperor cashiered with ignominy. To seduce the men to his purposes, he forged letters from Vespasian, promising ample rewards to such as went over to his party. Claudius Apollinaris was, at that time, commander of the fleet; a man inclined to treachery, but wanting resolution to be forward in guilt. It happened that Apinius Tiro, who had discharged the office of prætor, was then at Minturnæ. He placed himself at the head of the revolters, and drew the neighbouring colonies and municipal towns into the confederacy. The inhabitants of Puteoli[1] declared with alacrity for Vespasian, while Capua, with equal vehemence, adhered to Vitellius. Those two cities had been long at variance, and now mingled with the rage of civil war all the rancour of their private animosities. In order to bring the revolters back to their duty, Vitellius fixed on Claudius Julianus, who had been prefect of the fleet at Misenum, and had the character of being mild in the exercise of his authority. He set out from Rome at the head of a city cohort, and a band of gladiators, over whom he had been, before that time, appointed commanding officer. He was no sooner in sight of the rebel camp, than he went over to Vespasian. The two parties, with their combined force, took possession of Tarracina, a city strong both by nature and art. In that place the revolters were more indebted for their security to the strength of the works, than to their own military talents.

LVIII. Vitellius, having received intelligence of these transactions, ordered part of his army to take post at Narnia, under the command of the prætorian prefects, while his brother Lucius Vitellius, at the head of six cohorts and five hundred horse, marched into Campania, to check the progress of the revolt. He himself, in the meantime, sunk into a state

[1] Now *Pozzuolo.*

of languor, overwhelmed with despair and melancholy, till the generous ardour of the soldiers and the clamours of the populace demanding to be armed, revived his drooping spirits. He flattered himself, that a turbulent multitude, bold in words, but without spirit in action, would be equal to the regular legions. To a mere mob he gave the name of an army. His freedmen were his only advisers. In such as professed to be his friends, he reposed no confidence. The truth is, all of that class, the higher they stood in rank, were the more ready to betray. By the advice of his servile counsellors, he ordered the people to be assembled in their tribes.[1] As they came forward to enrol their names, he received the oath of fidelity; but the crowd pressing too thick upon him, he grew weary of the task, and left the business of completing the new levy to the two consuls. The senators were required to bring in a quantity of silver, and a certain number of slaves. The Roman knights made a voluntary offer to serve with their lives and fortunes. The freedmen, in a body, desired to be admitted to the same honour. This humour continued, till what at first proceeded from servility and fear, grew serious in the end, and became real ardour. The greater part, notwithstanding, felt no affection for the prince; indifferent about the man, they grieved to see the humiliating condition to which the empire was reduced. Vitellius, on his part, omitted nothing that could conciliate the public favour. He appeared with a dejected air: he spoke in a pathetic tone; he tried the force of tears; he made ample promises, lavish of words, and, as is usually the case with men in distress, generous beyond all bounds. He now desired to assume the title of Cæsar. His superstitious veneration for a name, in which he thought there was something sacred, made him willing to accept what he had often rejected. The public clamour was an additional motive. The populace thought it proper, and, in cases of extreme danger, the voice of the rabble is equal to the wisest counsels. But the spirit, which at the flood was violent, soon began to ebb away. The senators and knights fell off by degrees, at first, in the absence of the prince, watching their opportunity with care and caution; but, in the end, not even managing appearances, with open and avowed indifference. Vitellius gave up his cause for lost. He saw that the prince demands in vain, when the people are no longer willing to comply.

[1] The people of Rome were divided into five-and-thirty tribes.

LIX. By taking possession of Mevania, Vitellius had struck all Italy with terror. The war seemed to revive with redoubled vigour, but, by his dastardly flight from the camp, he lost every advantage. Vespasian's interest gained additional strength. The people, throughout the country, went over to his party with uncommon ardour. The Samnites, the Pelignians, and the Marsians, saw, with regret, the prompt alacrity with which the inhabitants of Campania had taken the lead in the revolt; and, to atone for their own remissness, declared for Vespasian with all the vehemence which a new passion inspires. Meanwhile, the army, in passing over the Apennine, suffered every extremity from the rigour of the winter. The difficulty with which, though unmolested by the enemy, they laboured through a waste of snow, plainly shows the dangers that surrounded them, if fortune, no less propitious to Vespasian than the wisdom of his counsels, had not drawn Vitellius from his post. During the march over the mountains, Petilius Cerealis, in the disguise of a common peasant, presented himself to the general. Being well acquainted with the course of the country, he had been able to elude the pursuit of the Vitellians. As he had the honour of being allied to Vespasian, and was besides an officer of distinguished merit, he was not only well received, but ranked with the commanders-in-chief. The writers of that day inform us, that Flavius Sabinus, and Domitian, had it in their power to escape out of Rome. Antonius, it is said, by his emissaries, invited them to a place of safety; but Sabinus declined the offer, alleging his ill state of health, and his want of vigour for so bold an enterprise. Domitian was not deficient either in spirit or inclination. Even the guards appointed by Vitellius to watch his motions, offered to join his flight; but he suspected an underhand design to draw him into a snare, and, for that reason, made no attempt. His fear, however, was ill founded. Vitellius felt a tender regard for his own family, and on their account meditated nothing against the life of Domitian.

LX. The army pursued their march as far as Carsulæ. At that place the generals thought fit to halt for some days, as well to rest the troops, as to wait the arrival of the eagles and standards of the legions. The situation afforded a pleasant spot for their camp, with an open champaign country on every side, abounding with plenty, and behind them a number of opulent and flourishing cities. Being then not more than ten miles distant from the Vitellian forces, they hoped, by intrigue and secret negotiation, to induce the whole party to lay down their arms. But the soldiers were impatient of delay. They wished to end the war by victory, not by compromise. They desired to be led against the enemy, before the arrival of their own legions, who would be sure to claim a share of the booty, though their assistance was not wanted. Antonius called the men together, and, in a public harangue, informed them, "that Vitellius had still numerous forces in reserve, all willing, if left to their own reflection, to hearken to terms of accommodation; but despair might rouse their courage. In the first movements of a civil war, much must be left to chance. To complete the conquest, is the province of wisdom and deliberate counsels. The fleet at Misenum, with the whole region of Campania, the fairest part of Italy, had already declared for Vespasian. Of the whole Roman world, the tract that lies between Narnia and Tarracina was all that remained in the hands of Vitellius. By the victory at Cremona enough of glory had been gained, and, by the demolition of that city, too much disgrace. Rome still flourishes in all its grandeur. To save that city, the seat of empire, from the like calamity, would be more for their honour than the wild ambition of taking it by assault. Their fame would stand on a more solid basis, and their reward would be greater, if, with the spirit of citizens, and without further effusion of blood, they protected the rights of the senate, and the Roman people."

LXI. By these remonstrances the fury of the soldiers was appeased. The legions arrived soon after, and, by the fame of their united force, struck the Vitellians with dismay. To hold out to the last extremity, was no longer the advice or exhortation of the officers. To surrender was thought the best measure. Numbers saw the advantage of going over to the enemy with their companies of foot, or their troops of horse, and by that service hoped to merit better terms for themselves. Advice was received, that four hundred of the enemy's cavalry were stationed in the neighbourhood, in garrison at *Interamna*. Varus, at the head of a detached party, marched against them. All who resisted were put to the sword; the greater part laid down their arms, and begged quarter. Some fled in a panic to the camp at Narnia, and there, by magnifying the numbers and courage of the enemy, endeavoured to palliate their own disgrace. In the Vitellian army defection and treachery were unpunished: guilt had nothing to fear from the officers, and from the victors it met with a sure reward. Who should be the most expeditious traitor, was now the only struggle. The tribunes and centurions deserted in open day, while the common soldiers adhered to Vitellius with undaunted resolution; but, at length, Priscus and Alphenus gave the finishing blow to all their hopes. Those two officers abandoned the camp, in order to return to Vitellius, and by that step made the apology of all who, being left without a leader, went over to the side of the strongest.

LXII. During these transactions, Fabius Valens was put to death in prison at Urbinum. A report had been spread abroad, that he made his escape into Germany, and was there employed in raising an army of veterans to renew the war. To clear up that mistake, and crush at once the hopes of the Vitellians, his head was exposed to public view. At the sight of that unexpected object, the enemy sunk down in deep despair, while the Flavian party considered that event as the end of all their labour.

Fabius Valens was a native of Anagnia, descended from a family of equestrian rank. His manners were corrupt and profligate, but to his vices he united no small degree of genius. A libertine in the pursuit of pleasure, he acquired an air of gaiety, and passed for a man of polite accomplishments. In the interludes, called Juvenalia,[1] which were exhibited in the reign of Nero, he appeared among the pantomime performers, at first with seeming reluctance, but afterwards of his own choice, displaying talents that gained applause, while they disgraced the man. Rising afterwards to the command of a legion under Verginius, he paid his court to that commander, and betrayed him. He seduced Fonteius Capito, or, perhaps, found him incorruptible, and, for one of those reasons, murdered him. False to Galba, yet faithful to Vitellius, he exhibited, in the last stage of life, a contrast to the general depravity of the times. The perfidy of others raised his reputation.

LXIII. The Vitellians, seeing all hopes cut off, determined to submit to the conqueror, and accordingly, to the utter disgrace of the party, descended into the plains of Narnia, with their colours displayed, there to make a voluntary surrender. Vespasian's army was drawn up in order of battle. They formed their lines on each side of the public road, and in the intermediate space received the vanquished troops. Antonius addressed them in a speech, that breathed moderation and humanity. They were quartered at different places; one division at Narnia, and the other at Interamna. A party of the victorious legions were stationed near them, not with a

[1] See *Annals*, xiv. 15; xvi. 21.

design to insult or irritate men in distress, but, in case of need, to preserve peace and good order. Antonius and Varus, in the meantime, did not neglect the opportunity of negotiating with Vitellius. By frequent messengers they offered for himself a supply of money, and a safe retreat in Campania, upon condition that he should lay down his arms, and surrender himself and his children to the discretion of Vespasian. Letters to the same effect were also sent to him by Mucianus. Vitellius listened to these proposals. He even went so far, as to amuse himself with settling the number of his train, and to talk of the spot on the sea-shore where he intended to fix his retreat. Such was the stupidity that benumbed his faculties: if others would not remember that he had been emperor of Rome, he himself was willing to forget it.

LXIV. At Rome, in the meantime, the leading men endeavoured, by secret exhortations, to incite Flavius Sabinus, the prefect of the city, to take an active part in the approaching revolution, and claim a share in the fame and splendour of so great an event. "The city cohorts," they said, "were all devoted to him; the soldiers of the night watch would join them; and their own slaves might be called forth. Everything favoured the enterprise, and nothing could withstand the victorious arms of a party, in whose favour fortune had already decided. Why leave to Varus and Antonius the whole glory of the war? Vitellius had but a few cohorts left, a mere handful of men, alarmed at the news from every quarter, and overwhelmed with fear. The minds of the populace were always wavering, fond of change, and ready to shift to the side of the strongest. Let Sabinus show himself, and the acclamations, now given to Vitellius, would be as loud for Vespasian. As to Vitellius, the tide of prosperity overpowered him; what must now be his case, when he sees destruction on every side? To end the war, be master of Rome; that will consummate all, and the merit as well as the glory will be yours. Who so fit as Sabinus to secure the sovereign power for his brother? And whom can Vespasian, with so much propriety, wish to see the second man in the empire."

LXV. These temptations, bright as they were, made no impression on Sabinus. Enfeebled by old age, he was no longer alive to motives of ambition. His inactivity was by some imputed to a jealous spirit, that wished to retard the elevation of his brother. Sabinus was the elder, and, while both remained in a private station, always took the lead, superior not only in point of fortune, but also in the opinion of the public. When Vespasian stood in need of pecuniary assistance, Sabinus supported his credit, but, according to report, secured himself by a mortgage on his brother's house and lands. From that time they lived on good terms, preserving the exteriors of friendship, while mutual animosity was supposed to be suppressed in silence. Such were the suspicions that prevailed at the time. The fair and probable construction is, that Sabinus, a man of a meek disposition, wished to spare the effusion of blood, and, with that intent, held frequent conferences with Vitellius, in order to compromise the dispute, and settle the terms of a general pacification. We are told, that, having agreed in private on the preliminary articles, they ratified a final treaty in the temple of Apollo[1] in the presence of Cluvius Rufus and Silius Italicus,[2] who attended as witnesses. The scene was not without a number of spectators, who stood at a distance, watching the looks and behaviour of the contracting parties. Vitellius showed in his countenance an air of sorrow and abject humility. Sabinus scorned to insult a man in distress; he seemed to feel for the unfortunate.

LXVI. Vitellius had long since divested himself of every warlike passion, and, if to persuade others had been as easy as to degrade himself, Vespasian's army might have taken possession of the city of Rome unstained with blood. But his friends were still firm in his interest; their zeal was not to be subdued; they rejected all terms of accommodation, and with warmth protested against a peace which brought with it no security, but depended altogether on the will and pleasure of the conqueror. "Was it probable that Vespasian would have the magnanimity to let his rival live secure in a private station? Would the vanquished bear it? The friends of a fallen emperor would commiserate his case, and that commiseration would be his certain ruin;[3] the ruin, it was true, of a man advanced in years, who had seen the vicissitudes of good and evil fortune. But what would be the situation of his son? What name, what rank, what character, could be bestowed on him, who had been

1 The temple of Apollo was on Mount Palatine, where Augustus formed a library. Horace says,

"Scripta Palatinus quæcumque recepit Apollo."

2 Silius Italicus, the poet.

3 If Vespasian suffered Vitellius to survive his grandeur, and live a private citizen, men would ascribe it to pride and arrogance, and the vanquished would not submit to see their emperor a living reproach to their whole party; and, consequently, Vitellius would be in danger from the commiseration of his friends.

already honoured with the title of Germanicus? The present offer promises a supply of money, a household train, and a safe retreat in the delightful regions of Campania; but when Vespasian seizes the imperial dignity, neither he, nor his friends, nor even his armies, will think themselves secure, till, by the death of a rival, they crush the seeds of future contention. Even Fabius Valens, though a prisoner, and, while they feared a reverse of fortune, reserved as a pledge in the hands of the enemy, was thought at last too formidable, and for that reason he fell a sacrifice. And is it to be imagined, that Antonius, and Fuscus, or Mucianus, that pillar of the party, will not make the same use of their power over Vitellius? Pompey was pursued to death by Julius Cæsar, and Mark Antony by Augustus. But, perhaps, superior sentiment and true greatness of soul are to be expected from Vespasian! Let us not deceive ourselves. He is now a new man, formerly the client,[1] the creature of Vitellius, who, at that time, was joined in the consulship with the emperor Claudius. All motives conspire to rouse and animate the emperor: the dignity of an illustrious line, the office of censor, three consulships held by his father, with the various honours heaped on his family. These are powerful incentives. They call aloud for some bold effort of courage, or, at the worst, of brave despair. The soldiers are still determined to meet every danger, and the fidelity of the people nothing can alter. In all events, no calamity can be so bad as that, into which Vitellius seems willing to plunge himself. If vanquished, we must perish by the sword; if we surrender, what will be the case? An ignominious death. To choose between infamy and glory, is all that now remains. The only question is, Shall we tamely resign our lives, amidst the scorn and insolence of the enemy? or shall we act like men, and die sword in hand, with honour and applause."

LXVII. Vitellius was deaf to every manly sentiment. An obstinate resistance might render the conqueror inexorable to his wife and children, and that consideration overpowered him with grief and tenderness. His mother was now no more. Worn-out with age, she died a few days before, happy not to behold the downfall of her family. From the elevation of her son she derived nothing, except the anxiety

[1] Vitellius had great weight and influence in the reign of Claudius. Vespasian, at that time, paid his court to the favourite, and also to Narcissus, the emperor's freedman.

that preyed upon her spirits, and the fame of a blameless character. On the fifteenth before the calends of January,[1] the defection of the legions and cohorts, that surrendered at Narnia, reached the ears of Vitellius. On receipt of that dismal intelligence, he went forth from his palace in mourning apparel, surrounded by his family in deep affliction. His infant son was carried in a small litter, with all the appearance of a funeral ceremony. The populace followed in crowds, with unavailing shouts, and flattery out of season. The soldiers marched in sullen silence.

LXVIII. In that vast multitude, no man was so insensible of the events and sudden revolutions of human life, as not to be touched by the misery of the scene before him. They saw an emperor, but a little before master of the Roman world, abandoning his palace, and, in the midst of a vast crowd of citizens assembled round him, proceeding through the streets of Rome to abdicate the imperial dignity. No eye had seen a spectacle so truly affecting; no ear had heard of so dismal a catastrophe. Cæsar, the dictator, fell by sudden violence; Caligula perished by a dark conspiracy; Nero fled through devious paths, while the shades of night concealed his disgrace; Piso and Galba may be said to have died in battle. Vitellius, before an assembly of the people called by himself, in the midst of his own soldiers, and in the presence of a concourse of women, who beheld the sad reverse of fortune, by his own act deposed himself. In a short but pathetic speech, he declared his voluntary abdication. "I retire," he said, "for the sake of peace and the good of the commonwealth; retain me still in your memory, and view with an eye of pity the misfortunes of my brother, my wife, and infant children. I ask no more." He raised his son in his arms, and showed him to the people; he turned to individuals; he implored the compassion of all. A gush of tears suppressed his voice: in that distress, taking his sword from his side, and addressing himself to Cæcilius Simplex, the consul, who stood near him, he offered to deliver it into his hands, as the symbol of authority over the lives of the Roman citizens. The consul refused to accept it, and the people, with violent uproar, opposed his resignation. Vitellius left the place. His intention was, to lay down all the ensigns of sovereignty in the temple of Concord, and seek an humble retreat in his brother's house.

[1] Vitellius abdicated on the 18th of December, A.D. 69, after a few months of anarchy, plunder, and massacre.

This again met with a strong opposition from the populace. The general cry was, that the house of a private citizen was not a proper mansion: all insisted on his returning to the palace. The crowd obstructed the streets, and no pass was left open, except that called the *Sacred Way*. In confusion, distracted, and left without advice, Vitellius returned to the palace.

LXIX. The abdication of the prince was soon known throughout the city. Upon the first intelligence, Flavius Sabinus sent orders in writing to the tribunes of the cohorts, commanding them to restrain the violent spirit of the soldiers. The leading members of the senate, as if the whole power of the state was falling at once into the hands of Vespasian, went in a body to the house of Sabinus. A numerous band of the equestrian order, with the city soldiers, and the night watch, followed the example of the fathers. They were there informed of the zeal of the people for Vitellius, and the menaces thrown out by the German cohorts. Sabinus was too far advanced to think of a retreat. Individuals trembled for themselves: if they dispersed, the Vitellians might seize the opportunity to lay a scene of blood. To prevent that terrible disaster, they urged Sabinus to take up arms, and show himself in force to the people. But, as often happens in pressing exigencies, all were ready to advise, and few to share the danger. Sabinus went forth at the head of a band of soldiers. Near the Fundane lake,[1] a bold and resolute party of the Vitellians advanced against him. A skirmish ensued. The Vitellians had the advantage. Sabinus retreated to the fort of the capitol, and in that stronghold shut himself up with his soldiers, and a small party of senators and Roman knights. A list of their names cannot be given with any precision, as numbers afterwards, in the reign of Vespasian, assumed a share of merit in that transaction. There were even women who dared to defy the danger of a siege. Among these the most distinguished was Verulana Gracilia, a woman of high spirit, who had neither children nor relations to attract her, but acted entirely on the impulse of her own intrepid genius. The Vitellians invested the citadel, but guarded the passes with so much negligence, that Sabinus, in the dead of night, was able to receive into the place his own children, and Domitian, his

[1] The lake was in the city of Rome, near the *Mons Quirinalis*. There were at least a thousand of those lakes at Rome, which ought more properly to be called fountains.

brother's son. At the same time, he sent despatches to the victorious army, to inform the chiefs of his situation, and the necessity of immediate relief. The besiegers attempted nothing during the night. Had Sabinus taken advantage of their inactivity, he might have made his escape through the passes neglected by a ferocious enemy, bold and resolute, but scorning all regular discipline and impatient of fatigue. It happened, besides, that a storm of rain fell with all the violence of the winter season. During the tempest, the men could neither see nor hear one another.

LXX. At the dawn of day, before hostilities commenced, Sabinus despatched Cornelius Martialis, a principal centurion, with instructions to represent to Vitellius the treachery of his conduct in open violation of a solemn treaty. "The late abdication was no better than a state farce, played in the face of mankind, to deceive the most illustrious citizens. For what other purpose did he wish to withdraw to his brother's house, so situated as to overlook the forum, and attract the eyes of the public? Why not rather choose the mansion of his wife, a sequestered station near Mount Aventine? For him who renounced the sovereign power, a place of obscurity was the fittest. But Vitellius sought the very reverse: he returned to his palace, the citadel, as it were, of the empire, and thence sent forth a military force to deluge the best part of the city with innocent blood. Even the capitol was no longer a sanctuary. During the rage of civil war, while the fate of empire hung suspended between Vespasian and Vitellius; while the legions drenched their swords in the blood of their fellow-citizens; while cities were taken by storm, and whole cohorts laid down their arms; the part which Sabinus acted, was that of a senator and a civil magistrate. Both the Spains, the Upper and Lower Germany, and all Britain, had revolted; and yet the brother of Vespasian preserved his fidelity to the reigning prince. If at length he entered into a negotiation, Vitellius invited him to the meeting. The stipulated terms were advantageous to the vanquished; and to the conqueror brought nothing but fame and honour. If Vitellius repented of that transaction, why point his arms against Sabinus, who had been the dupe of insidious policy? Why besiege the son of Vespasian, a youth not yet grown up to the age of manhood? By the murder of an old man, and the death of a stripling, what advantage could be gained? It would be more for the honour of Vitellius to make head against the legions, and decide the contest in the field of battle. A single victory would end the war, and everything would fall to the lot of the conqueror." Vitellius listened to this remonstrance with visible marks of fear. He endeavoured in few words to clear his own conduct, imputing the whole mischief to the soldiers, whose intemperate zeal was no longer subject to his authority. He advised Martialis to depart through a private part of the house, lest the soldiers in their fury should destroy the negotiator of a peace which they abhorred. He himself remained in his palace, unable to command or to prohibit any measure whatever; a mere phantom of power, no longer emperor, but still the cause of civil dissension.

LXXI. Martialis had no sooner entered the capitol, than the Vitellian soldiers appeared before it; no chief to lead them on; all rushing forward with impetuous fury, and every man his own commanding officer. Having passed the forum, and the temples [1] that surround it, they marched up the hill that fronts the capitol, and, after halting there to form their ranks, advanced in regular order to the gates of the citadel. On the right side of the ascent, a range of porticos had been built in ancient times. From the top of those edifices the besieged annoyed the enemy with stones and tiles. The assailants had no weapons but their swords. To wait for warlike engines seemed a tedious delay to men impatient for the assault. They threw flaming torches into the portico nearest at hand; and, seeing the destruction made by the devouring flames, were ready to force their way through the gate, if Sabinus had not thrown into a heap all the statues that adorned the place, and, with those venerable monuments of antiquity, blocked up the passage. The Vitellians pushed on the assault in two different quarters; one near the grove of the asylum,[2] and the other near the hundred steps of the Tarpeian rock.[3] Both attacks were unforeseen. Near the asylum grove the affair grew serious. On that side of the hill, the houses which had been built during a long peace, were raised as high as the foundation of the capitol. The besiegers climbed to the top of those buildings, in spite of every effort to stop their

[1] The forum was surrounded by a number of temples; such as the temple of FORTUNE, of JUPITER TONANS, of SATURN, the temple of CONCORD, and several others.

[2] The *Lucus Asyli* was so called, because it was made a sanctuary by Romulus, to invite a conflux of foreigners to his new state. It stood between the two rocks of the Capitoline hill, on one of which was built the temple of JUPITER CAPITOLINUS; on the other the temple of FERETRIAN JOVE.

[3] The Tarpeian rock, with its hundred steps, was on the west side of the Capitoline hill, and from that eminence malefactors were thrown headlong into the Tiber.

progress. The roofs were immediately set on fire, but whether by the besieged, or the besiegers,[1] is uncertain. The current opinion ascribed it to the former. The flame soon reached the contiguous porticos, and, in a short time, spread to the eagles (a set of pillars so called) that supported the buildings. The wood, being old and dry, was so much fuel to increase the fire. In the conflagration that followed, the capitol, with all its gates shut, and neither stormed by the enemy, nor defended by Sabinus, was burned to the ground.

LXXII. From the foundation of the city to that hour, the Roman people had felt no calamity so deplorable, no disgrace so humiliating. Without the shock of a foreign enemy, and, if we except the vices of the age, without any particular cause to draw down the wrath of heaven, the temple of Jupiter, supreme of gods; a temple built in ancient times, with solemn rites and religious auspices, the pledge of future grandeur; which neither Porsena,[2] when Rome surrendered to his arms, nor the Gauls, when they took the city by storm, had dared to violate; that sacred edifice was now demolished by the rage of men contending for a master to reign over them. The capitol, it is true, was once before destroyed by fire during the violence of a civil war;[3] but the guilt was then confined to the treachery of a few incendiaries, the madness of evil-minded men. In the present juncture it was besieged with open hostility, and in the face of day involved in flames. And what adequate motive? what object in view to atone for so wild a frenzy? Was the sword drawn in the cause of public liberty?

Tarquinius Priscus, during the war which he waged against the Sabines, bound himself by a vow to build that sacred structure. He afterwards laid the foundation, on a plan suggested by his own vast idea of the rising grandeur of the empire, but inconsistent with the circumstances of an infant state. Servius Tullius, assisted by the zeal of the allies of Rome, went on with the work, and after him Tarquin the proud, with the spoils of Suessa Pometia,[4] added to the magnificence of the building. But the glory of completing the design was reserved

[1] Pliny the elder says, the capitol was set on fire by the Vitellians. Josephus gives the same account.

[2] It is not strictly true that Porsena became master of the city. He was at the gates, but, instead of advancing, received hostages, and raised the siege.

[3] In the civil war between Sulla and Marius, the capitol was destroyed by fire. The Sibylline books perished in the flames.

[4] Suessa Pometia, a city of ancient Latium, about fifty miles from Rome, on the Appian road.

for the era of liberty, when kings were deposed and banished for ever. It was under the republic that Horatius Pulvillus, in his second consulship, performed the ceremony of dedicating the temple, at that time finished with so much grandeur, that the wealth of after ages could do no more than grace it with new embellishments: to its magnificence nothing could be added. Four hundred and fifteen years afterwards, in the consulship of Lucius Scipio and Caius Norbanus, it was burnt to the ground, and again rebuilt on the old foundation. Sulla, who in that juncture had triumphed ever all opposition to his arms, undertook the care of the building: the glory of dedicating it would have crowned his felicity; but that honour was reserved for Lutatius Catulus, whose name, amidst so many noble monuments of the Cæsars, remained in legible characters till the days of Vitellius. Such was the sacred building, which the madness of the times reduced to ashes.

LXXIII. The fire, when it first began to rage, threw the combatants into the utmost confusion, but on the part of the besieged the distress was greatest. The Vitellian soldiers, in the moment of difficulty, wanted neither skill nor courage. In the opposite party the men were seized with a panic, and the commander had neither spirit nor presence of mind. Benumbed and torpid, he lost his powers of speech, and even the faculties of eyes and ears. No resources in himself, he was deaf to the advice of others. Alarmed by every sudden noise, he went forward, he returned; he ordered what he had forbidden, and countermanded what he had ordered. In this distraction all directed, and none obeyed. They threw down their arms, and each man began to shift for himself. They fled, they hid themselves in lurking-places; the Vitellians burst in with fire and sword; a scene of carnage followed. A few gallant spirits made a brave resistance, and perished in the attempt. The most distinguished were Cornelius Martialis, Æmilius Pacensis, Casperius Niger, and Didius Scæva: all these met their fate with undaunted courage. Flavius Sabinus, without his sword, and not so much as attempting to save himself by flight, was surrounded by a band of the Vitellians. Quinctius Atticus, the consul, was also taken prisoner. The ensigns of his magistracy discovered him to the soldiers; and the haughty style in which he had issued several edicts, in their tenor favourable to Vespasian, and injurious to Vitellius, made him an object of resentment. The rest by various stratagems made their escape; some in the disguise of slaves; others assisted by the fidelity of their friends, and by their care concealed under the baggage. A few, who had caught the military word by which the Vitellians knew each other, used it with confidence in their questions and answers to all that came in their way. The boldness of the experiment saved their lives.

LXXIV. Domitian, on the first irruption of the besiegers, was conveyed to the apartments of the warden of the temple, and there protected till one of his freedmen had the address to conduct him, clad in a linen vestment, amidst the band of sacrificers, to the place called *Velabrum*, where he lodged him safe under the care of Cornelius Primus, a man firmly attached to Vespasian. Domitian, during the reign of his father, threw down the warden's lodge, and on the same spot built a chapel to JUPITER THE CONSERVATOR, with a marble altar, on which the story of his escape was engraved at length. Being afterwards invested with the imperial dignity, he dedicated a magnificent temple to JUPITER THE GUARDIAN, and a statue representing the god with the young prince in his arms. Sabinus and Quinctius Atticus were conducted in fetters to the presence of Vitellius. He received them without a word of reproach, or so much as an angry look, though the soldiers, with rage and vociferation, insisted on their right to murder both, demanding, at the same time, the reward due to them for their late exploits. The inferior populace, with violent uproar, called for immediate vengeance on Sabinus, not forgetting to mingle with their fury the language of adulation to Vitellius, who endeavoured to address them from the stairs of the palace: but the storm was too outrageous. The mob fell upon Sabinus. He died under repeated blows. The assassins cut off his head, and dragged the mangled body to the common charnel.

LXXV. Such was the end of a man who merited a better fate. He had carried arms five-and-thirty years in the service of his country, distinguished by his civil and military conduct. His integrity and love of justice were never questioned. His fault was that of talking too much. In the course of seven years, during which he administered the province of Mæsia, and twelve more, while he was governor of Rome, malice itself could find no other blemish in his character. In the last act of his life he was condemned for inactivity and want of spirit; others saw in his conduct a man of moderation, who wished to prevent the effusion of Roman blood. Before the elevation of Vespasian, all agree that he was the head and ornament of his family. That his fall was matter of joy to

Mucianus, seems well attested. In general, his death was considered as an event of public utility, since all emulation between two men likely to prove dangerous rivals, one as the emperor's brother, and the other as a colleague in power, was now extinguished. The consul, Quinctius Atticus, was the next victim demanded by the populace. Vitellius opposed their fury. He thought himself bound in gratitude to protect a man, who, being interrogated concerning the destruction of the capitol, avowed himself the author of the misfortune, and by that truth, or well-timed lie, took upon himself the whole load of guilt, exonerating the Vitellian party.

LXXVI. During these transactions, Lucius Vitellius, having pitched his camp in the neighbourhood of Feronia, formed a design to storm the city of Tarracina. The garrison, consisting of marines and gladiators, remained pent up within the walls, not daring to sally out and face the enemy in the open field. The gladiators, as has been mentioned, were under the command of Julianus, and the marines under that of Apollinaris; two men, immersed in sloth and luxury, by their vices more like common gladiators than superior officers. No sentinels stationed, no night watch to prevent a sudden alarm, and no care taken to guard the works, they passed both day and night in drunken jollity. The windings of that delightful coast resounded with notes of joy, and the soldiers were spread about the country to provide for the pleasures of the two commanders, who never thought of war except when it became the subject over their bottle. Apinius Tiro had left the place a few days before, in order to procure supplies for the commanding officers. By exacting presents and contributions from the municipal towns, he inflamed the prejudices of the people, gaining ill-will in every quarter, and for his party no accession of strength.

LXXVII. Things remained in this posture, when a slave belonging to Verginius Capito deserted to Lucius Vitellius, with an offer to head a detachment, and, by surprise, make himself master of the citadel, unprovided, as it then was, with a sufficient force to guard the works. His proposal was accepted. In the dead of night he set out with a party of light-armed cohorts, and, having gained the summit of the hill, took his station over the heads of the enemy. From that eminence the soldiers poured down with impetuous fury, not to a battle, but to a scene of carnage and destruction. They fell upon a defenceless multitude, the greatest part unarmed, some running to snatch up their weapons, others scarce awake, and all thrown into consternation by the general uproar, by the darkness, the clangour of trumpets, and the shouts of the enemy. A few of the gladiators made a brave resistance, and sold their lives at the dearest rate. The rest fled to the ships. Terror and confusion followed them. The peasants of the neighbourhood were intermixed with the troops, and all together fell in one promiscuous slaughter. In the beginning of the tumult, six light galleys broke loose from their moorings. On board of one of them, Apollinaris, the commander of the fleet, made his escape. The rest were either taken, or, by the weight of the crowd that rushed on board, sunk to the bottom. Julianus was conducted to Lucius Vitellius, and, in his presence, first ignominiously scourged, and then put to death. Triaria, the wife of Lucius the commanding officer, was accused of exulting with pride and cruelty amidst the carnage that laid waste the city of Tarracina. She is said to have appeared with a sword girt by her side, adding mockery and insult to the horrors of that tragic scene. The general, to mark so brilliant a victory, sent a letter wreathed with laurel to his brother, desiring, at the same time, to know whether he should march directly forward to Rome, or stay to finish the entire reduction of Campania. The delay was of the greatest moment, not only to Vespasian's party, but to the commonwealth. A fierce and savage soldiery, flushed with success, and to their natural ferocity adding the insolence of victory, had they been immediately led to Rome, would, beyond all doubt, have renewed the war with dreadful havoc, and, perhaps, the destruction of the city. On such an occasion, Lucius Vitellius was an officer to be dreaded. Though his character was decried and infamous, he wanted neither talents nor vigour of mind. Like all who succeed by prosperous wickedness, he had raised himself to eminence, and what good men obtain by their virtues he accomplished by his vices.

LXXVIII. Meanwhile, Vespasian's army, inactive ever since their departure from Narnia, loitered away the time at Oriculum,[1] amusing themselves with the celebration of the Saturnalian festival.[2] To wait for the arrival of Mucianus, was the ostensible reason for this ill-timed delay. Motives of a different nature were imputed to Antonius. Vitellius, it was said, had tampered with him by letters, and, to entice him from his party, promised the consulship, and his daughter in marriage, with a splendid fortune. With a considerable

[1] Now Otricoli.

[2] The Saturnalian festival began on the 17th of December.

number, this accusation had no kind of weight. They treated it as a mere calumny, the invention of artful men, who wished to pay their court to Mucianus. Many were of opinion, that the whole was a deliberate plan, settled by all the general officers, who rather chose to alarm the city of Rome with distant terrors, than to carry desolation within the walls; especially since the strongest cohorts had abandoned Vitellius, and that prince, left as he was, without hopes of succour, would probably end the contest by a voluntary abdication. This design, however wise and prudent, was defeated, at first, by the rashness, and, in the end, by the irresolution, of Sabinus. That officer had taken up arms with a show of courage, and yet was not able, against so small a force as three cohorts, to defend the capitol; a fortress strong enough to stand the shock of powerful armies, and always deemed impregnable. But the truth is, where all were guilty of misconduct, the blame cannot well be fixed on any one in particular. Mucianus, by the studied ambiguity of his letters, checked the progress of the victorious army: and Antonius, by obsequious compliances, or, perhaps, with a design to blacken the character of Mucianus, was willing to incur the imputation of inactivity. The rest of the officers concluded hastily that the war was ended, and, by that mistake, occasioned all the disasters that closed the scene. Even Petilius Cerealis, who had been sent forward at the head of a thousand horse, with orders to proceed by rapid marches through the country of the Sabines, and to enter Rome by the Salarian road, did not push on with vigour. The chiefs heard, at last, that the capitol was besieged; and that intelligence roused them from their lethargy.

LXXIX. Antonius, in the night-time, made a forward movement towards the city of Rome. He pursued the Flaminian road, and, by a forced march, arrived at the RED ROCKS; but the mischief had already happened. At that place he received intelligence, that Sabinus was murdered; that the capitol lay smoking on the ground; that the populace, joined by the slaves, had taken up arms for Vitellius, and that all Rome was wild with consternation. At the same time, Petilius Cerealis met with a defeat. That general, despising an enemy whom he considered as already conquered, advanced incautiously to attack a party of horse and infantry. The battle was fought at a small distance from Rome, at a place where the land was divided into gardens, intersected by narrow roads, and covered with buildings; a spot well known to the Vitellians, but, to men unacquainted with the defiles, every way disadvantageous. Nor did the cavalry under Cerealis act with unanimity or equal ardour. They had among them a party of them who laid down their arms at Narnia, and all of that description waited to see the issue of the battle. Tullius Flavianus, who commanded a squadron of Vespasian's horse, was taken prisoner. The rest fled with precipitation. The conquering troops pursued the runaways as far as Fidenæ.

LXXX. The success of the Vitellians in this engagement inspired the partisans at Rome with new courage. The populace had recourse to arms. A few were provided with shields; the rest snatched up whatever weapons fell in their way. With one voice they demanded the signal for the attack. Vitellius commended their zeal, and ordered them to exert themselves in the defence of the city. In the meantime he convened the senate. The fathers sent ambassadors to the several chiefs, with instructions to propose, in the name of the commonwealth, a plan of pacification. The deputies chosen for this purpose were variously received. In the camp of Petilius Cerealis they were in danger of their lives. The soldiers disdained all terms of accommodation, and, in their fury, attacked the ambassadors. The prætor Arulenus Rusticus was wounded. By this outrage the rights of ambassadors were violated, and, in the personal dignity of the man, virtue itself was insulted. The attendants in his train were obliged to fly. The lictor who attempted to open a passage through the crowd, was murdered on the spot; and, if the guard appointed by Cerealis had not interposed in time, the law of nations, ever respected by the most hostile states, had been trampled under foot, and the ambassadors, in the face of their country, under the very walls of Rome, must have fallen victims to the brutal rage of frantic men. The deputies who went to the camp of Antonius met with a more gentle reception; but were indebted for it, not to the pacific temper of the soldiers, but to the authority of the commander-in-chief.

LXXXI. It happened that Musonius Rufus,[1] a Roman knight, followed in the train of the ambassadors. He professed himself devoted to the study of philosophy, and in particular to the doctrines of the Stoic sect. Full of his boasted system, he mixed among the soldiers, and, reasoning much concerning good and evil, began a dissertation on the

[1] Musonius Rufus has occurred, *Annals*, xiv. 59 and xv. 71.

blessings of peace, and the calamities of war. Men under arms, and fierce with victory, were not likely to relish a moral lecture. His pedantry tired the patience of the soldiers, and became a subject of ridicule. The philosopher was in danger of being roughly treated, if the advice of the more considerate, and the menaces of others, had not taught him to suppress his ill-timed maxims of wisdom.

The vestal virgins went in procession to the camp, with letters from Vitellius addressed to Antonius, in substance requesting a cessation of arms for a single day. In the interval a compromise might take place, and prevent the havoc of decisive action. The vestal train received every mark of respect. An answer in writing was sent to Vitellius, informing him, that the murder of Sabinus, and the destruction of the capitol, made all terms of accommodation inadmissible.

LXXXII. Antonius, in the meantime, called an assembly of the soldiers, and, in a soothing speech, endeavoured to infuse into their minds a spirit of moderation. He advised them to encamp at the Milvian bridge, and not to think of entering Rome till the next day. An enraged soldiery, forcing their way sword in hand, he had reason to fear, would rush on with impetuous fury, and give no quarter to the people or the senate. Even the temples and altars of the gods might fall in one promiscuous ruin. But the impatience of the army was not to be restrained. Eager for victory, they thought themselves ruined by delay. A display of colours and ensigns was seen glittering on the hills, followed indeed, by an undisciplined rabble; but the appearance announced the preparations of an enemy. The conquerors advanced in three divisions; the first from their station on the Flaminian road; the second marched along the banks of the Tiber; and the third, towards the gate Collina, by the Salarian way. On the first onset the mob was put to flight by the cavalry. The Vitellian soldiers ranged themselves in three columns. The entrance of the city was obstinately disputed. Several sharp engagements followed before the walls, with various success, but for the most part favourable to Vespasian's men, supported as they were by able officers. A party wheeled round to the left side of the city, towards the Sallustian gardens, and, being engaged in slippery and narrow passes, were roughly handled. The Vitellians had taken possession of the gardens, and, from the tops of the walls, were able, with stones and spears, to annoy the troops beneath them. The advantage was on their side, till, towards the close of day, a party of Vespasian's cavalry forced their way through the Collinian gate, and fell upon the enemy in the rear. A battle was also fought in the field of Mars. The good fortune that hitherto attended Vespasian's cause, gave him a decided victory. The Vitellians fought with obstinacy to the last. Despair lent them courage. Though dispersed and routed, they rallied within the walls of the city, and once more returned to the charge.

LXXXIII. The people flocked in crowds to behold the conflict, as if a scene of carnage were no more than a public spectacle exhibited for their amusement. Whenever they saw the advantage inclining to either side, they favoured the combatants with shouts, and theatrical applause. If the men fled from their ranks, to take shelter in shops or houses, they roared to have them dragged forth, and put to death like gladiators for their diversion. While the soldiers were intent on slaughter, these miscreants were employed in plundering. The greatest part of the booty fell to their share. Rome presented a scene truly shocking, a medley of savage slaughter and monstrous vice; in one place war and desolation; in another, bathing, riot, and debauchery. Heaps of slain lay weltering in the streets, and blood flowed in torrents, while harlots and abandoned women wandered about with lascivious impudence. Whatever the libidinous passions can inspire in the hour of peace, was intermixed with all the horrors of war, of slaughter, and destruction. The whole city seemed to be inflamed with frantic rage, and, at the same time, intoxicated with bacchanalian pleasures. Before this period, Rome had seen enraged armies within her walls; twice under Sulla, and once after the victory obtained by Cinna. Upon those occasions the same barbarity was committed; but the unnatural security and inhuman indifference that now prevailed, were beyond all example. In the midst of rage and massacre, pleasure knew no intermission. A dreadful carnage seemed to be a spectacle added to the public games. The populace enjoyed the havoc; they exulted in the midst of devastation; and, without any regard for the contending parties, triumphed over the miseries of their country.

LXXXIV. Vespasian's party had now conquered everything but the camp.[1] That difficult and arduous task still remained. The bravest of the Vitellians were still in possession. They considered it as their last resort, and were therefore determined to make a vigorous stand. The conquering troops advanced

[1] The camp of the prætorian guards.

with determined fury to the attack, and the old prætorian cohorts with inflamed resentment. Whatever the military art had invented against places of the greatest strength, was employed by the assailants. They advanced under the shell; they threw up mounds; they discharged missive weapons and flaming torches; "all declaring aloud, that one glorious effort would put an end to their toil and danger. To the senate and people of Rome they had restored their city, and to the gods their altars and their temples. It now remained to gain possession of the camp, the soldier's post of honour, his country, and the seat of his household gods. They must either carry the intrenchments by assault, or pass the night under arms." The spirit of the Vitellians was broken, but not subdued. To sell the victory at the dearest rate, and delay the return of peace, was the effort of expiring rage; and to stain the houses and altars with an effusion of blood, was the last consolation of despair. The towers and ramparts were covered with heaps of slain. The gates of the camp were forced. The few that still survived had the courage to maintain their post. They fell under honourable wounds, prodigal of life, and to the last tenacious of their glory.

LXXXV. Vitellius, seeing the city conquered, went in a litter, by a private way at the back of the palace, to his wife's house on Mount Aventine, with intent, if he could lie concealed during the rest of the day, to fly for refuge to his brother and the cohorts under his command at Tarracina. His natural irresolution returned upon him. He dreaded everything, and, with the usual distraction of fear, what was present alarmed him most. He returned to his palace, and found it a melancholy desert. His slaves had made their escape, or shunned the presence of their master. Silence added to the terror of the scene. He opened the doors of his apartments, and stood aghast at the dreary solitude. All was desolation round him. He wandered from room to room, till his heart sunk within him. Weary, at length, of his wretched condition, he chose a disgraceful lurking-place,[1] and there lay hid with abject fear, till Julius Placidus, the tribune of a cohort, dragged him forth. With his hands bound behind him, and his garment torn, he was conducted, a wretched spectacle, through crowds insulting his distress, and not a friend to pity his misfortunes. A catastrophe so mean and despicable moved no passion but contempt. A German

[1] The porter's lodge.

soldier, either in wrath, or to end his misery, struck at him with his sabre, and, missing his aim, cut off the ear of a tribune. Whether his design was against that officer, cannot now be known. For his attempt he perished on the spot. Vitellius was dragged along amidst the scoffs and insults of the rabble. With swords pointed at his throat, they forced him to raise his head, and expose his countenance to scorn and derision; they made him look at his statues tumbling to the ground; they pointed to the place of public harangues, and showed him the spot where Galba perished. In this manner they hurried him to the charnel,[1] where the body of Flavius Sabinus had been thrown amongst the vilest malefactors. An expression fell from him, in the last extremity, that bespoke a mind not utterly destitute of sentiment. A tribune insulted him in his misery; "and yet," said Vitellius, "I have been your sovereign." He died soon after under repeated wounds. The populace, who had worshipped him in the zenith of his power, continued, after his death, with the same depravity, to treat his remains with every mark of scorn and insolence.

LXXXVI. He was the son, as already mentioned, of Lucius Vitellius, and had completed the fifty-seventh year of his age. He rose to the consulship, to pontifical dignities, and a name and rank amongst the most eminent citizens, without industry or personal merit. The splendid reputation of the father laid open the road to honours for the son. The men who raised him to the imperial dignity, did not so much as know him. By his vices, and luxurious ease, he gained an ascendant over the affections of the army, to a degree rarely attained by the virtue of the ablest generals. Simplicity, frankness, and generosity, must not be denied to him; but those qualities, when not under the curb of discretion, are always equivocal, and often ruinous. He endeavoured to conciliate friendships, not by his virtues, but by boundless liberality, and no wonder if he missed his aim: he deserved friends, but never had them. That his power should be overturned, was, no doubt, the interest of the commonwealth; but the men who figured in that important scene could claim no merit with Vespasian, since, with equal versatility, they had been traitors to Galba.

The day being far spent, and the fathers and chief magistrates having either fled from the city in a panic, or concealed

[1] Gemoniæ, the charnel of malefactors.

themselves in the houses of their friends, the senate could not be assembled. The rage of slaughter being appeased, and all hostilities ceasing, Domitian presented himself before the leaders of the party. He was saluted by the title of Cæsar, and a band of soldiers under arms conducted him to his father's house.

BOOK IV

CONTENTS

I. *Cruelties committed at Rome by Vespasian's army.*—II. *Lucius Vitellius surrenders with all his forces, and is put to death.*—III. *Affairs in Campania composed by Lucilius Bassus—The sovereignty of Vespasian confirmed by the senate with demonstrations of obsequious duty.*—IV. *Honours conferred on Mucianus in his absence—Antonius and Arrius Varus raised to dignities—The capitol to be rebuilt: Helvidius Priscus displays a spirit of liberty.*—V. *The character of Helvidius Priscus—His contest with Eprius Marcellus.*—IX. *A debate concerning the public expenditure.*—X. *Musonius Rufus attacks Publius Celer, the informer, who ruined Bareas Soranus.*—XI. *Mucianus enters the city of Rome—He assumes the whole power of the state—Calpurnius Galerianus put to death, and also Asiaticus the freedman.*—XII. *A war breaks out in Germany—The causes of it—Claudius Civilis, a Batavian, heads the revolt.*—XIV. *The Batavians under Civilis, and the Caninefates under Brinno, the first to take up arms.*—XV. *The Frisians join the league—A fortress of the Romans demolished; their garrisons cut off—A victory obtained by Civilis.*—XVII. *The German nations take up arms—Civilis applies to the states of Gaul for their assistance.*—XVIII. *The inactivity of Hordeonius Flaccus—Mummius Lupercus gives battle to Civilis. The veteran cohorts of the Batavians in the service of Rome go over to the enemy—The Romans routed—They escape to the old camp called Vetera.*—XIX. *Some cohorts of the Caninefates and Batavians, on their march to Rome, drawn over by Civilis to his party—They return in spite of Hordeonius Flaccus towards the lower Germany, and defeat the Romans at Bonn.*—XXI. *Civilis, to conceal his real design, pretends to espouse the cause of Vespasian.*—XXII. *He lays siege to the old camp called Vetera.*—XXIV. *Hordeonius Flaccus driven from his command by a mutiny in his camp: he resigns his authority to Vocula.*—XXVI. *Herennius Gallus associated with Vocula—The army encamps at Gelduba—A ship loaded with corn drawn away from the Romans to the opposite bank of the Rhine—Herennius Gallus receives violent blows from his own soldiers, and is thrown into prison, but released by Vocula.*—XXIX. *Civilis attempts in the night-time to storm the old camp.*—XXXI. *By letters from Antonius the Romans receive intelligence of the victory at Cremona—The auxiliaries from Gaul renounce the cause of Vitellius—Hordeonius Flaccus enforces the oath of fidelity to Vespasian.*—XXXII. *Montanus, who commanded a Vitellian cohort at Cremona, is sent to Civilis to require that chief to lay down his arms—Civilis inflames the turbulent spirit of Montanus.*—XXXIII. *Civilis sends a detachment against Vocula—A battle is fought, prosperous at first on the side of the Germans—The Romans prevail at last—Vocula makes no use of his victory.*—XXXVI.

Civilis makes himself master of Gelduba—A fresh sedition among the Romans—The soldiers murder Hordeonius Flaccus—Vocula in the disguise of a slave makes his escape.—XXXVII. *Vocula resumes the command, and marches to raise the siege of Magontiacum—The Treverians revolt to Civilis.*—XXXVIII. *Transactions at Rome—Vespasian and Titus declared consuls in their absence—A famine dreaded at Rome, and Africa supposed to be in arms.*—XXXIX. *Domitian prætor—Mucianus jealous of Antonius Primus, and Arrius Varus—He lessens the power of both—Part of the army ordered back to Germany, and tranquillity thereby restored at Rome.*—XL. *Honour done to the memory of Galba—Musonius Rufus renews his accusation against Publius Celer—Celer condemned.*—XLII. *Messala intercedes for his brother Aquilius Regulus, a notorious informer—Curtius Montanus makes a vehement speech against Regulus.*—XLIII. *Eprius Marcellus is again attacked by Helvidius Priscus—Domitian proposes a general oblivion of all past grievances—A few offenders ordered to return to their place of exile.*—XLV. *A senator complains of having been beat by the inhabitants of Sienna—The guilty brought to Rome and punished.*—XLVI. *A violent sedition among the prætorian bands quelled by Mucianus—The order of succession to the consulship established by Vitellius declared void—The funeral of Flavius Sabinus performed with the honours usually paid to the rank of censor.*—XLVIII. *Assassination of Lucius Piso in Africa.*—L. *War between the Æensians and the people of Leptis prevented by Festus the commander of the legions—The Garamantes put to flight.*—LI. *Vespasian informed of the death of Vitellius—Succours offered by the Parthian king, but refused.*—LII. *Vespasian exasperated by the accounts of Domitian's conduct at Rome—Titus endeavours to mitigate the anger of his father, and sets out to conduct the wars against the Jews.*—LIII. *The rebuilding of the capitol entrusted to Lucius Vestinus.*—LIV. *Two wars at once in Germany and Gaul, occasioned by the death of Vitellius—Civilis avows his hostile intentions—The Treverians and Lingones revolt from the Romans, under the influence of Classicus, Tutor, and Julius Sabinus—The other states of Gaul on the point of revolting.*—LVIII. *Vocula harangues his soldiers—He is slain by an emissary sent by Classicus—The soldiers declare for the empire of the Gauls.*—LX. *The legions, besieged in the old camp, submit in like manner to the Gauls.*—LXI. *Vow of Civilis to let his beard grow: after the defeat of the legions, he thinks his vow complete—He is said to have given certain Roman prisoners to his infant son, to divert himself with shooting arrows at them—He sends presents to Veleda, the German prophetess; Marcus Lupercus sent to her as a present; he is killed on the road—Veleda had foretold the destruction of the legions, and her authority increases throughout Germany.*—LXII. *The captive legions march in a dismal procession from Novesium to the Theverian territories—Magnanimous behaviour of the Picentinian squadron of horse.*—LXIII. *The Agrippinian colony in danger from the nations beyond the Rhine.*—LXVI. *Civilis gives battle to Claudius Labio; and, having routed him, receives the Batavians and Tungrians under his protection.*—LXVII. *The Lingones defeated by the Sequanians—Julius Sabinus, the Lingonian chief, escapes, and lives in subterraneous caves for nine years afterwards—The memorable constancy of his wife, Eponina.*—LXVIII. *At Rome the empire thought to be in danger—Mucianus and Domitian prepare to set out for Gaul—The Gauls call a general assembly of the states—They prefer peace to the dangers of war.*—LXX. *Civilis and Tutor differ in their opinions about the conduct of the war—Classicus agrees with Tutor, and they resolve to hazard a battle.*—LXXI. *Petilius Cerealis arrives at Magontiacum—He gains a complete victory over the Treverians at Rigodulum, on the banks of the Moselle—Valentinus, the Treverian chief, taken prisoner.*—LXXII. *The legions that had revolted return to their duty, and are received into the Roman camp.*—LXXIII. *Cerealis receives the Treverians and Lingones under his protection.*—LXXV. *Cerealis gives battle to Civilis and Classicus: the beginning of the conflict doubtful, but the issue favourable to the Romans.*—LXXIX. *The Agrippinians desert the cause of the Germans.*—LXXX. *Mucianus orders the son of Vitellius to be put to death—Antonius Primus, resenting the behaviour of Mucianus, proceeds to Vespasian, but is not well received.*—LXXXI. *Miracles performed by Vespasian at Alexandria—He visits the temple of Serapis.*—LXXXIII. *An account of the origin and superstitious worship paid by the Egyptians to that god.*—LXXXV. *Near the foot of the Alps, Valentinus is brought a prisoner before Mucianus and Domitian—He is condemned to die—The firmness with which he meets his fate.*—LXXXVI. *Domitian arrives at Lyons—He attempts to prevail on Cerealis to resign the command of the army in Germany—His dissimulation, and pretended love of studious retirement, the better to hide his real passions.*

These transactions passed partly during the civil war between Vespasian and Vitellius, in the year of Rome 822; and partly after the elevation of Vespasian, in the

Year of Rome.	Of Christ.	Consuls.
823	70	Flavius Vespasianus, Titus, his son.

I. Though the war, by the death of Vitellius, was completely ended, peace was by no means established. The victorious troops, with minds envenomed, fierce, and unrelenting, continued prowling about the streets of Rome in quest of the Vitellians. Every part of the city presented a scene of carnage; the forum and the temples were dyed with blood, and all who fell in the way of the conquerors were put to the sword without distinction. From the streets and public places the soldiers rushed into private houses, and, in their fury, dragged forth the unhappy victims. Whoever was grown up to manhood, citizen or soldier, was butchered on the spot. The fury of the men was at length glutted with blood, and the love of plunder succeeded. Nothing was suffered to remain concealed, nothing unviolated. Under colour of detecting the partisans of Vitellius, they broke open every secret recess in quest of booty.

Houses were pillaged, and all who attempted to resist died by the edge of the sword. The vile and indigent joined in the fray; slaves discovered the wealth of their masters, and numbers suffered by the treachery of their friends. The groans of despair were heard in every quarter, and Rome was filled with all the horrors of a city taken by storm. In comparison with the present barbarity, the people regretted the licentiousness of the Othonian and Vitellian soldiers. The leading chiefs, who had succeeded so well in kindling the flame of war, had now no authority to check the insolence of victory. In the hour of tumult and public distraction, the bold and desperate take the lead; peace and good order are the work of virtue and ability.

II. Domitian fixed his residence in the imperial palace, enjoying the name of Cæsar, but without aspiring to a share in the cares of government. Riot and debauchery gave the first impression of the emperor's son. The command of the prætorian bands was assigned to Arrius Varus, while the supreme authority rested with Antonius, who, in haste to enrich himself, seized the treasure and the slaves of the prince, as if they were the spoils of Cremona. The other officers, who, through their own moderation or want of spirit, were undistinguished during the war, remained in obscurity, unnoticed and unrewarded. The people, still in consternation, and ready to crouch in servitude, expressed their wishes that Lucius Vitellius, then advancing with the cohorts from Tarracina, might be intercepted on his march, in order, by that blow, to end the war. The cavalry was sent forward to Aricia,[1] and the legions took their station at Bovillæ.[2] But Lucius Vitellius was no longer disposed to maintain the conflict. He and his cohorts surrendered at discretion. The soldiers, abandoning an unfortunate cause, laid down their arms with indignation rather than fear. They entered the city of Rome in a long dismal procession, guarded on each side by a file of troops under arms. In their looks no sign of repentance, no dejected passion; they retained an air of ferocity, and heard the taunts of the vulgar with sullen contempt. A few broke from their ranks to repress the insolence of the populace, but were overpowered by numbers. The rest were secured in prison. Not a word escaped from any of them unworthy of their warlike character. They were unfortunate, but still respected for their valour. Lucius Vitel-

[1] Aricia in Latium.

[2] Bovillæ, about ten miles from Rome.

lius was put to death. In vice and profligacy he was equal to his brother; in vigour and industry, his superior; by the splendour of success no way benefited; in the day of adversity a sharer in the general ruin.

III. Campania was still in agitation. The disturbances in that country were not so much occasioned by a spirit of opposition to the new prince, as by the internal dissensions of the municipal cities, all at variance among themselves. To compose those differences, and restore public tranquillity, Lucilius Bassus[1] was despatched with a party of light-armed cavalry. On the first appearance of a military force, a perfect calm succeeded. The cities of inferior note were treated with indulgence: but the third legion was stationed in winter quarters at Capua, in order to bridle the principal families, who, by consequence, felt the weight of oppression. To the sufferers at Tarracina no relief was extended; so true it is, that men are more willing to retaliate an injury than to requite an obligation: obligation implies a debt, which is a painful sensation; by a stroke of revenge something is thought to be gained. The people of Tarracina saw the slave of Verginius Capito, who, as already mentioned, betrayed them to the enemy, hanging on a gibbet, with the rings on his fingers which he received from Vitellius as the reward of his perfidy. That act of justice was all that was done to assuage the sorrows of a city in distress.

At Rome, in the meantime, the senate, conceiving hopes of the new establishment, decreed to Vespasian all the honours which custom had hitherto granted to the reigning prince. The flame of war which first broke out in Spain and Gaul, and, after spreading into Germany and Illyricum, blazed out in Egypt, Judæa, and Syria, involving the several provinces and armies of the empire, seemed at length, by a severe lustration, to have expiated the crimes of mankind. The joy occasioned by that pleasing prospect, was heightened by letters from Vespasian; though, by the contents, it did not appear that he knew the issue of the war. As if that event had not yet reached his ear, he wrote in the style and language of an emperor; of himself he spoke with moderation; of the commonwealth with pomp and dignity. Nor was the senate backward in demonstrations of obsequious duty. They decreed the consulship to Vespasian and his son Titus. Domitian was made prætor with consular authority.

IV. Mucianus had also thought fit to write to the senate.

[1] For Lucilius Bassus, see ii. 100; and iii. 12.

His letters gave room for various reflections. Men observed, "If he was still a private citizen, why aspire above his rank, and usurp the prerogative of the sovereign? What he had to communicate, might have been reserved till he took his seat in the senate. His strain of invective against Vitellius came too late, and, after that emperor's death, gave no proof of his ardour in the cause of liberty. His vainglorious boast, that, having the sovereign power in his own disposal, he resigned it to Vespasian, was deemed an insult to the commonwealth, and, as far as it related to the prince, highly arrogant." But the senate acted with dissimulation; they murmured in private, and spoke aloud the language of flattery. They decreed triumphal decorations to Mucianus, in fact, for his conduct in the civil war; but his expedition against the Sarmatians [1] was the ostensible reason. The consular ornaments were voted to Antonius Primus, and the prætorian to Cornelius Fuscus and Arrius Varus.

The gratitude due to the gods was the next object of their care. They resolved to rebuild the capitol. The several motions were made by Valerius Asiaticus, consul elect. The fathers in general signified their assent by a nod of approbation, or by holding up their hands. A few, who valued themselves for their rank and dignity, or, by their eloquence, were able to give new graces to adulation, made elaborate speeches. Helvidius Priscus, prætor elect, delivered his sentiments in a manly strain. His speech was the panegyric of a virtuous prince, without a tincture of flattery. He was heard with applause by the whole assembly; and yet that day, so truly illustrious, may be called the first of his danger as well as glory.

V. As we shall have frequent occasion, in the course of our history, to speak of this excellent man,[2] it may be proper, in this place, to touch the features of his character, his conduct in life, and the fortune that attended him. Helvidius Priscus was born in the municipal city of Tarracina. His father, Cluvius, was a centurion of principal rank. Blessed with talents and an early genius, Helvidius applied himself to speculations of the sublimest kind; not with a design, as many have done, to grace a life of indolence with the name of abstract philosophy, but to bring with him into public business a mind provided with science and prepared to

[1] Triumphs and triumphal ornaments were never granted for a victory over Roman citizens.

[2] Helvidius Priscus has been mentioned, *Annals*, xvi. 35.

meet every danger. He adopted the tenets of those philosophers who maintain that nothing can be deemed an evil but vice; and nothing a positive good but what is fair and honourable; who place in the class of things indifferent all external advantages; and consider power, wealth, and nobility, as foreign to the soul, mere adventitious circumstances, in themselves equivocal, neither good nor evil. He had risen no higher than the quæstorian rank, when Pætus Thrasea[1] gave him his daughter in marriage. Of all the virtues of his father-in-law, he imbibed none so deeply as the spirit of liberty, which animated that extraordinary man. He performed the relative duties of every station with the strictest attention; citizen, senator, husband, friend, and son-in-law, he discharged all parts with equal lustre; despising riches; in the cause of truth inflexible; and, when danger threatened, erect and firm.

VI. The love of fame was by some objected to him as his strongest motive, his ruling passion. But the love of fame, it should be remembered, is often the incentive of the wise and good, the great principle of the noble mind, and the last which it resigns. When his father-in-law fell a victim to his enemies, Helvidius was driven into exile; but, being afterwards recalled by Galba,[2] he stood forth the accuser of Eprius Marcellus, the informer who wrought the downfall of Pætus Thrasea. By that vindictive measure, as bold as it was just, the senate was divided into contending factions. The ruin of Marcellus, it was clearly seen, would draw after it the whole legion of informers. The cause, however, went on, supported on both sides with equal ardour and consummate eloquence. Galba balanced between the parties, and the leading senators interposed to end the contest. At their request Helvidius desisted from the prosecution. His conduct, as usual, underwent various constructions; some commending the moderation of his temper, while others condemned him for his want of firmness. The day at length arrived, when the senate met to confirm the imperial dignity to Vespasian. It was agreed that deputies should be sent to congratulate the prince on his accession. In the debate upon this occasion, a sharp conflict ensued between Helvidius Priscus and Eprius Marcellus. The former proposed that the ambassadors should be named by magistrates sworn for the purpose. The latter was for

[1] For Pætus Thrasea, see *Annals*, xvi. 28 and 35.
[2] Helvidius was banished by Nero.

drawing the names by lot, as had been proposed by Valerius Asiaticus, the consul elect, who first moved in the business.

VII. Marcellus contended the point with force and vehemence. If an open election took place, he dreaded the disgrace of being rejected. The dispute, at first, was carried on in short but passionate onsets; from altercation it rose to the form of regular speeches. "Why," said Helvidius, "does Marcellus decline the judgment of the magistrates? The influence of wealth is on his side; the fame of eloquence gives him great advantages; but, perhaps, the memory of his guilt is not yet effaced. By drawing names out of an urn, no distinction of character is made. The mode of open suffrages is an appeal to the judgment of the senate, and in that way of proceeding, the fame and morals of men are brought to the test. It is for the interest of the community, and the honour of the prince, that such as approach him on so important an event should be chosen with discrimination, men of fair integrity, who are known to carry with them sentiments and principles worthy of the imperial ear. Vespasian had been, heretofore, in habits of friendship with Thrasea, with Soranus, and Sentius; and if the informers who ruined those excellent men are not to suffer the punishment due to their crimes, let them not expect, in the opening of a new reign, to play the first characters in the state. By the choice of the senate, the prince would see a line of distinction between the men whom he may safely trust, and such as deserve to be removed for ever from his presence. Virtuous friends are the true support of an upright government. Marcellus may rest satisfied with the exploits of his life: he incited Nero to the murder of the most illustrious citizens; that was his victory; let him enjoy the rewards of his guilt; let him triumph with impunity; but let him leave Vespasian to better men than himself."

VIII. Marcellus observed in reply, "that the motion, which was opposed with so much warmth, did not originate with himself. It was proposed by the consul elect, in conformity to ancient precedents, by which, to prevent intrigue and cabal, the choice of ambassadors had been wisely left to be decided by lot. And is there now any reason to warrant a departure from a system so long established, with intent, under colour of doing honour to the prince, to give a stab to the character of individuals? To pay due homage to the prince, was competent to all without distinction. The danger to be apprehended at present, is, that by the sullen humour of discontented men, an impression may be made on the mind of an emperor, new to the cares of state, and for that reason jealous of all, balancing their words, and forming a judgment of their looks and most frivolous actions. For himself, he knew the temper of the times in which he lived, nor was he a stranger to the form of government established by the old republic: he admired the past, and submitted to the present system, wishing, at all times, for a race of virtuous princes, but willing to acquiesce under the worst. The fall of Thrasea could not, with any colour of reason, be imputed to him:[1] the fathers heard the cause, and pronounced judgment against him. Nero, it was well known, amused mankind with a show of justice, while under the forms of law, he practised the most unrelenting cruelty. Nor did others suffer more by the pains and penalties of exile than he himself had felt from the dangerous friendship of that emperor. Let Helvidius, if he will have it so, be ranked with Cato and with Brutus; in courage and unshaken fortitude let him rival those exalted worthies: for himself, he pretended to be no more than one of that very senate, which submitted with passive obedience to the reigning prince. But, if he might presume to advise Helvidius, he would caution him not to aspire above his sovereign, nor affect, with airs of superior wisdom, to give dogmatical lessons to a prince advanced in years, who had gained triumphal honours, and was the father of two princes flourishing in the prime of life. For though it be true, that despotic power is the constant aim of the worst princes; it is equally true, that liberty, without due limitations, is never agreeable even to the best." Such were the arguments urged on both sides. The fathers heard the debate with divided sentiments. The party that inclined to the old practice of drawing the names by lot, prevailed in the end, supported, as they were, by the most illustrious members, who foresaw the danger of giving umbrage to numbers, if the choice was decided by a majority of voices.

IX. This debate was followed by another no less warm and spirited. The prætors, who at that time conducted the department of the treasury,[2] after giving a gloomy picture

[1] See the speech of Eprius Marcellus against Thrasea, *Annals*, xvi. 28.

[2] For the managers of the *Ærarium*, or the public treasury, see *Annals*, xiii. 29.

of the distress and poverty of the state, proposed a plan of public economy. The consul elect opposed the motion. The business, he said, was in itself of so much magnitude, and the remedy so nice and difficult, that the question ought to be reserved for the consideration of the prince. Helvidius Priscus was of a contrary opinion. To make new regulations, he contended, was the duty and the province of the senate. The consuls put the question, and were proceeding to collect the votes, when Volcatius Tertullinus, a tribune of the people, interposed his authority, that in so arduous a business nothing might be determined in the absence of the emperor. Helvidius had moved another resolution, importing that the capitol should be rebuilt by the public, with the voluntary aid of Vespasian. No debate ensued. Men of moderation wished to give their silent negative, and consign the motion to oblivion: but certain busy memories hoarded it up for a future day.

X. Musonius Rufus took this opportunity to fall on Publius Celer,[1] whom he charged with having, by false testimony, taken away the life of Bareas Soranus.[2] A prosecution of this kind tended to revive the resentments of the public against the whole race of informers; but an offender so vile, and so detested, could not be screened from justice. The memory of Soranus was held in veneration, and in the conduct of Celer there were circumstances that aggravated his crime. Professing to be a teacher of wisdom and philosophy, he took up the trade of an informer. He affected to explain the laws of friendship, and, in open violation of his own rules, became a traitor to the pupil whom it was his duty to protect. The cause was appointed to be heard at the next meeting of the senate. In the meantime the minds of men were eager with expectation, not only to see Musonius and Publius Celer engaged in a public controversy, but also to behold Helvidius Priscus returning to the charge against Eprius Marcellus, and the rest of that detested crew.

XI. In this distracted state of affairs, when the senate was divided into factions; when a ruined party still breathed resentment, and the conquerors were without authority; when no law was in force, and no sovereign at the head of the government; Mucianus entered the city, and soon engrossed into his own hands the whole power of the state.

[1] Egnatius Celer; *Annals*, xvi. 32.
[2] For Bareas Soranus, see *Annals*, xii. 53; xvi. 21 and 23.

The influence of Antonius, with that of Arrius Varus, vanished at once. Mucianus, harbouring secret animosity, amused them with a specious show of friendship; but a fair face could not disguise the malice of his heart. The people of Rome, ever quick to discern the spirit of parties, transferred their homage to Mucianus. He was now the rising sun. All degrees and ranks of men paid court to him alone. Mucianus, on his part, omitted nothing that could add to the grandeur of his appearance. He appeared in public attended by guards; he removed from one palace to another, and resorted to different gardens: his train, his equipage, and his pompous display, announced the ambition of the man. He assumed the majesty of empire, renouncing the title only. His first act of power struck a general terror. He ordered Calpurnius Galerianus[1] to be put to death. The unfortunate victim was the son of Caius Piso. His popularity, his youth, and the graces of his person, were his only crimes. In a city like Rome, still in agitation, prone to change, and listening with greedy ears to every rumour, Calpurnius was marked out, by the discourse of shallow politicians, as a person likely to succeed to the sovereign power. By order of Mucianus he was taken into custody, and, under a military guard, conveyed to a place forty miles distant on the Appian road. His veins were there opened, and he bled to death. Mucianus did not choose to hazard so tragical a scene in the city of Rome. Julius Priscus, who commanded the prætorian bands under Vitellius, without any urgent necessity, but conscious of various iniquities, despatched himself with his own hand. Alphenus Varus preferred a life of disgrace and infamy. Asiaticus, the freedman, suffered the punishment of common slaves, and, by that ignominious end, made atonement for the abuse of his ill-gotten power.

XII. About this period, the report which had prevailed for some time, of a dreadful defeat in Germany, was confirmed by fresh advices. The news made no impression at Rome. Men talked with calm indifference of the revolt of the provinces in Gaul, of the slaughter of armies, and of legions stormed in their winter quarters. Distant events were not considered as calamities. The flame of war being kindled in Germany, the occasion requires that we here explain the causes of that convulsion, which involved the allies of Rome,

[1] Calpurnius Galerianus was the son of Calpurnius Piso, who despatched himself to avoid Nero's cruelty.

and armed whole nations of barbarians against the Roman empire.

The Batavians,[1] while they dwelt beyond the Rhine, were a part of the people called the Cattians. Driven from their native country by intestine commotions, they settled on a waste tract of land bordering on the confines of Gaul, and, at the same time, took possession of an island washed at the northern extremity by the ocean, and at the back, and on both sides, by two branches of the Rhine. They formed a treaty of alliance with the Romans, and did not suffer by their friendship. A supply of men and arms was the whole of their contribution. In the wars in Germany they learned to be soldiers. They passed afterwards into Britain,[2] under the command of their own chiefs (according to their peculiar custom), and added new laurels to their former fame. In their own country they maintained a chosen body of cavalry, so expert in the art of swimming, that in whole squadrons, encumbered with their arms, and moving in regular order, they could dash across the current of the Rhine.

XIII. The leading chieftains of the nation were Julius Paulus and Claudius Civilis, both of royal descent. The former, under a false charge of rebellion, was put to death by Fonteius Capito. Civilis was sent in irons to be disposed of by Nero: Galba released him from his fetters. Under Vitellius, he was again in danger from the fury of the Roman soldiers, who called aloud for his execution. Hence his hatred of the Roman name, and his hopes of success founded on the distractions of the empire. Disfigured by the loss of an eye, he took occasion from that blemish to call himself a second Sertorius, or another Hannibal. Politic beyond the reach of barbarians, he wished to avoid an open rupture with Rome, and, to that end, affected to espouse the cause of Vespasian. To this conduct some colour was given by the letters which he received from Antonius, directing him to make a diversion in Germany, in order to prevent the succour of the legions expected by Vitellius. Hordeonius Flaccus gave the same order in person. That general was a friend to Vespasian's cause, but chiefly zealous in the cause of his country. If such prodigious numbers made an irruption into Italy, he trembled for the fate of the empire.

XIV. Civilis had taken his resolution to throw off the yoke. With a bold, but concealed, plan of ambition, he looked for-

[1] For the Batavi and the Catti, see the Manners of the Germans, 29.
[2] The Batavians served in Britain as the allies and auxiliaries of Rome.

ward to future contingencies, and took his measures in the following manner. By order of Vitellius, new levies were to be made, and the youth of Batavia was to be called out. This expedient, harsh in itself, was rendered still more so by the avarice and profligacy of the Roman officers. By their direction the aged and infirm were pressed into the service, in order to extort from them a stipulated price for their dismission. Boys of tender years, but advanced in their growth (as is generally the case in that country), were dragged away to gratify the criminal passions of their masters. Hence murmurs, jealousies, and grievous complaints. The leaders of the conspiracy saw their opportunity, and, by their advice, the people refused to be enrolled. Civilis, under the pretext of a convivial meeting, drew together the prime nobility, and the bravest of the nation, to a banquet in a sacred grove. At a late hour, when wine and midnight revelry had inflamed their spirits, he took occasion to expatiate on the fame and military exploits of the Batavians, artfully making a transition to the sufferings of his countrymen, the depredations of the Romans, and the cruel tyranny under which the nation groaned. "Rome," he said, "no longer treats us as allies and friends: we are reduced to the vilest bondage. The commanders of legions were wont to come among us with their train of attendants, always a grievous burthen; but even that honour is now withheld. We are turned over to centurions and subaltern officers. Those petty tyrants are no sooner enriched with plunder, and pampered with our blood, than they are recalled, to make way for new oppressors. Rapacity follows in succession; and, to varnish their new guilt, new expedients are found, and new names for extortion. A project is now on foot to recruit their armies, and for that purpose, the country must be drained of inhabitants; sons must be torn from their parents, and brothers from their brothers. And yet the Romans were never, at any period, in so feeble a condition. Behold their winter quarters: besides their old men, and their stores of plunder, what have they to exhibit to our view? Dare to lift your eyes, and you will see the phantom of an army, mere nominal legions. Our forces are in vigour; we have both infantry and cavalry: the Germans are our kinsmen; the Gauls think as we do: and even the Romans themselves invite us to the war. If we fail, our zeal for Vespasian will plead our excuse; if we succeed, Victory gives no account of her actions."

XV. This speech was received with shouts of approbation.

Civilis, taking advantage of the impression he had made, bound them all in a solemn league, with oaths and imprecations, according to the custom of barbarians. Deputies were sent to the Caninefates, to invite them into the confederacy. That nation occupies part of the island, in their origin, their manners, language, and military virtue, equal to the Batavians, but inferior in point of numbers. The Batavian cohorts, formerly sent to serve in Britain, as already mentioned, returned from that expedition, and were quartered at Magontiacum. By secret practices Civilis engaged them in the revolt. The leading chieftain among the Caninefates was known by the name of Brinno; a man of brutal and ferocious bravery, and by his birth illustrious. His father had been often in arms against the Romans, and, after many signal exploits, laughed at the ridiculous expedition and the mock triumph of Caligula. The descendant of a rebel family wanted no recommendation to his countrymen. Brinno was placed on a shield, according to the custom of the nation, and being carried in triumph on the shoulders of the men, was declared commander-in-chief. He was soon after joined by the Frisians, a people beyond the Rhine. With this reinforcement he found means to storm the winter quarters of two cohorts, which, except the extremity next to the sea, lay open and defenceless. The assault was not foreseen, nor were the Romans in force to maintain their post. The camp was taken and pillaged. The victuallers, and Roman traders, who had spread themselves over the country, were the next victims. That the castles and forts, built along the coast, might not fall into the hands of the enemy, the Roman officers, seeing an attack intended, ordered them all to be burnt to the ground. Aquillius, a principal centurion, collected together all the colours and standards, and, with the remnant of his forces, chose a station on the upper part of the island, exhibiting rather the name than the strength of an army. The flower of the cohorts had been drawn away by Vitellius, and, to fill up the companies, a set of raw recruits, from the neighbouring villages of the Nervians and Germans, were compelled to take up arms. But arms in the hands of men not inured to discipline, were an unwieldy burthen.

XVI. Civilis, still thinking it his interest to disguise his real intentions, complained aloud of the Roman officers, who had deserted their posts. With the cohort under his command, he would undertake to quell the insurrection of the Caninefates: the Romans, therefore, would do well to return to their quarters. The policy of this advice was too apparent. The cohorts, dispersed and weakened by division, might fall an easy prey; and from various circumstances, which the martial spirit of the Germans could not suppress, it soon transpired, that Civilis, and not Brinno, was at the head of the revolt. At length that enterprising chief, finding that he gained nothing by his wily arts, resolved to throw off the mask. He drew up his army in three divisions, consisting of the Caninefates, the Frisians, and Batavians, all distinguished by their proper colours and standards. The Romans appeared in order of battle on the banks of the Rhine, while their ships, which, after setting fire to the forts and castles, had been collected together, advanced up the river to second the operations of the army. A battle ensued, and had not lasted long, when a cohort of Tungrians, with their ensigns displayed, went over to Civilis. By this unexpected treachery the Roman army was thrown into confusion. The soldiers found themselves beset on every side. They were slaughtered by their friends and enemies. Nor did the fleet behave with more fidelity. Numbers of the men at the oars were Batavians: they began, as it were through ignorance and want of skill, to counteract the mariners and sailors, till, at length, turning the prows of the vessels, they bore away to the opposite shore. The pilots and centurions who dared to oppose them, were put to death; and thus the whole fleet, to the number of four and twenty ships, was either taken, or went over to the enemy.

XVII. This victory was splendid, and at the same time brought with it solid advantages. The Batavians were in want of arms and shipping, and they were now supplied with both. Their fame resounded throughout Gaul and Germany. Both nations honoured them as the assertors of public liberty. The Germans, by their ambassadors, offered to espouse their cause, and the Gauls were already inclined to join the confederacy. Civilis had the address to allure that nation to his interest. To such of their officers as were taken prisoners, he granted liberty to return to their native country, and the cohorts had their option either to depart, or to join the victorious army. Those who remained were employed honourably in the service, and such as preferred their dismission went off loaded with the spoils of the Romans. Before their departure, Civilis laboured, in secret conferences, to inflame their indignation. "Call to mind," he said, "the miseries which you have endured for a series of years. Your condition, during that period, was a state of bondage, and you gave it the name of peace. The Batavians were exempt from taxes and tributes, and yet they took up arms against the oppressors of mankind. In the first engagement, the Romans fled before the sons of freedom. Let the Gauls shake off the yoke, and what must be the consequence? The resources of Italy are exhausted. It is by the blood of the provinces that the provinces have been wrested from us. For the defeat of Vindex[1] the Romans have no reason to triumph. That victory was gained by the Batavian cavalry: by them the Æduans and Avernians were put to the rout. Among the auxiliaries led by Verginius on that occasion, the Belgic Gauls were his strongest force. Gaul, it may be truly said, was conquered by herself. At present, one common interest unites us all, and we have this further advantage; whatever of useful discipline was to be found in the Roman camps, we have made that our own. Their military skill is on our side. The veteran cohorts, before whom Otho's legions were obliged to fly, have declared for us. Syria and Asia, and the oriental nations, may, if they will, bow down in slavery, and stretch their necks to the yoke: under their own despotic kings they have been taught to crouch in bondage. In Gaul there are men still living, who were born in freedom, before tributes, imposts, and other badges of Roman tyranny, were invented. By the overthrow of Varus and his legions, slavery was driven out of Germany. In that juncture, it was not with a Vitellius that the assertors of freedom were to contend: the struggle was with Augustus Cæsar. Against that emperor the Germans fought for liberty, that best gift, dealt out by the impartial hand of nature, even to the brute creation. Man has the addition of courage and virtue to defend his rights; and all who have the fortitude to stand forth in that glorious cause, are sure to be favoured by the gods. Let us rise at once, and, sword in hand, attack a people weakened by their own divisions. Our strength is unimpaired; the Romans are exhausted; they are divided between Vespasian and Vitellius; and, while they are fighting for a master, they offer themselves to the just vengeance of an injured people."

XVIII. While Civilis, in this manner, endeavoured to rouse the states of Gaul and Germany, the ambition of that politic warrior inspired all his measures. If his project succeeded, he thought of nothing less than making himself king of those

[1] The defeat of Vindex at Visontium in Gaul.

rich and powerful nations. Hordeonius Flaccus affected, for some time, to have no suspicion of Civilis. He soon, however, received intelligence that the camp was taken by storm, the cohorts put to the sword, and the Roman name exterminated from the isle of Batavia. In this alarming crisis, he ordered Mummius Lupercus, with two legions, then under his command in winter quarters, to march against the enemy. That officer obeyed with prompt alacrity. With the forces in his camp, with the Ubians, who were near at hand, and the Treverian cavalry, drawn from an inconsiderable distance, he passed over into the island. He added to his army a squadron of Batavian horse, already corrupted by the wily arts of Civilis. These men made a show of zeal in the service of the Romans, to the end that, on the day of battle, they might enhance the value of their treachery. Civilis prepared to receive the enemy. Near his person he displayed the banners taken from the vanquished cohorts, that the sight of those glorious trophies might inspire his troops with ardour, and depress a conquered enemy by the recollection of their late calamity. In the rear he placed his mother and his sisters, with the wives and children of the soldiers, that they might there inflame the ardour of the combatants, and, by their reproaches, prevent an ignominious flight. The field resounded with the war-song of the soldiers, and the savage howlings of the women. The Romans returned a feeble shout. The Batavian cavalry went over to their countrymen, and by that desertion the left wing of the Roman army was exposed to the enemy. The legionary soldiers, though pressed on every side, preserved their ranks, and showed an intrepid countenance. The Ubian and Treverian auxiliaries fled with precipitation. The Germans pursued them with determined fury. The legions, in the meantime, seized the opportunity, and retreated in good order to the station known by the name of VETERA, or the old camp. After this victory, a struggle for power and pre-eminence broke out between Civilis and Claudius Labeo, who commanded the Batavian cavalry. Civilis did not judge it safe to put his rival to death: an act of violence might provoke the popular hatred; and yet, if he suffered him to remain with the army, internal discord might be productive of quarrels and confusion. Labeo was removed to the country of the Frisians.

XIX. Such was the posture of affairs when the Caninefates and a detachment of Batavian cohorts, by order of Vitellius, set out on their march for Rome. A messenger despatched by Civilis overtook them with the news of his victory. The intelligence filled the soldiers with arrogance and ferocity. They demanded a recompense for their march, the donative promised by Vitellius, with double pay, and an augmentation of their cavalry. In making these demands, they had no hopes of success; a pretext for sedition was all they wanted. Hordeonius Flaccus yielded in several instances; but his concessions provoked ulterior demands, which the men knew would not be granted. At length throwing aside all respect for the general, they resolved to join Civilis, and accordingly bent their course towards the Lower Germany. Flaccus called a council of the tribunes and centurions, to deliberate whether it were expedient to reduce the mutineers by force of arms. His natural timidity returned upon him, and his officers had no resolution. They suspected the fidelity of the auxiliary forces, and knew besides that the legions were chiefly filled with raw recruits. Flaccus resolved to keep his men within their intrenchments; but he resolved without decision, and the next moment repented. The very officers who advised the measure were the first to condemn it. The general sent off despatches to Herennius Gallus, then at the head of the first legion stationed at Bonn, with orders to oppose the march of the Batavians, while he himself with his whole army hung upon their rear. The plan was, no doubt, well concerted. Had both generals advanced with their troops, the revolters must have been hemmed in, and cut to pieces. Flaccus once more changed his mind. In a second letter to Gallus, he directed that officer not to obstruct the Batavians in their march. By this fluctuation of councils, both the generals were brought under a cloud of suspicion. The war and all its consequences were imputed, not to the inactive spirit of the soldiers, nor yet to the superior bravery of the insurgents, but to the perfidy of the commanding officers.

XX. The Batavians, as soon as they drew near to the camp at Bonn, sent a message to Herennius Gallus, importing "that they had no hostile design. They had often fought for the Romans, and did not mean to make war against them. Worn out in a long and painful service, they desired nothing but a retreat from labour in their native country. Their march, if not obstructed, would leave behind no trace of mischief; but if their passage was disputed, they were determined to cut their way sword in hand." The Roman general was staggered by these menaces; but his soldiers, eager for action, obliged him to hazard a battle. The whole army rushed out at the several gates of the camp, in number three thousand legionary soldiers, some Belgic cohorts raised by sudden levies, and a large body of peasants and followers of the camp, an undisciplined band, before the onset brave and insolent, and in the heat of action the first to betake themselves to flight. The Romans hoped to surround an enemy whom they knew to be inferior in number. The Batavians, whom a life of warfare had made soldiers, formed their ranks with skill; the front, the flanks, and the rear, prepared to meet the enemy. The Roman lines were too much extended into length. The Batavians attacked with fury, and soon broke through the ranks. The Belgic cohorts gave way on the first impression. The rout of the legions followed. All endeavoured to regain their camp. In the intrenchments a dreadful slaughter followed. The fosse was filled with mangled bodies, nor was the havoc made by the Batavians only: numbers, in that wild confusion, perished by the hands of their comrades. The conquerors pursued their march, avoiding the road to the Agrippinian colony, and, during the rest of their way, committed no act of hostility. They even endeavoured to exculpate themselves from all imputation in their late encounter at Bonn, alleging that they were, on that occasion, under the necessity of acting on the defensive, when peace was humbly offered, and haughtily refused.

XXI. Civilis, being now reinforced by these veteran cohorts, found himself at the head of a regular army. His resolution, notwithstanding, began to falter. The weight and power of the Romans presented themselves to his mind; he balanced all consequences, and, still remaining indecisive, judged it best to save appearances by making his whole army take the oath of fidelity to Vespasian. He also sent a deputation to the two legions, which after their late defeat retired to the old camp, inviting them to follow his example, and acknowledge the title of the new emperor. The legions returned for answer, "that it was not their custom to adopt the counsels of an enemy, much less of a traitor. Vitellius was their sovereign, and in his cause they would stand firm to the last. It was not for a deserter, a Batavian fugitive, to assume the style and character of an arbiter in the affairs of Rome. The punishment due to his crimes was what he had to expect." Enraged by this reply, Civilis roused the whole Batavian nation. The Bructerians and Tencterians[1] entered into the league, and by agents, despatched for the

[1] For the Bructeri and Tencteri, see *Annals*, xiii. 56.

purpose, all Germany was invited to share in the spoil and glory of the conquest.

XXII. Mummius Lupercus and Numisius Rufus, the two Roman generals, saw a storm gathering round them, and, to maintain their post against the combined forces of the enemy, began to strengthen the fortifications of the old camp. A number of buildings, during a long peace, had been erected near the intrenchments, so thick as to resemble a municipal town; but, in time of war, they might favour the approach of an enemy, and, for that reason, were levelled to the ground. But a sufficient store of provisions was not laid up in the camp. The soldiers were permitted to seize the whole stock, as lawful plunder; and by consequence, that which might have held out for a considerable time, was in a few days entirely consumed. Civilis advanced with the main body of his army. He commanded the centre in person, at the head of the select Batavian forces. To strike the Romans with terror, he lined both banks of the Rhine with battalions of Germans, and ordered the cavalry to scour the country round. His fleet, at the same time, advanced against the current. To increase the pomp and terror of the war, the colours taken from the cohorts were displayed to view, and the images of wild beasts were brought forth from the sacred groves, according to the custom of those barbarous nations rushing to a battle. The besieged saw the appearance of a civil and a foreign war upon their hands at once. The extent of the intrenchments, designed at first for the reception of two legions, and now defended by scarce five thousand men, inspired the Barbarians with hope and courage. It is true, that within the lines there was a numerous body of sutlers and followers of the army, who, on the first alarm, had fled to the camp for protection, and from those men some kind of service was expected.

XXIII. The camp stood partly on the side of a hill, that rose with a gentle acclivity, and partly on the level plain: originally the design of Augustus Cæsar, who had conceived, that the legions stationed there in winter quarters would be able to bridle both the Germanies. That emperor did not foresee the time when the Barbarians would dare to seek the legions in their intrenchments. It followed, by consequence, that no pains were employed to add to the natural strength of the place; no works were thrown up to secure the ramparts; courage and military discipline were deemed a sufficient bulwark. The Batavians, and the troops from beyond the Rhine, did not advance to the attack in one united body. Jealous of their national honour, and eager to distinguish themselves by brave exploit, the several nations formed their lines in separate divisions. The assault began with missive weapons lanced at a distance; but no impression was made. The darts hung without effect upon the towers and pinnacles of the walls, while the discharge of stones from the fortifications overwhelmed all beneath. The Barbarians resolved to storm the works. They rushed to the attack, rending the air with wild and furious howlings; they advanced their scaling-ladders, and formed a military shell. Some boldly gained the top of the parapet, but were driven back at the point of the sword, or beat down with bucklers. As they fell, numbers were crushed with stakes and javelins. Their own impetuous fury hurried them into danger. Encouraged by their former success, and sure of victory, they rushed on to the assault with that undaunted courage with which the thirst of prey inspires the minds of Barbarians. Under every disadvantage, they still thought of plunder. They attempted, for the first time, to make use of battering-engines, but without sufficient skill. They were taught by prisoners and deserters to raise, with rude materials, a platform, in the shape of a bridge, and to move it forward upon wheels. From the top of the arch, as from a rampart, some were able to annoy the besieged, while others, under cover, endeavoured to sap the walls. But the weight of stones discharged from the engines of the Romans broke down and crushed the enormous fabric. The Batavians, however, did not desist. They began to prepare penthouses, and to form a covered way with hurdles. The besieged attacked them with a volley of flaming javelins, and poured such an incessant fire, that the assailants were on every side enveloped by the flames. In despair of carrying the works by force, they turned their thoughts to a regular blockade. They knew that the besieged had but a scanty store of provisions, by no means equal to the subsistence of a vast unwarlike multitude. Famine, they had no doubt, would conspire with the natural treachery of the slaves to kindle the flame of sedition in the camp. They relied, besides, on the unforeseen events of war, and had no doubt of being in a short time masters of the place.

XXIV. Hordeonius Flaccus, having received intelligence that the old camp was invested, sent despatches into Gaul for a reinforcement, and ordered Dillius Vocula, who commanded the eighteenth legion, to proceed at the head of a chosen detachment, by rapid marches along the banks of the Rhine; while he himself, disabled by bodily infirmity, and detested by his men, sailed down the river, to follow the motions of the army. The complaints of the soldiers against their general were loud and violent. "It was by his connivance that the Batavian cohorts departed from Magontiacum; he was blind, or pretended to be so, to the machinations of Civilis; and he wilfully suffered the German nations to be drawn into the revolt. Neither Antonius Primus, nor Mucianus, by their vigour and activity, so effectually served the interest of Vespasian. Open hostility declares itself at once, and men are on their guard: fraud works in secret, and the blow, because concealed, is not easily warded off. Civilis has thrown off the mask; above disguise, an open enemy, he heads his army in the field. Hordeonius Flaccus wages war in his chamber; he gives his orders in bed, and favours the operations of the enemy. And shall so many brave and warlike soldiers languish under a wretched valetudinarian, a superannuated general? Better to strike at once, and, by the death of a traitor, deliver the army from an impotent chief, under whose inauspicious banners they had nothing to expect but disgrace and ruin." While by these and suchlike discourses the minds of the legions kindled to a blaze, letters from Vespasian added fuel to the flame. The receipt of those letters could not be concealed from the army. Flaccus, for that reason, read them to a full assembly of the soldiers, and sent the messengers bound in chains to Vitellius.

XXV. That proceeding had its effect: the men were pacified, and soon after arrived at Bonn, the winter station of the first legion. The soldiers at that place were still more enraged against the general. To his misconduct they imputed their late defeat. "By his order they marched out to offer battle to the Batavians, expecting, while they engaged the enemy in front, that the troops from Magontiacum were to fall upon the rear. But no succours arrived; the men fell a sacrifice to the treachery of the general. The other armies, wherever stationed, were kept in ignorance of all that passed, nor was any account transmitted to Vetellius. And yet it was evident, that, by the vigorous efforts of the adjoining provinces, the rebellion might have been crushed in the bud." To appease these discontents, Flaccus produced, and read, in the presence of the army, copies of the several letters by which he had endeavoured to obtain succours from Britain, Spain, and Gaul. He descended to other compliances still more pernicious and disgraceful. He established a new rule, by which it was settled, that for the future, all letters should be delivered to the eaglebearers of the legions, to be by them communicated to the soldiers, before they underwent the inspection of the general officers. He then ordered one of the mutineers to be loaded with irons; not that the man was the only incendiary, but the general meant, by that act, to retain some shadow of authority. From Bonn the army proceeded to the Agrippinian colony. At that place they were joined by numerous succours that came pouring in from Gaul, where, in the beginning of the troubles, the people still adhered to the interest of Rome. But in a short time afterwards, when they saw the efforts of the Germans crowned with success, the different states of that country had recourse to arms, determined to recover their liberty, and, if the enterprise succeeded, with the ambitious design of imposing upon others the yoke which they shook off from their own shoulders. The fury of the legions was far from being appeased. The example of a single offender bound in chains made no impression. That very man was hardy enough to turn his own particular case into an argument against his general. He had been, he said, the confidential messenger between Flaccus and Civilis; and now, to hinder the truth from being brought to light, his testimony was to be suppressed by an unjust and cruel sentence. The wickedness of this incendiary roused the indignation of Vocula. That spirited officer mounted the tribunal with a firmness that struck a general awe. He ordered the miscreant to be seized, and, notwithstanding the violence of his shrieks, sent him to instant execution. The seditious were overawed, and the well-disposed obeyed with alacrity. Vocula was now the favourite of the army. The soldiers, with one voice, insisted that he should be their general, and Flaccus resigned the command.

XXVI. The minds of the soldiers were still in agitation, and various causes conspired to inflame their discontents. Their pay was in arrear; provisions were scarce; the Gauls were not in a temper to pay their tribute, or to furnish supplies of men; the Rhine, by a long course of dry weather, almost unknown in that climate, was sunk so low as to be hardly navigable; supplies for the army were conveyed with difficulty; to hinder the Germans from fording over, a chain of posts was necessary on the banks of the river; and, by consequence, there was a dearth of grain, and many mouths to demand it. With vulgar minds, the shallowness of the stream passed for a prodigy. According to their interpretation, the very rivers deserted the Romans, and the ancient boundaries of the empire disappeared. That, which in time of peace would have been no more than the effect of natural causes, was now called fate, and the wrath of the gods. The army marched to Novesium, and was there joined by the thirteenth legion, under the command of Herennius Gallus, who was now associated with Vocula. The two generals were not inclined to seek the enemy. They pitched their camp at a place called Gelduba, and, to keep their men in exercise, employed them in forming the line of battle, in digging trenches, throwing up ramparts, and other military works. To give them an opportunity to plunder, and by that incentive to animate their courage, Vocula marched with the main body into the territory of the Gugernians,[1] a people leagued with Civilis. Gallus, in the meantime, with part of the troops, kept possession of the camp.

XXVII. It happened that a barge, laden with grain, was stranded in a shallow part of the river, at a small distance from the camp. The Germans exerted themselves to draw the vessel to their own bank. Gallus despatched a cohort to prevent the disgrace. The Germans poured down in great numbers. Succours arrived on both sides. An engagement followed. The Germans, after making a prodigious slaughter, secured the vessel. The Romans imputed their defeat not to their own want of valour, but to the treachery of the general. This, in all calamities, was the constant language of the army. The soldiers in their fury dragged Gallus out of his tent; they tore his clothes, and fell on him with blows, demanding who were the accomplices combined with him to betray the army? and what was the price of his perfidy? Their rage against Hordeonius Flaccus broke out again with increasing violence. He was the author of the crime, and Gallus was an instrument in his hands. In this extremity, to deliver himself from instant death, the general was obliged to yield to the passions of the men, and give his testimony against Hordeonius Flaccus. He was, notwithstanding, loaded with fetters, and not released till Vocula returned to the camp. That general, on the following day, ordered the ringleaders of the mutiny to be put to death. Such was the wonderful diversity of temper that showed itself in that army; at one moment, rage and madness, and, in quick succession, patience

[1] Originally a people of Germany.

and resignation. The common men, beyond all doubt, were devoted to Vitellius, while the most distinguished officers inclined to Vespasian. Hence that astonishing medley of guilt and punishment, of dutiful behaviour and savage ferocity. The men were unwilling to be governed, and yet submitted to correction.

XXVIII. Civilis, in the meantime, grew every day more formidable. All Germany espoused his cause, and succours arrived from every quarter. The states beyond the Rhine delivered their prime nobility as hostages to bind the league in closer union. Civilis issued his orders, that the confederates, who lay contiguous to the Ubians and Treverians, should harass the people by frequent incursions, and carry slaughter and devastation through their country. At the same time he gave directions that a strong party should pass over the Meuse, to invade the Menapians, the Morinians, and the frontiers of Gaul. The soldiers in every quarter were enriched with plunder. The Ubians, in particular, felt the vengeance of the ravaging parties. Though they were originally of German extraction, they had renounced their country, and, proud of a Roman name, styled themselves the Agrippinian colony. Their cohorts, posted at a distance from the Rhine, and in that station thinking themselves secure, were surprised at the town of Marcodurum, and cut to pieces. The Ubians, in their turn, penetrated into Germany, and at first committed depredations with impunity, till, in the end, they were overpowered by superior numbers. Through the whole of the war their fidelity to Rome was unshaken; but a train of misfortunes was their only recompense. Flushed with success, and pleased with the defeat of the Ubians, Civilis pressed the siege of the old camp with the utmost vigour. His first care was to cut off all communication, that no intelligence of intended succours might reach the garrison. The management of the battering-engines and other warlike preparations he left to the Batavians; and seeing that the forces from beyond the Rhine were eager for action, he ordered them to advance to the intrenchments, and by a sudden assault to force the works. They were repulsed, and by his order returned to the charge. In so numerous an army men might be sacrificed, and yet the loss not be felt.

XXIX. The night afforded no pause from the attack. The Barbarians set fire to the clumps of wood, which they had ranged along the intrenchments, and betook themselves to feasting and revelry. Growing warm with liquor, they rushed with headlong fury to assault the works. Their darts were thrown at an enemy safe in obscurity, while the Romans were enabled by the glaring fires to view the scene of action, and take aim at the combatants, who made themselves conspicuous by their valour or the splendour of their arms. Civilis saw the disadvantage, and ordered the fires to be extinguished. Confusion, darkness, and wild uproar, followed. Dissonant shouts were heard; random blows were given; chance directed, and none could see where to press or avoid the enemy. Where the noise was loudest, they faced about to that quarter, and discharged their weapons in the dark. Valour was undistinguished, and the bravest often fell by the hand of the coward. The Germans fought with the rage of madmen; the Romans with their usual discretion, like soldiers inured to danger. Their poles pointed with iron were never darted at random, nor did they discharge their massy stones without being sure of their effect. Whenever they heard the Barbarians sapping the foundations of the walls, or found their scaling-ladders applied to the ramparts, they made sure of their blow, and with their bucklers or their javelins drove the assailants headlong down the steep. Some gained the summit of the walls, and perished on the spot. The night passed in this manner, and the day brought on a new mode of attack.

XXX. A tower with two floors for the soldiers, had been constructed by the Barbarians. With this huge machine they now advanced against the works at the prætorian gate, the ground on that side of the camp being smooth and level. The Romans directed their strong beams and other instruments with so much force that the whole structure was crushed to pieces, and the soldiers, who had been posted in the galleries, lay buried under the ruins. In that moment the besieged made a successful sally. The legionary soldiers, in the meantime, framed with skill a number of new machines. One, in particular, struck the enemy with terror and amazement. This was so constructed, that an arm, projecting from the top, waved over the heads of the Barbarians, till, being suddenly let down, it caught hold of the combatants, and, springing back with sudden elasticity, carried them up in the air, in the view of the astonished Germans, and, turning round with rapidity, threw them headlong into the camp. Civilis found himself baffled in every attempt. He despaired of carrying the place by storm, and once more turned the siege into a close blockade; in the meantime tampering with the garrison, and, by false intelligence as well as ample promises, endeavouring to seduce the men from their duty.

XXXI. The transactions, which we have here related, happened in Germany before the battle of Cremona. The first account of the victory at that place was sent by Antonius Primus, with Cæcina's proclamation annexed to his letters. The news was further confirmed by Alpinus Montanus, the commander of one of the vanquished cohorts, who, after the defeat, made the best of his way into Germany. By this event the minds of the Roman army were thrown into violent agitations. The auxiliaries from Gaul, a mercenary band, who neither loved one party nor hated the other, mere soldiers of fortune, without sentiment or principle, were soon persuaded by their officers to abandon the cause of Vitellius. The veteran soldiers remained for some time in suspense. Overruled at length by Herdeonius Flaccus, and importuned by the tribunes, they swore fidelity to Vespasian; but with an air of reluctance, and a stern ferocity, that plainly showed their hearts were not in unison with their words. In repeating the form of the oath, they faltered at the name of Vespasian, never pronouncing it distinctly, but muttering to themselves, and, in general, passing it over in silence.

XXXII. A letter from Antonius to Civilis was read to a full assembly of the legions. The style in which that active partisan was treated as a friend to the new emperor, while the legions were considered as enemies, excited a general indignation. An account of these transactions was soon after transmitted to the camp at Gelduba, where the same compliance, and the same discontents, prevailed. Montanus was deputed to Civilis, with instructions to require that he would "lay down his arms, and cease to varnish hostile intentions with the specious pretence of fighting in the cause of Rome. If, in fact, he meant to serve Vespasian, that end was answered, and it was time to sheathe the sword." To this message Civilis replied with guarded subtlety; but perceiving in Montanus an active genius, and a spirit of enterprise, he opened his mind without reserve. "I have served," he said, "in the Roman armies for five-and-twenty years: in that time I have encountered various perils; and what has been my reward? I have seen the death of a brother; I have been loaded with fetters; and I have heard the clamours of the Roman army, with rage and violence demanding my blood. If, in return, I seek the blood of my enemies, I stand justified by the law of nations. As to you, ye Treverians, and you, ye abject nations, who can tamely submit to a foreign master, what do you expect will be the fruit of all your toil, and all your blood lavished in the service of Rome? Endless warfare, eternal tributes, the lictor's rod, the axe, and the wanton cruelty of your imperious masters; those are the rewards that wait you. Behold in me the prefect of a single cohort; behold the Caninefates and the Batavian forces: they are but a mere handful of men, a small portion of Gaul: and yet, what have we not achieved? That spacious camp, the proud display of Roman labour, is, at this moment, tottering to its fall. If their legions hold out, famine will devour them; if famine forbears, the sword must end them. In a word, by daring nobly, we shall recover our liberty: if we fail, our condition cannot be worse than it was before." By this animated speech Civilis roused the ambition of Montanus. He then dismissed him, with directions to report his answer in milder terms. Montanus obeyed his orders, content with reporting that he failed in his negotiation. He suppressed the rest; but the whole broke out afterwards with redoubled fury.

XXXIII. Civilis turned his attention to the motions of Vocula and his army. Having reserved for himself a sufficient force, he despatched to Gelduba his veteran cohorts, and the bravest of the Germans, under the command of Julius Maximus and Claudius Victor. The last was nephew to Civilis, being a sister's son. The two chiefs arrived at Asciburgium, and there stormed the winter encampment of a squadron of horse. From that place they made a forced march, and fell with such unexpected fury on the camp at Gelduba, that Vocula had neither time to harangue his men, nor to form his line of battle. All he could do, was to order the legionary soldiers to draw up in the centre. The auxiliaries, in a tumultuary manner, ranged themselves in the wings. The cavalry advanced to the attack; but making no impression on the well-embodied ranks of the Germans, they soon gave ground, and fled with precipitation. From that moment, it was a scene of slaughter, not a battle. The Nervians quitted their post through fear or treachery, and, by their flight, left the flank of the Romans open to the enemy. The Barbarians following their advantage, penetrated to the centre. They drove the legions into their intrenchments; they seized their standards, and made a dreadful carnage. But a reinforcement coming up in time, the fortune of the day was changed. The Gascon cohorts,[1]

[1] The Vascones inhabited the country of *Navarre.*

formerly levied by Galba, had received orders to join the army. Hearing, as they approached the camp, the din of arms, and the uproar of battle, they advanced to the attack, and charged the Batavians in the rear. The terror that seized the enemy, was greater than could be expected from so small a number. Some imagined that succours arrived from Novesium; others thought of nothing less than the whole army from Magontiacum. The mistake revived the drooping courage of the Romans. Depending on the valour of others, they began to exert their own. The Batavian infantry was put to the rout. Their cavalry escaped, and carried with them the prisoners and standards, which they had taken in the beginning of the action. The number slain on the part of the Romans greatly exceeded the loss of the enemy; but the slaughter fell on the worst of their troops, whereas the Germans lost the flower of their army.

XXXIV. The commanders on both sides were equally in fault. By their misconduct, they deserved the check they met with; and, when fortune favoured their arms, neither of them knew how to improve his advantage. Had Civilis sent into the field a stronger force, it is evident that his men could not have been hemmed in by so small a number. Having forced the intrenchments, he might have razed them to the ground. On the other hand, Vocula had sent out no scouts to watch the motions of the enemy. Taken by surprise, he marched out of his camp, and was defeated. Having afterwards gained a victory, he made no use of it, but lost several days before he made a forward movement. Had he pursued his advantage, and given the enemy no time to rest, one vigorous effort would have raised the siege of the camp. Civilis exerted every effort, determined to profit by the inactivity of the Roman general. He endeavoured, by his messengers, to shake the firmness of the garrison; he represented the forces under Vocula as entirely overthrown; he boasted of a complete victory; he displayed the banners taken from the enemy, and, with ostentation, made a show of the prisoners. The spirit with which one of them behaved deserves to be recorded. With a clear and audible voice, he called out to the besieged, and told them the event of the late battle. For this gallant action, he was butchered on the spot. That act of vengeance gave credit to his story. The besieged, at the same time, saw the blaze of villages on fire, and the country laid waste on every side. This announced the approach of a victorious army. Vocula commanded his men to halt in the sight of the camp, and, having erected his standards, ordered a fosse to be made, and a palisade to be thrown up, that, the baggage being safely deposited, he might offer battle with greater security. The soldiers thought it loss of time, they desired to be led on to the attack; and, according to custom, threats of vengeance resounded through the army. No order of battle was formed. Fatigued by their march, and their ranks in confusion, they rushed on with impetuous fury. Civilis was in force, and ready to receive them. He relied no less on the vices of his enemy, than on the valour of his own troops. The Romans fought with various turns of fortune. The bold and forward in sedition were cowards in the field. A sense of honour prevailed with some. They remembered their late exploits, and, flushed with victory, maintained their post; they attacked the Barbarians, and by deeds of valour roused the spirit of their comrades. Having restored the broken ranks, and renewed the battle, they waved their hands to the besieged, inviting them to sally out, and use their opportunity. The legions from their ramparts saw the scene of action, and rushed out at every gate. An accident disconcerted Civilis. His horse fell under him. A report that he was slain, or dangerously wounded, ran through both armies. Consternation covered the Batavian ranks, and joy inspired the Romans with new ardour.

XXXV. Vocula did not think fit to harass the Barbarians in their retreat. Instead of hanging on their rear, he amused himself with repairing the works of the camp, as if he expected a second siege. The consequence was that he who so often neglected to make use of his victory, was thought no enemy to a lingering war. The scarcity of provisions was what chiefly distressed the Roman army. To remedy the evil, Vocula sent off all his useless people, with the waggons, as far as Novesium, with intent that, by the return of the same convoy, a supply of corn might be brought to the camp. The conveyance by land was necessary, as the enemy were masters of the river. The first attempt succeeded, Civilis not having then recovered his strength. Being informed soon after that a second party was on their way to Novesium, with a few cohorts marching in all the negligence of a profound peace, their colours and standards thinly guarded, their arms laid up in the waggons, and the men scattered in loose disorder, he resolved to attack them by surprise. Having first secured the bridges over the river, and the defiles of the country, he advanced in order of battle. The Romans, though their lines were stretched to a vast length, made a brave resistance, till night put an end to the conflict. The cohorts arrived at Gelduba, and found the intrenchments and the garrison in good condition. The difficulty of returning, after this check, to the old camp was now too apparent. Vocula resolved to march to their assistance. For this purpose he drafted from the fifth and fifteenth legions a thousand chosen men, who had stood the siege in the old camp, and were distinguished by their rancorous animosity to their commanding officers. These he added to his army. A number of others, without orders, thought fit to follow, declaring aloud that they would neither bear the distress of famine, nor the treachery of their chiefs. Among those who remained behind, the spirit of discontent was no less violent. They complained, that, by drawing off a part, the whole was weakened. Hence two seditions raged at the same time; one demanding the return of Vocula, and the other resolved never again to enter the camp.

XXXVI. Civilis, in the meantime, returned to the siege. Vocula retired to Gelduba, and thence to Novesium. Civilis took possession of Gelduba, and soon after, in an engagement of the cavalry, near Novesium, gained a victory. All events, whether prosperous or otherwise, were now alike to the Romans, incensed on every occasion against their general officers. Being reinforced by the detachment from the fifth and fifteenth legions, they grew more outrageous than ever: and having gained intelligence that a sum of money was sent by Vitellius, they clamoured loudly for the immediate discharge of their donative. Hordeonius Flaccus complied without hesitation, but in the name of Vespasian. By this step the flame of sedition was kindled to a blaze. The men betook themselves to feasts and revelling; they caroused during the night, and, in their liquor, their old antipathy to Flaccus revived with all its virulence. They rushed to his tent; the darkness of the night served to muffle their horrible design, and no sense of shame remained. Neither tribune nor centurion dared to interpose. They dragged their general out of his bed, and murdered him on the spot. The same catastrophe was prepared for Vocula; but that officer, in the disguise of a slave, made his escape. The fury of the mutineers began to relent: fear succeeded to rage; they dreaded the consequences, and, in their distress, despatched some of the centurions with letters to the states of Gaul, requesting a supply of men and money.

XXXVII. Being left without a leader, they were no better than a senseless multitude, bold and wavering, rash and cowardly, by turns. Civilis advanced to offer battle; they seized their arms, they laid them down, and betook themselves to flight. Even in distress they could not act with a spirit of union; they quarrelled among themselves, and the soldiers from the upper Rhine abandoned the common cause. The images of Vitellius were, notwithstanding, set up in the camp, and the adjacent Belgic cities; but Vitellius was then no more. The soldiers of the first, the fourth, and the eighteenth legions, returning to a sense of their duty, put themselves under the command of Vocula, and having, by his direction, taken the oath of fidelity to Vespasian, marched to raise the siege of Magontiacum. A motley army of the Cattians, the Usipians, and the Mattiaci had invested the place; but, on the approach of the Romans, they decamped with a load of booty. The legions fell in with their straggling parties, and put a great number to the sword. The Treverians had sunk a fence and raised a palisade, to defend the frontier of their country against the inroads of the Germans, whom they attacked with alternate success, and no small effusion of blood. In the end, they deserted from the Romans, and, by their perfidy, sullied the lustre of all their former services.

XXXVIII. Meanwhile, Vespasian and his son Titus, though both absent from Rome, entered on the year of their joint consulship.[1] A melancholy gloom hung over the city. The minds of men were distracted with different apprehensions, and to their natural fears imagination added a train of groundless terrors. It was supposed that Africa,[2] at the instigation of Lucius Piso, was in open rebellion. Piso was, at that time, governor of the province; but the love of innovation made no part of his character. It happened that the roughness of the winter interrupted the navigation, and, the corn ships not arriving regularly, the populace, who have never more than one day's provision, dreaded an approaching famine. Of all that concerns the public, the price of grain is their only care. Their fear at present was, that, to cut off supplies from Rome, the coast of Africa was guarded; and what they feared, they easily believed. The Vitellians, not having yet renounced the spirit of party, did what in them

[1] A.D. 70.
[2] The province of Africa, now *Tunis*.

lay to confirm the report. Even the conquerors did not dislike the news. Convulsions of the state were not unwelcome to men of their description, whose avarice no foreign conquest could appease, and no civil war could satisfy.

XXXIX. On the calends of January, the senate, convened by Julius Frontinus, the city prætor, passed a vote of thanks to the general officers, the armies, and the kings in alliance with Rome. Tertius Julianus, who had quitted the legion under his command, as soon as the men declared for Vespasian, was, for that offence, deprived of the prætorship. Plotius Griphus succeeded to the office. Hormus was raised to the equestrian rank. Upon the voluntary abdication of Frontinus, Domitian, who had the additional title of Cæsar, assumed the dignity of city prætor. From that time, all edicts and public instruments were issued in his name; but the authority of government still centred in Mucianus, though sometimes counteracted by Domitian. That young prince, encouraged by his friends, or spurred on by his own ambition, by fits and starts assumed the character of first minister. But Antonius Primus and Arrius Varus were the persons whom Mucianus viewed with a jealous eye. They were both recent from the field of glory; both covered with laurels, idolised by the army, and, as all the blood they had spilt was in the field of battle, they were both respected by the populace. Antonius, it was confidently said, had invited Scribonianus Crassus[1] to the head of the commonwealth. Crassus was descended from an illustrious line of ancestors, and derived additional lustre from his brother, whom Galba made, by adoption, heir-apparent of the empire. Thus distinguished, he would not have wanted partisans; but he was deaf to all temptation. A man of his way of thinking, who would have refused himself to a party already formed, was not to be dazzled by a distant and uncertain prospect. Mucianus found that he had, in the person of Antonius, a powerful rival. To ruin him by open hostility were a dangerous attempt. He resolved to act by stratagem; accordingly, in the senate, grew lavish in his praise. He amused him in private with splendid promises; he offered him the government of the nethermost Spain, then vacant by the absence of Cluvius Rufus, and bestowed favours on his friends, assigning to some the rank of prefect, and raising others to military honours. He flattered the ambition of

[1] Scribonianus Crassus was the brother of Piso, whom Galba adopted.

Antonius, and was, at the same time, at work to undermine him. He sent the seventh legion, known to be devoted to his rival, into winter quarters. The third was in the interest of Arrius Varus, and for that reason sent into Syria. Part of the army was ordered back to Germany; and, the seeds of tumult and sedition being in this manner removed, the city began to resume its ancient form: the laws revived, and the magistrates discharged the functions of their office.

XL. Domitian, on the day of his first appearance in the senate, lamented, in a short speech, the absence of his father and his brother Titus. Of himself he spoke with becoming diffidence. His deportment was graceful, and his manner interesting. The vices of his heart being then unknown, the blush of youth was considered as the mark of an ingenuous mind. He proposed that the name of Galba should be revived with all the honours due to his memory. Curtius Montanus added to the motion the name of Piso. A decree was passed accordingly, but, as far as it related to Piso, never executed. A number of commissioners were drawn by lot; some with power to restore to the lawful owners the property wrested from them during the violence of civil war; others, to inspect the tables of brass, on which the laws were engraved, and to repair such as were defaced by the injuries of time; to examine the public registers, and erase the expressions of servile adulation, with which, at different periods, they were all contaminated; and finally, to set due limits to the public expenditure. Tertius Julianus, it now appeared, fled from his legion, to join the banners of Vespasian, and thereupon the prætorian dignity was restored to him; but the honours of that rank were by a decree confirmed to Griphus. The prosecution commenced by Musonius Rufus against Publius Celer was resumed, and brought to a hearing. Celer was convicted, and by the sentence of condemnation he made atonement to the manes of Soranus. This act of justice was honourable to the fathers, and not less so to Musonius. Men applauded the constancy with which he vindicated the memory of his friend. Nothing could equal his glory, except the infamy that attended Demetrius, a professor of the cynic philosophy, who, with more ambition than virtue, employed his eloquence in the cause of a notorious criminal, who, in the hour of danger, had neither courage nor ability to defend himself. The event gave the signal for a general attack on the whole race of informers; and, accordingly, Junius Mauricus moved for an order to lay the journals of the late emperors before the senate, that in those records it might be seen, who were the men of a persecuting spirit, and against whom their malice had been levelled. Domitian was of opinion, that in a matter of such magnitude, the emperor ought to be consulted.

XLI. The senate, on the motion of some of the leading members, devised a new form of oath, by which they called the gods to witness, that no man by any act of theirs had been aggrieved, and that they themselves had derived no kind of advantage from the calamity of the times. The magistrates took this oath with the most ready compliance; and the fathers, in regular succession, followed their example. Some, whom their conscience reproached in secret, endeavoured, by various subtleties, to weaken or to vary the form of the words. The remorse of scrupulous minds the fathers approved, but equivocal swearing they condemned as perjury. That judgment, delivered by the highest authority, fell with weight upon Sariolenus Vocula, Nonius Actianus, and Cestius Severus, three notorious informers in the reign of Nero. The first of these offenders added to his former practices the recent guilt of attempting the same iniquity under Vitellius. The fathers, fired with indignation, threatened to lay violent hands on him, and never desisted till they forced him to withdraw from the senate-house. Pactius Africanus was the next object of resentment. It was he, they said, who made Nero sacrifice to his cruelty the two Scribonii, those excellent brothers, not more distinguished by the splendour of their fortunes, than by their affection for each other. The miscreant had not the contumacy to avow the fact, and to deny it was not in his power. He turned short upon Vibius Crispus, who pressed him with pointed questions; and, since he could not justify his own conduct, he contrived, by blending it with the guilt of his accuser, to soften resentment against himself.

XLII. In the debates of that day, Vipstanius Messala, though a young man, not yet of senatorian age,[1] gained immortal honour, not only by his eloquence, but for natural affection and the goodness of his heart. He had the spirit to stand forth for his brother, Aquilius Regulus,[2] and to implore, in his behalf, the lenity of the fathers. By the ruin of the ancient family of the Crassi, and the illustrious house of Orphitus,[3] Regulus had drawn upon himself the public

1 That is, not five-and-twenty. 2 A practised informer.

3 Crassus Camerinus and Scribonianus Camerinus were accused by Regulus in the reign of Nero, and put to death. See Pliny, lib. i. epist. 5.

detestation. Of his own motion he undertook the prosecution against those eminent citizens. He had no motives of fear, no danger to ward off from himself. The early genius of the man made him an informer from his youth; and by the destruction of others he hoped to open his road to honours. His brother, notwithstanding, interceded for him; but, on the other hand, Sulpicia Prætextata, the widow of Crassus, with her four fatherless children, attended the senate, ready, if the cause came to a hearing, to demand the vengeance due to his crimes. Messala did not enter into the merits of the cause. Without attempting to make a defence, he sued for mercy, and succeeded so well, that many of the fathers were softened in his favour. To counteract that impression, Curtius Montanus rose, and, in a speech of great warmth and vehemence, went so far as to charge, in direct terms, that Regulus, as soon as Galba was despatched, gave a purse of money to the ruffian that murdered Piso, and, throwing himself on the body with unheard-of malice, gnawed the head with his teeth. "This," he said, "was an act of barbarity not imputable to Nero. Did that tyrant order it, or did you, Regulus, advance your dignity by that atrocious deed? Did your personal safety require it? Let us, if you will, admit, in some cases, the plea of necessity: let those, who, to save themselves, accomplish the ruin of others, be allowed, by such excuses, to extenuate their guilt. You, Regulus, have not that apology: after the banishment of your father, and the confiscation of his effects, you lived secure, beyond the reach of danger. Excluded by your youth from public honours, you had no possessions to tempt the avarice of Nero; no rising merit to alarm his jealousy. A rage for blood, early ambition, and avarice panting for the wages of guilt, were the motives that urged you on. Unknown at the bar, and never so much as seen in the defence of any man, you came upon mankind with talents for destruction. The first specimen of your genius was the murder of illustrious citizens. The commonwealth was reduced to the last gasp, and that was the crisis in which you plundered the remaining spoils of your country. You seized the consular ornaments, and, having amassed enormous riches, swelled your pride with the pontifical dignities. Innocent children, old men of the first eminence, and women of illustrious rank, have been your victims. It was from you that Nero learned a system of compendious cruelty. The slow progress with which he carried slaughter from house to house, did not satisfy your thirst for blood. The emperor, according to your doctrine, fatigued himself and his band of harpies, by destroying single families at a time, when it was in his power, by his bare word, to sweep away the whole senate to destruction. Retain amongst you, conscript fathers, if such be your pleasure, retain this son of mischief, this man of despatch, that the age may have its own distinctive character, and send down to posterity a model for imitation. Marcellus and Crispus gave lessons of villainy to your fathers: let Regulus instruct the rising generation. We see, that daring iniquity, even when unsuccessful, has its followers: when it thrives and flourishes, will it want admirers? We have before us a man, no higher at present than the rank of quæstor; and if we are now afraid of proceeding against him, what think you will be the case, when we see him exalted to the prætorian and the consular dignity? Do we flatter ourselves, that the race of tyrants ended with Nero? The men who survived Tiberius reasoned in that manner; after the death of Caligula they said the same; but another master succeeded, more cruel, and more detestable. From Vespasian we have nothing to fear. He is at the time of life when the passions subside; the virtues of moderation and humanity are his: but virtue operates slowly while pernicious examples remain in force, and teach a system of cruelty when the tyrant is no more. As to us, conscript fathers, we have lost all our vigour; we are no longer the senate that condemned Nero to death, and in the spirit of ancient times called aloud for vengeance on the ministers and advisers of that evil period. The day that succeeds the downfall of a tyrant is always the best."

XLIII. This speech was heard with such marks of general approbation, that Helvidius Priscus, taking advantage of the temper of the fathers, thought it a fair opportunity to have his full blow at Eprius Marcellus. He began with an encomium on the character of Cluvius Rufus; a man of wealth and distinguished eloquence, yet never known, through the whole reign of Nero, to have employed his talents against the life or fortune of any person whatever. As a contrast to this bright example, he painted forth, in glaring colours, the flagitious practices of Marcellus. The fathers heard the charge with indignation. Marcellus saw the temper of the assembly, and, rising in his place, addressed himself to Helvidius: "I withdraw," he said, "and leave you to give your laws to the senate. Preside if you will, and, even in the presence of the emperor's son, usurp the supreme authority." He spoke, and quitted his seat. Vibius Crispus followed him; both enraged, but with different passions in their looks; Marcellus with eyes that darted fire: Crispus, with a malignant smile. Their friends prevailed on them to return to their places. The whole assembly was in a flame. The men of integrity were on one side, and formed the largest party: the opposite faction were few in number, but they had weight and influence. A violent contest followed, and ended in nothing. The day was lost in altercation.

XLIV. At the next meeting of the senate, Domitian proposed a general amnesty, in order to bury in oblivion all complaints, all resentments, and all the grievances of former times. Mucianus went at large into the case of the informers, and, in a tone of mild persuasion, entreated such as wanted to revive dormant prosecutions to desist from their purpose. The fathers had hitherto entertained hopes of recovering the independent exercise of their rights; but the present opposition convinced them, that liberty was not to be favoured. Mucianus apprehending, that, by this check, a blow might appear to be given to the authority of the senate, and that, by consequence, impunity would be claimed by all the delinquents of Nero's time, remanded to the islands, to which they had been banished, Octavius Sagitta, and Antistius Sosianus, both of senatorian rank. The former had lived in a course of adultery with Pontia Posthumia; and not being able to prevail on her to marry him, in the fury of disappointed love murdered the woman whom he adored. Sosianus, by his evil practices, had been the ruin of numbers. Both had been condemned by a solemn decree of the senate; and though, in other instances, similar judgments had been remitted, against these two offenders the law was enforced with rigour. Mucianus expected that these measures would soften prejudice, and conciliate the public favour; but his plan did not succeed. Sosianus and Sagitta might have been allowed to remain at Rome without any disadvantage to the public. They were men despised, and must have lived in obscurity. The grievance, under which the people laboured, arose from the encouragement given to the tribe of informers. The talents, the riches, and the influence of that pernicious crew, spread a general terror through the city.

XLV. A cause, which was soon after brought forward, and heard in due form, according to ancient usage, contributed, in some degree, to calm the discontents of the senate. A complaint was made to that assembly, by Manlius Patruitus, a member of their body, that, at a meeting of the people in the colony of the Senensians, he was assaulted, and even struck, by order of the magistrates. Nor did the injury stop there: they buried him in effigy in his own presence, compelling him not only to be a spectator of the scene, but to bear the insulting mockery of funeral lamentations, to see the images of his ancestors carried in a ludicrous procession, and to hear a torrent of opprobrious language thrown out against the senate. The parties accused were cited to appear. The cause was heard, and the guilty suffered condign punishment. The fathers added a decree, by which the people of the colony were required to be more observant of decency and good order. About the same time, Antonius Flamma, at the suit of the inhabitants of Cyrene, was convicted of extortion, and, his case being aggravated by acts of cruelty, the fathers ordered him into banishment.

XLVI. During these transactions, a violent uproar broke out in the camp, and almost rose to open sedition. The soldiers, disbanded by Vitellius, and afterwards embodied in the service of Vespasian, claimed a right to their former rank in the prætorian guards. At the same time, a number of others, who had been drafted from the legions, under a promise of being promoted to that station, demanded their right, and the pay annexed to it. In this dilemma another difficulty occurred. The soldiers who had been retained in the army by Vitellius, could not be dismissed without great hazard and even bloodshed. Mucianus entered the camp. In order to ascertain the period of time during which they all had carried arms, he directed that the victorious troops, leaving proper distances between the respective companies, should be drawn up under arms, with all their military ornaments. The Vitellians, who, as has been mentioned, surrendered at Bovillæ, together with all the stragglers that could be found either at Rome, or in the neighbourhood, advanced forward in one collected body. Nothing could be more wretched than their appearance; all in a ragged condition, and almost naked. Such of them as came from Britain, from Germany, or any other province, had orders to range themselves in separate divisions. The field presented an awful spectacle. The Vitellians saw before them the victors in the late battle, arrayed in terror, and brandishing their arms. They looked around, and found themselves inclosed, in a defenceless state, displaying their nakedness and deformity. Being ordered to remove to different parts of the field, they were seized with a general panic. The Germans, in particular, thought themselves led forth to slaughter; they embraced their comrades; they hung about their necks; and, with prayers and tears, implored their fellow-soldiers not to desert them in the last distress. Their cause, they said, was common, and why should their fate be different from the rest? They appealed to Mucianus; they invoked the absent prince; they offered up their supplications to the gods. Mucianus appeased their fears: he told them, they were all fellow-soldiers in the service of the same prince, all bound by the common obligation of the same military oath. The victors were touched with sympathy, and by their acclamations, showed that they felt for the unhappy. Nothing further happened on that day. In a short time afterwards, Domitian addressed them in a public harangue. The men had recovered their courage. They listened to the young prince with an air of confidence firm and intrepid. Domitian proposed an allotment of lands: they refused the offer, desiring to continue in the service, and receive the arrears of their pay. They made their request in an humble style; but the request was in the nature of a demand, not to be resisted. They were all incorporated with the prætorian guards. The superannuated, and such as had served out their time, were discharged with honour from the service. Some were cashiered for misbehaviour, but by slow degrees, and without disgrace. They were weeded out man by man; a sure expedient to prevent cabals and factions in the army.

XLVII. The poverty of the public treasure, real, or, for political reasons, pretended, was brought forward in the senate. A scheme was proposed for raising by a loan from private persons, the sum of six hundred thousand sesterces. The management of the business was committed to Poppæus Silvanus; but the project was soon after dropped, the plea of necessity ceasing, or the motives for dissimulation being removed. A law was proposed by Domitian, and enacted by the senate, by which the several successions to the consulship, as they stood appointed by Vitellius, were declared null and void. The funeral of Flavius Sabinus was performed with all the pomp annexed to the censorian dignity; a striking instance of the caprice of fortune, which, like the tempest, mixing the highest and the lowest in wild confusion, sunk Sabinus to the depth of misery, and, after his death, raised him to unavailing honours.

XLVIII. About this time, Lucius Piso, the proconsul, was

murdered. The particulars of that tragic event I shall relate with the fidelity of an historian; and if I go back to trace the origin and progress of all such atrocious deeds, the inquiry will not be without its use. By the policy of Augustus, and afterwards by the same system continued under Tiberius, the legion quartered in Africa, together with the auxiliaries employed to defend the frontier of the province, obeyed the sole authority of the proconsul. The wild and turbulent genius of Caligula changed that arrangement. Suspecting Marcus Silanus, then governor of Africa, he transferred the command of the legion to an imperial lieutenant, whom he sent into Africa for the purpose. By that measure, the power of granting military preferment was divided between two rivals: a struggle for pre-eminence soon took place; their orders clashed; strife and emulation followed, and passions on both sides inflamed the dispute. In process of time, the imperial lieutenant gained the ascendant. His continual residence on the spot gave him the advantage, and, as is usual in subordinate stations, the second in authority was the most eager to grasp at power. The proconsuls, conscious of their own dignity, despised the little arts of aggrandising themselves. They took care to act with circumspection, and, content with personal safety, formed no schemes of ambition.

XLIX. During Piso's administration in Africa, Valerius Festus had the command of the legion; a young man of unbounded expense; a voluptuous prodigal, and an aspiring genius. He was nearly allied to Vitellius, and that circumstance filled him with disquietude. Whether it be true, that, in private conferences, he endeavoured to incite Piso to a revolt, or, on the other hand, that, being himself solicited, he withstood the temptation, must remain uncertain. No man was admitted into their secrets. After the death of Piso, the public was disposed to think favourably even of the murderer. The natives of the province, as well as the soldiers, were disaffected to Vespasian. It is likewise certain, that the partisans of Vitellius, who escaped from Rome, endeavoured to fire the ambition of Piso. They represented Gaul on the eve of revolt, and the Germans ready to take up arms; they stated the dangerous situation in which Piso stood, and open war, they said, was preferable to a dangerous peace. In that juncture, Claudius Sagitta, who commanded the squadron of horse called PETRINA, arrived in Africa. Favoured with a quick passage, he got the start of Papirius, a centurion, despatched by Mucianus, with secret instructions, as Sagitta affirmed, to assassinate Piso. He added, that Galerianus, the proconsul's near relation, and also his son-in-law, had already met his fate. For the proconsul himself, there remained nothing but a bold and daring enterprise. For this purpose two schemes presented themselves; one, by calling forth the province under arms; the other, by passing over into Gaul, there to show himself at the head of the Vitellian party. Piso remained deaf to these remonstrances. In the meantime, the centurion sent by Mucianus arrived in Africa. He landed at Carthage, and no sooner entered that city, than he proclaimed, with an air of joy, that Piso's affairs were in a prosperous train, and that the imperial dignity was already his. The people stood astonished at a revolution so unexpected. The centurion desired them to spread the news, with shouts and demonstrations of joy, and, accordingly, the credulous multitude rushed to the forum, calling aloud on Piso to make his appearance. The city rung with acclamations. About the truth no man inquired: all pressed forward to pay their court to the new emperor. Piso, in the meantime, alarmed by the evidence of Sagitta, or, perhaps, restrained by his own native modesty, resolved not to stir from his house. He examined the centurion; and finding that the whole was a snare to involve him in a rash attempt, and thereby give a colour to the intended murder, he ordered the ruffian to be put to death; not imagining that, by that vindictive measure, he could save his own life, but because he saw with indignation the assassin of Clodius Macer ready to imbrue his hands in the blood of the proconsul. Having made this sacrifice to justice, he issued a proclamation, in strong terms condemning the rash behaviour of the Carthaginians. From that moment, renouncing all the duties of his station, he confined himself to his own house, determined that nothing on his part should be the occasion of new disturbances.

L. Festus was duly apprised of all that passed. The excesses committed by the populace, the death of the centurion, and other reports, magnified, as usual, by the voice of fame, determined him to cut off the proconsul without delay. He despatched a party of horse to perpetrate the deed. The assassins made a rapid march in the night, and at the dawn of day rushed, sword in hand, into Piso's house. Being men picked for the purpose from the Carthaginian or the Moorish auxiliaries, they did not so much as know the person whom they intended to murder. Near his chamber-door they met one of the slaves, and sternly asked him, Who are you? and where is Piso? With a generous and splendid falsehood, the man replied, "I am Piso." He was butchered on the spot. Piso in a short time after met his fate. It happened that he was known to one of the ruffians, by name Bebius Massa,[1] an imperial procurator in Africa, even then the avowed enemy of every worthy character, and, in the miseries that followed, an actor frequently to appear in scenes of blood and cruelty. Meanwhile, Festus remained at Adrumetum, waiting for the issue of the business. Having received intelligence, he proceeded to the legion, and there ordered Cetronius Pisanus, the prefect of the camp, to be loaded with fetters. His motive for this proceeding was a personal grudge, disguised, however, under a pretended charge, that the prisoner was the friend and partisan of Piso. He punished some of the soldiers, and rewarded others, with no good reason for either, but purely to give himself the important air of having crushed a civil war. A quarrel subsisted between the Œensians and the people of Leptis; but by the interposition of Festus the dispute was compromised. Those cities complained of depredations committed in their respective territories, and both were preparing to hazard a battle. The Œensians were, in fact, inferior in number to their adversaries; but they had formed a league with the Garamantes, a fierce and savage race, that lived altogether by plunder, and, by consequence, the people of Leptis were reduced to the last extremity. They saw their lands laid waste, and were obliged to take shelter in their fortified towns, till the Roman cohorts and cavalry advanced to their relief. The Garamantes abandoned the siege, leaving behind them the whole of their booty, except what some of their flying parties had conveyed to their huts in the midst of deserts, or sold to the inhabitants of distant regions.

LI. Vespasian, at this time, had received intelligence of the victory at Cremona, and the success of his arms in every quarter. The death of Vitellius was announced to him by men of rank and condition, who had the spirit, in that rough season of the year, to undertake a voyage, in order to be the first to communicate that important event. Vologeses, the Parthian king, offered by his ambassadors to assist him with forty thousand of his cavalry. Nothing could be more glorious than the situation in which Vespasian stood: the allies paid their court, and he was in no need of their assistance. He returned thanks to Vologeses, desiring, at the same time, since the peace

[1] For more of Bebius Massa, see *Life of Agricola*, 45. He is mentioned by Juvenal as a noted informer.

of the empire was now established, that he would send ambassadors to the senate. Vespasian now began to turn his thoughts towards Italy, and the affairs of Rome. The accounts which he received concerning his son Domitian were by no means favourable. The young prince was said to assume beyond his years, and to tower above the rank even of the emperor's son. For the present, Vespasian thought fit to place his son Titus at the head of the army, and leave him to carry on the war against the Jews.

LII. Titus, we are told, before he set out to take upon him the command, used his best influence to mitigate his father in favour of Domitian. "The tales," he said, "of insidious whisperers ought not to be regarded: a son may fairly claim a right to be heard in his defence, nor should a father harbour prejudices against him. Fleets and armies are not always the strongest bulwarks: the best resources of the sovereign are in his own family. Friends moulder away; time changes the affections of men; views of interest form new connections; the passions fluctuate; desires arise that cannot be gratified; misunderstandings follow, and friendships are transferred to others; but the ties of blood still remain in force, and in that bond of union consists the security of the emperor. In his prosperity numbers participate; in the day of trouble, who, except his relations, takes a share in his misfortunes? Even between brothers, concord and unanimity are seldom lasting; and how should it be otherwise, if the father ceases to give a laudable example?"

Vespasian listened to these remonstrances, charmed with the amiable disposition of his son, yet not reconciled to Domitian. He desired Titus to banish all anxiety, and proceed, with a mind firm and erect, in the great work of enlarging the dominion and the glory of the empire. For himself, it should be his business to improve the arts of peace, and secure the welfare of his family. Vespasian's next care was to provide a supply of grain for the city of Rome. He ordered a number of swift-sailing vessels to be loaded with corn, and, though it was still the tempestuous season of the year, to put to sea without delay. Rome, in that juncture, was reduced to an alarming situation, not having in the public granaries, when the fleet arrived, more than ten days' provision.

LIII. The care of rebuilding the capitol was committed to Lucius Vestinus, a man no higher than the equestrian rank, but in credit and dignity of character equal to the first men in Rome. Under his direction the soothsayers were convened.

Their advice was, that the ruins of the former temple should be removed to the marches, and that the new structure should be raised on the old foundation; for the gods would not permit a change of the ancient form. On the eleventh day before the calends of July, the sky being remarkably serene, the ground assigned for the foundation was encompassed with ribbons and chaplets of flowers. Such of the soldiers as had names of auspicious import[1] entered within the inclosure, bearing in their hands branches from the favourite trees of the gods. The vestal virgins followed in procession, with a band of boys and girls, whose parents, male and female, were still living. They sprinkled the place with water drawn from three clear fountains, and three rivers. Helvidius Priscus, the prætor, preceded by Plautius Ælianus, the pontiff, sacrificed a swine, a sheep, and a bull; and, having spread the entrails upon the green turf, invoked Jupiter, Juno, and Minerva, praying of them, and all the tutelar deities of Rome, that they would favour the undertaking, and, with their divine assistance, carry to perfection a work begun and consecrated by the piety of man.

After this solemn prayer, Helvidius laid his hand upon the fillets that adorned the foundation-stone, and also the cords by which it was to be drawn to its place. In that instant, the magistrates, the priests, the senators, the Roman knights, and a number of citizens, all acting with one effort, and general demonstrations of joy, laid hold of the ropes, and dragged the ponderous load to its destined spot. They then threw in ingots of gold and silver, and other metals, which had never been melted in the furnace, but still retained, untouched by human art, their first formation in the bowels of the earth. The soothsayers had directed, that neither stone nor gold, which had been applied to other uses, should profane any part of the building. The walls were raised higher than before. Religion allowed no other alteration. To the magnificence of the former structure nothing but elevation could be added; and that, in a place designed for the reception of prodigious multitudes, was allowed to be necessary.

LIV. Meanwhile, the news of Vitellius's death, spreading through Gaul and Germany, gave rise to two wars at once. Civilis, no longer managing appearances, declared open hostility against the Romans; and the Vitellian soldiers, rather than acknowledge Vespasian, were ready to submit to slavery under

[1] Upon all solemn occasions the Romans made choice of men whose names they thought auspicious.

a foreign yoke. The Gauls began to breathe new life and vigour, persuaded that the Roman armies, wherever stationed, were broken and dispirited. A rumour was current among them, and universally believed, that the Dacians and Sarmatians had laid siege to the encampments in Mæsia and Pannonia. Affairs in Britain were supposed to be in no better situation. Above all, the destruction of the capitol announced the approaching fate of the Roman empire. The Druids,[1] in their wild enthusiasm, sung their oracular songs, in which they taught, that, when Rome was formerly sacked by the Gauls, the mansion of Jupiter being left entire, the commonwealth survived that dreadful shock; but the calamity of fire, which had lately happened, was a denunciation from heaven, in consequence of which, power and dominion were to circulate round the world, and the nations on their side of the Alps were in their turn to become masters of the world. A report prevailed, at the same time, that the chieftains of Gaul, who had been employed by Otho against Vitellius, bound themselves by solemn league, if the civil dissensions of Rome continued, to watch their opportunity, and by one brave effort, recover their natural independence.

LV. Before the murder of Hordeonius Flaccus, this confederacy was a profound secret. That tragic event no sooner happened, than a negotiation took place between Civilis and Classicus, who commanded a squadron of Treverian horse, and was, at that time, a leading chief among the Gauls, in fame and wealth surpassing the rest of his countrymen. He derived his origin from a royal line; a race of men who had made themselves famous for the wisdom of their counsels, and their courage in the field. Thus descended, Classicus made his boast, that he was the hereditary enemy, not the ally, of Rome. His plot was strengthened by the accession of Julius Tutor and Julius Sabinus; the former a Treverian; the latter, one of the Lingones. Tutor had been preferred by Vitellius to a command on the banks of the Rhine. Sabinus to his natural vanity united the pride, however ill-founded, of an illustrious descent. He pretended, that his great-grandmother attracted the regard of Julius Cæsar during his wars in Germany, and from that embrace he deduced his pedigree.

The conspirators made it their business, in secret conferences, to sound the temper of others; and, having drawn into their plot a number of accomplices, held a general meeting in the

[1] The order of Druids had been suppressed in Gaul by Tiberius.

Agrippinian colony. A private house was their scene of action. In that city the public mind abhorred all dangerous conspiracies. There were, notwithstanding, some of the inhabitants, and a party of Tungrians, present at the meeting: but the Treverians and Lingones gave life and vigour to the cause. Men of their spirit thought they lost their time in debate. They broke out at once, declaring with vehemence, "that Rome was brought, by the madness of her own intestine divisions, to the brink of ruin; her armies were cut to pieces; Italy was laid waste, and the city taken by storm. In other parts of the empire the legions have different wars upon their hands; what then remains but to take possession of the Alps? Secure the passes over those mountains, and Gaul will not only recover her liberty, but establish an independent empire. She may then deliberate where to fix the extent and boundaries of her own dominions."

LVI. This great and daring project was approved as soon as heard. How to dispose of the remaining Vitellian soldiers, was the next consideration. A general massacre was proposed. All agreed, that men of their description, seditious, turbulent, void of principle, the murderers of their superior officers, deserved no quarter. And yet there were political reasons for extending mercy: "The Vitellians might be roused to an act of brave despair. It were better to entice them into the confederacy. Let their officers bleed, and, after that sacrifice, the common men, conscious of their crimes, yet entertaining hopes of impunity, would be ready to join in any great and daring enterprise." Such was the plan of their revolt. Their next step was, by their agents and emissaries, to kindle the flame of discord all over Gaul. The conspirators, in the meantime, with a specious show of duty, submitted to the commands of Vocula, determined to deceive him at first, and ruin him in the end. The plot, however, was not entirely concealed from the Roman general: he received intelligence, but in a difficult juncture, when his legions were incomplete, and wavering in their duty. Vocula found himself surrounded with perfidious soldiers, and secret conspirators. In that distress he judged it best to play against his enemies their own insidious game. With this design he set out for the Agrippinian colony. At that place he met Claudius Labeo, who, as already mentioned, had been sent by Civilis to be detained in custody by the Frisians. Having corrupted his guard, this man made his escape and fled for refuge to the Romans. He now was willing to assist their cause. To that end he offered, at the head of a detachment, to penetrate into Batavia, and, by his influence, to engage the chiefs of the country in the interest of Rome. He obtained a small party of foot and cavalry, and with that force passed over into the island, but attempted nothing against the Batavians. The whole of his service consisted in prevailing on a party of the Nervians and Betasians to take up arms. With that reinforcement he ventured to atttack the Caninefates and Marsacians, not indeed in an open and regular war, but in the style of a freebooter, by sudden incursions.

LVII. The Gauls found means to impose upon Vocula. That commander fell into the snare, and marched in quest of the enemy. As soon as he approached the old camp, called VETERA, Classicus and Tutor, under colour of exploring the motions of the enemy, advanced to a considerable distance from the army, and, having there concluded a treaty with the German chiefs, threw off the mask at once. They encamped apart, and began to throw up intrenchments. Vocula, with indignation, exclaimed against the measure. "Rome," he said, "was not so humbled by her own divisions as to become the scorn of the Treverians and Lingones. She had still great resources, a number of provinces firm in her interest; victorious armies, and the auspicious fortune of the empire. The avenging gods were still on her side. The fate of Sacrovir and the treacherous Æduans may be still remembered. The overthrow of Vindex is a more recent instance. A single battle was sufficient to quell those insurrections; and what have the violators of all good faith to expect at present? The same gods, the same vengeance, the same fate, awaits them. Julius Cæsar was the person who best understood the national character of the Gauls. He knew how to deal with a perfidious race. Augustus followed his example. Galba granted an exemption from tributes, and, by that indulgence, gave encouragement to sedition. Your burden has been lessened, and rebellion is your gratitude: when you are once more subdued, and reduced to poverty, you will then be taught that submission is the duty of the vanquished." The tone of firmness, and even ferocity, with which this speech was uttered, made no impression on Classicus and Tutor. Vocula marched back to Novesium. The Gauls encamped at the distance of two miles. The centurions and soldiers visited them without restraint, and settled the price for which they were willing to sell themselves. In that vile bargain and sale, a Roman army, with a baseness of spirit till then unheard of, submitted to swear fidelity to a foreign power; and, to ratify the horrible contract, agreed to murder their officers, or deliver them up bound in chains. In this distress, Vocula was advised to save himself by flight; but that general was resolved to face every danger. With a mind superior to distress, he called his men together, and harangued them as follows:

LVIII. "I have often addressed you, my fellow-soldiers, but never with so much anxiety for your welfare; never with so little concern for myself. You have conspired against me, and I hear it without regret. Encompassed as I am by so many enemies, I can welcome death as the end of human misery. But I feel for you: for you my heart bleeds inwardly. You are neither going forth to the attack, nor does the enemy offer battle. In either case, that would be the lot of war, and I should be willing to share the danger. You are now to draw your unhallowed swords against your country: Classicus expects it; he hopes to make you traitors and parricides. He places before your eyes the empire of Gaul; he invites you to swear fidelity to that imaginary state. But still reflect for a moment: if fortune has deserted you, if your courage fails, are there no bright examples transmitted to you by your ancestors, to rouse your valour? Have you forgot how often the Roman armies, rather than desert their post, have died bravely sword in hand? The allies of Rome have seen their cities wrapped in fire, and, with their wives and children, perished in the flames: and what was their motive? They preserved their faith inviolate, and they died with glory. Even at this moment you have before your eyes the noblest example: in the old camp, the legions, amidst the horrors of a siege and the miseries of famine, still maintain their post, undismayed by danger, unseduced by promises. We have arms and men; a camp well fortified, and provisions sufficient for a long and tedious war. That there is no want of money, yourselves are witnesses: you have received your donative; and whether you impute it to Vespasian or Vitellius, it is the bounty of the emperor. And will you, my fellow-soldiers, after all your victories, after routing the enemy at Gelduba and the old camp, will you now shrink at once, and sully all your fame? If you dread an engagement, behold your walls and fortifications, your trenches and palisades: those will defend you; with those advantages you may stand at bay till succours arrive from the neighbouring provinces. Does your general displease you? There are other officers; there are tribunes, centurions, and, if you will, there are common men, to take the command. In all events, let not the world hear the monstrous story, that Classicus and Civilis, with Roman arms and Roman soldiers, have invaded Italy.

"But let me ask you: Should the Gauls and Germans be able to conduct you to the walls of Rome, will you there lift your impious hands against your country? My heart recoils with horror from the thought. Shall Roman soldiers be placed as sentinels at the tent of Tutor the Treverian? Shall a Batavian give the word of command? Will you serve as recruits to complete the German battalions? And what is to be the issue? When the Roman legions appear before you in order of battle, what part will you act? Deserters already, will you become so a second time? From traitors to your country, will you turn traitors to your new allies? Bound by your former oaths, distracted by your last, and between both confounded, you will be lost in a maze of guilt, detesting yourselves, and still more detested by the gods. Immortal Jove, supreme of gods, to whom, for so many triumphs during a space of eight hundred and twenty years, Rome has bowed down with praise and adoration! thee I invoke; and thee too, Romulus, thou mighty founder of the Roman name! on thee I call: if it is your awful will, that, under my command, this camp shall not remain inviolate, yet hear my humble prayer; preserve it from the pollution of Barbarians; save it from such men as Tutor and Classicus. To these my fellow-soldiers, grant unshaken virtue; or, if that cannot be, inspire them with remorse, that they may see their error, and avert the horror of flagitious deeds."

LIX. This speech was heard with various emotions. Hope, fear, and shame, rose in the minds of the soldiers. Vocula retired, with his own hand determined to deliver himself from a seditious army. His slaves and freedmen interposed, but their officious care reserved him for a harsher fate. Classicus despatched his assassin, by name Æmilius Longinus, a deserter from the first legion. That ruffian struck the fatal blow. Herennius and Numisius, who had each the command of a legion, were secured in chains. Classicus, in a short time afterwards, entered the camp, with the pomp and apparel of a Roman commander; and though he brought with him a mind prompt and daring, he made no attempt to harangue the men, content with repeating the words of the oath. The soldiers swore fidelity to the empire of the Gauls. The murderer of Vocula was raised to rank in the army. The rest were rewarded in proportion to their crimes. Tutor and Classicus took their different shares in the conduct of the war. Tutor proceeded with a strong force to the Agrippinian colony, and, having invested the place, compelled the inhabitants to bind themselves by an oath to the new empire. He exacted the same submission from the soldiers stationed on the Upper Rhine. Classicus marched to Magontiacum, and, by his order, the tribunes who refused obedience were put to death. The prefect of the camp betook himself to flight. From those who submitted, Classicus selected the most distinguished for their profligacy, and sent them to the old camp, with directions to promise a free pardon to all who were willing to surrender, and, in case of wilful obstinacy, to give notice, that famine, the devouring sword, and all the horrors of military vengeance, would be their portion. To these instructions the messengers added their own example, and the motives that influenced their conduct.

LX. The besieged were now in the last distress. Their sense of duty was still an active principle, and, on the other hand, famine stared them in the face. Between honour and infamy they were held in suspense, and the conflict was for some time undecided. Their store of provisions was exhausted. They were in want, not only of common food, but even of such as necessity might suggest. They had lived on horse-flesh; their beasts of burden were consumed, and even of animals impure and filthy none remained. Reduced to this extremity, they tore up shrubs by the root; they broke down twigs and branches; they gathered the wretched herbs that grew penuriously between the stones. A generous band! exhibiting, in the last distress, an example of patience and heroic fortitude! Men for ever memorable, if they had not at last, by sending deputies to sue for mercy, tarnished all their glory. The haughty Batavian refused to listen to their supplications till they swore fidelity to the empire of Gaul. By the terms of the capitulation, everything in the camp was to be delivered up to Civilis. A band of soldiers was, accordingly, sent to guard the money, the slaves, the victuallers, and the baggage. The legions marched out destitute of everything, with a strong party to escort them. They had not proceeded above five miles, when the Germans, contrary to all good faith, attacked them with sudden fury. The brave and resolute died on the spot; others betook themselves to flight, and were cut off by the pursuers; the survivors made their way back to the camp. Civilis called the behaviour of the Germans a violation of the law of nations: but whether he was acting a part, or, in fact, had not sufficient authority to restrain a body of undisciplined Barbarians, must remain problematical. Having pillaged the camp, the Batavians threw in combustibles, and the whole was reduced to ashes. All who had lately escaped from the fury of the sword, perished in the flames.

LXI. Civilis, when he first took up arms against the Romans, bound himself by a solemn vow, according to the custom of those barbarous nations, to cherish the growth of his hair, which was now waving about his shoulders, dishevelled, long, and red. Thinking himself absolved by the slaughter of the legions, he cut it short for the first time during the war. He is said to have given to his infant son some Roman prisoners, as a mark to be levelled at with little darts and arrows, for the diversion of a child. It is worthy of notice, that in the height of his zeal for the empire of Gaul, he neither swore fidelity himself, nor required that act of submission from the Batavians. He relied on the valour of the Germans; and should it be necessary to contend for the sovereign power, he considered his own abilities, and his fame in arms, as a decided superiority. Mummius Lupercus, the commander of a legion, was sent, among a number of ample presents, as a gift to Veleda, a prophetess of the Bructerian nation.[1] She ruled over a large tract of territory. Her name was held in veneration throughout Germany. The superstition of the country ascribed to numbers of women a preternatural insight into future events; and, in consequence of that persuasion, many have been revered as goddesses. Veleda, at that time, was the oracle of Germany. She had foretold the success of her countrymen, and the destruction of the legions. Her name, in consequence of that prediction, rose to the highest pitch. Lupercus was murdered on the road. A few centurions and tribunes, who were natives of Gaul, were reserved as hostages in the hands of Civilis, to bind the alliance between the two nations. The winter camps of the cohorts, the cavalry, and the legions, excepting one at Magontiacum, and another at Vindonissa, were levelled to the ground, or destroyed by fire.

LXII. The thirteenth legion, with the auxiliaries that surrendered at the same time, received orders to march, on a day appointed, from Novesium to the colony of the Treverians. The interval was big with anxiety, terror, and distraction. The dastardly thought of nothing but the massacre of the old camp, and expected to have that scene renewed. The better sort,

[1] For *Veleda* and other prophetic women, see the Manners of the Germans, 8.

who still retained some sense of honour, blushed to see the humiliating condition to which they were reduced. "What kind of march were they to undertake? and who was to conduct them? It was their own act, they said, that made the Barbarians arbiters of life and death: everything depends upon their will and pleasure." Others cared for nothing but their money and their effects. To pack up what they valued most, and brace it round their bodies, was their only employment. About shame and dishonour they felt no solicitude. A few prepared their arms, as if for the field of battle. The fatal day arrived, more dismal and afflicting than their imaginations had represented it. In the camp their wretched appearance passed without notice: the open field and the glare of day displayed a scene of deformity. The images of the emperors were torn down from the ensigns; and the Roman standards, stripped of their ornaments, seemed to droop in disgrace, while the colours of the Gauls fluttered in the air, and glittered to the eye. The march was slow, silent, melancholy; a long and dismal train, resembling a funeral procession. Claudius Sanctus, a man deformed by the loss of an eye, of a ferocious countenance, and remarkable stupidity, was their leader. Their disgrace was aggravated by the arrival of another legion from the camp at Bonn. This wretched state of captivity was rumoured about the country, and the people, who a little before shuddered at the Roman name, flocked together in crowds to behold their reverse of fortune. The fields were deserted; houses were left empty; a prodigious multitude assembled from all quarters to enjoy the novelty of the spectacle. The insolence of the rabble was more than the squadron of horse, called PICENTINA, had patience to endure. They marched off in disdain, directing their route towards Magontiacum; nor could Sanctus, their commander, by threats or menaces, divert them from their purpose. In their way they met Longinus, the murderer of Vocula, and killed him on the spot. By that sacrifice they began to expiate their own disgrace. The legions, without altering their course, proceeded to the city of the Treverians, and pitched their tents under the walls.

LXIII. Civilis and Classicus, elated with success, had it in contemplation to give the Agrippinian colony to the fury of the soldiers. Their own natural ferocity and love of plunder conspired to prompt them to this act of barbarity; but motives of policy counterbalanced their inclinations. They knew that to the founders of a new empire the fame of clemency is always an advantage. Civilis had other reasons: his son, on the first breaking out of the war, was taken into custody by the Agrippinians, and treated with marks of respect. Civilis felt the obligation, and gratitude touched his heart; but the nations beyond the Rhine saw the opulence of the place, and the increase of population, with an eye of envy. They insisted that, to terminate the war, it was necessary either to make it an open city for all Germany, or to demolish it at once, and, by that stroke, exterminate the Ubian race.

LXIV. The Tencterians, a people dwelling on the opposite bank of the Rhine, thought fit to send ambassadors to the Agrippinian colony, with directions to explain to an assembly of the state the sentiments of the German nations. The person among the deputies most distinguished by his ferocity spoke as follows: "That you have restored yourselves to your country, and are become Germans in fact as well as in name, we return thanks to the gods, whom we adore in common, and in particular to Mars, the supreme of deities. We congratulate you on this great occasion; you will live, henceforward, among nations born in freedom, and you will enjoy your natural rights. The Romans hitherto were masters of our lands, our rivers, and even of the elements over our heads. They excluded us from all intercourse with you: if at any time we were allowed access to your city, it was under the eye of a guard; and, what to a warlike people was the worst indignity, we were forced to visit you without arms, defenceless and almost naked, nay, obliged to pay a tax for the favour. Would you now establish our mutual friendship on a firm foundation? These are the conditions: demolish the walls of your city, those monuments of your former slavery. The fiercest animals, if you keep them close confined, grow mild in time, and forget their nature. Rise at once, and by a general massacre extirpate the Roman race. Liberty and the presence of a master are incompatible. When you have destroyed your enemies, let their goods be brought into a common stock; allow no embezzlement, nor suffer any man to think of his own private advantage. Our common ancestors enjoyed both banks of the Rhine: let those rights be now restored. The use of light and air is given by nature to us all, and the same liberal hand has opened to the brave and valiant a free passage to every region of the globe. Revive the customs of your ancestors: restore the primitive laws, and renounce the charm of baneful pleasures. The Romans, hitherto, have waged a war of luxury, and have succeeded more by their vices than by their valour. Prove yourselves Germans, shake off the yoke; be a regenerated, a brave, unmixed, and warlike people; you will then be upon a footing of equality with your neighbours: in time, perhaps, you may rise to the dignity of giving laws to others."

LXV. The Agrippinians desired time for deliberation. If they complied with the terms, they trembled at the consequences; and, in their present condition, a peremptory refusal was more than they dared to hazard. Their answer was as follows: "As soon as we perceived the dawn of returning liberty, we seized the opportunity, with more zeal than prudence, to make common cause with you and the rest of our German relatives. But when the Roman armies are assembling on every side, is that a time to demolish our fortifications? The juncture requires that we should rather add to their strength. If, heretofore, there have been within our territories emigrants from Italy and the provinces of Rome, the rage of war has destroyed them, or they have made their escape to their native home. As to those who formerly transplanted their families, and settled amongst us, they have been for a long time part of the colony, intermixed and blended with us by intermarriages and the ties of consanguinity. Their descendants are our own progeny: this is their native land, and this their country. And are we now required to cut the throats of our fathers, our brothers, and our children? That black design cannot be imputed to the Tencterians. A free commerce shall be established: all duties, that are a restraint on trade and liberty, shall be repealed. Our city shall be open to you, but with this restriction: you must come unarmed, and in open day, that these regulations, at present new and therefore feeble, may gain strength from time, and grow into established usage. We desire that Civilis and Veleda may arbitrate between us. Under their sanction the treaty shall be ratified." The Tencterians acquiesced. Ambassadors were sent with presents to Civilis and Veleda, and, by their mediation, all matters were adjusted to the satisfaction of the Agrippinians. The deputies, however, were not admitted to the presence of Veleda. To increase the veneration paid to her character, all access to her person was denied. She resided in the summit of a lofty tower. A near relation, chosen for the purpose, conveyed to her several questions, and from that sanctuary brought back oracular responses, like a messenger who held commerce with the gods.

LXVI. Strengthened by his alliance with the Agrippinian

colony, Civilis turned his thoughts to the neighbouring states; determined, if gentle measures proved ineffectual, to subdue them by force. The Sunicians had already submitted to his arms, and he had formed the youth of the country capable of bearing arms into regular cohorts. To oppose his progress, Claudius Labeo advanced at the head of a considerable body of Betasians, Tungrians, and Nervians, raised by sudden levies. Having taken an advantageous post, where he commanded the bridge over the Meuse, he ventured an engagement. The battle was, for some time, fought in a narrow defile with doubtful success, till the Germans, with their usual dexterity in swimming, crossed the river, and charged Labeo's forces in the rear. Civilis, with a bold effort of courage, or in consequence of a preconcerted measure, rushed among the Tungrians, proclaiming aloud, "that the object of the war was not to procure for the Batavians and Treverians dominion over the nations. We have no such arrogance, no such wild ambition. We court your alliance: I am ready to join you; your general, if you will; if not, a common soldier." This speech had its effect. The common men felt the impression, and sheathed their swords. In that moment, Campanus and Juvenalis, the leading chieftains of the Tungrians, on behalf of themselves and their whole nation, submitted to Civilis. Labeo made his escape. The Betasians and the Nervians in like manner surrendered. Civilis incorporated them with his army, and, in a tide of success, saw his strength increasing every day. The adjacent nations were overawed by the terror of his arms, or voluntarily entered into the confederacy.

LXVII. Meanwhile, Julius Sabinus, having destroyed all public monuments of the alliance between Rome and the Lingones, caused himself to be proclaimed by the title of Cæsar. He put himself, soon after, at the head of an undisciplined multitude of his countrymen, and marched against the Sequanians, a neighbouring state, at that time faithful to Rome. The Sequanians did not decline the conflict. Fortune favoured the juster cause. The Lingones were defeated. The rashness with which Sabinus rushed on to the attack, was equalled by nothing but the precipitation with which he fled the field. He escaped to a cottage, and, in order to spread a report of his death, set fire to the place. It was generally believed that he perished in the flames. He lived nine years afterwards. The various arts by which he protracted his days, and the subterraneous places in which he lay concealed, together with the constancy of his friends, and the memorable example of his wife Epponina, shall be recorded in their proper place. The victory obtained by the Sequanians checked the progress of the war. The states of Gaul began to think with moderation, and to reflect on the law of nations and the faith of subsisting treaties. The people of Rheims set the example. By a proclamation dispersed through Gaul, they summoned a convention of delegates from the several provinces, in order to consult which was most for the general interest, a settled peace, or a vigorous effort for the recovery of their liberty.

LXVIII. At Rome, in the meantime, these transactions, exaggerated always beyond the truth, kept Mucianus in a state of anxiety. He had already appointed Annius Gallus and Petilius Cerealis to command the German armies; but, though they were both officers of distinguished merit, there was reason to fear that they would prove unequal to the weight of the war. Rome, at the same time, could not be left without a ruler. From the unbridled passions of Domitian everything was to be apprehended. Antonius Primus and Arrius Varus were both suspected. The latter commanded the prætorian guards, and by consequence, had arms and men in his power. Mucianus removed him from his office, and, to soften his fall, made him superintendent of the public granaries. To reconcile Domitian, the known friend of Varus, to the measure, he gave the vacant post to Arretinus Clemens, a man nearly related to the house of Vespasian, and high in favour with the young prince. His father, in the reign of Caligula, held the same command, with considerable reputation. The name, Mucianus observed, would be welcome to the soldiers; and the new officer, though a member of the senate, would be able to discharge the duty of both stations. An expedition against the Germans was now a settled measure. The principal men at Rome had notice to attend the army. Numbers offered themselves with views of ambition. Domitian and Mucianus prepared to set out, but with different motives; the prince with the ardour of youth, panting for the novelty of enterprise; Mucianus, with studied delays, endeavouring to protract the time, in order to allay the impetuosity of Domitian. A young man of his rank, hurried away by his passions, or misled by evil counsellors, might, at the head of the army, so embarrass everything, that it would be impossible either to wage war with advantage, or to conclude an honourable peace.

Two of the victorious legions, namely, the sixth and eighth, with the twenty-first from the Vitellian party, and the second from the forces lately raised, had orders to march into Gaul by different routes; some over the Pennine and Cottian Alps, and others over the Graian mountains. The fourteenth legion was recalled from Britain, and the sixth and tenth from Spain. Alarmed by these preparations, the states of Gaul, already disposed to pacific measures, held a convention at Rheims. The deputies of the Treverians attended the meeting, and with them Tullius Valentinus, a fierce incendiary, and the most active promoter of the war. In a speech prepared for the purpose, he poured forth a torrent of declamation, abounding with all the topics of invective usually urged against the authority of extensive empires, and all the injurious reflections that could be cast on the Roman name. To inflame sedition was the talent of the man. Possessing a daring genius and a turbulent vein of eloquence, no wonder that he was the favourite orator of the vulgar.

LXIX. Julius Auspex, a leading chief among the people of Rheims, rose in opposition to the Treverian. He painted forth the power of the Romans, and the blessings of peace. "Nations," he said, "might be involved in all the calamities of war by men of no account in the field. The coward may begin hostilities, but the brave and valiant are left to shed their blood in the quarrel. Even then the Roman legions were advancing, and to oppose them would be a vain attempt." He urged the faith of treaties, and by that consideration succeeded with men of sober judgment: the young and ardent were restrained by the magnitude of the approaching danger. All admired the spirit of Valentinus, but the advice of Auspex was adopted. The states of Gaul had not forgotten, that, in the commotions excited by Vindex, the Treverians and Lingones had sided with Verginius, and that conduct was still felt with resentment. The mutual jealousy with which the several provinces beheld each other, was still another reason to prevent their acting in concert. "Who was to have the conduct of the war? Under whose auspices were the troops to take the field? And, if their efforts were crowned with success, where were they to fix the seat of empire?" By this spirit of emulation all were thrown into violent debate; they had gained no victory, and yet were quarrelling for the spoils. One state talked of its alliances; another was rich and powerful; a third boasted of its ancient origin, and all with arrogance claimed the superiority. The result was a general resolution to prefer their present condition to the uncertain issue of a dangerous war. Letters were despatched to the Treverians in the name of the states of Gaul, requiring them to lay down their arms, while repentance might obtain their pardon, and their friends were ready to solicit for them. Valentinus opposed all terms of accommodation. His countrymen, by his advice, were deaf to all remonstrances. But war was not the talent of their leader. Skilled in debate, he was a factious demagogue, and an inactive soldier.

LXX. The exertions of the Treverians, the Lingones, and other revolted states, were in no proportion to the importance of the occasion. Between their generals no concerted plan, no union of counsels. Civilis traversed the defiles and devious parts of Belgia,[1] with no object in view but that of making Labeo his prisoner, or forcing him to fly the country. Classicus loitered away the time in indolence, pleased with his imaginary empire, and swaying a sceptre not yet in his possession. Even Tutor neglected to secure the banks of the Upper Rhine, and the passes of the Alps. In the meantime, the one and twentieth legion, by the way of Vindonissa, penetrated into Gaul, and Sextilius Felix, with the auxiliary cohorts, forced his way through Rhætia.[2] He was joined by a squadron of horse, embodied first by Vitellius, and afterwards listed under Vespasian. Their commanding officer was Julius Briganticus, whose mother was the sister of Civilis. The uncle and the nephew hated each other; and, as is often the case in family quarrels, their animosity was deep, envenomed, and implacable. Tutor found means to augment his army by new musters in the country of the Vangiones, the Caracatians, and Tribocians. He added a body of Roman veterans, both horse and foot, whom he had either inveigled by promises, or compelled by menaces. A cohort detached by Sextilius Felix appeared in sight. The veteran legionaries put the whole corps to the sword; but seeing the approach of Roman generals and a Roman army they went over to that side, and by a second desertion atoned for the disgrace of the first. The Tribocians, the Vangiones, and the Caracatians followed their example.

Tutor, being now deserted by all but his countrymen the Treverians, thought it best to make his retreat. He avoided

[1] The country about *Bruges*.

[2] The Rhæti, now the *Grisons*.

Magontiacum, and made the best of his way to Bingium, where, having destroyed the bridge over the river Nava, he thought himself posted to advantage. Felix, with a cohort under his command, hung closely on his rear. Having found a fordable place, his men crossed the river, and rushed on to the attack. Tutor was put to the rout, and totally defeated. The Treverians, struck with terror, laid down their arms, and dispersed themselves about the country. Some of their chiefs, to claim the merit of a voluntary submission, fled for refuge to such states as had not joined the revolt. The legions which had been removed, as already mentioned, from Novesium and Bonn to the territory of the Treverians, seized their opportunity to renew their oath of fidelity to Vespasian. Valentinus was absent in some other quarter. He returned breathing vengeance, and bent on new commotions; but the legions quitted the country, and pursued their route to Mediomatricum,[1] a city in alliance with Rome. By the zeal and ardour of Tutor and Valentinus, the Treverians were once more incited to take up arms. To strengthen the bond of union by cutting off all hopes of pardon, they murdered Herennius and Numisius, two commanders of legions; and by that exploit hoped to rouse the desperate valour of their countrymen.

LXXI. Such was the state of the war when Petilius Cerealis reached Magontiacum. By his arrival the face of things was changed. That general, always eager to give battle, and, by his natural temper, more disposed to hold the enemy in contempt than to prevent a surprise, harangued his men, and by his manly eloquence inspired them with new ardour. He desired that they would hold themselves in readiness for action, as he was resolved to seize the first opportunity that offered. The levies, which had been raised in Gaul, he ordered back to their own country, with directions to publish everywhere, that the legions were sufficient to defend the empire; and, therefore, that the allies might return to the employments of peace, secure from danger, since the Roman armies had taken the field. By this message the Gauls were wrought to a more pacific temper. Their young men being thus restored to their country, they felt their tribute lighter; and, their service being no longer wanted, their zeal rose in proportion.

Civilis and Classicus saw the sad reverse of their affairs. Tutor was defeated, the Treverians were cut to pieces, and

[1] Metz.

fortune began to smile on the Roman arms. In this distress, they drew together their scattered forces; taking care, in the meantime, to warn Valentinus, by repeated messengers, not to stand the hazard of a decisive engagement. Cerealis was the more impatient to strike a sudden blow. He despatched proper officers to Mediomatricum, with orders to bring forward the legions from that place, by the shortest route. Having, in the meantime, united the soldiers stationed at Magontiacum with the forces which he brought with him from Italy, he proceeded by rapid marches, and in three days arrived at Rigodulum. At that place Valentinus, at the head of a large body of Treverians, had taken post in a strong situation, defended on one side by the Moselle, and in other parts enclosed by mountains. To the natural strength of the place he added a deep fosse, and a rampart of stones piled on one another. The Roman general was determined to surmount all difficulties. He ordered the infantry to rush on to the assault, while the cavalry gained the higher ground. He despised an enemy consisting of new levies; an undisciplined army, to whom their fortifications could give no advantage which Roman valour was not able to conquer. The first ascent was difficult. For some time the soldiers were retarded by the missive weapons of the enemy; but in spite of every obstacle they gained the summit. A close engagement followed. The Barbarians were hurled headlong from the steep, as if their fortifications tumbled down in ruins. In the meantime a party of the cavalry, having circled round the smooth edges of the hill, made the principal Belgic chiefs prisoners of war, with Valentinus, their general, in the number.

LXXII. On the following day Cerealis entered the capital of the Treverians. The soldiers panted for the destruction of the city. "It was the birthplace of Classicus and of Tutor. By them the legions had been besieged and massacred. What was the guilt of Cremona? That unfortunate city checked the career of a victorious army for a single night, and, for that offence, was swept from the bosom of Italy. And shall a hostile city, standing on the confines of Germany, be allowed to subsist, and even to flourish, rich with the spoil of plundered armies, and reeking with the blood of slaughtered generals? Let the booty be added to the public treasure; but let the place be wrapt in flames, and the whole colony laid in ruins. That just revenge would atone for the loss of so many Roman camps. The soldiers ask no more." Cerealis dreaded the consequence of suffering his army to retaliate by acts of cruelty, which, he knew, would brand his name with infamy. He checked the fury of his men, and they obeyed. The rage of civil war was over, and against foreign enemies there was nothing to embitter the soldier's mind. There was, besides, another object, that touched every heart with compassion. The legions from Mediomatricum presented a spectacle truly wretched. Conscious of their guilt, they stood with their eyes fixed on the ground. Between the two armies no mutual salutation passed. The men in disgrace heard the words of consolation from their friends, and made no answer. They retired in silence to their tents, wishing to hide themselves from the face of day. Fear made no part of their distress. They felt the infamy of their conduct, and shame and anguish of heart overwhelmed them. Even the men who were flushed with their recent victory, stood at gaze in mute astonishment. They pitied their fellow soldiers, but did not dare to raise their voices in their favour. They showed their compassion by their pathetic silence, and interceded for them with their tears. Cerealis removed all cause of apprehension. He declared that all that had happened, either in consequence of dissensions among the superior officers, by sedition among the soldiers, or the treachery of the enemy, was the effect of fatal necessity. "But now," he said, "the revolted soldiers are once more the soldiers of their country. From this day you are enlisted in the service, and from this day you are bound by the oath of fidelity. The emperor has forgot all that has happened, and your general will remember nothing." The penitent troops were admitted into the camp; and the general gave out in orders to every company, that no man should presume, upon any occasion, public or private, to mention the revolt of the legions, or the disasters that happened afterwards.

LXXIII. Cerealis, without loss of time, called an assembly of the Treverians and Lingones. His speech was to the following effect: "Eloquence is not my province: it is a talent which I never cultivated. Arms have been my profession: in the field of battle I have given you proof of Roman valour. But words, and what you call eloquence, are, in your estimation, superior gifts, of power to change the colours of good and evil. It is not by the nature of things that you form your judgment: the speech of a seditious incendiary has more weight and influence. But a few plain words may prove a seasonable antidote. I shall, therefore, explain myself to you on certain points, which, now the war is over, it will be more your interest to hear, than mine to enforce. When the Roman generals at the head of their armies entered your territories, and the other provinces of Gaul, they were neither led by their own ambition, nor the lust of conquest. They were invited by your ancestors, at that time torn by intestine divisions, and driven to the brink of ruin. You had called the Germans to your aid, and those Barbarians proved the worst of tyrants: they enslaved, without distinction, those who invited them, and those who resisted. The battles which Rome has fought with the Teutones and the Cimbrians, need not be mentioned. Her wars in Germany, and the toil and vigour of her legions, with the various events that followed, are all sufficiently known. If the legions seized the banks of the Rhine, can the defence of Italy be deemed the motive? The protection of Gaul was the object, that another Ariovistus [1] may not aspire to reign over you. And do you now imagine that Civilis, or the Batavians, or the nations beyond the Rhine, have that affection for you and your welfare which your forefathers never experienced from their ancestors? The same motives that first incited the Germans to cross the Rhine, will ever subsist: ambition, avarice, and the love of new settlements, will be perpetual incentives. The Germans will be ready, at all times, to change their swampy fens and barren deserts for your fertile plains and fruitful valleys. On your own soil they wish to lord it over you. They come to ravage your lands, and liberty is the pretext. But the rights of man, and other specious names, are the language of all who want to usurp dominion over others.

LXXIV. "Your country, till you put yourselves under our protection, was at all times harassed with wars, and oppressed by tyrants. Rome has been often insulted, often provoked, by the unruly spirit of the Gauls; and what has been the use of her victories? She required no more at your hands than what was necessary for the aid of a government that defends and protects you. To maintain the tranquillity of nations, arms are necessary; soldiers must be kept in pay; and without a tribute from the provinces, how are supplies to be raised? In common with the citizens of Rome, you enjoy every benefit. Our legions are often commanded by you; you are governors of your own provinces, and even of others subject to the empire. All posts of honour are open to you; nothing is precluded. Does a virtuous prince reign at Rome;

[1] For Ariovistus, the German chief, see Cæsar, *De Bell. Gall.*, i. 31.

though placed at a distance, you feel the mildness of his government. Does a tyrant rule with an iron rod, his weight is felt by those immediately within his reach. Natural evils, such as incessant rains, and barren seasons, you are forced to bear: political evils, such as the avarice and prodigality of princes, should in like manner be endured. As long as there are men, there will be vices. But vice is not without interruption. Better times succeed, and the virtue of a good prince atones for antecedent evils. But, perhaps, you expect from Tutor and Classicus a mild and equitable reign. Under their auspices armies must be raised to repel the Germans and the Britons; and this, you fancy, will be done with lighter taxes than you pay at present. Overturn the Roman power (may the gods avert so dire a calamity!) and what think you will be the consequence? The nations will rise in arms, and the world will be a theatre of war. During a space of eight hundred years, the mighty fabric of the empire has been raised by the valour of the legions, and a series of victories; nor can that fabric be rent from its foundation, without burying all who prevail against it in one general ruin. In that scene of wild commotion, Gaul will be the sufferer. You have gold and riches, those great incentives of ambition, and the prime cause of war. Peace is your interest. Cherish it, therefore, and honour the city of Rome: a city, that protects her subjects, and is ever ready to receive the conquered upon equal terms with her own inhabitants. Take warning from your own experience; you have known the smiles and the frowns of fortune; it will now be yours to show that you have the wisdom to prefer to a revolt, which may involve you all in ruin, a pacific temper, and a due regard to your own internal happiness." This speech revived the drooping spirits of the Gauls. They expected to be treated with rigour, and their fears were dissipated.

LXXV. The Romans were in possession of the Treverian state, when Cerealis received letters from Civilis and Classicus, in substance as follows: "Vespasian is no more; though the secret is suppressed with care, the fact is well known. Italy and Rome are reduced to the last extremity by their own dissensions. Domitian and Mucianus are high-sounding names, yet signify nothing. If Cerealis aspired to the sovereignty of Gaul, Civilis and Classicus would rest contented with the Batavian dominions. If he preferred the decision of the sword, they were willing to try the fortune of the field." To this message Cerealis returned no answer, but sent the letter, and the person who brought it, to Domitian. Meanwhile, the Barbarians, in detached parties, came pouring down from every quarter. Cerealis was censured for suffering an army to be assembled, when he might have attacked the enemy in separate divisions, before they formed a junction. He had even neglected to fortify his camp, and at last contented himself with a fosse and a palisade.

LXXVI. The chiefs of the German army were divided in opinion about their future operations. Civilis was for waiting till the nations arrived from the other side of the Rhine. "The Romans," he said, "would shrink with terror from the approach of those gallant warriors. The Gauls were of no account; a race of dastards, and the ready prey to the conqueror. The Belgians are the strength of their nation; and yet those states are either in arms against the Romans, or with us in their hearts." Tutor opposed this advice. "By protracting the war, the enemy would gain time to augment their army. Their legions were advancing on every side. One was already arrived from Britain, others were on their march from Spain, and more from Italy; all hardy veterans, inured to the fatigue and the perils of war. The Germans, for whom we are desired to wait, are strangers to discipline; men unaccustomed to obey their officers, without any other guide than their own caprice, and the impulse of the moment. Besides this, they are a venal race; money is their passion, and with those sinews of war the Romans are best provided. And when the price of inactivity is equal to the wages of war, what soldier will not prefer the former? If we offer battle, what force has Cerealis to bring against us? His legions are the poor remains of the German army, the refuse of the sword, all lately bound by solemn oaths to the empire of the Gauls. On what does the Roman found his hopes? He put to the rout an undisciplined handful of men under the conduct of Valentinus: but that very circumstance will be his ruin. The general and his army are inspired with a fit of valour, and will soon have reason to repent of their rashness. Let him hazard an engagement; it will not be with Valentinus, a young orator, fluent in words, but of no skill in war: the affair will be with Civilis and with Classicus. The sight of those chiefs will cover the legions with consternation: their defeat, their flight, their famine, and their ignominious surrender, will all be present to their minds, and all will plunge them in despair. As to the Treverians and Lingones, will they be faithful to the

Romans? Remove their fears, and the next moment they are on our own side." Such was the advice of Tutor. Classicus adopted it, and the measure was forthwith carried into execution.

LXXVII. The chiefs drew up their men in order of battle. In the centre they stationed the Ubians and Lingones, the Batavian cohorts in the right wing, the Bructerians and Tencterians in the left. They resolved to attack the Romans in their camp. One division poured down from the hills, while the rest advanced with rapidity over the plain that lay between the high road and the Moselle. The blow was struck with such sudden vigour, that Cerealis, who passed the night out of his camp, received in bed the news of the attack and the defeat. He gave no credit to the account, but persisted with anger to condemn the folly of the messengers, till he saw a scene of carnage. The Germans had forced the intrenchments; the cavalry was routed; and the bridge over the Moselle, which made a communication between the Treverians and the Agrippinians, was in possession of the enemy. Undismayed in the moment of danger, he rushed forward, without waiting for his armour, to retrieve the loss. He threw himself into the middle of the fray, and faced every danger, defying darts and javelins, animating the brave, and stopping such as fled from their post. His example roused a spirit of emulation. Numbers went to his assistance. His happy temerity recovered possession of the bridge, and that important pass was secured by a chosen band.

Cerealis returned to the camp. He there saw the legions which had been captured at Novesium and Bonn, dispersed in wild disorder, their standards well-nigh abandoned, and the eagles in danger of falling into the hands of the enemy. Enraged at the sight, he exclaimed aloud, "It is not Flaccus, it is not Vocula, whom you thus abandon; against me you have no charge of treachery. The confidence which I reposed in you is my only crime. I was weak enough to believe that you repented of your submission to the empire of Gaul; I thought you capable of remembering, with remorse, your violated oath of fidelity to your country: but I was too credulous. Add me to the list of your murdered generals; stretch me in death with Herennius and Numisius; let it be the fate of all your commanders to perish by the hands of their soldiers, or to be butchered by the enemy. Go, tell Vespasian, or, if you will, tell Classicus and Civilis (for they are nearer), tell the Barbarians, all your brave exploits, and make it a merit with them that you have deserted your general. But remember that the legions are at hand. They will revenge my death, and your crimes will not remain unpunished."

LXXVIII. These reproaches were founded in truth: the tribunes and other officers urged the same topics. The soldiers rallied, but could only form in cohorts, or in separate companies. Surrounded as they were by the enemy, and forced to engage within their intrenchments, amidst the tents and baggage, they were not able to present a regular line of battle. Tutor, Classicus, and Civilis, at the head of their respective divisions, enacted wonders. They invited the Gauls to liberty, the Batavians to immortal glory, and the Germans to the plunder of the camp. All things conspired in their favour, till the one-and-twentieth legion, finding an open space, drew up in regular order, and, after sustaining for some time the shock of superior numbers, turned the fortune of the day. The gods, in that moment, became propitious to the cause of Rome. Nothing but their special protection could work that wonderful change, in consequence of which, the conquerors, who the instant before were bearing down all opposition, fled in a sudden panic from inferior numbers. Their consternation, as they declared afterwards, was occasioned by the cohorts that rallied after their defeat, and showed themselves on the ridge of the hills. They seemed to the Batavians a reinforcement just arrived. But the fact is, their love of plunder was the cause of their ruin. When they had gained the advantage, and ought to have pursued it, they began to quarrel among themselves for their share of the booty. On the other hand, Cerealis, by his negligence, well-nigh lost his army; but his bravery afterwards redeemed his character. Determined to make the best use of his victory, he took the enemy's camp on that very day, and razed it to the ground.

LXXIX. The interval allowed to the soldiers to repose from their fatigue was but short. Cerealis marched to the Agrippinian colony, where the inhabitants were ready to deliver up the wife and sister of Civilis, with the daughter of Classicus, all three left in their hands as hostages for the due performance of mutual treaties. They had, at this time, massacred all the Germans throughout their colony. For this act they dreaded the vengeance of an enraged nation, and applied for succours, before the enemy could be again in force to renew the campaign, and revenge their slaughtered countrymen. For that purpose Civilis had already planned his measures. He depended on the assistance of a cohort of distinguished bravery, composed of Chaucians and Frisians, and, as he imagined, safely posted at Tolbiacum, in the Agrippinian territory. At the head of this resolute band he had projected a sudden attack, but, on the road, had the mortification to hear that those gallant soldiers were all destroyed. They had been invited by the Agrippinians to a sumptuous feast, and, in the night, as they lay oppressed with sleep and wine, their cottages being set on fire, the whole cohort perished in one general conflagration. At the same time Cerealis made a forced march to the relief of the city. Civilis had now another care to distract his attention. He saw that the fourteenth legion, co-operating with the fleet from Britain, might harass the Batavians on the sea-coast, and lay waste the country. That legion, however, marched overland, under the conduct of Fabius Priscus, to invade the Tungrians and the Nervians. These two states submitted to the Romans. The Caninefates, in the meantime, attacked the fleet, and either took or sunk the greatest part. By the same people a large body of the Nervians, who had taken up arms in favour of the Romans, was totally overthrown. Classicus, in another part of the country, fell in with a party of horse, detached by Cerealis to Novesium, and engaged them with good success. These, it is true, were petty advantages; but, being frequent, they tarnished the fame of the victory lately obtained by Cerealis.

LXXX. During these transactions, Mucianus, who was still at Rome, ordered the son of Vitellius [1] to be put to death. Political necessity was the colour which he gave to this proceeding: if the seeds of discord were not destroyed, the rude scene of civil commotion would never be closed. He still continued to foster ill-will to Antonius, and, for that reason, excluded him from the train appointed to attend Domitian into Gaul. The affections of the army, he well knew, were fixed on a general who had led them on to victory; and such was the pride of Antonius, that, so far from bending to a superior, he could not brook an equal. Being superseded by Mucianus, he set out, in disgust, to join Vespasian. The reception which he met with from the emperor, though it bore marks of displeasure, did not, however, answer his expectation. Vespasian was divided between opposite motives: he knew that the services of Antonius were too glaring to be overlooked, and that the war was terminated

[1] Germanicus: *Hist.* ii. 59.

by his ability; but still Mucianus, by his letters, continued to infuse the rancour of his own private animosity. The courtiers were also leagued against Antonius: they represented him in odious colours, as a man of high ambition, fierce, and overbearing. Nor did their malice fail to revive the reproaches of his former conduct. Antonius was at no pains to soften prejudice. His arrogance provoked new enemies. He magnified his own exploits, and talked in degrading terms of other officers, particularly of Cæcina, a man, he said, of an abject spirit, who had surrendered with disgrace. By this conduct Antonius gave umbrage to all. His consequence declined, and the emperor, still preserving the exteriors of friendship, lost all affection for his person.

LXXXI. Vespasian passed some months at Alexandria, having resolved to defer his voyage to Italy till the return of summer, when the winds, blowing in a regular direction, afforded a safe and pleasant navigation. During his residence in that city, a number of incidents, out of the ordinary course of nature, seemed to mark him as the particular favourite of the gods. A man of mean condition, born at Alexandria, had lost his sight by a defluxion on his eyes. He presented himself before Vespasian, and, falling prostrate on the ground, implored the emperor to administer a cure for his blindness. He came, he said, by the admonition of Serapis, the god whom the superstition of the Egyptians holds in the highest veneration. The request was, that the emperor, with his spittle, would condescend to moisten the poor man's face and the balls of his eyes. Another who had lost the use of his hands, inspired by the same god, begged that he would tread on the part affected. Vespasian smiled at a request so absurd and wild. The wretched objects persisted to implore his aid. He dreaded the ridicule of a vain attempt; but the importunity of the men, and the crowd of flatterers, prevailed upon the prince not entirely to disregard their petition.

He ordered the physicians to consider among themselves, whether the blindness of the one, and the paralytic affection of the other, were within the reach of human assistance. The result of the consultation was, "that the organs of sight were not so injured, but that, by removing the film or cataract, the patient might recover. As to the disabled limb, by proper applications and invigorating medicines, it was not impossible to restore it to its former tone. The gods, perhaps, intended a special remedy, and chose Vespasian to be the instrument of their dispensations. If a cure took place, the glory of it would add new lustre to the name of Cæsar; if otherwise, the poor men would bear the jests and raillery of the people." Vespasian, in the tide of his affairs, began to think that there was nothing so great and wonderful, nothing so improbable or even incredible, which his good fortune would not accomplish. In the presence of a prodigious multitude, all erect with expectation, he advanced with an air of serenity, and hazarded the experiment. The paralytic hand recovered its functions, and the blind man saw the light of the sun. By living witnesses, who were actually on the spot, both events are confirmed at this hour, when deceit and flattery can hope for no reward.[1]

LXXXII. Vespasian was now determined to visit the sanctuary of Serapis, in order to consult the god about the future fortune of the empire. Having given orders to remove all intruders, he entered the temple. While he adored the deity of the place, he perceived, in the midst of his devotion, a man of principal note among the Egyptians advancing behind him. The name of this person was Basilides, who, at that moment, was known to be detained by illness at the distance of several miles. Vespasian inquired of the priests, whether they had seen Basilides that day in the temple. He asked a number of others, whether they had met him in any part of the city. At length, from messengers whom he despatched on horseback, he received certain intelligence, that Basilides was no less than fourscore miles distant from Alexandria. He concluded, therefore, that the gods had favoured him with a preternatural vision, and from the import of the word BASILIDES, he inferred an interpretation of the decrees of Heaven in favour of his future reign.

LXXXIII. Concerning the origin of the god Serapis, a subject hitherto untouched by the Roman writers, the account given by the priests of Egypt is as follows: At the time when Ptolemy, the first of the Macedonian race, who settled the government of Egypt, had raised walls and ramparts to defend the newly-built city of Alexandria, and afterwards gave a temple and the rites of national worship, a youth of graceful mien, and size above the human form, appeared to him in a midnight vision, commanding him to send some of his trusty friends as far as Pontus, to bring from that place into Egypt the statue of the preternatural being then before him. By his compliance with those directions the prosperity of the

[1] Tacitus wrote his *History* in the reign of Trajan, when the Vespasian or Flavian family was extinct.

whole kingdom would be advanced, and the city which should be so happy as to possess that valuable treasure, would be great among the nations. In that instant the youth was seen mounting to heaven in a column of fire. Ptolemy had recourse to the Egyptian priests, the usual interpreters of dreams and prodigies. But those religionists had no knowledge of Pontus, nor of any foreign modes of worship. Timotheus, the Athenian, a man descended from the race of the Eumolpides, was called in to their assistance. Ptolemy had, before this time, invited him from the city of Eleusis, to preside over the mysteries and the established worship of the country. He now desired Timotheus to explain what god had visited the king in his dreams, and what were the rites and ceremonies of his new religion. Timotheus addressed himself to such as had travelled into Pontus, and, upon inquiry, learned that there was in those parts a city called Sinope,[1] and near it a temple of great celebrity, sacred to Pluto. Such was the opinion of the natives, founded on tradition, and confirmed by the statue of the god erected in the temple, with a female form at his side, supposed to be Proserpina. Ptolemy, like other kings, was easily alarmed; but, soon recovering from his apprehensions, forgot the whole business, addicting himself entirely to his pleasures, and little solicitous about religious matters. The same form appeared to him a second time, arrayed in terror, and in a tone of menace denouncing vengeance on the king and his whole empire, if the orders already given were not obeyed. After this visitation Ptolemy sent his deputies with magnificent presents to Scydrothemis, the prince then on the throne of Sinope. The ambassadors had it in their instructions to touch at the isle of Delos, there to consult the Pythian Apollo. They sailed with favourable winds, and had a quick passage. The answer of the oracle was in explicit terms: "Pursue your course, carry off the statue of my father, and let that of my sister be unremoved."

LXXXIV. Having reached Sinope, they presented their gifts, and opened their commission to Scydrothemis. That monarch hesitated for some time. He dreaded the displeasure of an angry deity; the clamours of his people alarmed him; and, at times, the gifts and presents of the ambassadors dazzled his imagination. The business remained three years in suspense. Ptolemy never desisted from his

1 Sinope, on the Euxine.

purpose. He renewed his entreaties; he omitted no arts of persuasion; he added new dignities to his embassy, increased the number of ships, and made his presents still more magnificent. A dreadful vision appeared to Scydrothemis, threatening dreadful consequences, if he persisted in his opposition to the measures of a god. The king fluctuated between opposite counsels. His delay was punished by a variety of disasters, by sore disease, the manifest signs of divine vengeance, and calamities increasing every day. In that distress he called an assembly of the people, and laid before them the orders of the god, the visions of Ptolemy, as well as those which he saw himself, and the miseries that threatened the whole community. The populace clamoured in opposition to their sovereign. They envied the Egyptian monarch, and, trembling for themselves, rushed in a body to guard the avenues of the temple. Common fame, at all times delighting in the marvellous, spread a report, that the god, of his own motion, quitted the temple, and embarked on board one of the vessels that lay at anchor in the harbour. To complete the miracle, though a large tract of sea divided Sinope from Alexandria, the voyage was performed in less than three days. A temple, such as suited a great and opulent city, was built at a place called Rhacotis, where, in ancient times, a chapel had been dedicated to Serapis and Isis.

Such is the history of the god Serapis, and his first introduction into Egypt. There is, however, a different account, which places the whole transaction in the reign of the third Ptolemy, who, it is said, brought the statue from Seleucia, a city of Syria: others assert, that it was found at Memphis, the celebrated capital of ancient Egypt. Concerning the god himself the opinions of antiquarians are not less at variance. On account of his healing art, he is by some called Æsculapius; by others, Osiris, the most ancient deity of the country; and many, who think him the governing mind of the universe, give him the name of Jupiter. But the prevailing doctrine maintains that Pluto is the true deity. That hypothesis is either founded on the reasoning of mystic interpreters, or confirmed by certain symbols, that manifest the attributes of the god.

LXXXV. We return to the affairs of Rome. Domitian and Mucianus set out on their expedition. They had hardly reached the foot of the Alps, when they received advice of the victory gained by Cerealis over the Treverians. Of this news they entertained no doubt when they saw Valentinus brought in a prisoner, loaded with irons. Even in ruin that gallant chief appeared with a mind unconquered. The spirit that animated him in the field, was still visible in his countenance. He was heard in vindication of his conduct; but curiosity and a desire to try the spirit of the man, were the only motives. Being condemned to suffer death, he persevered with unshaken constancy. In his last moments he was told, with an air of insult, that his country was reduced to subjection; he calmly answered, "You have reconciled me to my fate: I die without regret." Mucianus thought it time to change the plan of his expedition. The design had been long rolling in his mind, though he now started it as a new scheme suggested by the events of war. "The gods (he said) had favoured the Roman arms, and crushed the turbulent spirit of the enemy. At such a time, it would ill become Domitian to snatch the laurel from the brow of the general who had fought with such brilliant success. If the majesty of the empire, or the security of the provinces of Gaul, were exposed to danger, the crisis would be worthy of the emperor's son; but the Caninefates and the Batavians were the proper quarry of inferior commanders. The prince might now proceed as far as Lyons. At that place he might display the pomp of imperial grandeur, superior to the little ambition of engaging in petty skirmishes, yet near at hand, and ready, if occasion called, to undertake a great and important enterprise."

LXXXVI. The veil was too thin to hide the designs of Mucianus; but to yield to his artifice, without seeming to detect it, was judged the best policy. Domitian proceeded to Lyons. At that place he is said, by secret messengers, to have tampered with Cerealis, in order to sound the disposition of that officer, and learn beforehand, whether, on the appearance of the prince at the head of the army, he would be willing to resign the command. Whether Domitian had it in contemplation to levy war against his father, or to strengthen himself against his brother Titus, remains uncertain. Cerealis had the wisdom to decline the overture, considering it as nothing more than the vain project of youth and inexperience. Domitian saw himself slighted by the superior officers, and, in disgust, withdrew from all public business, never interfering afterwards, nor taking upon him to direct in such inferior matters as had been heretofore committed to his authority. With a specious appearance of humble content and modesty, he chose to live in solitude pretending that poetry and literary pursuits were his only passion. Under this artful disguise he hoped to conceal the native passions of his heart, and to give no jealousy to his brother. From his own frame of mind he judged of Titus, commenting with malignity on the milder virtues that adorned the character of that amiable prince.

BOOK V

CONTENTS

Titus undertakes the conduct of the war against the Jews—He enters Judæa—The number of his forces—He encamps before the walls of Jerusalem.—II. *The origin of the Jews; their customs, institutions, and religion.*—VI. *Their territory, and boundaries; the palm and balm tree; Mount Libanus; the river Jordan; the lake that throws up pitch; the vast tract of barren land; the sands at the mouth of the river Belus of use in making glass.*—VIII. *Jerusalem the capital city —Immense riches of the temple—Condition of the Jews under the Assyrians, the Medes, the Persians, the Macedonians—An account of their kings.*—IX. *Pompey the first Roman general that besieged and took the city of Jerusalem—Herod raised to the throne by Mark Antony —Caligula ordered his statue to be placed in the temple—The Jews refused to comply—A new dispute with Gessius Florus, the Roman governor—Vespasian sent by Nero to conduct the war.*—XI. *Titus lays siege to Jerusalem—Strength and fortifications of the city, and the temple—Three armies in the town under three different generals.*—XIII. *Prodigies before the siege began, but all neglected by the Jews—An ancient prophecy misinterpreted.*—XIV. *Further account of the war under Civilis in Germany.*—XV. *Civilis and Cerealis have various success in different battles.*—XIX. *Civilis with his whole force enters the island of Batavia, and attacks the Roman garrisons.*—XXI. *Cerealis marches to the relief of the Romans.*—XXII. *Cerealis by his want of caution in danger of being taken by surprise, and carried off by the enemy in the night-time.*—XXIII. *Civilis equips a naval armament on the vast bay near the mouth of the Meuse—Cerealis collects a number of vessels, and offers battle—A slight naval engagement—This the last attempt of Civilis—He retires beyond the Rhine—The Romans in great danger from the floods by which Batavia was laid under water.*—XXVI. *Civilis inclined to terms of peace—A conference between him and Cerealis.* The rest of this book is lost.

These transactions passed in the

Year of Rome.	Of Christ.	Consuls.
823	70	Flavius Vespasianus, Titus, his son.

I. In the beginning of this year, Titus was appointed by his father to complete the reduction of Judæa. This young commander, while Vespasian was yet no higher than a subject, had gained a reputation for brave exploit and military talents.[1]

[1] Titus served with his father in Britain, in Germany, and Judæa.

His fame and authority were now in their meridian splendour. The armies of the empire and the several provinces exerted themselves with emulation to assist him in his enterprise. Titus, on his part, made it his study to show himself superior to the fortuitous advantages of his station. Active in the field and elegant in his manners, he endeavoured to merit esteem by affability and a strict discharge of his duty. He attended the works; he marched in the ranks, and mixed with the common soldiers, without impairing the dignity of his character. He was received in Judæa at the head of three legions, the fifth, the tenth, and the fifteenth;[1] all experienced veterans who had served under Vespasian. To these were added the twelfth, from Syria; and the third and twenty-second, from Alexandria. He had, besides, twenty cohorts of the allies and eight squadrons of horse. The two kings, Agrippa and Sohemus, joined his standard. Antiochus sent the forces of his kingdom. A formidable body of Arabs, with that animosity which often embitters neighbouring nations against each other, took the field as avowed enemies of the Jewish nation. The number that passed over from Rome and Italy, to serve as volunteers under a prince not yet decided in his friendships, was considerable. With this force Titus advanced into the enemy's country in order of battle, by his scouts exploring the motions of the enemy, and always prepared for action. In this manner he arrived at Jerusalem, and encamped before the town.

II. Being now to relate the progress of a siege that terminated in the destruction of that once celebrated city, it may be proper to go back to its first foundation, and to trace the origin of the people. The Jews, we are told, were natives of the isle of Crete. At the time when Saturn was driven from his throne by the violence of Jupiter, they abandoned their habitations, and gained a settlement at the extremity of Libya. In support of this tradition, the etymology of their name is adduced as a proof. Mount Ida, well known to fame, stands in the isle of Crete: the inhabitants are called Idæans; and the word, by a barbarous corruption, was changed afterwards to that of Judæans. According to others, they were a colony from Egypt, when that country, during the reign of Isis, overflowing with inhabitants, poured forth its redundant numbers under the conduct of Hierosolymus and Juda. A third hypothesis makes them originally Ethiopians, compelled by the tyranny of

[1] See an account of the army under Titus; Josephus, *Bell. Jud.*, lib. v. cap. 6.

Cepheus, the reigning monarch, to abandon their country. Some authors contend that they were a tribe of Assyrians, who for some time occupied a portion of Egypt, and, afterwards transplanting themselves into Syria, acquired in their own right a number of cities, together with the territories of the Hebrews. There is still another tradition, which ascribes to the Jews a more illustrious origin, deriving them from the ancient Solymans so highly celebrated in the poetry of Homer.[1] By that people the city was built, and from its founder received the name of Hierosolyma.

III. In this clash of opinions, one point seems to be universally admitted. A pestilential disease, disfiguring the race of man, and making the body an object of loathsome deformity, spread all over Egypt. Bocchoris, at that time the reigning monarch, consulted the oracle of Jupiter Hammon, and received for answer, that the kingdom must be purified, by exterminating the infected multitude, as a race of men detested by the gods. After diligent search, the wretched sufferers were collected together, and in a wild and barren desert[2] abandoned to their misery. In that distress, while the vulgar herd was sunk in deep despair, Moses, one of their number, reminded them, that, by the wisdom of his counsels, they had been already rescued out of impending danger. Deserted as they were by men and gods, he told them, that if they did not repose their confidence in him, as their chief by divine commission, they had no resource left. His offer was accepted. Their march began, they knew not whither. Want of water was their chief distress. Worn-out with fatigue, they lay stretched on the bare earth, heart-broken, ready to expire, when a troop of wild asses, returning from pasture, went up the steep ascent of a rock covered with a grove of trees. The verdure of the herbage round the place suggested the idea of springs near at hand. Moses traced the steps of the animals, and discovered a plentiful vein of water. By this relief the fainting multitude was raised from despair. They pursued their journey for six days without intermission. On the seventh they made halt, and, having expelled the natives, took possession of the country, where they built their city, and dedicated their temple.

IV. In order to draw the bond of union closer, and to

[1] Homer was held in such high veneration throughout Greece, that his verses often decided the limits of disputed lands, and threw a lustre round every state or people recorded in his poems.

[2] In the wide plains of Arabia.

establish his own authority, Moses gave a new form of worship, and a system of religious ceremonies, the reverse of everything known to any other age or country. Whatever is held sacred by the Romans, with the Jews is held profane: and what in other nations is unlawful and impure, with them is fully established. The figure of the animal[1] that guided them to refreshing springs, is consecrated in the sanctuary of their temple. In contempt of Jupiter Hammon, they sacrifice a ram. The ox, worshipped in Egypt for the god Apis, is slain as a victim by the Jews. From the flesh of swine they abstain altogether. An animal, subject to the same leprous disease that infected their whole nation, is not deemed proper food. The famine, with which they were for a long time afflicted, is frequently commemorated by a solemn fast. Their bread, in memory of their having seized a quantity of grain to relieve their wants, is made without leaven. The seventh day is sacred to rest, for on that day their labours ended; and such is their natural propensity to sloth, that, in consequence of it, every seventh year is devoted to repose and sluggish inactivity. For this septennial custom some account in a different manner; they tell us, that it is an institution in honour of Saturn, either because the Idæans expelled, as has been mentioned, from the isle of Crete, transmitted to their posterity the principles of their religious creed, or because, among the seven planets that govern the universe, Saturn moves in the highest orbit, and acts with the greatest energy. It may be added, that the period in which the heavenly bodies perform their revolutions, is regulated by the number seven.

V. These rites and ceremonies, from whatever source derived, owe their chief support to their antiquity. They have other institutions, in themselves corrupt, impure, and even abominable, but eagerly embraced, as if their very depravity were a recommendation. The scum and refuse of other nations, renouncing the religion of their country, flocked in crowds to Jerusalem, enriching the place with gifts and offerings. Hence the wealth and grandeur of the state. Connected amongst themselves by the most obstinate and

[1] The veneration here said to have been paid in the temple to the image of an ass, is refuted by Tacitus himself, who says in the following chapter, that the Jews suffered no consecrated statues or images to be erected either in their cities or their temples. *Nulla simulacra urbibus suis, nedum templis sinunt.* He tells us afterwards, that when Pompey conquered Jerusalem, and made his entry into the temple, he found neither statues nor images, but a void and empty tabernacle. *Nulla intus deum effigie, vacuam sedem, et inania arcana.* See this book, chap. ix.

inflexible faith, the Jews extend their charity to all of their own persuasion, while towards the rest of mankind they nourish a sullen and inveterate hatred. Strangers are excluded from their tables. Unsociable to all others, they eat and lodge with one another only; and, though addicted to sensuality, they admit no intercourse with women from other nations. Among themselves their passions are without restraint. Vice itself is lawful. That they may know each other by distinctive marks, they have established the practice of circumcision. All who embrace their faith, submit to the same operation. The first elements of their religion teach their proselytes to despise the gods, to abjure their country, and forget their parents, their brothers, and their children. To encourage their own internal population is a great object of their policy. No man is allowed to put his children to death. The souls of such as die in battle, or by the hand of the executioner, are thought to be immortal. Hence two ruling passions; the desire of multiplying their species, and a fixed contempt of death. The bodies of the deceased are never burned: they choose rather to inter them, after the example of the Egyptians. With that people they agree in their belief of a future state; they have the same notion of departed spirits, the same solicitude, and the same doctrine. With regard to the Deity, their creed is different. The Egyptians worship various animals, and also certain symbolical representations, which are the work of man; the Jews acknowledge one God only, and him they see in the mind's eye, and him they adore in contemplation, condemning, as impious idolaters, all who, with perishable materials wrought into the human form, attempt to give a representation of the Deity. The God of the Jews is the great governing mind, that directs and guides the whole frame of nature, eternal, infinite, and neither capable of change, nor subject to decay. In consequence of this opinion, no such thing as a statue was to be seen in their city, much less in their temples. Flattery had not learned to pay that homage to their own kings, nor were they willing to admit the statues of the Cæsars. Their priests, it is true, made use of fifes and cymbals: they were crowned with wreaths of ivy, and a vine wrought in gold was seen in their temple. Hence some have inferred, that Bacchus, the conqueror of the east, was the object of their adoration. But the Jewish forms of worship have no conformity to the rites of Bacchus. The latter have their festive days, which are always celebrated with mirth and carousing banquets. Those of the Jews are a gloomy ceremony, full of absurd enthusiasm, rueful, mean, and sordid.[1]

VI. The country of Judæa is bounded on the east by Arabia; on the south by Egypt; on the west by Phœnicia and the sea; the northern frontier stretches to a great length along the confines of Syria. The natives are strong, and patient of labour. The climate is dry and sultry; rain is seldom seen, and the soil is rich and fertile. Besides the fruits known in Italy, the palm and balm tree flourish in great luxuriance. The palm is beautiful as well as lofty; the balm is of moderate growth. Its branches, when the juices circulate, seem to call for an incision, but they dread the application of steel; the veins shrink from its approach. The operation is performed with a shell, or pointed stone. The liquor that distils from the wound is of use in medicine. Libanus is the highest mountain in the country. It rises to a great height, affording shade under its verdant groves, and, even in the ardent heat of that sultry region, covered at the top with eternal snow. From this mountain the river Jordan derives its source, and the abundance of its waters. The stream does not discharge itself into the sea: it runs into two different lakes, preserving through both a clear and unmixed current, till it loses itself in a third. The last of these lakes is of immense extent, resembling a sea, but more nauseous to the taste, and, by its fetid exhalations, pernicious to the neighbourhood. The winds occasion no undulation: the surface is never ruffled. No fish can live in these waters. The birds that love to dip the wing, avoid the place. The fluid element, for it can scarce be called water, supports, as it were on a solid expanse, whatever is thrown in. Between those who cannot swim, and the perfect masters of the art, there is no difference: all float with equal ease. At certain seasons of the year, the lake throws up a quantity of pitch, or bitumen. Experience, the mother of all useful arts, has taught men how to gather it. It is a liquid substance, naturally of a black hue. The infusion of vinegar gives cohesion to the parts. When thus condensed, it floats on the surface, and you may grasp it with your hand. Those who make it their business to collect it, draw one end into their boats; the rest of the mass follows

[1] The Roman *dies festus* signified a day consecrated to joy, and song, and dance, and public spectacles. It was otherwise with the Jews. At stated periods they commemorated public misfortunes; and grief and fasting, sackcloth and ashes, distinguished their religious ceremonies, wholly different from the rites of Bacchus, and therefore called absurd and sordid. Tacitus, it must be said, has given us an unfavourable picture of the Jews.

without toil or difficulty, and continues loading the vessel, till the viscous substance is cut in two. The separation is neither made with iron nor with brass. Touch it with blood, or with linen tinged with menstrual evacuations, and the parts instantly divide. Such is the account transmitted to us by ancient authors. We learn, however, from modern experience, that this extraordinary substance, floating in heaps up and down the lake, is driven towards the shore, or easily drawn by the hand; and when the vapour that exhales from the land, or the heat of the sun, has sufficiently dried and hardened it, it is then cut asunder, like wood or stone, by wedges, or the stroke of the hatchet.

VII. At a small distance from the lake lie those wide-extended plains, which tradition says were formerly a rich and fruitful country, abounding with populous cities, but long since destroyed by fire from heaven, and now a barren desert. Amidst the ruins, which still remain, we are told that the marks of celestial vengeance may be clearly traced, and that the soil, consumed and parched, has lost the powers of vegetation. Whatever the earth produces, whether by the prolific vigour of nature, or the cultivation of man, nothing ripens to perfection. The herbage may shoot up, and the trees may put forth their blossoms; they may even attain the usual appearance of maturity; but, with this florid outside, all within turns black, and moulders into dust. To speak my own opinion, though it be true that great and flourishing cities have been destroyed by fire from heaven, yet the desolation here described may be accounted for from natural causes. The exhalations from the lake seem sufficient to blast the vital principle of the soil, and to infect the whole atmosphere. By consequence, all manner of grain, and the fruits of the autumn, naturally perish in a climate so hostile to vegetation. The river Belus empties itself into the sea that washes the coast of Judæa. The sands, which the stream carries down in large quantities, are taken up at its mouth, and, being mixed with nitre, dissolve by the action of fire, and soon afterwards harden into glass. The shore is of small extent, and, though constantly searched, these ingredients still remain unexhausted.

VIII. The face of the country is covered with villages. There are likewise towns of considerable note. Jerusalem is the capital. The temple is distinguished by its wealth, no less than by its magnificence. The fortifications of the city are its first defence; the royal palace is the second; the enclosure, where the temple stands, forms the third. Even a

Jew is not admitted beyond the portal. No man, except the priests, has access to the interior parts. While the Assyrians, and after them the Medes and Persians, were masters of the oriental world, the Jews, of all the nations then held in subjection, were deemed the vilest. At a subsequent period, when the Macedonian monarchy was established, Antiochus, the reigning king, formed a plan to weed out the superstition of the country. To reform, if possible, so corrupt a race, he intended to introduce the manners and institutions of Greece; but a war with the Parthians (Arsaces being then in arms) rendered that design abortive. In process of time, when the Macedonians were by degrees enfeebled, when the Parthian state was in its infancy, and the Romans were yet at a distance, the Jews seized the opportunity to erect a monarchy of their own.[1] Their kings were soon deposed by the caprice and levity of the people. They returned, however, in a short time, and, having recovered the throne by force of arms, made the people feel the weight of their resentment. A scene of oppression followed; citizens were driven into exile; whole cities were demolished; brothers, wives, and parents, were put to death; and, in short, every species of cruelty, usual among despotic kings, was enforced with rigour by the usurpers. They saw that superstition is among the instruments of tyranny; and, to strengthen their ill-gotten power, they not only supported the national rites and ceremonies, but united in their own persons the sacerdotal and regal functions.

IX. Pompey was the first Roman[2] that subdued the Jews. By right of conquest he entered their temple. It is a fact well known, that he found no image, no statue,[3] no symbolical representation of the Deity; the whole represented a naked dome; the sanctuary was unadorned and simple. By Pompey's orders the walls of the city were levelled to the ground, but the temple was left entire. In the civil wars that afterwards shook

[1] Justin informs us, that the power of Demetrius I. and his successors, kings of Syria, not being supported with vigour, the Jews took their opportunity to shake off a foreign yoke, and assert their liberty. See Justin, lib. xxxvi. ver. 1 and 3. In confirmation of this, we read in Maccabees a treaty between Demetrius and Simon the high-priest, B.C. 143; and thus *the yoke of the heathen was taken away from Israel, and the people of Israel began to write in their instruments and contracts, In the first year of Simon the high-priest, the governor and leader of the Jews.* 1 Maccabees xiii. 41, 42.

[2] Pompey made himself master of Jerusalem, B.C. 63. He entered the temple and the holy of holies; but, according to Josephus (*Jewish Antiquities*, xiv. 4), abstained from plunder, content with imposing an annual tribute.

[3] This passage affords another proof that the effigy of an ass was not consecrated in the temple, as mentioned by Tacitus.

the empire, when the eastern provinces fell to the lot of Mark Antony, Pacorus, the Parthian king, made himself master of Judæa; but being, in a short time after, put to death by Ventidius, his forces retired beyond the Euphrates. Caius Sosius once more reduced the Jews to obedience. Herod[1] was placed on the throne by Mark Antony, and Augustus confirmed the sceptre in his hand. On the death of Herod, a man of the name of Simon, without deferring to the authority of the emperor, usurped the sovereignty. He, however, was punished for his ambition by Quinctilius Varus, the governor of Syria; and the kingdom, by an equal partition, was divided between the three sons of Herod. During the reign of Tiberius things remained in a state of tranquillity. Caligula[2] ordered his statue to be erected in the temple. The Jews, rather than submit, had recourse to arms. Caligula was assassinated, and the contest died with him. In the following reign, the Jewish kings being either dead, or their dominion reduced to narrow limits, the rest of Judæa[3] was converted into a Roman province. Claudius committed the administration to Roman knights, or to his favourite freedmen. Antonius Felix was of the latter description; a man who, from low beginnings, rose to power, and, with the true genius of a slave, exercised the tyranny of an eastern prince. He married Drusilla, the grand-daughter of Antony and Cleopatra. Mankind had then two extraordinary objects to gaze at; one in the person of Claudius, emperor of Rome; and the other, an enfranchised slave; each the grandson of Mark Antony.

X. The Jews, though harassed by various acts of oppression, continued to give proofs of their patient spirit, till Cassius Florus, in the character of procurator, took upon him the administration of the province. Under him a war broke out. Cestius Gallius, the governor of Syria, endeavoured to crush the revolt. He fought a number of battles, in most of them unsuccessful. After his death, which was, perhaps, hastened by disappointment and vexation, Vespasian, by the appointment of Nero, succeeded to the command. Supported by his great military character, and the good fortune that attended his arms, with the additional advantage of able officers under him, that general, in two summer campaigns, overran the

[1] Herod was raised to the throne by Mark Antony, and his title was confirmed by a decree of the senate.

[2] Caligula had the frantic ambition to have his statue placed in the temple of Jerusalem: but the Jews had recourse to arms; another proof of their resolution not to suffer the tabernacle to be profaned by images of any kind.

[3] See *Annals*, xii. 23.

whole country, and made himself master of all the inferior cities. Jerusalem was the only place that held out. In the following year, the war with Vitellius engaged his attention, and the Jews enjoyed an interval of repose. The peace of Italy being at length restored, foreign affairs demanded his immediate care. The Jews were the only nation that refused to submit. The obstinacy of that stubborn people filled Vespasian with resentment. But what sudden emergencies might involve a new reign in difficulties, could not be foreseen. In order to be prepared for all events, Vespasian judged it the wisest measure to leave his son Titus at the head of the army. The prince, as already mentioned, encamped under the walls of Jerusalem, and drew out his legions in the face of the enemy.

XI. The Jews appeared in force on the plains under the ramparts, determined, if successful, to push their advantage, and, if obliged to give ground, sure of a retreat within their fortifications. The Roman cavalry, with a detachment from the light-armed cohorts, advanced to the attack. A battle was fought, but with doubtful success. The Jews took shelter within their walls, venturing, however, for several days afterwards, to sally out in small parties, till, tired by repeated losses, they resolved to shut themselves up within their fortifications. Titus prepared to carry the place by storm. To linger before it, till famine compelled a surrender, appeared unworthy of the Roman name. The soldiers were eager to brave every danger: courage, ferocity, and the hope of gaining the rewards of victory, inspired the whole army. Titus had his private motives: Rome was before his eyes; wealth and magnificence dazzled his imagination; and pleasure had its allurements. If the city was not taken by assault, a siege in form would detain him too long from the splendid scene that lay before him. But Jerusalem stood upon an eminence, difficult of approach. The natural strength of the place was increased by redoubts and bulwarks, which, even on the level plain, would have made it secure from insult. Two hills that rose to a prodigious height, were enclosed by walls constructed with skill, in some places projecting forward, in others retiring inwardly, with the angles so formed, that the besiegers were always liable to be annoyed in flank. The extremities of the rock were sharp, abrupt, and craggy. In convenient places, near the summit, towers were raised sixty feet high, and others, on the declivity of the sides, rose no less than a hundred and twenty feet. These works presented a spectacle altogether astonishing. To the distant eye they seemed to be of equal elevation. Within the city, there were other fortifications enclosing the palace of the kings. Above all was seen, conspicuous to view, the tower Antonia, so called by Herod, in honour of the triumvir, who had been his friend and benefactor.

XII. The temple itself[1] was a strong fortress, in the nature of a citadel. The fortifications were built with consummate skill, surpassing, in art as well as labour, all the rest of the works. The very porticos that surrounded it were a strong defence. A perennial spring supplied the place with water. Subterraneous caverns were scooped under the rock. The rain-water was saved in pools and cisterns. It was foreseen by the founders of the city, that the manners and institutions of the nation, so repugnant to the rest of mankind, would be productive of frequent wars; hence so many precautions against a siege. Since the reduction of the place by Pompey, experience taught the Jews new modes of fortification; and the corruption and venality that pervaded the whole reign of Claudius, favoured all their projects. By bribery they obtained permission to rebuild their walls. The strength of the works plainly showed that, in profound peace, they meditated future resistance. The destruction of the rest of their cities served to increase the number of the besieged. A prodigious conflux poured in from all quarters, and among them the most bold and turbulent spirits of the nation. The city, by consequence, was distracted by internal division. They had three armies, and as many generals. The outward walls, forming the widest extent, were defended by Simon: John, otherwise called Bargioras, commanded in the middle precinct: Eleazar kept possession of the temple. The two former commanded the greatest number of soldiers; the latter had the advantage of situation. The three parties quarrelled among themselves. Battles were fought within the walls; stratagems were practised; conflagrations destroyed parts of the city, and a large quantity of grain was consumed in the flames. Under colour of performing a sacrifice, John contrived to send a band of assassins, to cut off Eleazar and his whole party in one general massacre. By this atrocious deed he gained possession of the temple. From that time two contending factions threw everything into confusion, till the enemy at their gates obliged them to unite in their common defence.

[1] For a description of the temple, see Josephus, *Bell. Jud.*, v. cap. 5.

XIII. Portents and prodigies announced the ruin of the city: but a people, blinded by their own national superstition, and with rancour detesting the religion of other states, held it unlawful by vows and victims to deprecate the impending danger. Swords were seen glittering in the air; embattled armies appeared, and the temple was illuminated by a stream of light, that issued from the heavens. The portal flew open, and a voice more than human denounced the immediate departure of the gods. There was heard, at the same time, a tumultuous and terrific sound, as if superior beings were actually rushing forth. The impression made by these wonders fell upon a few only: the multitude relied upon an ancient prophecy, contained, as they believed, in books kept by the priests, by which it was foretold, that, in this very juncture, the power of the east would prevail over the nations, and a race of men would go forth from Judæa to extend their dominion over the rest of the world. The prediction, however, couched in ambiguous terms, related to Vespasian and his son Titus.[1] But the Jewish mind was not to be enlightened. With the usual propensity of men ready to believe what they ardently wish, the populace assumed to themselves the scene of grandeur which the fates were preparing to bring forward. Calamity itself could not open their eyes. The number besieged in Jerusalem, including both sexes and every age, amounted, according to the best accounts, to no less than six hundred thousand. All who were capable of serving appeared in arms. The number of effective men was beyond all proportion greater than could be expected, even in so vast a multitude. The women, no less than the men, were inflamed with zeal and ardour. If doomed to quit their country, life, they declared, was more terrible than death itself. Against a city so strongly fortified, and defended by such an obstinate race, Titus saw that nothing could be done, either by surprise or a general assault. He threw up mounds and ramparts, and prepared battering-engines. He stationed the legions at different posts, and assigned to each a distinct share of the duty. For some time no attack was made. In

[1] Tacitus condemns the Jews for not rightly understanding a prophecy which he himself has misapplied. But it is evident that it could not relate to the short reigns of Vespasian and his two sons. The Christian religion was at that time striking root in Judæa, and we know it has been since extended over the world. We cannot, however, wonder at the misconception of Tacitus, when it is considered that Josephus, willing, perhaps, to pay his court to the imperial family, did not hesitate to say that the prophecy related to Vespasian. *Bell. Jud.*, vi. cap. 5.

the interval, the Romans prepared all the machines of war, which either the ancients had employed, or modern genius invented.

XIV. It will now be proper to return to the affairs of Germany. Civilis, after the check which he received in the country of the Treverians, recruited his army by levies made in Germany. With these forces he fixed his station in the old camp, called VETERA, depending on the strength of the place. The exploits already performed on that very spot, he hoped, would rouse the valour of his men. Cerealis followed him by rapid marches, with an army more than double his former number, having been joined by the second, the sixth, and the fourteenth legions. To these were added the cohorts and cavalry, which had some time before received orders to come up to his assistance. They did not immediately obey; but since his victory they lost no time. The commanders on both sides were eager to engage. Delay was not the genius of either; but the two armies were separated by a marshy plain of vast extent. The natural humidity of the soil was increased by the skill of Civilis, who had contrived, by obstructions thrown across the bed of the Rhine, to stop the current, and discharge a vast body of water on the neighbouring plains. A treacherous spot like this, covered with an inundation that concealed the solid ground, was highly disadvantageous to the Romans, who carried a weight of armour, and had no skill in swimming. The Germans, on the contrary, had everything in their favour. To make their way through the floods and rivers was their usual practice. They were lightly armed, and their size and stature enabled them to wade through the waters.

XV. The Batavians advanced near enough to insult the Romans. An engagement followed. The legions were thrown into disorder. Their arms and horses were swallowed up in the fens, while the Barbarians, acquainted with the shallows and fordable places, advanced with alacrity, yet not daring to attack the front of the lines, but making their impression on the flank and rear. The conflict had no appearance of two armies engaged on a solid plain: it resembled a naval fight, where the combatants are driven at the mercy of the waves. Wherever a firm footing could be found, to that spot every effort was directed. The sound, the wounded, those who could swim, and those who were unused to the waters, were all, without distinction, involved in one general scene of distress. The slaughter, however, was inconsiderable. The Germans, not daring to hazard a battle out of their fens, returned to their camp. The event of the day made the generals on both sides wish for a decisive action; but they wished with different motives. Civilis wanted to pursue his advantage, and Cerealis to retrieve his honour. Success inspired the Barbarians; the Romans were roused by a sense of shame. The night was passed by both armies in a very different manner. War-songs and savage uproar resounded from the German camp; the Romans continued silent, breathing revenge, and meditating future carnage.

XVI. At the return of day, Cerealis drew out his army. In the front he placed the cavalry and auxiliary cohorts, and, to support them, the legions in the rear. He took post himself at the head of a chosen band, to act as occasion might require. Civilis, instead of presenting a regular line, formed his men in separate divisions. On the right stood the Batavians and Gugernians; the left was occupied by the Germans, with the Rhine on their flank. No general harangue was made to either army. The commanders, on both sides, passed through the ranks, exhorting their men as the occasion prompted. Cerealis called to mind the glory of the Roman name, and the victories of ancient as well as modern date. "You may now," he said, "by one vigorous effort, exterminate a base, a treacherous, and a vanquished race. It is not a battle you are to expect: you are going forth the avengers of your country, to punish a rebellious crew. In the late engagement you were inferior in number, and yet their bravest troops fled before you. You see the refuse of your swords; a set of runaways, who in their minds still bear the galling memory of their late defeat, and on their backs the print of ignominious wounds." He next addressed the legions, in the style peculiarly suited to each. The fourteenth he called the conquerors of Britain. The sixth raised Galba to the imperial dignity. The soldiers of the second were now to flesh their maiden swords, and in that field to consecrate their banners and their eagle. From the legions he passed to the German army, and, with hands outstretched, pointed to the fields around, and there, he said, "There is your station; that bank of the Rhine, and that camp, was yours; wade through the blood of your enemies, and recover your own." The general was heard with shouts of applause. The whole army panted for the onset: those who were weary of a long peace, were eager to signalise their valour; while others, harassed out with the toils of war, hoped, by one glorious victory, to find the end and recompense of all their labours.

XVII. In the opposite army Civilis was neither silent nor inactive. "These fields," he said, "have seen your brave exploits. The Batavians and the Germans, at every step they take, tread on the monuments of their own fame, and the bones of slaughtered legions. The Romans, whichever way they turn their eyes, have nothing before them but memorials of their own captivity, their defeat, and their disgrace. If in the Treverian territories the issue of the battle was unpropitious, the event of that day ought to make no impression. In that field the Germans conquered; but, too eager for plunder, they suffered the victory to be snatched out of their hands. From that moment we have been in a train of success, while the Romans have had to struggle with every difficulty. Whatever could be done by the skill of your general, has been provided for you. Fens and marshes are the spot where you are to engage. The depths and shallows are known to you, and they will be the grave of the Romans. The Rhine, and the gods of Germany, are before you. In their view, and under their protection, rush on to the charge; and let each man remember, that on his sword depends the welfare of his parents, his wife, his children, and the liberty of his country. This day, my friends, this important day, will either prove us the glorious rivals of our famed forefathers, or send down our names with disgrace and infamy to the latest posterity." The Barbarians, according to their custom, applauded by clanking their arms, and dancing in wild distortion. They rushed on to the attack, discharging a volley of stones, and leaden balls, and other missive weapons. By this artifice they hoped to bring on an engagement in the fens: but the Romans, aware of the stratagem, remained on the solid ground.

XVIII. The Barbarians exhausted their store of darts, when the battle growing warm, they could no longer restrain their ardour. They rushed forward with impetuous fury. Their huge stature gave them every advantage. With their long spears they were able to goad and pierce the Romans, who with difficulty kept their footing on the slippery soil. A band of Bructerians had the spirit to quit the dam erected across the Rhine, and swim to the shore. The Romans were thrown into disorder. The auxiliary cohorts began to give way, when the legions advanced to sustain the fight, and stopped the progress of the enemy. The battle was now on equal terms. In that moment, a Batavian deserter informed Cerealis, that a party of cavalry might with ease wheel round the marsh, and at the farther extremity attack the enemy in the rear. The ground, he said, was in that part dry and firm, and there the Gugernians might be taken by surprise. Two squadrons of horse, with the deserter for their guide, reached the place, and surrounded the enemy. A shout of victory gave notice of this advantage. The legions, at the same time, charged in front. The Barbarians fled with precipitation towards the Rhine. Had the fleet been put in motion to second the operations of the army, that day would have closed the war. The approach of night, and a sudden storm of rain, hindered the cavalry from mixing in the action.

XIX. On the following day, the tenth legion being arrived from Spain, Cerealis detached the fourteenth to reinforce Annius Gallus in the upper province. Civilis at the same time was reinforced by the Chaucians; but, even with those succours, he did not think himself in force to protect the Batavian cities. Content with carrying off whatever was portable, he set fire to the rest, and retired to the island. The Romans, he well knew, could not follow him without throwing up a bridge, and for that purpose they had no boats in readiness. As a further security, he had the precaution to destroy the great dam formerly laid across the Rhine by Drusus Germanicus, leaving the river, thus freed from obstruction, to flow in its natural channel towards the confines of Gaul. The consequence was that, the current taking a new course, the body of water, which separated the island from the mainland, sunk into a scanty stream, and the space between Germany and Batavia seemed to be one continued continent. Tutor and Classicus passed over the Rhine, followed by no less than a hundred and thirteen Treverian senators. Alpinus Montanus, the deputy sent, as above mentioned, from Cremona by Antonius Primus to the states of Gaul, was one of the number. He was accompanied by his brother Decimus Alpinus. These men dispersed themselves among the neighbouring nations, urging every topic that could excite compassion; and by their gifts and presents, in a country fond of tumult and commotion, they raised considerable levies.

XX. Civilis found himself in a condition to rekindle the war. He formed four divisions of his army, with intent to attack on one and the same day the Roman cohorts, the cavalry, and the legions at four different posts; the tenth legion at Arenacum; the second at Batavodurum; and the auxiliaries in their intrenchments at Grinnes and Vada. In this enterprise, Civilis headed one of the divisions; Verax, his sister's son, led the second; Classicus and Tutor had their separate commands. In these several attempts, complete success was not expected; but where much was hazarded, the issue in some quarter might be prosperous. The enemy knew that Cerealis was not an officer of the strictest caution; and therefore hoped, that, while he was distracted by different tidings, and, by consequence, obliged to hasten from one post to another, he might be somewhere intercepted on his march. The party destined to storm the quarters of the tenth legion, judging it an enterprise of too much danger, desisted from the project; content with falling on such as were employed at a distance from the camp in hewing wood for the use of the army. In this attack, the prefect of the camp, five principal centurions, and a few soldiers, were cut to pieces. The rest took shelter within the intrenchments. At Batavodurum the push of the enemy was to destroy a bridge, which the Romans had in part constructed over the river. A fierce engagement followed, but the approach of night left it undecided.

XXI. The attack at Vada, under the conduct of Civilis, and at Grinnes, led on by Classicus, were attended with greater danger to the Romans. At each place the assault was made with resistless fury. The best and bravest of the soldiers perished on the spot. Among them fell Briganticus, at the head of a squadron of horse; a man, as already stated, distinguished by his zeal in the service of Rome, and his avowed hatred of Civilis, his uncle.[1] While the Romans were pressed on every side, Cerealis, with a select body of cavalry, came up to their relief. The fortune of the day was instantly changed. The Germans in a panic plunged into the river. Civilis attempted to stop their flight. His person being known, a shower of darts was discharged against him. He quitted his horse, and saved himself by swimming across the river. The Germans escaped by the same expedient. Tutor and Classicus were conveyed away in boats. The Roman fleet, notwithstanding positive orders, failed again to co-operate with the land forces. Several of the mariners were dispersed on different duties, and fear restrained the rest. It was the constant fault of Cerealis, never to allow due time for the execution of his orders. His designs were always sudden, but the issue crowned him with glory. Where his conduct was liable to

[1] See iv. 70.

censure, fortune seemed willing to repair his error. Success made him over-sanguine, and, by consequence, discipline fell into neglect. It was but a few days after his victory, that he narrowly escaped being made a prisoner. His address saved him from the hands of the enemy, but not from the disgrace of his own misconduct.

XXII. He had been as far as Bonn and Novesium to inspect the camps then carrying on at those places, for the winter quarters of the legions. He chose to return by water. Among the troops that followed his boats along the banks of the Rhine, no order was observed, no discipline, no night-watch. The Germans saw their negligence, and took their measures accordingly. They chose a night remarkably dark, and sailed down the river. They landed without opposition, and rushed immediately to the intrenchments. They began with art and stratagem. They cut the cords of the tents, and butchered the men as they lay struggling under the load. Another party, in the meantime, attacked the fleet. They fastened their grappling instruments, and began to haul off the vessels. Their first approach was conducted in silence; but the slaughter was no sooner begun, than, to increase the terror, they rent the air with shouts and savage uproar. Roused by the anguish of their wounds, the Romans started from their beds; they grasped their arms, and ran wild about the avenues of their camp; some completely armed, but the greatest part with their clothes thrown on in their hurry, and their swords in their hands. Cerealis, half asleep, and almost naked, owed his safety to a mistake. The Barbarians saw the prætorian ship with a flag displayed, and, from that circumstance inferring that the general was on board, took possession of the vessel. Cerealis had passed the night in another quarter. A woman from the country of the Albians, known by the name of Claudia Sacatra, had attracted his notice; and the report of the army was, that when the attack began, he was happy in her embrace. The sentinels, who had neglected the duty of their watch, made an excuse that did no honour to the general. That they might not disturb his rest, their orders were to observe the strictest silence, and, by consequence, making no signal, and using no watchword, they themselves were overpowered with sleep. It was broad daylight when the Germans sailed back, leading with them the captured vessels, and among them the prætorian galley, which they afterwards sent by the river Luppia, as a present to Veleda.

XXIII. Civilis had the ambition to display his naval armament. For this purpose he equipped all the vessels that carried two ranks of oars, or even one. To these he added a prodigious number of small craft, among which were thirty or forty fitted out like the Roman Liburnian galleys. The vessels lately taken from the Romans carried sails made with German mantles, and, with their diversity of colours, presented a spectacle not unpleasing to the eye. The place chosen for this naval show was the vast bay, resembling a sea, where the Rhine discharges itself through the mouth of the Meuse into the ocean. For fitting out this fleet Civilis had two motives; one, to gratify the national vanity of the Batavians; the second, more important, to intercept the provisions sent from Gaul for the use of the Roman army. Cerealis, at the sight of this unexpected parade, was struck with wonder; but nothing could shake his resolution. He prepared to meet the Barbarians on their new element. He ordered out his fleet, inferior in number, but in the skill of the mariners, the experience of the pilots, and the size of the vessels, greatly superior. The Romans sailed with the current; the enemy had the wind in their favour. A slight engagement followed. The two fleets exchanged a flight of darts; they passed each other, and parted. This was the last effort of Civilis. He gave up all hope, and retired beyond the Rhine. Cerealis laid waste the isle of Batavia, leaving, however, the lands and houses of Civilis free from injury. This policy is not unusual among general officers. It was now the latter end of autumn; the rainy season set in, and the river, swelled above its banks, caused an inundation throughout the island. The face of the country, naturally low and swampy, presented a vast sheet of water. No ships were at hand; the army was distressed for provisions; and the tents and baggage were washed away by the flood.

XXIV. Civilis asserted afterwards, that the Roman army, in this juncture, might have been utterly destroyed, and that the Germans actually intended it, if he himself had not diverted them from the enterprise. The surrender of that chief, which followed soon after, made this account not improbable. Cerealis, by his secret agents, offered terms of peace to the Batavians; he tempted Civilis with a promise of pardon; and to Veleda and her family he held forth the advantages to be gained by terminating a war, which brought nothing but slaughter and calamity. "Her best policy," he said, "would be, to entitle herself, by some meritorious act, to the favour and protection of Rome. The Treverians were cut to pieces, the Ubians submitted, and the Batavians were expelled from their country. By the friendship of Civilis, Germany had gained nothing but slaughter, ruin, and the desolation of families. Where is Civilis now? He roams about, a helpless wanderer, destitute of means, a burden to his friends. After passing the Rhine so often, the Germans may now be satisfied. Fresh hostilities would add to their guilt. The insolence and the crime would be on their side; on that of Rome the indignation of the legions, and the vengeance of the gods."

XXV. With this menacing strain Cerealis had the art to intermix soothing promises. The nations beyond the Rhine were weary of war. The Batavians began to open their eyes. "To persist," they said, "were to provoke their utter ruin. A single nation could not undertake to deliver the world from bondage. By the slaughter of the legions, and the destruction of the Roman camps, what had been gained? New legions, with greater vigour and superior numbers, were poured in upon them. If the war was waged for Vespasian, the end was answered: Vespasian is master of the empire. If to oppose the Roman people was the real object, the Batavians are but a handful of men, unequal to the task. Let us turn our eyes to Rhætia, to Noricum, and the other allies of Rome. They are loaded with various imposts. From the Batavians Rome exacts no tribute: men and valour are all she asks. This may be called a state of freedom; at the worst, it borders on civil liberty. And if we are to choose who shall rule over us, is it not more honourable to submit to the emperor of Rome, than, like the Germans, to bear the infamy of a female reign?" Such was the reasoning of the Batavian people. The nobles of the country charged everything to the account of Civilis: "By his headlong violence they were hurried into the war. In the miseries of his country that restless chief hoped to find a remedy for his ruined fortunes. In evil hour the Batavians were advised to besiege the legions, and to murder the commanding officers: the gods, in that moment, denounced their vengeance on the whole nation. The war was necessary for one man, and it has been the ruin of his country. We are now on the brink of destruction: repentance may expiate our guilt, and, by delivering up the author of all calamity, we may atone for past misconduct."

XXVI. Civilis knew the temper of his countrymen, and took his measures to prevent the blow. A long train of adversity had sunk the vigour of his mind; and the love of life, a passion which often enervates the noblest minds, began to exert its influence. He desired a conference. Cerealis granted it. The bridge over the Wahal was broken down in the middle. The two chiefs advanced to the extreme points. In that situation Civilis spoke as follows: "Were I to plead my cause before an officer in the interest of Vitellius, I should give myself up as lost. Pardon I should not expect, nor would any credit be given to what I have to offer. Vitellius and I were mortal foes. We acted with open, with avowed hostility. The quarrel was begun by him; it was inflamed by me. With Vespasian I lived on other terms; my respect for his person has long been known. While he was yet a private man, he ranked me in the number of his friends. Antonius Primus knew our connection. By letters from that officer I was urged to kindle the flame of war. I was desired to find employment for the German legions and the states of Gaul, that none might pass over the Alps into Italy. The advice of Antonius, communicated by his letters, was seconded by Hordeonius Flaccus in person. I complied with their wishes: I appeared in arms, and did in Germany what was accomplished by Mucianus in Syria, by Aponius in Mæsia, and by Flavianus in Pannonia."[1]

[1] The rest of the *History* is lost, and with it the siege of Jerusalem, with the reigns of Vespasian, Titus, and Domitian.

A TREATISE ON THE SITUATION, MANNERS, & PEOPLE OF GERMANY

A TREATISE ON THE SITUATION, MANNERS, & PEOPLE OF GERMANY[1]

CONTENTS

---

[1] The time when the treatise on the German manners was written, is fixed by Lipsius in the fourth consulship of Nerva, and the second of Trajan, A.D. 98. A passage in section 37, where Tacitus mentions the second consulship of Trajan, clearly shows that the piece was composed in that year, or soon after. It is a draft of savage manners, delineated by a masterly hand; the more interesting, as the part of the world which it describes was the seminary of the modern European nations; the VAGINA GENTIUM, as historians have emphatically called it. The work is short, but, as Montesquieu observes, it is the work of a man who abridged everything, because he knew everything.

disallowed—Constancy of the German wives.—XIX. *Punishment of adultery inflicted by the husband.*—XX. *Education of youth, and rules of succession to the property of the father.*—XXI. *Duty of adopting the friendship and feuds of parents and relations—Composition for homicide, and other crimes—Their love of hospitality.*—XXII. *Convivial meetings; the custom of drinking deep; quarrels in their liquor, and even their public debates.*—XXIII. *The liquor and food of the Germans.*—XXIV. *Public spectacles, and their rage for gaming.*—XXV. *The slaves are prædial servants; the master has not the power of life and death over his slaves—Condition of the freedmen.*—XXVI. *Partition and cultivation of the lands—The year divided into three seasons: autumn unknown.*—XXVII. *Their funeral ceremonies without pomp or ostentation.*—XXVIII. *Thus far the general manners: particular description of the several nations—The Gauls and Germans reciprocally passed over the Rhine in quest of habitations—The Helvetians, the Boians, originally Gauls—The Araviscians and Osians of doubtful extraction—The Treverians, Nervians, Vangiones, Trebocians, Nemetes, and Ubians, all natives of Germany.*—XXIX. *The Batavians possessed of an island formed by the branches of the Rhine: a brave and warlike people—Community of the Matiaci: the decuman lands, a tract of country subject to an impost of one tenth.*—XXX. *The Cattians, a brave and warlike people, famous for the discipline of their infantry—Their vows to let their hair and beard grow till they kill an enemy.*—XXXII. *The Usipians and Tencterians: the strength of the latter consists in cavalry.*—XXXIII. *The Bructerians expelled from their territory by the Chamavians and Angrivarians.*—XXXIV. *The Dulgibinians and Chasuarians; the Greater and Lesser Frisia.*—XXXV. *The Chaucians, bounded at the farthest extremity by the Northern Sea; a people renowned for their love of justice.*—XXXVI. *The Cheruscans and Fosians subdued by the Cattians.*—XXXVII. *The Cimbrians, dwelling on the borders of the Northern Ocean; now an inferior state, but their ancient glory still survives.*—XXXVIII. *The Suevians, the greatest and most extensive state in all Germany—Their dress and manners.*—XXXIX. *The Semnones, a part of the Suevian nation: their religious rites, human sacrifices, and other acts of superstition.*—XL. *The Langobards, the Reudignians, the Aviones, Angles, Varinians, Eudosians, Nuithones, and Suardonians—The worship paid to Herth, or the goddess of the earth.*—XLI. *The Hermundurians.*—XLII. *The Nariscans, Marcomanians, and Quadians.*—XLIII. *The Marsignians, and Gothinians, Osians, and Burians—Their manners, and the national character of each—The territory of the Lygians, with their inferior tribes, such as the Arians, the Helvecones, the Manimians, Elysians, and Naharvalians; the worship of Alcis, supposed to be Castor and Pollux—Particular description of the Arians—The Gothones, the Rugians, and Lemivians, all under regal government.*—XLIV. *The Suiones bordering on the ocean: their naval strength—Their kings despotic.*—XLV. *The sea without undulation: the Æstians, and their plenty of amber on the shore—The formation of amber, and its natural causes—The Sitones, subject to female government.*—XLVI. *The Peucinians, the Venedians and Fennians: their filth and poverty—Accounts of the Helusians, the Oxiones, and others too fabulous to be related.*

This tract was composed by Tacitus in the

Year of Rome.	Of Christ.	Consuls.	
851	98	Nerva, the 4th time.	Trajan, the 2nd.

I. THE whole vast country of Germany[1] is separated from Gaul,[2] from Rhætia, and Pannonia, by the Rhine and the Danube; from Dacia and Sarmatia, by a chain of mountains,[3] and, where the mountains subside, mutual dread forms a sufficient barrier. The rest is bounded by the ocean, embracing in its depth of water several spacious bays,[4] and islands of prodigious extent, whose kings and people are now, in some measure, known to us, the progress of our arms having made recent discoveries. The Rhine has its source on the steep and lofty summit of the Rhætian Alps, from which it precipitates, and, after winding towards the west, directs its course through a long tract of country, and falls into the Northern Ocean. The Danube, gushing down the

[1] It is material in this place to observe, that Augustus Cæsar divided part of Belgic Gaul into two provinces, distinguished by the names of Upper and Lower Germany. Many of the new settlers in those parts were originally Germans, and, when the whole country was reduced under subjection to the Roman empire, the people, unwilling to pass for natives of Gaul, still retained their original name. Those two provinces called the Upper and Lower Germany (being, in fact, part of Gaul) are not comprised in the account given by Tacitus.

[2] Gaul, according to Cæsar, was divided into three parts, namely, 1, Belgic Gaul, bounded by the Seine, the Marne, the mountains of Vauge, the Rhine, and the ocean; 2ndly, Celtic Gaul, bounded by the ocean, the Seine, the Marne, the Saone, the Rhone, and the Garonne; 3rdly, Aquitania, bounded by the Atlantic Ocean, the Garonne, and the Pyrenees.

Rhætia was bounded towards the east by the Alps; by Italy towards the south; by the Rhine on the west; and by the country of the Vindelici towards the north. It is now the country of the Grisons.

Pannonia was an extensive country, having Dalmatia on the south, Illyricum on the west, Mæsia on the east, and the Danube on the north. And thus, as Tacitus says, Germany is divided from Gaul by the Rhine, and from Rhætia and Pannonia by the Danube.

[3] Dacia, in a short time after Tacitus wrote this treatise, was reduced by the emperor Trajan to a Roman province. It lay on the other side of the Danube, extending northward to the Carpathian mountains. Sarmatia was formerly divided into European and Asiatic. The European division is here intended by Tacitus. It had the Vistula, and a chain of mountains, for its western boundary, and extended to the northern part of Europe. The mountains, which in part divided these nations from Germany, are now called the Carpathian mountains.

[4] The Baltic Sea was probably thought in the time of Tacitus to be the Northern Ocean. The deep gulfs were those of Bothnia and Finland. Sweden, Norway, and Finland, were anciently called Scandinavia, and supposed by the Romans to be a large island.

soft and gentle declivity of the mountain Abnoba,[1] visits several nations in its progress, and at last, through six channels (the seventh is absorbed in fens and marshes), discharges itseif into the Pontic Sea.

II. The Germans, there is reason to think, are an indigenous race,[2] the original natives of the country, without any intermixture of adventitious settlers from other nations. In the early ages of the world, the adventurers who issued forth in quest of new habitations, did not traverse extensive tracts of land;[3] the first migrations were made by sea. Even at this day the Northern Ocean, vast and boundless, and, as I may say, always at enmity with mariners,[4] is seldom navigated by ships from our quarter of the world. Putting the dangers of a turbulent and unknown sea out of the case, who would leave the softer climes of Asia, Africa, or Italy, to fix his abode in Germany? where nature offers nothing but scenes of deformity: where the inclemency of the seasons never relents; where the land presents a dreary region, without form or culture, and, if we except the affection of a native for his mother-country, without an allurement to make life supportable. In all songs and ballads,[5] the only memorials of antiquity amongst them, the god Tuisto, who was born of the Earth, and Mannus, his son, are celebrated as the founders of the German race. Mannus, it is said, had three sons, from whom the Ingævones, who bordered on the sea-coast; the Hermiones, who inhabit the midland country; and the Istævones, who occupy the remaining track, have all respectively derived their names. Some indeed, taking advantage of the obscurity that hangs over remote and fabulous ages, ascribe to the god Tuisto a more numerous issue, and thence trace the names of various tribes, such as the Marsians, the Gambrivians, the Suevians, and the Vandals.[6] The ancient date and authenticity of those names are, as they contend, clearly ascertained.

[1] Called by the Germans Schwartzwald, and by the French the Black Forest.

[2] The inhabitants of every nation, that had no literary monuments, were by the ancients deemed the immediate offspring of the soil.

[3] The first migrations could not be made by sea in those early ages, when the use of shipping was little known.

[4] Drusus, the father of Germanicus, was the first Roman commander who ventured to explore those seas. *Oceanum septentrionalem primus Romanorum ducum navigavit*, says Suetonius.

[5] Songs and rude poetry have been in all savage countries the memorials of public transactions.

[6] The Vandals are the same as the *Vindili* mentioned by Pliny; a brave and warlike race, who afterwards overran Gaul, Spain, and Italy, and were finally destroyed in Africa.

The word Germany is held to be of modern addition. In support of this hypothesis, they tell us that the people who first passed the Rhine, and took possession of a canton in Gaul, though known at present by the name of Tungrians, were, in that expedition, called Germans, and thence the title assumed by a band of emigrants, in order to spread a general terror in their progress, extended itself by degrees, and became, in time, the appellation of a whole people. They have a current tradition that Hercules visited those parts. When rushing to battle, they sing, in preference to all other heroes, the praises of that ancient worthy.

III. The Germans abound with rude strains of verse, the reciters of which, in the language of the country, are called BARDS. With this barbarous poetry they inflame their minds with ardour in the day of action, and prognosticate the event from the impression which it happens to make on the minds of the soldiers, who grow terrible to the enemy, or despair of success, as the war-song produces an animated or a feeble sound. Nor can their manner of chanting this savage prelude be called the tone of human organs: it is rather a furious uproar; a wild chorus of military virtue. The vociferation used upon these occasions is uncouth and harsh, at intervals interrupted by the application of their bucklers to their mouths, and by the repercussion bursting out with redoubled force. An opinion prevails among them, that Ulysses, in the course of those wanderings which are so famous in poetic story, was driven into the Northern Ocean, and that, having penetrated into the country, he built, on the banks of the Rhine, the city of Asciburgium,[1] which is inhabited at this day, and still retains the name given originally by the founder. It is further added, that an altar dedicated to Ulysses, with the name of Laertes, his father, engraved upon it, was formerly discovered at Usciburgium. Mention is likewise made of certain monuments and tombstones, still to be seen on the confines of Germany and Rhætia, with epitaphs or inscriptions in Greek characters. But these assertions it is not my intention either to establish or to refute; the reader will yield or withhold his assent, according to his judgment or his fancy.

IV. I have already acceded to the opinion of those, who think that the Germans have hitherto subsisted without intermarrying with other nations, a pure, unmixed, and independent

[1] The love of fabulous history, which was the passion of ancient times, produced a new Hercules in every country, and made Ulysses wander in every sea.

race, unlike any other people, all bearing the marks of a distinct national character. Hence, what is very remarkable in such prodigious numbers, a family likeness throughout the nation; the same form and feature, stern blue eyes, ruddy hair, their bodies large and robust, but powerful only in sudden efforts. They are impatient of toil and labour; thirst and heat overcome them; but, from the nature of their soil and climate, they are proof against cold and hunger.

V. The face of the country, though in some parts varied, presents a cheerless scene, covered with the gloom of forests, or deformed with wide-extended marshes; towards the boundaries of Gaul, moist and swampy; on the side of Noricum[1] and Pannonia, more exposed to the fury of the winds. Vegetation thrives with sufficient vigour. The soil produces grain, but is unkind to fruit-trees;[2] well stocked with cattle, but of an under-size, and deprived by nature of the usual growth and ornament of the head. The pride of a German consists in the number of his flocks and herds: they are his only riches, and in these he places his chief delight. Gold and silver are withheld from them; is it by the favour or the wrath of Heaven? I do not, however, mean to assert that in Germany there are no veins of precious ore; for who has been a miner in those regions? Certain it is, they do not enjoy the possession and use of those metals with our sensibility. There are, indeed, silver vessels to be seen amongst them, but they were presents to their chiefs or ambassadors; the Germans regard them in no better light than common earthenware. It is, however, observable, that near the borders of the empire, the inhabitants set a value upon gold and silver, finding them subservient to the purposes of commerce. The Roman coin is known in those parts, and some of our specie is not only current, but in request. In places more remote, the simplicity of ancient manners still prevails: commutation of property is their only traffic. Where money passes in the way of barter, our old coin is the most acceptable, particularly that which is indented at the edge, or stamped with the impression of a chariot and two horses, called the SERRATI and BIGATI. Silver is preferred to gold, not from caprice or fancy, but because the inferior

[1] Noricum was bounded towards the north by the Danube, on the east by Pannonia, on the south by a range of the Alps, and on the west by the country of the Vindelici. It contained a great part of Austria and Bavaria.

[2] The Germans attended to nothing but the production of corn. Their country, like Canada, was covered over with immense tracts of forest, and, till the ground was cleared, and the cold, by consequence, abated of its rigour, cultivation could not be carried on with any kind of advantage.

metal is of more expeditious use in the purchase of low-priced commodities.

VI. Iron does not abound in Germany, if we may judge from the weapons in general use. Swords and large lances are seldom seen. The soldier grasps his javelin, or, as it is called in their language, his FRAM; an instrument tipped with a short and narrow piece of iron, sharply pointed, and so commodious, that, as occasion requires, he can manage it in close engagement, or in distant combat. With this, and a shield, the cavalry is completely armed. The infantry have an addition of missive weapons. Each man carries a considerable number, and, being naked, or, at least, not encumbered by his light mantle, he throws his weapon to a distance almost incredible. A German has no attention to the ornament of his person: his shield is the object of his care, and this he decorates with the liveliest colours. Breastplates are uncommon. In a whole army you will not see more than one or two helmets. Their horses have neither swiftness nor elegance of shape, nor are they trained to the various evolutions of the Roman cavalry. To advance in a direct line, or wheel suddenly to the right, is the whole of their skill, and this they perform in so compact a body, that not one is thrown out of his rank. According to the best estimate, the infantry form the national strength, and, for that reason, always fight intermixed with the cavalry. The flower of their youth, able by their vigour and activity to keep pace with the movements of the horse, are selected for this purpose, and placed in the front of the lines. The number of these is fixed and certain: each canton sends a hundred, from that circumstance called HUNDREDERS [1] by the army. The name was at first numerical only: it is now a title of honour. Their order of battle presents the form of a wedge. To give ground in the heat of action, provided you return to the charge, is military skill, not fear, or cowardice. In the most fierce and obstinate engagement, even when the fortune of the day is doubtful, they make it a point to carry off their slain. To abandon their shield is a flagitious crime. The person guilty of it is interdicted from religious rites, and excluded from the assembly of the state. Many, who survived their honour on the day of battle, have closed a life of ignominy by a halter.

VII. The kings in Germany owe their election to the nobility of their birth; the generals are chosen for their valour. The

[1] Germany was divided into states or communities, each state into cantons, and each canton into hundreds, or a hundred families.

power of the former is not arbitrary or unlimited;[1] the latter command more by warlike example than by their authority. To be of a prompt and daring spirit in battle, and to attack in the front of the lines, is the popular character of the chieftain: when admired for his bravery, he is sure to be obeyed. Jurisdiction is vested in the priests. It is theirs to sit in judgment upon all offences. By them, delinquents are put in irons, and chastised with stripes. The power of punishing is in no other hands. When exerted by the priests, it has neither the air of vindictive justice, nor of military execution; it is rather a religious sentence, inflicted with the sanction of the god, who, according to the German creed, attends their armies on the day of battle. To impress on their minds the idea of a tutelar deity, they carry with them to the field certain images and banners, taken from their usual depository, the religious groves.[2] A circumstance which greatly tends to inflame them with heroic ardour, is the manner in which their battalions are formed. They are neither mustered nor embodied by chance. They fight in clans, united by consanguinity, a family of warriors. Their tenderest pledges[3] are near them in the field. In the heat of the engagement, the soldier hears the shrieks of his wife, and the cries of his children. These are the darling witnesses of his conduct, the applauders of his valour, at once beloved and valued. The wounded seek their mothers and their wives: undismayed at the sight, the women count each honourable scar, and suck the gushing blood. They are even hardy enough to mix with the combatants, administering refreshment, and exhorting them to deeds of valour.

VIII. From tradition, they have a variety of instances of armies put to the rout, and by the interposition of their wives and daughters again incited to renew the charge. Their women saw the ranks give way, and rushing forward in the instant, by the vehemence of their cries and supplications, by opposing their breasts to danger, and by representing the horrors of slavery, restored the order of the battle. To a

[1] Cæsar says, that Ambiorix, king of the Eburones, a German nation, described his authority so limited, that, though he governed, the people in their turn gave laws to the prince.

[2] The figures of savage animals were deemed religious symbols; see *Hist.*, iv. 12. It was also a custom to deposit the standards taken from the enemy in their sacred groves, *Annals*, i. 59. These they carried with them to their wars.

[3] The Germans felt themselves inflamed with enthusiastic ardour, when their wives and children surveyed the field of battle. Many instances of this occur in Tacitus. See *Hist.*, iv. 18.

German mind the idea of a woman led into captivity is insupportable. In consequence of this prevailing sentiment, the states which deliver as hostages the daughters of illustrious families, are bound by the most effectual obligation. There is, in their opinion, something sacred in the female sex,[1] and even the power of foreseeing future events. Their advice is, therefore, always heard; they are frequently consulted, and their responses are deemed oracular. We have seen, in the reign of Vespasian, the famous Veleda revered as a divinity by her countrymen. Before her time, Aurinia and others were held in equal veneration; but a veneration founded on sentiment and superstition, free from that servile adulation which pretends to people heaven with human deities.

IX. Mercury is the god chiefly adored in Germany. On stated days they think it lawful to offer to him human victims. They sacrifice to Hercules and Mars such animals as are usually slain in honour of the gods. In some parts of the country of the Suevians, the worship of Isis is established. To trace the introduction of ceremonies, which had their growth in another part of the world, were an investigation for which I have no materials: suffice it to say, that the figure of a ship (the symbolic representation of the goddess) clearly shows that the religion was imported into the country. Their deities are not immured in temples, nor represented under any kind of resemblance to the human form. To do either, were, in their opinion, to derogate from the majesty of superior beings. Woods and groves[2] are the sacred depositories; and the spot being consecrated to those pious uses, they give to that sacred recess the name of the divinity that fills the place, which is never profaned by the steps of man. The gloom fills every mind with awe; revered at a distance, and never seen but with the eye of contemplation.

X. Their attention to auguries, and the practice of divining by lots, is conducted with a degree of superstition not exceeded by any other nation. Their mode of proceeding by lots is wonderfully simple. The branch of a fruit-tree is cut into small pieces, which, being all distinctly marked, are thrown at random on a white garment. If a question of

[1] Tacitus in his *History* observes, that most of the German women were considered as prophetesses, and, in particular, that *Veleda* was worshipped as a goddess. *Hist.*, iv. 61 and 65.

[2] The younger Pliny (Epist. 12) says concisely, We adore the gloom of woods, and the silence that reigns around us. *Lucos, atque in iis silentia ipsa adoramus.*

public interest be depending, the priest of the canton performs the ceremony; if it be nothing more than a private concern, the master of the family officiates. With fervent prayers offered up to the gods, his eyes devoutly raised to heaven, he holds up three times each segment of the twig, and as the marks rise in succession, interprets the decrees of fate. If appearances prove unfavourable, there ends all consultation for that day: if, on the other hand, the chances are propitious, they require, for greater certainty, the sanction of auspices. The well-known superstition, which in other countries consults the flight and notes of birds, is also established in Germany; but to receive intimation of future events from horses[1] is the peculiar credulity of the country. For this purpose a number of milk-white steeds, unprofaned by mortal labour, are constantly maintained at the public expense, and placed to pasture in the religious groves. When occasion requires, they are harnessed to a sacred chariot, and the priest, accompanied by the king, or chief of the state, attends to watch the motions and the neighing of the horses. No other mode of augury is received with such implicit faith by the people, the nobility, and the priesthood. The horses, upon these solemn occasions, are supposed to be the organs of the gods, and the priests their favoured interpreters. They have still another way of prying into futurity, to which they have recourse, when anxious to know the issue of an important war. They seize, by any means in their power, a captive from the adverse nation, and commit him in single combat with a champion selected from their own army.[2] Each is provided with weapons after the manner of his country, and the victory, wherever it falls, is deemed a sure prognostic of the event.

XI. In matters of inferior moment the chiefs decide; important questions are reserved for the whole community. Yet even in those cases where all have a voice, the business is discussed and prepared by the chiefs. The general assembly, if no sudden alarm calls the people together, has its fixed and stated periods, either at the new or full moon. This is thought the season most propitious to public affairs. Their account of time differs from that of the Romans: instead of

[1] Instances of this superstition are recorded among the Persians. Darius was elected king by the neighing of a horse.

[2] Montesquieu observes, that this was the origin of duelling, and also of the heroic madness of knight-errantry. It was considered by the superstition of the times as an appeal to heaven.

days they reckon the number of nights.[1] Their public ordinances are so dated; and their proclamations run in the same style. The night, according to them, leads the day. Their passion for liberty is attended with this ill consequence: when a public meeting is announced, they never assemble at the stated time. Regularity would look like obedience: to mark their independent spirit, they do not convene at once, but two or three days are lost in delay. When they think themselves sufficiently numerous, the business begins. Each man takes his seat, completely armed. Silence is proclaimed by the priests, who still retain their coercive authority. The king, or chief of the community,[2] opens the debate: the rest are heard in their turn, according to age, nobility of descent, renown in war, or fame for eloquence. No man dictates to the assembly: he may persuade, but cannot command. When anything is advanced not agreeable to the people, they reject it with a general murmur. If the proposition pleases, they brandish their javelins. This is their highest and most honourable mark of applause: they assent in a military manner, and praise by the sound of their arms.

XII. In this council of the state, accusations are exhibited, and capital offences prosecuted. Pains and penalties are proportioned to the nature of the crime. For treason and desertion, the sentence is to be hanged on a tree: the coward, and such as are guilty of unnatural practices, are plunged under a hurdle into bogs and fens. In these different punishments, the point and spirit of the law is, that crimes which affect the state may be exposed to public notoriety: infamous vice cannot be too soon buried in oblivion. He who is convicted of transgressions of an inferior nature, pays a mulct of horses, or of cattle. Part of that fine goes to the king or the community, and part to the person injured or to his family. It is in these assemblies that princes are chosen and chiefs elected to act as magistrates in the several cantons of the state. To each of these judicial officers, assistants are appointed from the body of the people, to the number of a hundred, who attend to give their advice, and strengthen the hands of justice.

XIII. A German transacts no business, public or private, without being completely armed. The right of carrying arms

[1] The Gauls, we find in Cæsar, *B. G.*, vi. 17, computed the time by nights, not by days.

[2] From this it is evident that not all the states of Germany were governed by kings.

is assumed by no person whatever, till the state has declared him duly qualified. The young candidate is introduced before the assembly, where one of the chiefs, or his father, or some near relation, provides him with a shield and javelin.[1] This, with them, is the manly gown:[2] the youth from that moment ranks as a citizen; till then he was considered as part of the household; he is now a member of the commonwealth. In honour of illustrious birth, and to mark the sense men entertain of the father's merit, the son, though yet of tender years, is called to the dignity of a prince or chief. Such as are grown up to manhood, and have signalised themselves by a spirit of enterprise, have always a number of retainers in their train. Where merit is conspicuous, no man blushes to be seen in the list of followers, or companions. A clanship is formed in this manner, with degrees of rank and subordination. The chief judges the pretensions of all, and assigns to each man his proper station. A spirit of emulation prevails among his whole train, all struggling to be the first in favour, while the chief places all his glory in the number and intrepidity of his COMPANIONS. In that consists his dignity; to be surrounded by a band of young men is the source of his power; in peace, his brightest ornament; in war, his strongest bulwark. Nor is his fame confined to his own country; it extends to foreign nations, and is then of the first importance, if he surpasses his rivals in the number and courage of his followers. He receives presents from all parts; ambassadors are sent to him; and his name alone is often sufficient to decide the issue of a war.

XIV. In the field of action, it is disgraceful to the prince to be surpassed in valour by his COMPANIONS; and not to vie with him in martial deeds, is equally a reproach to his followers. If he dies in the field, he who survives him survives to live in infamy. All are bound to defend their leader, to succour him in the heat of action, and to make even their own actions subservient to his renown. This is the bond of union, the most sacred obligation. The chief

1 This seems to be the origin of CHIVALRY, that institution which spread over the greatest part of Europe in the eleventh century. It is related of Charlemagne, that he gave a sword with great pomp and solemnity to his son, Prince Lewis.

2 When the young men of Rome attained the age of seventeen years, they changed their dress, called the *prætexta*, for the *toga virilis*, the manly gown. On that occasion the youth was conducted by his friends into the forum (or sometimes into the capitol), where with much solemnity he changed his habit, and the day was called *dies tirocinii*, or the day on which he was capable of being a *cadet* in the army.

fights for victory; the followers for their chief. If, in the course of a long peace, the people relax into sloth and indolence, it often happens that the young nobles seek a more active life in the service of other states engaged in war. The German mind cannot brook repose. The field of danger is the field of glory. Without violence and rapine, a train of dependants cannot be maintained. The chief must show his liberality, and the follower expects it. He demands, at one time this warlike horse, at another, that victorious lance imbrued with the blood of the enemy. The prince's table, however inelegant, must always be plentiful: it is the only pay of his followers. War and depredation are the ways and means of the chieftain. To cultivate the earth, and wait the regular produce of the seasons, is not the maxim of a German: you will more easily persuade him to attack the enemy, and provoke honourable wounds in the field of battle. In a word, to earn by the sweat of your brow, what you might gain by the price of your blood, is, in the opinion of a German, a sluggish principle, unworthy of a soldier.

XV. When the state has no war to manage, the German mind is sunk in sloth. The chase does not afford sufficient employment. The time is passed in sleep and gluttony. The intrepid warrior, who in the field braved every danger, becomes in time of peace a listless sluggard. The management of his house and lands he leaves to the women, to the old men, and the infirm part of his family. He himself lounges in stupid repose, by a wonderful diversity of nature exhibiting in the same man the most inert aversion to labour, and the fiercest principle of action. It is a custom established in the several states, to present a contribution of corn and cattle to their chieftains. Individuals follow the example, and this bounty proves at once an honour to the prince, and his best support. Presents are also sent from the adjacent states, as well by private persons, as in the name of the community. Nothing is so flattering to the pride of the chiefs as those foreign favours, consisting of the best horses, magnificent armour, splendid harness, and beautiful collars. The Romans have lately taught them to receive presents of money.[1]

XVI. The Germans, it is well known, have no regular cities; nor do they allow a continuity of houses. They dwell in separate habitations, dispersed up and down, as a

[1] This was a dangerous lesson, which has been followed in every age and country. Herodian says of the Germans in his time, that they were greedy of money, and always ready for gold to barter a peace with the Romans.

grove, a meadow, or a fountain, happens to invite. They have villages, but not in our fashion, with a series of connected buildings. Every tenement stands detached, with a vacant piece of ground round it, either to prevent accidents by fire, or for want of skill in the art of building. They neither know the use of mortar nor of tiles. They build with rude materials, regardless of beauty, order, and proportion. Particular parts are covered over with a kind of earth so smooth and shining, that the natural veins have some resemblance to the lights and shades of painting. Besides these habitations, they have a number of subterraneous caves, dug by their own labour, and carefully covered over with dung; in winter their retreat from cold, and the repository of their corn. In those recesses they not only find a shelter from the rigour of the season, but in times of foreign invasion, their effects are safely concealed. The enemy lays waste the open country, but the hidden treasure escapes the general ravage; safe in its obscurity, or because the search would be attended with too much trouble.

XVII. The clothing in use is a loose mantle, made fast with a clasp, or when that cannot be had, with a thorn. Naked in other respects, they loiter away whole days by the fireside. The rich wear a garment, not, indeed, displayed and flowing, like the Parthians, or the people of Sarmatia, but drawn so tight, that the form of the limbs is palpably expressed. The skins of wild animals are also much in use. Near the frontier, on the borders of the Rhine, the inhabitants wear them, but with an air of neglect, that shows them altogether indifferent about the choice. The people who live more remote, near the northern seas, and have not acquired by commerce a taste for new-fashioned apparel, are more curious in the selection. They choose particular beasts, and, having stripped off the furs, clothe themselves with the spoil, decorated with parti-coloured spots, or fragments taken from the skins of fish that swim the ocean as yet unexplored by the Romans. In point of dress there is no distinction between the sexes, except that the garment of the women is frequently made of linen, adorned with purple stains, but without sleeves, leaving the arms and part of the bosom uncovered.

XVIII. Marriage is considered as a strict and sacred institution. In the national character there is nothing so truly commendable. To be contented with one wife, is peculiar to the Germans. They differ, in this respect, from all other savage nations. There are, indeed, a few instances of polygamy; not, however, the effect of loose desire, but occasioned by the ambition of various families, who court the alliance of the chief distinguished by the nobility of his rank and character. The bride brings no portion; she receives a dowry from her husband. In the presence of her parents and relations, he makes a tender of part of his wealth; if accepted, the match is approved. In the choice of the presents, female vanity is not consulted. There are no frivolous trinkets to adorn the future bride. The whole fortune consists of oxen, a caparisoned horse, a shield, a spear, and a sword. She in return delivers a present of arms, and, by this exchange of gifts, the marriage is concluded. This is the nuptial ceremony, this the bond of union, these their hymeneal gods. Lest the wife should think her sex an exemption from the rigours of the severest virtue, and the toils of war, she is informed of her duty by the marriage ceremony, and thence she learns, that she is received by her husband to be his partner in toil and danger, to dare with him in war, and suffer with him in peace. The oxen yoked, the horse accoutred, and the arms given on the occasion, inculcate this lesson; and thus she is prepared to live, and thus to die. These are the terms of their union: she receives her armour as a sacred treasure, to be preserved inviolate, and transmitted with honour to her sons, a portion for their wives, and from them descendible to her grandchildren.

XIX. In consequence of these manners, the married state is a life of affection and female constancy. The virtue of the woman is guarded from seduction; no public spectacles to seduce her; no banquets to inflame her passions; no baits of pleasure to disarm her virtue. The art of intriguing by clandestine letters is unknown to both sexes. Populous as the country is, adultery is rarely heard of: when detected, the punishment is instant, and inflicted by the husband. He cuts off the hair of his guilty wife, and, having assembled her relations, expels her naked from his house, pursuing her with stripes through the village. To public loss of honour no favour is shown. She may possess beauty, youth, and riches; but a husband she can never obtain. Vice is not treated by the Germans as a subject of raillery, nor is the profligacy of corrupting and being corrupted called the fashion of the age. By the practice of some states, female virtue is advanced to still higher perfection: with them none but virgins marry. When the bride has fixed her choice, her hopes of matrimony are closed for life. With one husband, as with one life, one mind, one body, every woman is satisfied; in him her happiness is centred; her desires extend no further; and the principle is not only an affection for her husband's person, but a reverence for the married state. To set limits to population, by rearing up only a certain number of children, and destroying the rest, is accounted a flagitious crime. Among the savages of Germany, virtuous manners operate more than good laws in other countries.

XX. In every family the children are reared up in filth. They run about naked, and in time grow up to that strength and size of limb which we behold with wonder. The infant is nourished at the mother's breast, not turned over to nurses and to servants. No distinction is made between the future chieftain and the infant son of a common slave. On the same ground, and mixed with the same cattle, they pass their days, till the age of manhood draws the line of separation,[1] and early valour shows the person of ingenuous birth. It is generally late before their young men enjoy the pleasures of love; by consequence, they are not enfeebled in their prime. Nor are the virgins married too soon. Both parties wait to attain their full growth. In the warm season of mutual vigour the match is made, and the children of the marriage have the constitution of their parents. The uncle by the mother's side regards his nephews with an affection nothing inferior to that of their father. With some, the relation of the sister's children to their maternal uncle is held to be the strongest tie of consanguinity, insomuch that in demanding hostages, that line of kindred is preferred, as the most endearing objects of the family, and, consequently, the most tender pledges. The son is always heir to his father. Last wills and testaments are not in use. In case of failure of issue, the brothers of the deceased are next in succession, or else the paternal or maternal uncles. A numerous train of relations is the comfort and the honour of old age. To live without raising heirs to yourself[2] is no advantage in Germany.

XXI. To adopt the quarrels as well as the friendships of

[1] The age of manhood seems to have commenced at the end of their twelfth year.

[2] Rome was divided into two classes; the rich, who amused their followers with expectations; and the legacy-hunters, who panted for sudden riches. Seneca has drawn, as it were in miniature, a striking picture of the avaricious sycophant: he is a vulture, lying in wait for a carcase. *Vultur est, cadaver expectat.* Horace, Juvenal, and Martial, have made both ranks of men a subject of ridicule. See *Annals*, iii. 25.

your parents and relations is held to be an indispensable duty. In their resentments, however, they are not implacable. Injuries are adjusted by a settled measure of compensation. Atonement is made for homicide by a certain number of cattle,[1] and by that satisfaction the whole family is appeased: a happy regulation, than which nothing can be more conducive to the public interest, since it serves to curb that spirit of revenge which is the natural result of liberty in the excess. Hospitality and convivial pleasures are nowhere so liberally enjoyed.[2] To refuse admittance to a guest were an outrage against humanity. The master of the house welcomes every stranger, and regales him to the best of his ability. If his stock falls short, he becomes a visitor to his neighbour, and conducts his new acquaintance to a more plentiful table. They do not wait to be invited, nor is it of any consequence, since a cordial reception is always certain. Between an intimate and an entire stranger no distinction is made. The law of hospitality is the same. The departing guest receives as a present whatever he desires, and the host retaliates by asking with the same freedom. A German delights in the gifts which he receives; yet by bestowing he imputes nothing to you as a favour, and for what he receives he acknowledges no obligation.

XXII. In this manner the Germans pride themselves upon their frankness and generosity. Their hours of rest are protracted to broad daylight. As soon as they rise, the first thing they do is to bathe, and generally, on account of the intense severity of the climate, in warm water. They then betake themselves to their meal, each on a separate seat, and at his own table.[3] Having finished their repast, they proceed completely armed to the despatch of business, and frequently to a convivial meeting. To devote both day and night to deep drinking is a disgrace to no man. Disputes, as will

[1] This mode of composition for crimes and injuries was adopted by the various communities in Germany; but their descendants, after the irruption into Gaul, Italy, and Spain, still claimed the right of waging private war for private injuries. Hostilities continued during a number of years, and the animosity of the contending parties laid a scene of blood. Charlemagne endeavoured by a positive law to abolish the mischief; but the genius of one man was not sufficient to eradicate a custom so firmly established.

[2] Tacitus is confirmed by Julius Cæsar, who says, the laws of hospitality are inviolable among the Germans. Their visitors are sure of a cordial reception. Their houses are open to every guest.

[3] The manner in which the Romans placed themselves at table, differed from most other nations. Three couches, called *triclinia*, were ranged in order, but so as to leave the end of the table open for the approach of the servants. Three persons lay on each of the couches.

be the case with people in liquor, frequently arise, and are seldom confined to opprobrious language. The quarrel generally ends in a scene of blood. Important subjects, such as the reconciliation of enemies, the forming of family alliances, the election of chiefs, and even peace and war, are generally canvassed in their carousing festivals. The convivial moment, according to their notion, is the true season for business, when the mind opens itself in plain simplicity, or grows warm with bold and noble ideas. Strangers to artifice, and knowing no refinement, they tell their sentiments without disguise. The pleasure of the table expands their hearts, and call forth every secret. On the following day the subject of debate is again taken into consideration, and thus two different periods of time have their distinct uses; when warm, they debate; when cool, they decide.

XXIII. Their beverage is a liquor drawn from barley or from wheat, and, like the juice of the grape, fermented to a spirit. The settlers on the banks of the Rhine provide themselves with wine. Their food is of the simplest kind; wild apples, the flesh of an animal recently killed, or coagulated milk.[1] Without skill in cookery, or without seasoning to stimulate the palate, they eat to satisfy nature. But they do not drink merely to quench their thirst. Indulge their love of liquor to the excess which they require, and you need not employ the terror of your arms; their own vices will subdue them.

XXIV. Their public spectacles boast of no variety. They have but one sort, and that they repeat at all their meetings. A band of young men make it their pastime to dance entirely naked amidst pointed swords and javelins. By constant exercise, this kind of exhibition has become an art, and art has taught them to perform with grace and elegance. Their talents, however, are not let out for hire.[2] Though some danger attends the practice, the pleasure of the spectator is their only recompense. In the character of a German there is nothing so remarkable as his passion for play. Without the excuse of liquor (strange as it may seem!), in their cool and sober moments they have recourse to dice, as to a serious and regular business, with the most desperate spirit

[1] What Tacitus calls *lac concretum*, coagulated milk, Cæsar calls by the name of cheese: *Major pars victus eorum lacte, et* CASEO, *et carne consistit.*

[2] Public exhibitions cost the Athenians more than their wars. At Rome the expense was enormous, and the profession of a player was so profitable, that, according to Pliny, Roscius gained annually a sum almost incredible. In the luxury of the times that followed, immense fortunes were acquired by the public performers.

committing their whole substance to chance, and when they have lost their all, putting their liberty and even their persons upon the last hazard of the die. The loser yields himself to slavery. Young, robust, and valiant, he submits to be chained, and even exposed to sale. Such is the effect of a ruinous and inveterate habit. They are victims to folly, and they call themselves men of honour. The winner is always in a hurry to barter away the slaves acquired by success at play; he is ashamed of his victory, and therefore puts away the remembrance of it as soon as possible.

XXV. The slaves in general are not arranged at their several employments in the household affairs, as is the practice at Rome. Each has his separate habitation, and his own establishment to manage. The master considers him as an agrarian dependant,[1] who is obliged to furnish a certain quantity of grain, of cattle, or of wearing apparel. The slave obeys, and the state of servitude extends no further. All domestic affairs are managed by the master's wife and children. To punish a slave with stripes, to load him with chains, or condemn him to hard labour, is unusual. It is true, that slaves are sometimes put to death, not under colour of justice, or of any authority vested in the master; but in a transport of passion, in a fit of rage, as is often the case in a sudden affray; but it is also true, that this species of homicide passes with impunity. The freedmen[2] are not of much higher consideration than the actual slaves; they obtain no rank in the master's family, and, if we except the parts of Germany where monarchy is established, they never figure on the stage of public business. In despotic governments they rise above the men of ingenuous birth, and even eclipse the whole body of the nobles. In other states the subordination of the freedmen is a proof of public liberty.

XXVI. The practice of placing money at interest, and reaping the profits of usury, is unknown in Germany; and that happy ignorance is a better prevention of the evil than a code of prohibitory laws. In cultivating the soil, they do

[1] See in Tacitus (*Annals*, xiv. 43) an account of Pedanius Secundus, who had fourscore servants in his family, with specific names for their several departments. This was called his city establishment, *familia urbana*. In the country the Romans had their rural slaves under different appellations. In Germany the slaves were prædial servants, not indeed at liberty, but annexed to the soil, *glebæ adscripti*. Their condition was the same as that of the vassals, or SERFS, who, a few centuries ago, were so numerous in every part of Europe.

[2] The slave at Rome, when manumitted, was called LIBERTUS, and his descendants were LIBERTINI.

not settle on one spot, but shift from place to place. The state or community takes possession of a certain tract proportioned to its number of hands; allotments are afterwards made to individuals according to their rank and dignity. In so extensive a country, where there is no want of land, the partition is easily made. The ground tilled in one year, lies fallow the next, and a sufficient quantity always remains, the labour of the people being by no means adequate to the extent or goodness of the soil. Nor have they the skill to make orchard plantations, to enclose the meadow grounds, or to lay out and water gardens. From the earth they demand nothing but corn. Hence their year is not, as with the Romans, divided into four seasons. They have distinct ideas of winter, spring, and summer, and their language has terms for each; but they neither know the blessings nor the name of autumn.

XXVII. Their funerals have neither pomp nor vain am bition.[1] When the bodies of illustrious men are to be burned, they choose a particular kind of wood for the purpose, and have no other attention. The funeral pile is neither strewed with garments nor enriched with fragrant spices. The arms of the deceased are committed to the flames, and sometimes his horse.[2] A mound of turf is raised to his memory, and this, in their opinion, is a better sepulchre than those structures of laboured grandeur, which display the weakness of human vanity, and are, at best, a burden to the dead. Tears and lamentations are soon at an end, but their regret does not so easily wear away. To grieve for the departed is comely in the softer sex. The women weep for their friends; the men remember them.

XXVIII. This is the sum of what I have been able to collect touching the origin of the Germans, and the general manners of the people. I now shall enter into a more minute description of the several states, their peculiar rites, and the distinctive character of each; observing at the same time, which were the nations that first passed the Rhine, and transplanted themselves into Gaul.[3] That the Gauls, in ancient times, were superior to the Germans, we have the

[1] The simplicity of the Germans is placed by Tacitus, as often as the occasion permits, in direct contrast to Roman luxury and magnificence.

[2] The things which a German valued most, were his arms and his horse. These were added to his funeral pile, with persuasion that the deceased would have the same delight in his new state of existence.

[3] We are now come to what may be called the second part of this treatise. The author has taken a survey of the general manners, and he now proceeds

authority of Julius Cæsar, that illustrious historian of his own affairs. From what is stated by that eminent writer, it is highly probable that colonies from Gaul passed over into Germany: for, in fact, how could a river check the migrations of either nation, when it increased in strength, and multiplied its numbers? So weak an obstacle could not repel them from taking possession of a country, not as yet marked out by power, and of course, open to the first occupant. We find, accordingly, that the whole region between the Hercynian forest,[1] the Maine and the Rhine, was occupied by the Helvetians, and the tract beyond it by the Boians; both originally Gallic nations. The name of BOIEMUM, which remains to this day, shows the ancient state of the country, though it has since received a new race of inhabitants. Whether the Araviscians, who settled in Pannonia, were originally a colony from the Osi, a people of Germany; or, on the other hand, whether the Osi overflowed into Germany from the Araviscians, cannot now be ascertained. Thus much is certain, the laws, the manners, and language of both nations are still the same. But which of them first passed the Danube? The same good and evil were to be found on both sides of the river; equal poverty and equal independence. To be thought of German origin is the ambition of the Treverians and the Nervians,[2] both conceiving, that the reproach of Gallic softness and effeminacy, which still infect their national manners, may be lost in the splendour of a warlike descent. The Vangiones, the Tribocians, and the Nemetes, who stretch along the banks of the Rhine, are, beyond all doubt, of German extraction. The Ubians, for their services, were made a Roman colony, and, with their own consent, became known by the name of AGRIPPINIANS, in honour of their founder; and yet they still look back with pride to their German origin. They issued formerly from that country, and, having given proof of their fidelity, obtained an allotment of territory on the banks of the Rhine, not so much with a view to their security, as to make them a guard to defend the Roman frontier.

XXIX. Of all these various nations the Batavians[3] are the

to give a distinct account of the several states that occupied the various divisions of the country.

1 The Hercynian forest, according to Cæsar's account, was about nine days' journey in breadth, and covered a vast tract of country.

2 The Treverians inhabited what is now called *the diocese of Treves;* the territory of the Nervians was near Cambray.

3 *i.e.* the Dutch, often celebrated by Tacitus for their bravery, their skill in swimming across rivers, and their faithful attachment to the interests of Rome.

most brave and warlike. Incorporated formerly with the Cattians, but driven out by intestine divisions, they took possession of an island, formed by the river Rhine, where, without any extent of land on the continent, they established a canton in alliance with the Romans. The honour of that ancient friendship they still enjoy, with the addition of peculiar privileges. They are neither insulted with taxes, nor harassed by revenue officers. Free from burdens, imposts, and tributes, they are reserved for the day of battle; a nursery of soldiers. The Mattiaci[1] are in like manner attached to the interest of the Romans. In fact, the limits of the empire have been enlarged, and the terror of our arms has spread beyond the Rhine and the former boundaries. Hence the Mattiaci, still enjoying their own side of the river, are Germans by their situation, yet in sentiment and principle the friends of Rome; submitting, like the Batavians, to the authority of the empire; but never having been transplanted, they still retain, from their soil and climate, all the fierceness of their native character. The people between the Rhine and the Danube, who occupy a certain tract, subject to an impost of one tenth, and therefore called the Decumate lands, are not to be reckoned among the German nations. The Gauls, from their natural levity prone to change, and rendered desperate by their poverty, were the first adventurers into that vacant region. The Roman frontier, in process of time, being advanced, and garrisons stationed at proper posts, that whole country became part of a province, and the inhabitants of course were reduced to subjection.

XXX. Beyond the Mattiaci lies the territory of the Cattians, beginning at the Hercynian forest, but not, like other parts of Germany, a wide and dreary level of fens and marshes. A continued range of hills extends over a prodigious tract, till growing thinner by degrees they sink at last into an open country. The Hercynian forest attends its favourite Cattians to their utmost boundary, and there leaves them, as it were, with regret. The people are robust and hardy; their limbs well braced; their countenance fierce, and their minds endowed with vigour beyond the rest of their countrymen. Considered as Germans, their understanding is quick and penetrating. They elect officers fit to command, and obey them implicitly; they keep their ranks, and know how to seize their opportunity;

[1] Their country was partly in Weteravie, and partly in Hesse.

they restrain their natural impetuosity, and wait for the attack; they arrange with judgment the labours of the day, and throw up intrenchments for the night; trusting little to fortune, they depend altogether on their valour; and, what is rare in the history of Barbarians, and never attained without regular discipline, they place their confidence, not in the strength of their armies, but entirely in their general. The infantry is their main strength. Each soldier carries, besides his arms, his provision and a parcel of military tools. You may see other armies rushing to a battle; the Cattians march to a war. To skirmish in detached parties, or to sally out on a sudden emergence, is not their practice. A victory hastily gained, or a quick retreat, may suit the genius of the cavalry; but all that rapidity, in the opinion of the Cattians, denotes want of resolution: perseverance is the true mark of courage.

XXXI. A custom, known, indeed, in other parts of Germany, but adopted only by a few individuals of a bold and ardent spirit, is with the Cattians a feature of the national character. From the age of manhood they encourage the growth of their hair and beard; nor will any one, till he has slain an enemy, divest himself of that excrescence, which by a solemn vow he has devoted to heroic virtue. Over the blood and spoils of the vanquished, the face of the warrior is, for the first time, displayed. The Cattian then exults; he has now answered the true end of his being, and has proved himself worthy of his parents and his country. The sluggard continues unshorn, with the uncouth horrors of his visage growing wilder to the close of his days. The men of superior courage and uncommon ferocity wear also an iron ring,[1] in that country a badge of infamy, and with that, as with a chain, they appear self-condemned to slavery, till by the slaughter of an enemy they have redeemed their freedom. With this extraordinary habit, the Cattians are in general much delighted. They grow grey under a vow of heroism, and by their voluntary distinctions render themselves conspicuous to their friends and enemies. In every engagement the first attack is made by them: they claim the front of the line as their right, presenting to the enemy an appearance

[1] This custom of voluntarily putting on a badge of slavery was observed by the descendants of the Germans in various parts of Europe, and in the times of chivalry seems to have grown into general use. It was then a mark of amorous gallantry.

wild and terrible. Even in the time of peace they retain the same ferocious aspect; never softened with an air of humanity. They have no house to dwell in, no land to cultivate, no domestic care to employ them. Wherever chance conducts them, they are sure of being maintained. Lavish of their neighbours' substance, and prodigal of their own, they persist in this course, till towards the decline of life their drooping spirit is no longer equal to the exertions of a fierce and rigid virtue.

XXXII. The Usipians and Tencterians border on the Cattians. Their territory lies on the banks of the Rhine, where that river, still flowing in one regular channel, forms a sufficient boundary. In addition to their military character, the Tencterians are famous for the discipline of their cavalry. Their horse is no way inferior to the infantry of the Cattians. The wisdom of their ancestors formed the military system, and their descendants hold it in veneration. Horsemanship is the pride of the whole country, the pastime of their children, the emulation of their youth, and the habit of old age. With their goods and valuable effects their horses pass as part of the succession, not however, by the general rule of inheritance, to the eldest son, but, in a peculiar line, to that son who stands distinguished by his valour and his exploits in war.

XXXIII. In the neighbourhood of the last-mentioned states formerly occurred the Bructerians, since that time dispossessed of their territory, and, as fame reports, now no longer a people. The Chamavians and Angrivarians,[1] it is said, with the consent of the adjacent tribes, invaded the country, and pursued the ancient settlers with exterminating fury. The intolerable pride of the Bructerians drew upon them this dreadful catastrophe. The love of plunder was, no doubt, a powerful motive; and, perhaps, the event was providentially ordained in favour of the Roman people. Certain it is, the gods have of late indulged us with the view of a fierce engagement, and a scene of carnage, in which above sixty thousand of the enemy fell a sacrifice, not to the arms of Rome, but, more magnificent still! to the rage of their own internal discord, all cut off, as it were in a theatre of war, to furnish a spectacle to the Roman army. May this continue to be the fate of foreign nations! If not the friends of Rome, let them be enemies

[1] The Chamavians occupied a territory near the banks of the Ems. The Angrivarians bordered on the Visurgis (the Weser).

to themselves. For in the present tide of our affairs, what can fortune have in store so devoutly to be wished for as civil dissension amongst our enemies?

XXXIV. At the back of the states, which I have now described, lie the Dulgibinians and the Chasuarians, with other nations of inferior note. In front occurs the country of the Frisians,[1] divided into two communities, called, on account of their degrees of strength, the Greater and the Lesser Frisia. Both extend along the margin of the Rhine as far as the ocean, enclosing within their limits lakes of vast extent, where the fleets of Rome have spread their sails. Through that outlet we have attempted the Northern Ocean, where, if we may believe the account of navigators, the Pillars of Hercules are seen still standing on the coast; whether it be, that Hercules did in fact visit those parts, or that whatever is great and splendid in all quarters of the globe is by common consent ascribed to that ancient hero. Drusus Germanicus was an adventurer in those seas.[2] He did not want a spirit of enterprise; but the navigation was found impracticable in that tempestuous ocean, which seemed to forbid any further discovery of its own element, or the labours of Hercules. Since that time no expedition has been undertaken: men conceived that to respect the mysteries of the gods, and believe without inquiry, would be the best proof of veneration.

XXXV. We have hitherto traced the western side of Germany. From the point where we stop, it stretches away with a prodigious sweep towards the north. In this vast region, the first territory that occurs is that of the Chaucians,[3] beginning on the confines of the Frisians, and, though at the extremity bounded by the sea-shore, yet running at the back of all the nations already described, till, with an immense compass, it reaches the borders of the Cattians. Of this immeasurable tract it is not sufficient to say that the Chaucians possess it: they even people it. Of all the German nations, they are, beyond all question, the most respectable. Their grandeur rests upon the surest foundation,

1 The Lesser Frisians were settled on the south-west side of the Zuyder Zee; the Greater Frisians were on the north-east of the lake or gulf, in the territory now called Groningen.

2 Drusus was the younger brother of Tiberius, and father of Germanicus.

3 The territory of the Chaucians extended from the Ems to the Elbe, and the German Ocean washed the northern extremity. The nation was distinguished into the Greater and the Lesser, divided from each other by the Visurgis (the Weser).

the love of justice; wanting no extension of territory, free from avarice and ambition, remote and happy, they provoke no wars, and never seek to enrich themselves by rapine and depredation. Their importance among the nations round them is undoubtedly great; but the best evidence of it is, that they have gained nothing by injustice. Loving moderation, yet uniting to it a warlike spirit, they are ever ready in a just cause to unsheathe the sword. Their armies are soon in the field. In men and horses, their resources are great, and even in profound tranquillity their fame is never tarnished.

XXXVI. Bordering on the side of the Chaucians, and also of the Cattians, lies the country of the Cheruscans;[1] a people by a long disuse of arms enervated and sunk in sloth. Unmolested by their neighbours, they enjoyed the sweets of peace, forgetting that amidst powerful and ambitious neighbours, the repose which you enjoy serves only to lull you into a calm, always pleasing, but deceitful in the end. When the sword is drawn, and the power of the strongest is to decide, you talk in vain of equity and moderation: those virtues always belong to the conqueror. Thus it has happened to the Cheruscans: they were formerly just and upright; at present they are called fools and cowards. Victory has transferred every virtue to the Cattians, and oppression takes the name of wisdom. The downfall of the Cheruscans drew after it that of the Fosi, a contiguous nation, in their day of prosperity never equal to their neighbours, but fellow-sufferers in their ruin.

XXXVII. In the same northern part of Germany we find the Cimbrians[2] on the margin of the ocean; a people at present of small consideration, though their glory can never die. Monuments of their former strength and importance are still to be seen on either shore. Their camps and lines of circumvallation are not yet erased. From the extent of ground which they occupied, you may even now form an estimate of the force and resources of the state, and the

[1] Arminius, their chief, made head against the Romans with distinguished bravery, and performed a number of gallant exploits, as related by Tacitus in the first and second book of the *Annals*. He was at last cut off by the treachery of his countrymen, and his character is given in lively colours in the last section of the second book. Varus and his legions were destroyed by the zeal and violent spirit of Arminius, as appears in the speech of Segestes, *Annals*, i. 58. The long peace, in which the vigour of this people sunk into sloth and indolence, was, perhaps, occasioned by the death of Arminius.

[2] The Cimbri inhabited the peninsula which, after their name, was called the Cimbric Chersonesus, and is now Jutland.

account of their grand army, which consisted of such prodigious numbers, seems to be verified. It was in the year of Rome six hundred and forty, in the consulship of Cæcilius Metellus and Papirius Carbo, that the arms of the Cimbrians first alarmed the world. If from that period we reckon to the second consulship of the emperor Trajan, we shall find a space of near two hundred and ten years: so long has Germany stood at bay with Rome! In the course of so obstinate a struggle, both sides have felt alternately the severest blows of fortune, and the worst calamities of war. Not the Samnite, nor the republic of Carthage, nor Spain, nor Gaul, nor even the Parthian, has given such frequent lessons to the Roman people. The power of the Arsacidæ was not so formidable as German liberty. If we except the slaughter of Crassus and his army,[1] what has the east to boast of? Their own commander, Pacorus, was cut off, and the whole nation was humbled by the victory of Ventidius. The Germans can recount their triumphs over Carbo, Cassius, Scaurus Aurelius, Servilius Cæpio, and Cneius Manlius,[2] all defeated, or taken prisoners. With them the republic lost five consular armies; and since that time, in the reign of Augustus, Varus perished with his three legions. Caius Marius,[3] it is true, defeated the Germans in Italy; Julius Cæsar made them retreat from Gaul: and Drusus, Tiberius, and Germanicus, overpowered them in their own country; but how much blood did those victories cost us! The mighty projects of Caligula ended in a ridiculous farce. From that period an interval of peace succeeded, till, roused at length by the dissensions of Rome, and the civil wars that followed, they stormed our legions in their winter quarters, and even planned the conquest of Gaul. Indeed we forced them to repass the Rhine; but from that time what has been our advantage? We have triumphed, and Germany is still unconquered.

XXXVIII. The Suevians are the next that claim attention.

[1] The slaughter of Crassus and his army is well known: but in revenge Pacorus, son of Orodes, the Parthian king, was put to death, and the kingdom was reduced to a lower condition than even that of Ventidius, who gained a complete victory.

[2] Marcus Scarus Aurelius gave battle to the Cimbrians, and his army was put to flight. He himself was taken prisoner. Being summoned to a consultation held by the enemy, he advised them not to think of passing the Alps, because the Romans were invincible. For that offence Boiorix, a young man of great ferocity, killed him on the spot.

[3] Marius, as has been mentioned, triumphed over the Teutones and the Cimbri.

Possessing the largest portion of Germany, they do not, like the Cattians and Tencterians, form one state or community, but have among themselves several subdivisions, or inferior tribes, known by distinct appellations, yet all comprehended under the general name of Suevians. It is the peculiar custom of this people to braid the hair, and tie it up in a knot. Between them and the rest of the Germans this is the mark of distinction. In their own country it serves to discriminate the free-born from the slave. If the same mode is seen in other states, introduced by ties of consanguinity, or, as often happens, by the propensity of men to imitate foreign manners, the instances are rare, and confined entirely to the season of youth. With the Suevians the custom is continued through life: men far advanced in years are seen with their hoary locks interwoven, and fastened behind, or sometimes gathered into a shaggy knot on the crown of the head. The chiefs are more nicely adjusted: they attend to ornament, but it is a manly attention, not the spirit of intrigue or the affectation of appearing amiable in the eyes of women. When going to engage the enemy, they fancy that from the high structure of their hair they appear taller and gain an air of ferocity. Their dress is a preparation for battle.

XXXIX. The Semnones are ambitious to be thought the most ancient and respectable of the Suevian nation. Their claim they think confirmed by the mysteries of religion. On a stated day a procession is made into a wood consecrated in ancient times, and rendered awful by auguries delivered down from age to age. The several tribes of the same descent appear by their deputies. The rites begin with the slaughter of a man, who is offered as a victim, and thus their barbarous worship is celebrated by an act of horror. The grove is beheld with superstitious terror. No man enters that holy sanctuary without being bound with a chain, thereby denoting his humble sense of his own condition, and the superior attributes of the deity that fills the place. Should he happen to fall, he does not presume to rise, but in that grovelling state makes his way out of the wood. The doctrine intended by this bigotry is, that from this spot the whole nation derives its origin, and that here is the sacred mansion of the all-ruling mind, the supreme God of the universe, who holds everything else in a chain of dependence on his will and pleasure. To these tenets much credit arises from the weight and influence of the Semnones, a populous nation, distributed into a hundred cantons, and by the vast extent of their territory entitled to consider themselves as the head of the Suevian nation.

XL. The Langobards exhibit a contrast to the people last described. Their dignity is derived from the paucity of their numbers. Surrounded as they are by great and powerful nations, they live independent, owing their security not to mean compliances, but to that warlike spirit with which they encounter danger. To these succeed in regular order the Reudignians, the Aviones, Angles, and Varinians: the Eudocians, Nuithones, and Suardonians, all defended by rivers, or embosomed in forests. In these several tribes there is nothing that merits attention, except that they all agree to worship the goddess Earth, or as they call her Herth, whom they consider as the common mother of all. This divinity, according to their notion, interposes in human affairs, and, at times, visits the several nations of the globe. A sacred grove on an island[1] in the Northern Ocean is dedicated to her. There stands her sacred chariot, covered with a vestment, to be touched by the priest only. When she takes her seat in this holy vehicle, he becomes immediately conscious of her presence, and in his fit of enthusiasm pursues her progress. The chariot is drawn by cows yoked together. A general festival takes place, and public rejoicings are heard, wherever the goddess directs her way. No war is thought of; arms are laid aside, and the sword is sheathed. The sweets of peace are known, and then only relished. At length the same priest declares the goddess satisfied with her visitation, and re-conducts her to her sanctuary. The chariot with the sacred mantle, and, if we may believe report, the goddess herself, are purified in a secret lake. In this ablution certain slaves officiate, and instantly perish in the water. Hence the terrors of superstition are more widely diffused; a religious horror seizes every mind, and all are content in pious ignorance to venerate that awful mystery, which no man can see and live. This part of the Suevian nation stretches away to the most remote and unknown recesses of Germany.

XLI. On the banks of the Danube (for we shall now pursue that river, in the same manner as we have traced the course of the Rhine), the first and nearest state is that

[1] The isle of Heligoland, which is not far from the mouth of the Elbe.

of the Hermundurians,[1] a people in alliance with Rome, acting always with fidelity, and for that reason allowed to trade not only on the frontier, but even within the limits of the empire. They are seen at large in the heart of our splendid colony in the province of Rhætia, without so much as a guard to watch their motions. To the rest of the Germans we display camps and legions, but to the Hermundurians we grant the exclusive privilege of seeing our houses and our elegant villas. They behold the splendour of the Romans, but without avarice, or a wish to enjoy it. Iu the territories of these people the Elbe takes its rise, a celebrated river, and formerly well known to the Romans. At present we only hear of its name.

XLII. Contiguous to the last-mentioned people lies the country of the Nariscans, and next in order the Marcomannians and the Quadians. Of these the Marcomannians are the most eminent for their strength and military glory. The very territory now in their possession is the reward of valour, acquired by the expulsion of the Boians. Nor have the Nariscans or Quadians degenerated from their ancestors. As far as Germany is washed by the Danube, these three nations extend along the banks, and from the frontier of the country. The Marcomannians and the Quadians, within our own memory, obeyed a race of kings, born among themselves, the illustrious issue of Maroboduus[2] and of Tudrus. Foreign princes at present sway the sceptre; but the strength of their monarchy depends upon the countenance and protection of Rome. To our arms they are not often indebted: we choose rather to supply them with money.

XLIII. At the back of the Marcomannians and Quadians lie several nations of considerable force, such as the Mar-

[1] We are now entering on what may be considered as the third part of this treatise. In the first the author has given a striking picture of the general manners of the whole nation, considered as a people living under the influence of the same rough northern climate. From the beginning of section xxviii. he has traced the several states from the head of the Rhine, in the country of the GRISONS, along the western side of Germany to where it branches off, and forms the isle of Batavia. From that place Tacitus has traced the several nations to the Elbe, and along the coast of the Baltic to the Vistula, the eastern boundary of Germany. In this third division of the work he pursues the course of the Danube, as long as it divides Germany from the Vindelici, from Noricum, and Pannonia. He then follows the eastern side of the country, where a chain of mountains, or, as he expresses it, mutual fear, draws the line of separation from Dacia and Sarmatia.

[2] Maroboduus was king of the Marcomannians. For an account of him, and his alliance with the Romans against Arminius, see *Annals*, ii. 46.

signians, the Gothinians, the Osians, and the Burians. In dress and language the two last resemble the Suevians. The Gothinians, by their use of the Gallic tongue, and the Osians by the dialect of Pannonia, are evidently not of German origin. A further proof arises from their submitting to the disgrace of paying tribute, imposed upon them as aliens and intruders, partly by the Sarmatians, and partly by the Quadians. The Gothinians have still more reason to blush; they submit to the drudgery of digging iron in mines. But a small part of the open and level country is occupied by these several nations: they dwell chiefly in forests, or on the summit of that continued ridge of mountains,[1] by which Suevia is divided and separated from other tribes that lie still more remote. Of these the Lygians[2] are the most powerful, stretching to a great extent, and giving their name to a number of subordinate communities. It will suffice to mention the most considerable; namely, the Arians, the Helvecones, the Manimians, the Elysians, and Naharvalians. The last show a grove famous for the antiquity of its religious rites. The priest appears in a female dress. The gods whom they worship are, in the language of the country, known by the name of Alcis, by Roman interpreters said to be Castor and Pollux. There are, indeed, no idols in their country; no symbolic representation; no traces of foreign superstition. And yet their two deities are adored in the character of young men and brothers. The Arians are not only superior to the other tribes above mentioned, but are also more fierce and savage. Not content with their natural ferocity, they study to make themselves still more grim and horrible by every addition that art can devise. Their shields are black; their bodies painted of a deep colour; and the darkest night is their time for rushing to battle. The sudden surprise and funereal gloom of such a band of sable warriors are sure to strike a panic through the adverse army, who fly the field, as if a legion of demons had broke loose to attack them; so true it is, that in every engagement the eye is first conquered. Beyond the Lygians the next state is that of the Gothones,[3] who live under regal government, and are, by consequence, ruled with a degree of power more rigorous

[1] These are the mountains between Moravia, Hungary, Silesia, and Bohemia.

[2] The nation of the Lygians inhabited part of Silesia, of Prussia, and Poland as far as the banks of the Vistula.

[3] The Gothones dwelt near the mouth of the Vistula, in part of Pomerania and the north-west of Poland.

than other parts of Germany, yet not unlimited, nor entirely hostile to civil liberty. In the neighbourhood of these people, we find, on the sea-coast, the Rugians[1] and Lemovians, both subject to royal authority. When their round shields and short swords are mentioned, there are no other particulars worthy of notice.

XLIV. The people that next occur are the Suiones,[2] who may be said to inhabit the ocean itself. In addition to the strength of their armies, they have a powerful naval force. The form of their ships is peculiar. Every vessel has a prow at each end, and by that contrivance is always ready to make head either way. Sails are not in use, nor is there a range of oars at the sides. The mariners, as often happens in the navigation of rivers, take different stations, and shift from one place to another, as the exigence may require. Riches are by this people held in great esteem; and the public mind, debased by that passion, yields to the government of one with unconditional, with passive obedience. Despotism is here fully established. The people are not allowed to carry arms in common, like the rest of the German nations. An officer is appointed to keep in a magazine all the military weapons, and for this purpose a slave is always chosen. For this policy the ostensible reason is, that the ocean is their natural fence against foreign invasions, and in time of peace the giddy multitude, with arms ready at hand, soon proceeds from luxury to tumult and commotion. But the truth is, the jealousy of a despotic prince does not think it safe to commit the care of his arsenal to the nobles or the men of ingenuous birth. Even a manumitted slave is not fit to be trusted.

XLV. At the further extremity beyond the Suiones there is another sea, whose sluggish waters seem to be in a state of stagnation. By this lazy element the globe is said to be encircled, and the supposition receives some colour of probability from an extraordinary phenomenon well known in those regions. The rays of the setting sun continue till the return of day to brighten the hemisphere with so clear a light, that the stars are imperceptible. To this it is added by vulgar credulity, that when the sun begins to rise, the sound of the emerging luminary is distinctly heard, and the very form of the horses, the blaze of glory round

[1] The Rugians were situated on the Baltic shore.

[2] The Suiones occupied Sweden, and the Danish isles of Funen, Langland, Zeeland.

the head of the god, is palpable to the sight. The boundaries of nature, it is generally believed, terminate here.[1]

On the coast to the right of the Suevian ocean, the Æstyans have fixed their habitation. In their dress and manners they resemble the Suevians, but their language has more affinity to the dialect of Britain. They worship the mother of the gods. The figure of a wild boar is the symbol of their superstition; and he, who has that emblem about him, thinks himself secure even in the thickest ranks of the enemy, without any need of arms, or any other mode of defence. The use of iron is unknown, and their general weapon is a club. In the cultivation of corn, and other fruits of the earth, they labour with more patience than is consistent with the natural laziness of the Germans. Their industry is exerted in another instance: they explore the sea for amber, in their language called GLESE, and are the only people who gather that curious substance. It is generally found among the shallows; sometimes on the shore. Concerning the nature or the causes of this concretion, the Barbarians, with their usual want of curiosity, make no inquiry. Amongst other superfluities discharged by the sea, this substance lay long neglected, till Roman luxury gave it a name, and brought it into request. To the savages it is of no use. They gather it in rude heaps, and offer it to sale without any form or polish, wondering at the price they receive for it. There is reason to think that amber is a distillation from certain trees, since in the transparent medium we see a variety of insects, and even animals of the wing, which, being caught in the viscous fluid, are afterwards, when it grows hard, incorporated with it. It is probable, therefore, that as the east has its luxuriant plantations, where balm and frankincense perspire through the pores of trees, so the continents and islands of the west have their prolific groves, whose juices, fermented by the heat of the sun, dissolve into a liquid matter, which falls into the sea, and, being there condensed, is afterwards discharged by the winds and waves on the opposite shore. If you make an experiment of amber by the application of fire, it kindles, like a torch, emitting a fragrant flame, and in a little time, taking the tenacious nature of pitch or rosin. Beyond the Suiones, we next find the nation of

[1] The ancients thought that the ocean was the boundary of nature, and that no land lay beyond it.

Sitones,[1] differing in nothing from the former, except the tameness with which they suffer a woman to reign over them. Of this people, it is not enough to say, that they have degenerated from civil liberty; they are sunk below slavery itself. At this place ends the territory of the Suevians.

XLVI. Whether the Peucinians, the Venedians, and Fennians, are to be accounted Germans, or classed with the people of Sarmatia, is a point not easy to be determined: though the Peucinians, called by some the Bastarnians, bear a strong resemblance to the Germans. They use the same language: their dress and habitations are the same, and they are equally inured to sloth and filth. Of late, however, in consequence of frequent intermarriages between their leading chieftains and the families of Sarmatia, they have been tainted with the manners of that country. The Venedians are a counterpart of the Sarmatians: like them they lead a wandering life, and support themselves by plunder amidst the woods and mountains that separate the Peucinians and the Fennians. They are, notwithstanding, to be ascribed to Germany, inasmuch as they have settled habitations, know the use of shields, and travel always on foot, remarkable for their swiftness. The Sarmatians, on the contrary, live altogether on horseback or in waggons. Nothing can equal the ferocity of the Fennians, nor is there anything so disgusting as their filth and poverty. Without arms, without horses, and without a fixed place of abode, they lead a vagrant life; their food the common herbage; the skins of beasts their only clothing; and the bare earth their resting-place. For their chief support they depend on their arrows, to which, for want of iron, they prefix a pointed bone. The women follow the chase in company with the men, and claim their share of the prey. To protect their infants from the fury of wild beasts, and the inclemency of the weather, they make a kind of cradle amidst the branches of trees interwoven together, and they know no other expedient. The youth of the country have the same habitation, and amidst the trees old age is rocked to rest. Savage as this way of life may seem, they prefer it to the drudgery of the field, the labour of building, and the painful vicissitudes of hope and fear, which always attend the defence and the acquisition of property. Secure against the passions of men, and fearing nothing from the anger of the gods, they have

[1] The Sitones, according to some, were the inhabitants of Norway.

attained that uncommon state of felicity, in which there is no craving left to form a single wish.

The rest of what I have been able to collect is too much involved in fable, of a colour with the accounts of the Hellusians and the Oxionians, of whom we are told, that they have the human face, with the limbs and bodies of wild beasts. But reports of this kind, unsupported by proof, I shall leave to the pen of others.

THE LIFE OF
CNÆUS JULIUS AGRICOLA

THE LIFE OF

CNÆUS JULIUS AGRICOLA[1]

CONTENTS

[1] This work is supposed by some commentators to have been written before the Treatise on the Manners of the Germans, in the third consulship of the emperor Nerva, and the second of Verginius Rufus, A.D. 97.

Ireland—He receives a petty king of that country under his protection, and is told that the island may be conquered by a single legion.—XXV. *Agricola explores the country beyond the Firth of Bodotria, and sends his fleet to annoy the coast.*—XXVI. *The Caledonians attack the ninth legion by surprise in the night—Agricola comes to the assistance of the legion: the Britons put to the rout; but soon after resume their courage, and form a general league against the Romans.*—XXVIII. *A cohort of the Usipians, levied in Germany, in a bold adventure, sail round the northern part of the island.*—XXIX. *Galgacus prepares to encounter the Romans, and takes post on the Grampian hills.*—XXX. *His admirable speech to his army.*—XXXIII. *Agricola harangues his men.*—XXXV. *A fierce and bloody battle.*—XXXVIII. *The Romans gain a complete victory—Agricola orders his fleet to sail round the whole island.*—XXXIX. *Domitian receives an account of Agricola's operations with pretended joy, and dissembled uneasiness.*—XL. *He grants triumphal ornaments and a statue to Agricola, but resolves to recall him from the command in Britain—Agricola returns to Rome, and meets with a cold reception from the emperor—His prudent plan of life.*—XLI. *The emperor and his courtiers hostile to virtue.*—XLII. *Agricola entitled by lot to the government of Asia or Africa; but Domitian by his emissaries contrives to dissuade him, and receives thanks for excusing him.*—XLIII. *The death of Agricola.*—XLIV. *His age, his form and stature, and his public dignities.*—XLV. *His loss the less to be regretted, as he escaped the horrid cruelties of Domitian, and the murder of the best men in Rome.—The beautiful and pathetic sentiments with which Tacitus concludes.*

The life of Agricola was written,

Year of Rome.	Of Christ.	Consuls.
850	97	Nerva, emperor, 3rd time. Verginius Rufus.

I. To transmit to posterity the lives and characters of illustrious men, was an office frequently performed in ancient times. Even in the present age, incurious as it is about its own concerns, the same good custom has prevailed, whenever a great and splendid virtue has been able to surmount those two pernicious vices, which not only infest small communities, but are likewise the bane of large and flourishing cities; I mean the vices of insensibility to merit, on the one hand, and envy, on the other. With regard to the usage of antiquity, it is further observable, that, in those early seasons of virtue, men were led by the impulse of a generous spirit to a course of action worthy of being recorded; and, in like manner, the writer of genius undertook to perpetuate the memory of honourable deeds, without any motives of flattery, and without views of private ambition, influenced only by the conscious pleasure of doing justice to departed merit. Many have been their own historians, persuaded that in speaking of themselves they should display an honest confidence in their morals, not a spirit of arrogance or vainglory. Rutilius and Scaurus left an account of their own lives, and the integrity of the narrative has never been called in question; so true it is, that the age which is most fertile in bright examples, is the best qualified to make a fair estimate of them. For the present undertaking, which professes to review the life of a great man now no more, I judged it necessary to premise an apology, led as I am, by the nature of my subject, to encounter an evil period,[1] in which every virtue struggled with adversity and oppression.

II. We have it upon record, that Arulenus Rusticus,[2] for the panegyric of Pætus Thrasea, and Herennius Senecio,[3] for that of Helvidius Priscus,[4] were both capitally convicted. Nor was it enough that those excellent authors fell a sacrifice to the tyrant's power; persecution raged against their books, and, by an order to the triumvirs, in the forum and the place of popular convention, the monuments of genius perished in the flames. The policy of the times, no doubt, intended that in the same fire the voice of the Roman people should be stifled, the freedom of the senate destroyed, and the sentiments of the human heart suppressed for ever. To complete the work, all sound philosophy was proscribed, every liberal art was driven into banishment, and nothing fair and honourable was suffered to remain. Of our passive temper we gave ample proof; and as former times had tasted of liberty even to a degree of licentiousness, so we exhausted the bitter cup of slavery to the very dregs. Restrained by the terrors of a merciless inquisition from the commerce of hearing and speaking, and, by consequence, deprived of all exchange of sentiment, we should have resigned our memory with our other faculties, if to forget had been as easy as to submit in silence.

[1] Agricola commanded in Britain in the time of Vespasian, Titus, and Domitian.

[2] Arulenus Rusticus was tribune of the people A.D. 66.

[3] Senecio was a native of Spain, born in the province of Bœtica, where he served the office of quæstor in the reign of Domitian, and never aspired to any higher honour. Not choosing to be a candidate for the magistracy, he was considered as an obstinate republican, hostile to the established government, and a friend to innovation.

[4] Helvidius Priscus, the subject of Senecio's panegyric, was born at Terracina, a municipal town in Italy. He was confirmed in the doctrines of the Stoic school by his father-in-law, Pætus Thrasea. His character, drawn by the masterly hand of Tacitus, may be seen, *Hist.* iv. 5.

III. At length, indeed, we begin to revive from our lethargy; but we revive by slow degrees, though the emperor Nerva,[1] in the beginning of this glorious era, found means to reconcile two things, till then deemed incompatible; namely, civil liberty and the prerogative of the prince; though his successor Trajan continues to heal our wounds, and by a just and wise administration to diffuse the blessings of peace and good order through every part of the empire; and though it is apparent, that hopes of the constitution are now conceived by all orders of men, and not only conceived, but rising every hour into confidence and public security.[2] And yet, such is the infirmity of the human mind, that, even in this juncture, the remedy operates more slowly than the disease. For as the body natural is tardy in its growth, and rapid in decay, so the powers of genius are more easily extinguished than promoted to their full maturity. There is a charm in indolence that works by imperceptible degrees; and that listless inactivity, which at first is irksome, grows delightful in the end.

Need I mention that in the course of fifteen years, a large portion of human life! many fell by unavoidable accidents, and the most illustrious men in Rome were cut off by the insatiate cruelty of the prince? A few of us, it is true, have survived the slaughter of our fellow-citizens; I had almost said, we have survived ourselves: for in that chasm, which slavery made in our existence, we cannot be said to have lived, but rather to have crawled in silence, the young towards the decrepitude of age, and the old to dishonourable graves. And yet I shall not regret the time I have spent in reviewing those days of despotism; on the contrary, it is my intention, even in such weak colouring as mine, to give a memorial of our slavery, that it may stand in contrast to the felicity of the present period.

In the meantime, the following tract is dedicated to the memory of Agricola, my father-in-law. The design, as it springs from filial piety, may merit a degree of approbation; it will, at least, be received with candour.

IV. Cnæus Julius Agricola was born at the ancient and respectable colony of Forojulium. His grandfather, by the maternal as well as the paternal line, served the office of

[1] On the death of Domitian, that emperor's acts were rescinded, and Nerva began his reign.

[2] The public security, *securitas publica*, was an inscription on the medals of the times.

imperial procurator; a trust of importance, which always confers the equestrian dignity. His father, Julius Græcinus, was a member of the senate, distinguished by his eloquence and philosophy. His merit gave umbrage to Caligula. Being commanded by that emperor to undertake the prosecution of Marcus Silanus,[1] he refused to comply, and was put to death. Julia Procilla, Agricola's mother, was respected for the purity of her manners. Under her care, and as it were in her bosom, the tender mind of the son was trained to science and every liberal accomplishment. His own ingenuous disposition guarded him against the seductions of pleasure. To that happy temperament was added the advantage of pursuing his studies at Marseilles, that seat of learning, where the refinements of Greece were happily blended with the sober manners of provincial economy.

He has often declared in my hearing, that in the first career of youth he felt himself addicted to philosophical speculations with more ardour than consisted with the duties of a Roman and a senator; but his taste was soon reformed by the admonitions of his mother. In fact, it cannot be matter of wonder, that a sublime and warm imagination, struck with the forms of moral beauty and the love of science, should aspire to reach the glory of the philosophic character. As he grew up to manhood, his riper judgment weaned him from vain pursuits, and during the rest of his life he preserved, what is difficult to attain, that temperate judgment, which knows where to fix the bounds even of wisdom itself.

V. His first rudiments of military knowledge were acquired in Britain, under the conduct of Suetonius Paulinus,[2] that experienced officer; active, vigilant, yet mild in command. Agricola was soon distinguished by his general, and selected to live with him at headquarters. Honoured in this manner, he did not, as is usual with young men, mix riot and dissipation with actual service; nor did he avail himself of his rank of military tribune to obtain leave of absence, in order to pass his time in idle pleasures and ignorance of his duty. To know the province, and make himself known to the army; to learn from men of experience, and emulate the best examples; to seek no enterprise with a forward spirit, and to decline none

[1] Marcus Silanus was highly respected, not only for his birth and rank, but also for his eminent virtues. He had the misfortune of being father-in-law to Caligula. He incurred the hatred of that tyrant by his honest counsels.

[2] Suetonius Paulinus was sent by Nero to command in Britain A.D. 61. Of this officer, one of the ablest that Rome produced during the first century of the Christian era, an ample character is given by Tacitus, *Annals*, xiv. 29.

with timid caution, were the rules he laid down to himself; prudent with valour, and brave without ostentation.

A more active campaign had never been known, nor was Britain at any time so fiercely disputed.[1] Our veteran forces were put to the sword; our colonies smoked on the ground; and the legions were intercepted on their march. The struggle was then for life; we fought afterwards for fame and victory. In a juncture so big with danger, though the conduct of the war was in other hands, and the glory of recovering the province was justly ascribed to the commander-in-chief, yet so fair an opportunity did not fail to improve a young officer, and plant in his mind the early seeds of military ambition. The love of fame took possession of him, that principle of noble minds, but out of season in an evil period when virtue suffered by sinister constructions, and from an illustrious name the danger was as great as from the most pernicious character.

VI. He returned from Britain to enter on the gradations of the civil magistracy, and married Domitia Decidiana, a lady of high rank and splendid descent. By that alliance he gained an accession of strength and credit, that served to forward him in the road to public honours. The conjugal state proved a source of domestic happiness. They lived in perfect harmony, endeared by the tenderest affection, and each ascribing to the other the felicity which they enjoyed. But the merit of Decidiana could not be too much acknowledged. The praise of a valuable wife should always rise in proportion to the weight of censure, that falls on such as violate the nuptial union.

Agricola obtained the office of quæstor;[2] and the province of Asia, of which Salvius Titianus was proconsul, fell to his lot. Neither the place nor the governor could warp his integrity. The wealth of the inhabitants invited the hand of rapacity; and Titianus, by the bias of his nature prone to acts

[1] While Suetonius was employed in the reduction of the Isle of *Mona*, now *Anglesey*, the chief seat of the Druids, and consequently the centre of superstition, the Britons, taking advantage of his absence, rose in arms; and headed by Boadicea, queen of the Iceni, attacked the Roman stations, and laid a scene of blood and carnage in every quarter. No less than 70,000 were put to the sword without distinction. Suetonius with his small army marched back through the heart of the country, to the protection of London, then a flourishing city; but he found on his arrival that the place was not tenable. He abandoned it to the merciless fury of the enemy, and it was accordingly reduced to ashes. But this cruelty was revenged by Suetonius in a great and decisive battle, in which 80,000 Britons are said to have perished. Boadicea put an end to her life by poison. See the account at large, *Annals*, xiv. 29.

[2] The quæstorship was the first office entered upon by those who aspired to the higher magistracies.

of avarice, was ready, on terms of mutual connivance, to cooperate in any scheme of guilt and plunder; but Agricola maintained his honour and his principles. During his stay in Asia his family was increased by the birth of a daughter, who proved soon after, when he lost his infant son, a source of consolation. The intermediate space between the expiration of his quæstorship and his advancement to the post of tribune of the people, he had the prudence to pass in calm tranquillity. Even during the year of his tribuneship he acted with the same reserve, aware of those disastrous times, when, under the tyranny of Nero's reign, the want of exertion was the truest wisdom. He discharged the office of prætor with the same moderation and silent dignity, having no occasion, as his good fortune would have it, to sit in judicature. That branch of the magistrate's business did not fall to his share. The pageantry of public spectacles, which belonged to his department, he conducted with economy and magnificence, short of profusion, yet with due regard to popularity. In the following reign, being appointed by Galba one of the commissioners to inspect the state of oblations to the several temples, he managed the inquiry with so much skill and well-tempered judgment, that no species of sacrilegious rapine, except the plunder committed by Nero, was suffered to pass without redress.

VII. In the course of the following year a dreadful misfortune happened in his family, and proved to him a severe stroke of affliction. A descent from Otho's fleet, which roved about in quest of depredations, was made on the coast of Liguria. The freebooters plundered the city of Intemelium,[1] and in their fury murdered Agricola's mother, then residing upon her own estate. They laid waste her lands, and went off with a considerable booty. Agricola set out immediately to pay the last tribute of filial piety, and being informed on his way that Vespasian aspired to the imperial dignity, he declared at once in favour of that party.

In the beginning of the new reign, the government of Rome, and the whole administration, centred in Mucianus, Domitian being at that time too young for business, and from the elevation of his father claiming no other privilege than that of being debauched and profligate without control. Agricola was despatched to raise new levies. He executed that commission with so much zeal and credit to himself, that Mucianus advanced him to the command of the twentieth legion, then

[1] Now called *Vintimiglia*.

quartered in Britain, and for some time unwilling to swear fidelity to Vespasian. The officer who had the command of that corps was suspected of seditious practices, and the men had carried their insolence to such a pitch, that they were even formidable to the consular generals. Their commander was of prætorian rank; but either on account of his own disaffection, or the turbulent spirit of the soldiers, his authority was too feeble. Agricola succeeded to the command of the legion, and to the task of punishing the guilty. He acquitted himself with consummate address, and singular moderation, wishing that the men should have the merit of voluntary compliance, and not seem to have yielded, with sullen submission, to the authority of their general.

VIII. The government of Britain was at that time committed to Vettius Bolanus, a man of milder disposition than consisted with the genius of those ferocious islanders. Agricola, that he might not seem to eclipse his superior officer, restrained his martial ardour, submitting with deference to his commander-in-chief, and, in every part of his conduct, uniting to his love of glory a due regard for the service. Bolanus was soon recalled, and Petilius Cerealis, an officer of consular rank, succeeded to the command. The field of warlike enterprise was laid open to Agricola. Under the new commander, he was, at first, no more than a common sharer in the dangers of the campaign; but in a short time his talents had their free career. The general, to make his experiment, sent him at the head of detached parties, and afterwards, encouraged by the event, employed him in more important operations. Agricola never betrayed a symptom of vain-glory. From the issue of his expeditions, however successful, he assumed no merit. It was the general that planned the measure, and he himself was no more than the hand that executed. By this conduct, vigorous in action, but modest in the report of his exploits, he gained a brilliant reputation, secure from the envy that attends it.

IX. On his return to Rome, Vespasian advanced him to the patrician rank, and soon after to the government of the province of Aquitania; an appointment of the first importance, leading directly to the honours of the consulship, to which he then aspired with the concurrence of the prince. The military mind, trained up in the school of war, is generally supposed to want the power of nice discrimination. The jurisdiction of the camp is little solicitous about forms and subtle reasoning; military law is blunt and summary, and where the sword resolves all difficulties, the refined discussions of the forum are never practised. Agricola, however, indebted to nature for a certain rectitude of understanding, was not out of his sphere even among men versed in questions of jurisprudence. His hours of business and relaxation had their stated periods. In the council of the province, or on the tribunal of justice, he discharged the duties of his station with awful gravity, intent to inquire, often severe, but more inclined to soften the rigour of the law. The functions of the magistrate being despatched, he divested himself of his public character; the man in authority was no longer seen. In his actions no tincture of arrogance, no spleen, no avarice was ever seen. Uncommon as it may appear, the sweetness of his manners took nothing from his authority, nor was the impression made by his amiable qualities lessened by the inflexibility of the judge.

To say of a character truly great, that integrity and a spirit above corruption made a part of it, were mere tautology, as injurious to his virtues, as it is unnecessary. Even the love of fame, that fine incentive of generous minds, could neither betray him into an ostentatious display of virtue, nor induce him to practise those specious arts that court applause, and often supply the place of merit. The little ambition of rising above his colleagues was foreign to his heart. He avoided all contention with the procurators of the prince. In struggles of that nature he knew that victory may be obtained without glory, and a defeat is certain disgrace. In less than three years he was recalled from his province, to take upon him the consular dignity. The voice of fame marked him out, at the same time, for the government of Britain: the report was current, but neither contrived, nor cultivated, by himself. He was mentioned, because he was worthy. Common fame does not always err: it often takes the lead, and determines the choice. During his consulship, though I was then very young, he agreed to a marriage between me and his daughter, who certainly might have looked for a prouder connection. The nuptial ceremony was not performed till the term of his consulship expired. In a short time after he was appointed governor of Britain, with the additional honour of a seat in the pontifical college.

X. If I here presume to offer a description of Britain and the manners of the people, it is not my intention to dispute with the number of authors, who have gone before me, either the fame of genius, or diligence in the research. The fact is, Britain was subdued under the conduct of Agricola, and that circumstance may justify the present attempt. Antecedent writers adorned conjecture with all the graces of language: what I have to offer will have nothing but the plain truth to recommend it.

Britain, of all the islands known to the Romans, is the largest. On the east, it extends towards Germany; on the west towards Spain; and on the south, it lies opposite to the coast of Gaul. The northern extremity is lashed by the billows of a prodigious sea, and no land is known beyond it. The form of the island has been compared by two eloquent writers (Livy among the ancients, and Fabius Rusticus among the moderns) to an oblong shield, or a two-edged axe. The comparison, if we except Caledonia, may be allowed to be just, and hence the shape of a part has been, by vulgar error, ascribed to the whole. Caledonia stretches a vast length of way towards the north. The promontories, that jut out into the sea, render the form of the country broken and irregular, but it sharpens to a point at the extremity, and terminates in the shape of a wedge.

By Agricola's order the Roman fleet sailed round the northern point, and made the first certain discovery that Britain is an island. The cluster of isles called the Orcades,[1] till then wholly unknown, was in this expedition added to the Roman empire. Thule,[2] which had lain concealed in the gloom of winter and a depth of eternal snows, was also seen by our navigators. The sea in those parts is said to be a sluggish mass of stagnated water, hardly yielding to the stroke of the oar, and never agitated by winds and tempests. The natural cause may be, that high lands and mountains, which occasion commotions in the air, are deficient in those regions; not to mention that such a prodigious body of water, in a vast and boundless ocean, is heaved and impelled with difficulty. But a philosophical account of the ocean and its periodical motions is not the design of this essay; the subject has employed the pen of others. To what they have said, I shall only add, that there is not in any other part of the world an expanse of water that rages with such uncontrollable dominion, now receiving the discharge of various rivers, and, at times, driving

[1] Now the *Orkney* islands.

[2] Much has been said by the Greek and Roman poets of a place in the northern regions, called Thule; but it is evident they did not all agree in the geographical description. Camden is of opinion that the *Thule* of Tacitus is one of the *Shetland* islands, which lie to the north of the Orcades, lat. 60°. The ancient poets heard of *Thule*, and made their own use of it, to adorn their verse. To fix the exact spot was not their business.

their currents back to their source. Nor is it on the coast only that the flux and reflux of the tide are perceived: the swell of the sea forces its way into the recesses of the land, forming bays and islands in the heart of the country, and foaming amidst hills and mountains, as in its natural channel.

XI. Whether the first inhabitants of Britain were natives of the island, or adventitious settlers, is a question lost in the mists of antiquity. The Britons, like other barbarous nations, have no monuments of their history. They differ in the make and habit of their bodies, and hence various inferences concerning their origin. The ruddy hair and lusty limbs of the Caledonians indicate a German extraction. That the Silures were at first a colony of Iberians is concluded, not without probability, from the olive tincture of the skin, the natural curl of the hair, and the situation of the country, so convenient to the coast of Spain. On the side opposite to Gaul the inhabitants resemble their neighbours on the continent; but whether that resemblance is the effect of one common origin, or of the climate in contiguous nations operating on the make and temperament of the human body, is a point not easy to be decided. All circumstances considered, it is rather probable that a colony from Gaul took possession of a country so inviting by its proximity. You will find in both nations the same religious rites, and the same superstition.[1] The two languages differ but little. In provoking danger they discover the same ferocity, and in the encounter, the same timidity. The Britons, however, not yet enfeebled by a long peace, are possessed of superior courage. The Gauls, we learn from history, were formerly a warlike people; but sloth, the consequence of inactive times, has debased their genius, and virtue died with expiring liberty. Among such of the Britons, as have been for some time subdued, the same degeneracy is observable. The free and unconquered part of the nation retains at this hour the ferocity of the ancient Gauls.

XII. The strength of their armies consists in infantry, though some of their warriors take the field in chariots. The person of highest distinction guides the reins, while his martial followers, mounted in the same vehicle, annoy the enemy.

[1] The Druids, according to Cæsar's account, believed in the transmigration of souls, and that doctrine they thought had a happy tendency to inspire men with courage, and a contempt of death. They taught their pupils a system of astronomy; they described the various revolutions of the planets, the dimensions of the globe, the operations of nature; they talked with reverence of the immortal gods, and initiated their youth in all their mysteries. Human sacrifices were part of their superstition.

The Britons were formerly governed by a race of kings:[1] at present they are divided into factions under various chieftains; and this disunion, which prevents their acting in concert for a public interest, is a circumstance highly favourable to the Roman arms against a warlike people, independent, fierce, and obstinate. A confederation of two or more states to repel the common danger is seldom known: they fight in parties, and the nation is subdued.

The climate is unfavourable; always damp with rains, and overcast with clouds. Intense cold is never felt. The days are longer than in our southern regions; the nights remarkably bright, and, towards the extremity of the island, so very short,[2] that between the last gleam of day and the returning dawn the interval is scarce perceptible. In a serene sky, when no clouds intervene to obstruct the sight, the sun, we are told, appears all night long, neither setting in the west, nor rising in the east, but always moving above the horizon. The cause of this phenomenon may be, that the surface of the earth, towards the northern extremities, being flat and level, the shade never rises to any considerable height, and, the sky still retaining the rays of the sun, the heavenly bodies continue visible.

The soil does not afford either the vine, the olive, or the fruits of warmer climates; but it is otherwise fertile, and yields corn in great plenty. Vegetation is quick in shooting up, and slow in coming to maturity. Both effects are reducible to the same cause, the constant moisture of the atmosphere and the dampness of the soil. Britain contains, to reward the conqueror, mines of gold and silver, and other metals. The sea produces pearls, but of a dark and livid colour. This defect is ascribed by some to want of skill in this kind of fishery: the people employed in gathering, content themselves in gleaning what happens to be thrown upon the shore, whereas in the Red Sea the shell-fish are found clinging to the rocks, and taken alive. For my part, I am inclined to think that the British pearl is of an inferior quality. I cannot impute to avarice a neglect of its interest.

[1] We read in the *Annals*, xii. 36, of Caractacus, king of the Silures; in xiv. 31, of Prasutagus, king of the Iceni; and in 35 of Boadicea, his widow, who succeeded to her husband's dominions. For Cartismandua, queen of the Brigantes, who delivered up Caractacus to the Romans, see *Annals*, xii. 36, and *Hist.* iii. 45.

[2] Tacitus, in this place, may be said to be out of his depth. His notions here, as well as in the passage concerning the Suiones in the Manners of the Germans, section 45, hold more of the poet than the philosopher.

XIII. The Britons are willing to supply our armies with new levies; they pay their tribute without a murmur; and they perform all the services of government with alacrity, provided they have no reason to complain of oppression. When injured, their resentment is quick, sudden, and impatient; they are conquered, not broken-hearted; reduced to obedience, not subdued to slavery. Even Julius Cæsar, the first of the Romans [1] who set his foot in Britain at the head of an army, can only be said by a prosperous battle to have struck the natives with terror, and to have made himself master of the sea-shore. The discoverer, not the conqueror of the island, he did no more than show it to posterity. Rome could not boast of a conquest. The civil wars broke out soon after, and, in that scene of distraction, when the swords of the leading men were drawn against their country, it was natural to lose sight of Britain. During the peace that followed, the same neglect continued: Augustus called it the wisdom of his counsels, and Tiberius made it a rule of state policy.

That Caligula meditated an invasion of Britain [2] is a fact well known; but the expedition, like his mighty preparations against Germany, was rendered abortive by the capricious temper of the man, resolving always without consideration and repenting without experiment. The grand enterprise was reserved for the emperor Claudius,[3] who transported into Britain an army composed of regular legions, besides a large body of auxiliaries. With the officers appointed to conduct the war he joined Vespasian, who there laid the foundation of that success which afterwards attended him. Several states were conquered, kings were led in captivity, and the Fates beheld Vespasian giving an earnest of his future glory.

XIV. The first officer of consular rank, that commanded in Britain, was Aulus Plautius.[4] To him succeeded Ostorius Scapula;[5] both eminent for their military character. Under

[1] Tacitus now proceeds to relate the progress of the Roman arms in Britain, from the first invasion of the island by Julius Cæsar to the time when Agricola became commander-in-chief.

[2] Caligula's threatened invasion of Britain ended in an idle and vain parade. History has no scene of folly to compare with it.

[3] The Britons, unmolested by the Romans, had enjoyed their liberty near a century, when, in the reign of Claudius, the project of subduing the island was concerted. The most stupid of the emperors was destined to be the conqueror of Britain.

[4] Aulus Plautius was commander-in-chief of the army sent by Claudius to the invasion of Britain, A.D. 43.

[5] An account of Ostorius Scapula and the brilliant success of his arms is given by Tacitus, *Annals*, xii. 31-39. He sent Caractacus a prisoner to Rome.

their auspices the southern part of Britain took the form of a province, and received a colony of veterans. Certain districts were assigned to Cogidunus, a king who reigned over part of the country. He lived within our own memory, preserving always his faith unviolated, and exhibiting a striking proof of that refined policy, with which it has ever been the practice of Rome to make even kings accomplices in the servitude of mankind.

The next governor was Didius Gallus. He preserved the acquisitions made by his predecessors, without aiming at an extension of territory, and without any advantage, except a few forts, which he built on the remote borders of the province, in hopes of gaining some pretension to the fame of having enlarged the frontier. Veranius succeeded to the command, but died within the year. Suetonius Paulinus was the next in succession. That officer pushed on the war in one continued series of prosperity for two years together. In that time he subdued several states, and secured his conquest by a chain of posts and garrisons. Confiding in the strength which he had thus established, he formed the plan of reducing the isle of Mona, the grand resource from which the malcontents drew their supplies. But having, in that expedition, turned his back on the conquered provinces, he gave an opportunity for a general revolt.

XV. The Britons, relieved from their fears by the absence of the commander-in-chief, began to descant on the horrors of slavery.[1] They stated their grievances, and, to inflame resentment, painted everything in the most glaring colours. "What was now the consequence of their passive spirit? The hand of oppression falls on the tame and abject with greater weight. Each state was formerly subject to a single king, but now two masters rule with an iron rod. The general gluts himself with the blood of the vanquished, and the imperial procurator devours our property. Those haughty tyrants may act in concert, or they may be at variance; but in either case the lot of the Britons is the same. The centurions of the general, and the followers of the tax-gatherer, add pride and insolence to injustice and rapacity. Nothing is safe from avarice, nothing by lust unviolated. In the field of battle, the booty is for the brave and warlike: at present, cowards and abject wretches seize the possessions of the

[1] The general revolt of the Britons, and the massacre of the Romans, that followed in consequence of the discontents here painted forth in the strongest colours, are related at large in the *Annals*, xiv. 31–38.

natives; to them the Britons tamely yield up their children; for them they make new levies, and, in short, the good of his country is the only cause in which a Briton has forgot to die. Compute the number of men born in freedom, who inhabit the island, and the Roman invaders are but a handful. It was thus the Germans argued, and they shook off the yoke.[1] No ocean rolled between them and the invader: they were separated by a river only. The Britons have every motive to excite their valour. They have their country to defend, and they have their liberty to assert; they have wives and children to urge them on; and they have parents, who sue to them for protection. On the part of the Romans, if we except luxury and avarice, what incentives are there to draw them to the field? Let British valour emulate the virtue of ancient times, and the invaders, like their own deified Cæsar, will abandon the island. The loss of a single battle, and even a second, cannot decide the fate of a whole people. Many advantages list on the side of misery. To attack with fury and persevere with constancy, belongs to men who groan under oppression. The gods, at length, behold the Britons with an eye of compassion: they have removed the Roman general from his station; they detain him and his army in another island. The oppressed have gained an advantage, too often difficult to obtain; they can now deliberate: they are met in council. In designs like these, the whole danger lies in being detected: act like men, and success will be the issue of the war."

XVI. Inflamed by these and such like topics, the spirit of revolt was diffused through the country. With one consent they took up arms, under the conduct of Boadicea,[2] a queen descended from a race of royal ancestors. In Britain there is no rule of distinction to exclude the female line from the throne, or the command of armies. The insurgents rushed to the attack with headlong fury; they found the Romans dispersed in their garrisons; they put all to the sword; they stormed the forts; they attacked the capital of the colony, which they considered as the seat of oppression, and with fire and sword laid it level with the ground. Whatever revenge could prompt, or victory inspire, was executed with unre-

[1] An allusion to the fate of Varus and his legions, which happened in the fortieth year of Augustus, A.D. 9.

[2] Boadicea was the daughter of Prasutagus, king of the Icenians: she succeeded to her father's dominions, and, being ignominiously treated by the Romans, headed the revolt, and in the field of action distinguished herself by her martial spirit.

lenting cruelty; and if Suetonius, on the first intelligence, had not hastened back by rapid marches, Britain had been lost. By the event of a single battle the province was recovered, though the embers of rebellion were not quite extinguished. Numbers of the malcontents, conscious of their share in the revolt, and dreading the vengeance of Suetonius, still continued under arms.

The truth is, notwithstanding the excellent qualities that distinguished the Roman general, it was the blemish of his character, that he proceeded always against the vanquished, even after they surrendered, with excessive rigour. Justice, under his administration, had frequently the air of revenge for a personal injury. In his public proceedings he mingled too much of his own passions, and was therefore recalled, to make way for Petronius Turpilianus, a man of less asperity, new to the Britons, and, having no resentments, likely to be satisfied on moderate terms. He restored the tranquillity of the island, and, without attempting anything further, resigned the province to Trebellius Maximus, an officer of no experience, by nature indolent and inactive, but possessed of certain popular arts that reconciled the minds of men to his administration. The Barbarians, at this time, had acquired a taste for elegant and alluring vices. The civil wars, which soon afterwards convulsed the empire, were a fair apology for the pacific temper of the general. His army, however, was not free from intestine discord. The soldiers, formerly inured to discipline, grew wanton in idleness, and broke out into open sedition. To avoid the fury of his men, Trebellius was obliged to save himself by flight. Having lain for some time in a place of concealment, he returned with an awkward air to take upon him the command. His dignity was impaired, and his spirit humbled. From that time his authority was feeble and precarious. It seemed to be a compromise between the parties; the general remained unmolested, the soldiers uncontrolled, and on these terms the mutiny ended without bloodshed. Vettius Bolanus was the next commander; but the distractions of the civil war still continuing, he did not think it advisable to introduce a plan of regular discipline. The same inactive disposition on the part of the general, and the same mutinous spirit among the soldiers, still prevailed. The only difference was, that the character of Bolanus was without a blemish. If he did not establish his authority, he lived on good terms with all; beloved, though not respected.

XVII. When Britain, with the rest of the Roman world,

fell to the lot of Vespasian, the ablest officers were sent to reduce the island; powerful armies were set in motion, and the spirit of the natives began to droop. In order to spread a general terror, Petilius Cerealis [1] fell with sudden fury on the Brigantes,[2] in point of numbers the most considerable state in the whole province. Various battles were fought, with alternate success, and great effusion of blood. At length the greatest part of that extensive country was either subdued, or involved in all the calamities of war. The fame of Cerealis grew to a size that might discourage the ablest successor; and yet under that disadvantage Julius Frontinus undertook the command. His talents did not suffer by the comparison. He was a man truly great, and sure to signalise himself, whenever a fair opportunity called forth his abilities. He reduced to subjection the powerful and warlike state of the Silures,[3] and, though in that expedition he had to cope not only with a fierce and obstinate enemy, but with the difficulties of a country almost impracticable, it was his glory that he surmounted every obstacle.

XVIII. Such was the state of Britain, and such the events of war, when Agricola arrived about the middle of summer, to take upon him the command. He found an army lulled in indolence and security, as if the campaign was at an end, while the enemy was on the watch to seize the first opportunity. The Ordivicians,[4] not long before his arrival, had fallen upon a party of horse, that happened to be quartered in their district, and put them almost all to the sword. By this blow the courage of the Britons was once more revived: the bold and resolute declared for open war, while others, less sanguine, were against unsheathing the sword, till the character and genius of the new governor should be better known.

Many things conspired to embarrass Agricola: the summer was far advanced; the troops were stationed at different quarters, expecting a cessation of arms during the remainder of the year: and to act on the defensive, content with strengthen-

[1] Petilius Cerealis served, at first, in Britain, under Suetonius Paulinus, *Annals*, xiv. 32. He fought afterwards on the side of Vespasian against Vitellius, *Hist*. iii. 59. He also commanded the legions in the Lower Germany, and, after his victory over Civilis, the Batavian chieftain, was sent by Vespasian to conduct the affairs of Britain, A.D. 70.

[2] The Brigantes inhabited the counties of York, Durham, Cumberland, Westmoreland, and Lancashire.

[3] The subjugation of the Silures, a fierce and obstinate enemy, gave the Romans quiet possession of the south of Britain.

[4] The Ordovices inhabited the counties of Flint, Denbigh, Caernarvon, Merioneth, and Montgomery, in North Wales.

ing the weakest stations, was in the opinion of the best officers the most prudent measure. These were circumstances unfavourable to a spirit of enterprise; but the general resolved to put his army in motion, and face the danger without delay. For this purpose, he drew together various detachments from the legions, and, with the addition of a body of auxiliaries, marched against the enemy. The Ordovicians continuing to decline an engagement on the open plain, he determined to seek them on their heights, and, to animate his men by his own example, he advanced at the head of the line. A battle ensued, and the issue was the destruction of the Ordovician state. Knowing of what moment it is to follow the first impressions of fame, and little doubting but that everything would fall before an army flushed with victory, Agricola formed a plan for the reduction of the isle of Mona, from which Paulinus had been recalled by the general insurrection of the province, as already mentioned.

For the execution of an enterprise so sudden and important, no measures had been concerted, and, by consequence, no vessels were ready to transport the troops. The genius and resolution of the general supplied all deficiencies. He drafted from the auxiliaries a chosen band, well acquainted with the fordable places, and inured to the national practice of swimming across lakes and rivers with such dexterity, that they could manage their arms and guide their horses at the same time. This select corps, free from the encumbrance of their baggage, dashed into the water, and made their way with vigour toward the island. This mode of attack astonished the enemy, who expected nothing less than a fleet of transports, and a regular embarkation. Struck with consternation, they thought nothing impregnable to men who waged so unusual a war. In despair they sued for peace, and surrendered the island. The event added new lustre to the name of Agricola, who had thus set out with a spirit of enterprise, and crowded so much glory into that part of the year, which is usually trifled away in vain parade and the homage of flatteries. The moderation with which he enjoyed his victory was remarkable. He had reduced the vanquished to obedience, and the act, he said, did not deserve the name of victory, nor even of an expedition. In his despatches to Rome he assumed no merit, nor were his letters, according to custom, decorated with sprigs of laurel: but this self-denial served only to enhance his fame. From the modesty of a commander who could undervalue such important services, men inferred that projects of vast extent were even then in his contemplation.

XIX. Agricola was well acquainted with the manners and national character of the Britons: he knew by the experience of past events, that conquest, while it loads the vanquished with injury and oppression, can never be secure and permanent. He determined, therefore, to suppress the seeds of future hostility. He began a reform in his own household; a necessary work, but attended often with no less difficulty than the administration of a province. He removed his slaves and freedmen from every department of public business. Promotions in the army no longer went by favour, or the partiality of the centurions; merit decided, and the man of worth, Agricola knew, would be the most faithful soldier. To know everything, and yet overlook a great deal; to forgive slight offences, and treat matters of importance with due severity, was the rule of his conduct; never vindictive, and in many instances disarmed by penitence. The prevention of crimes was what he wished, and to that end, in the disposal of offices, he made choice of men, whose conduct promised to supersede the necessity of punishment.

The exigencies of the army called for large contributions of corn and other supplies, and yet he lightened the burden by just and equal assessments, providing at the same time against the extortion of the tax-gatherer, more odious and intolerable than even the tax itself. It had been the settled practice of the collectors to engross all the corn, and then, adding mockery to injustice, to make the injured Briton wait at the door of the public granary, humbly supplicating that he might be permitted to re-purchase his own grain, which he was afterwards obliged to sell at an inferior price. A further grievance was, that instead of delivering the requisite quantity of corn at the nearest and most convenient magazines, the Britons were forced to make tedious journeys through difficult cross-country roads, in order to supply camps and stations at a remote distance; and thus the business, which might have been conducted with convenience to all, was converted into a job to gratify the avarice of a few.

XX. In the first year of Agricola's administration these abuses were all suppressed. The consequence was, that peace, which, through the neglect or connivance of former governors, was no less terrible than war itself, began to diffuse its blessings, and to be relished by all. As soon as the summer[1] opened, he assembled his army, and marched in quest of the enemy. Ever present at the head of the lines, he encouraged the strenuous by commendation; he rebuked the sluggard who fell from his rank; he went in person to mark out the station for encampments; he sounded the estuaries, and explored the woods and forests.[2] The Britons, in the meantime, were by sudden incursions kept in a constant alarm. Having spread a general terror through the country, he then suspended his operations, that, in the interval of repose, the Barbarians might taste the sweets of peace. In consequence of these measures, several states, which till then had breathed a spirit of independence, were induced to lay aside their hostile intentions, and to give hostages for their pacific behaviour. Along the frontier of the several districts which had submitted, a chain of posts was established with so much care and judgment, that no part of the country, even where the Roman arms had never penetrated, could think itself secure from the vigour of the conqueror.

XXI. To introduce a system of new and wise regulations was the business of the following winter. A fierce and savage people, running wild in woods, would be ever addicted to a life of warfare. To wean them from those habits, Agricola held forth the baits of pleasure, encouraging the natives, as well by public assistance as by warm exhortations, to build temples, courts of justice, and commodious dwelling-houses. He bestowed encomiums on such as cheerfully obeyed; the slow and uncomplying were branded with reproach; and thus a spirit of emulation diffused itself, operating like a sense of duty. To establish a plan of education, and give the sons of the leading chiefs a tincture of letters, was part of his policy. By way of encouragement, he praised their talents, and already saw them, by the force of their natural genius, rising superior to the attainments of the Gauls. The consequence was, that they who had always disdained the Roman language, began to cultivate its beauties. The Roman apparel was seen without prejudice, and the toga became a fashionable part of dress. By degrees the charms of vice gained admission to their hearts: baths, and porticos, and elegant banquets, grew into vogue; and the new manners, which, in fact, served only to

[1] This was the second summer after Agricola arrived in Britain, A.D. 79.

[2] Agricola, as appears from all circumstances, marched his army from Anglesey, which had surrendered to his army, through North Wales, on his way to Caledonia.

sweeten slavery, were by the unsuspecting Britons called the arts of polished humanity.

XXII. In the course of the third year[1] the progress of the Roman arms discovered new nations, whose territories were laid waste as far as the estuary called the firth of Tay. The legions had to struggle with all the difficulties of a tempestuous season; and yet the Barbarians, struck with a general panic, never dared to hazard an engagement. The country, as far as the Romans advanced, was secured by forts and garrisons. Men of skill and military science observed that no officer knew better than Agricola, how to seize, on a sudden view, the most advantageous situation, and, accordingly, not one of the stations, fortified by his direction, was taken by storm; not one was reduced to capitulate; not one was surrendered or abandoned to the enemy. At every post, to enable the garrison to stand a siege, a year's provision was provided, and each place having strength sufficient, frequent sallies were made; the besiegers were repulsed; and the Romans passed the winter secure from danger. The consequence of these precautions was, that the enemy, who had been accustomed to retrieve in the winter what they lost in the antecedent summer, saw no difference of seasons: they were defeated everywhere, and reduced to the last despair. Avarice of fame was no part of Agricola's character; nor was he ever known to arrogate to himself the praises due to other officers. From the commander of a legion to the lowest centurion, all found in their general a willing witness of their conduct. In his manner of expressing his disapprobation, he was thought to mix a degree of asperity. The truth is, his antipathy to bad men was equalled by nothing but his politeness to the deserving. His anger soon passed away, and left no trace behind. From his silence you had nothing to fear. Scorning to disguise his sentiments, he acted always with a generous warmth, at the hazard of making enemies. To harbour secret resentment was not in his nature.

XXXIII. The business of the fourth campaign was to secure the country, which had been overrun, not conquered, in the preceding summer; and if the spirit of the troops and the glory of the Roman name had been capable of suffering any limits, there was in Britain itself a convenient spot, where the boundary of the empire might have been fixed. The place for that purpose was, where the waters of the Glota and

[1] Agricola's third year was A.D. 80.

Bodotria,[1] driven up the country by the influx of two opposite seas, are hindered from joining by a narrow neck of land, which was then guarded by a chain of forts. On the south side of the isthmus, the whole country was bridled by the Romans, and evacuated by the enemy, who was driven, as it were, into another island.

XXIV. In the fifth summer, Agricola made an expedition by sea. He embarked in the first Roman vessel that ever crossed the estuary,[2] and having penetrated into regions till then unknown, he defeated the inhabitants in several engagements, and lined the coast, which lies opposite to Ireland, with a body of troops; not so much from an apprehension of danger, as with a view to future projects. He saw that Ireland, lying between Britain and Spain, and at the same time convenient to the ports of Gaul, might prove a valuable acquisition, capable of giving an easy communication, and, of course, strength and union, to provinces disjoined by nature.

Ireland is less than Britain, but exceeds in magnitude all the islands of the Mediterranean. The soil, the climate, the manners and genius of the inhabitants, differ little from those of Britain. By the means of merchants resorting thither for the sake of commerce, the harbours and approaches to the coast are well known. One of their petty kings, who had been forced to fly from the fury of a domestic faction, was received by the Roman general, and, under a show of friendship, detained to be of use on some future occasions. I have often heard Agricola declare that a single legion, with a moderate band of auxiliaries, would be sufficient to complete the conquest of Ireland. Such an event, he said, would contribute greatly to bridle the stubborn spirit of the Britons, who, in that case, would see, with dismay, the Roman arms triumphant, and every spark of liberty extinguished round their coast.

XXV. In the campaign which began in the sixth summer,[3] having reason to apprehend a general confederacy of the nations beyond the firth of Bodotria, and fearing, in a country not yet explored, the danger of a surprise, Agricola ordered his ships to sail across the gulf, and gain some knowledge of those new regions. The fleet, now acting for the first

[1] The *Clota* is now the Clyde. The *Bodotria* is the river Forth.

[2] We are now to see Agricola penetrating farther into North Britain, but the laconic style of the author does not distinctly tell us on which side of the country the attempt was made.

[3] Agricola's sixth campaign was A.D. 83, the second year of Domitian's reign.

time in concert with the land-forces, proceeded in sight of the army, forming a magnificent spectacle, and adding terror to the war. It frequently happened that in the same camp were seen the infantry and cavalry intermixed with the marines, all indulging their joy, full of their adventures, and magnifying the history of their exploits; the soldier describing, in the usual style of military ostentation, the forests which he had passed, the mountains which he climbed, and the Barbarians whom he put to the rout; while the sailor, no less important, had his storms and tempests, the wonders of the deep, and the spirit with which he conquered winds and waves.

At the sight of the Roman fleet, the Britons, according to intelligence gained from the prisoners, were struck with consternation, convinced that every resource was cut off, since the sea, which had always been their shelter, was now laid open to the invader. In this distress, the Caledonians resolved to try the issue of a battle. Warlike preparations were instantly begun with a degree of exertion, great in reality, but, as is always the case in matters obscure and distant, magnified by the voice of fame. Without waiting for the commencement of hostilities, they stormed the Roman forts and castles,[1] and by provoking danger, made such an impression, that several officers in Agricola's army, disguising their fear under the specious appearance of prudent counsels, recommended a sudden retreat, to avoid the disgrace of being driven back to the other side of the firth. Meanwhile Agricola received intelligence that the enemy meditated an attack in various quarters at once, and thereupon, lest superior numbers, in a country where he was a stranger to the defiles and passes, should be able to surround him, he divided his army, and marched forward in three columns.

XXVI. The Caledonians, informed of this arrangement, changed their plan, and, in the dead of night, fell with their united force upon the ninth legion, then the weakest of the Roman army. They surprised the advanced guard, and having, in the confusion of sleep and terror, put the sentinels to the sword, they forced their way through the intrenchments. The conflict was in the very camp, when Agricola, who had been informed that the Barbarians were on their march, and instantly pursued their steps, came up to the relief of the legion. He ordered the swiftest of the horse and light infantry to advance with expedition, and charge the

[1] Traces of these forts and castles are still extant.

enemy in the rear, while his whole army set up a general shout. At break of day the Roman banners glittered in view of the Barbarians, who found themselves hemmed in by two armies, and began to relax their vigour. The spirit of the legion revived. The men perceived that the moment of distress was over, and the struggle was now for glory. Acting no longer on the defensive, they rushed on to the attack. In the very gates of the camp a fierce and obstinate engagement followed. The besieged legion, and the forces that came to their relief, fought with a spirit of emulation; the latter contending for the honour of succouring the distressed, and the former to prove that they stood in no need of assistance. The Caledonians were put to the rout; and if the woods and marshes had not favoured their escape, that single action had put an end to the war.

XXVII. By this victory, so complete and glorious, the Roman army was inspired with confidence to such a degree, that they now pronounced themselves invincible. Nothing could stand before them: they desired to be led into the recesses of the country, and, by following their blow, to penetrate to the extremity of the island. Even the prudent of the day before changed their tone with the event, and talked of nothing but victory and conquest. Such is the tax, which the commanders of armies must always pay; the merit of success is claimed by all; calamity is imputed to the general only.

The Caledonians, notwithstanding their defeat, abated nothing from their ferocity. Their want of success, they said, was not to be ascribed to superior courage; it was the chance of war, or, perhaps, the skill of the Roman general. In this persuasion they resolved to keep the field. They listed the young men of their nation; they sent their wives and children to a place of safety; they held public conventions of the several states, and with solemn rites and sacrifices formed a league in the cause of liberty. The campaign ended in this manner, and the two armies, inflamed with mutual animosity, retired into winter quarters.

XXVIII. In the course of the same summer, a cohort of the Usipians which had been raised in Germany, and thence transported to serve in Britain, performed an exploit so daring and extraordinary, that in this place it may be allowed to merit attention. Having murdered the centurion who was left in the command, and also the soldiers, who, for the purpose of introducing military discipline, had been incorporated with the several companies,[1] they seized three light galleys, and forcing the masters on board, determined to sail from the island. One of the pilots made his escape, and suspicion falling on the other two, they were both killed on the spot. Before their design transpired, the deserters put to sea, to the astonishment of all who beheld their vessels under way.

They had not sailed far, when they became the sport of winds and waves. They made frequent descents on the coast in quest of plunder, and had various conflicts with the natives, victorious in some places, and in others beat back to their ships. Reduced at length to the extremity of famine, they fed on their companions, at first devouring the weakest, and afterwards deciding among themselves by lot. In this distress they sailed round the extremity of the island, and, through want of skill in navigation, were wrecked on the continent, where they were treated as pirates, first by the Suevians, and afterwards by the Frisians. Being sold to slavery, and in the way of commerce turned over to different masters, some of them reached the Roman settlements on the banks of the Rhine, and there grew famous for their sufferings, and the bold singularity of their voyage.

In the beginning of the following summer Agricola met with a stroke of affliction by the loss of a son, about a year old. He did not upon this occasion affect, like many others, the character of a man superior to the feelings of nature; nor yet did he suffer his grief to sink him down into unbecoming weakness. He felt the impression, but regret was lost in the avocations of war.

XXIX. In the opening of the campaign, he despatched his fleet, with orders to annoy the coast by frequent descents in different places, and spread a general alarm. He put himself, in the meantime, at the head of his army equipped for expedition, and taking with him a select band of the bravest Britons, of known and approved fidelity, he advanced as far as the Grampian hills, where the enemy was already posted in force. Undismayed by their former defeat, the Barbarians expected no other issue than a total overthrow, or a brave revenge. Experience had taught them that the common cause required a vigorous exertion of their united strength. For this purpose, by treaties of alliance, and by deputations to the several cantons, they had drawn together the strength of

[1] The *Manipuli* were companies of foot, as the *Turmæ* were of the cavalry.

their nation. Upwards of thirty thousand men appeared in arms, and their force was increasing every day. The youth of the country poured in from all quarters, and even the men in years, whose vigour was still unbroken, repaired to the army, proud of their past exploits, and the ensigns of honour which they had gained by their martial spirit. Among the chieftains distinguished by their birth and valour, the most renowned was Galgacus. The multitude gathered round him, eager for action, and burning with uncommon ardour. He harangued them to the following effect:

XXX. "When I consider the motives that have roused us to this war; when I reflect on the necessity that now demands our firmest vigour, I expect everything great and noble from that union of sentiment that pervades us all. From this day I date the freedom of Britain. We are the men, who never crouched in bondage. Beyond this spot there is no land, where liberty can find a refuge. Even the sea is shut against us, while the Roman fleet is hovering on the coast. To draw the sword in the cause of freedom is the true glory of the brave, and, in our condition, cowardice itself would throw away the scabbard. In the battles, which have been hitherto fought with alternate vicissitudes of fortune, our countrymen might well repose some hopes in us; they might consider us as their last resource; they knew us to be the noblest sons of Britain, placed in the last recesses of the land, in the very sanctuary of liberty. We have not so much as seen the melancholy regions where slavery has debased mankind. We have lived in freedom, and our eyes have been unpolluted by the sight of ignoble bondage.

"The extremity of the earth is ours: defended by our situation, we have to this day preserved our honour and the rights of men. But we are no longer safe in our obscurity; our retreat is laid open; the enemy rushes on, and, as things unknown are ever magnified, he thinks a mighty conquest lies before him. But this is the end of the habitable world, and rocks and brawling waves fill all the space behind. The Romans are in the heart of our country; no submission can satisfy their pride; no concessions can appease their fury. While the land has anything left, it is the theatre of war; when it can yield no more, they explore the sea for hidden treasure. Are the nations rich, Roman avarice is their enemy. Are they poor, Roman ambition lords it over them. The east and the west have been rifled, and the spoiler is still insatiate. The Romans, by a strange singularity of nature, are the only people who invade, with equal ardour, the wealth and the poverty of nations. To rob, to ravage, and to murder, in their imposing language, are the arts of civil policy. When they have made the world a solitude, they call it peace.

XXXI. "Our children and relatives are dear to us all. It is an affection planted in our breast by the hand of nature. And yet those tender pledges are ravished from us to serve in distant lands. Are our wives, our sisters, and our daughters, safe from brutal lust and open violation? The insidious conqueror, under the mask of hospitality and friendship, brands them with dishonour. Our money is conveyed into their treasury, and our corn into their granaries. Our limbs and bodies are worn out in clearing woods, and draining marshes: and what have been our wages? Stripes and insult. The lot of the meanest slave, born in servitude, is preferable to ours: he is sold but once, and his master maintains him; but Britain every day invites new tyrants, and every day pampers their pride. In a private family the slave who is last bought in, provokes the mirth and ridicule of the whole domestic crew; and in this general servitude, to which Rome has reduced the world, the case is the same: we are treated at first as objects of derision, and then marked out for destruction.

"What better lot can we expect? We have no arable lands to cultivate for a master; no mines to dig for his avarice; no harbours to improve for his commerce. To what end should the conqueror spare us? Our virtue and undaunted spirit are crimes in the eyes of the conqueror, and will render us more obnoxious. Our remote situation, hitherto the retreat of freedom, and on that account the more suspected, will only serve to inflame the jealousy of our enemies. We must expect no mercy. Let us therefore dare like men. We all are summoned by the great call of nature; not only those who know the value of liberty, but even such as think life on any terms the dearest blessing. The Trinobantes,[1] who had only a woman to lead them on, were able to carry fire and sword through a whole colony. They stormed the camps of the enemy, and, if success had not intoxicated them, they had been, beyond all doubt, the deliverers of their country. And shall not we, unconquered, and undebased by slavery, a nation ever free, and struggling now, not to recover, but to ensure our liberties, shall we not go forth the champions of our country? Shall we not, by one generous effort, show

[1] The people of Essex.

the Romans, that we are the men whom Caledonia has reserved to be assertors of the public weal?

XXXII. "We know the manners of the Romans: and are we to imagine that their valour in the field is equal to their arrogance in time of peace? By our dissensions their glory rises; the vices of their enemies are the negative virtues of the Roman army; if that may be called an army, which is no better than a motley crew of various nations, held together by success, and ready to crumble away in the first reverse of fortune. That this will be their fate, no one can doubt, unless we suppose that the Gaul, the German, and (with shame I add) the Britons, a mercenary band, who hire their blood in a foreign service, will adhere from principle to a new master, whom they have lately served, and long detested. They are now enlisted by awe and terror: break their fetters, and the man who forgets to fear, will seek revenge.

"All that can inspire the human heart, every motive that can excite us to deeds of valour, is on our side. The Romans have no wives in the field to animate their drooping spirit; no parents to reproach their want of courage. They are not listed in the cause of their country: their country, if any they have, lies at a distance. They are a band of mercenaries, a wretched handful of devoted men, who tremble and look aghast as they roll their eyes around, and see on every side objects unknown before. The sky over their heads, the sea, the woods, all things conspire to fill them with doubt and terror. They come like victims delivered into our hands by the gods, to fall this day a sacrifice to freedom.

"In the ensuing battle be not deceived by false appearances; the glitter of gold and silver may dazzle the eye; but to us it is harmless, to the Romans no protection. In their own ranks we shall find a number of generous warriors ready to assist our cause. The Britons know that for our common liberties we draw the avenging sword. The Gauls will remember that they once were a free people; and the Germans, as the Usipians lately did, will desert their colours. The Romans have left nothing in their rear to oppose us in the pursuit; their forts are ungarrisoned; the veterans in their colonies droop with age; in their municipal towns, nothing but anarchy, despotic government, and disaffected subjects. In me behold your general; behold an army of freeborn men. Your enemy is before you, and, in his train, heavy tributes, drudgery in the mines, and all the horrors of slavery. Are those calamities to be entailed upon us? Or shall this day relieve us by a brave revenge? There is the field of battle, and let that determine. Let us seek the enemy, and, as we rush upon him, remember the glory delivered down to us by our ancestors; and let each man think that upon his sword depends the fate of all posterity."

XXXIII. This speech was received, according to the custom of Barbarians, with war songs, with savage howlings, and a wild uproar of military applause. Their battalions began to form a line of battle; the brave and warlike rushed forward to the front, and the field glittered with the blaze of arms. The Romans on their side burned with equal ardour. Agricola saw the impatient spirit of his men, but did not think proper to begin the engagement, till he confirmed their courage by the following speech: "It is now, my fellow-soldiers, the eighth year of our service in Britain. During that time, the genius and good auspices of the Roman empire, with your assistance and unwearied labour, have made the island our own. In all our expeditions, in every battle, the enemy has felt your valour, and by your toil and perseverance the very nature of the country has been conquered. I have been proud of my soldiers, and you have had no reason to blush for your general. We have carried the terror of our arms beyond the limits of any other soldiers, or any former general; we have penetrated to the extremity of the land. This was formerly the boast of vain-glory, the mere report of fame; it is now historical truth. We have gained possession sword in hand; we are encamped on the utmost limits of the island. Britain is discovered, and by the discovery conquered.

"In our long and laborious marches, when you were obliged to traverse moors, and fens, and rivers, and to climb steep and craggy mountains, it was still the cry of the bravest amongst you, When shall we be led to battle? When shall we see the enemy? Behold them now before you. They are hunted out of their dens and caverns; your wish is granted, and the field of glory lies open to your swords. One victory more makes this new world our own; but remember that a defeat involves us all in the last distress. If we consider the progress of our arms, to look back is glorious; the tract of country that lies behind us, the forests which you have explored, and the estuaries which you have passed, are monuments of eternal fame. But our fame can only last, while we press forward on the enemy. If we give ground, if we think of a retreat, we have the same difficulties to surmount again. The success, which is now our pride, will in that case be our worst misfortune. We are not sufficiently acquainted with the course of the country; the enemy knows the defiles and marshes, and will be supplied with provisions in abundance. We have not those advantages, but we have hands that can grasp the sword, and we have valour, that gives us everything. With me it has long been a settled principle, that the back of a general or his army is never safe. Which of you would not rather die with honour, than live in infamy? But life and honour are this day inseparable; they are fixed to one spot. Should fortune declare against us, we die on the utmost limits of the world; and to die where nature ends, cannot be deemed inglorious.

XXXIV. "If our present struggle were with nations wholly unknown; if we had to do with an enemy new to our swords, I should call to mind the example of other armies. At present what can I propose so bright and animating as your own exploits? I appeal to your own eyes: behold the men drawn up against you: are they not the same, who last year, under covert of the night, assaulted the ninth legion, and, upon the first shout of our army, fled before you? A band of dastards! who have subsisted hitherto, because of all the Britons they are the most expeditious runaways.

"In woods and forests the fierce and noble animals attack the huntsmen, and rush on certain destruction; but the timorous herd is soon dispersed, scared by the sound and clamour of the chase. In like manner, the brave and warlike Britons have long since perished by the sword. The refuse of the nation still remains. They have not stayed to make head against you; they are hunted down; they are caught in the toils. Benumbed with fear, they stand motionless on yonder spot, which you will render for ever memorable by a glorious victory. Here you may end your labours, and close a scene of fifty years by one great, one glorious day. Let your country see, and let the commonwealth bear witness, if the conquest of Britain has been a lingering work, if the seeds of rebellion have not been crushed, that we at least have done our duty."

XXXV. During this harangue, whilst Agricola was still addressing the men, a more than common ardour glowed on every countenance. As soon as the general ended, the field rung with shouts of applause. Impatient for the onset, the soldiers grasped their arms. Agricola restrained their violence, till he formed his order of battle. The auxiliary infantry, in number about eight thousand, occupied the centre; the wings consisted of three thousand horse. The legions were stationed in the rear, at the head of the intrenchments, as a body of reserve to support the ranks, if necessary, but otherwise to remain inactive, that a victory, obtained without the effusion of Roman blood, might be of higher value.

The Caledonians kept possession of the rising grounds, extending their ranks as wide as possible, to present a formidable show of battle. Their first line was ranged on the plain, the rest in a gradual ascent on the acclivity of the hill. The intermediate space between both armies was filled with the charioteers and cavalry of the Britons, rushing to and fro in wild career, and traversing the plain with noise and tumult. The enemy being greatly superior in number, there was reason to apprehend that the Romans might be attacked both in front and flank at the same time. To prevent that mischief, Agricola ordered his ranks to form a wider range. Some of the officers saw that the lines were weakened into length, and therefore advised that the legions should be brought forward into the field of action. But the general was not of a temper to be easily dissuaded from his purpose. Flushed with hope, and firm in the hour of danger, he immediately dismounted, and, dismissing his horse, took his stand at the head of the colours.

XXXVI. The battle began, and at first was maintained at a distance. The Britons neither wanted skill nor resolution. With their long swords, and targets[1] of small dimension, they had the address to elude the missive weapons of the Romans, and at the same time to discharge a thick volley of their own. To bring the conflict to a speedy decision, Agricola ordered three Batavian and two Tungrian cohorts to charge the enemy sword in hand. To this mode of attack those troops had been long accustomed, but to the Britons it was every way disadvantageous. Their small targets afforded no protection, and their unwieldy swords, not sharpened to a point, could do but little execution in a close engagement. The Batavians rushed to the attack with impetuous fury; they redoubled their blows, and with the bosses of their shields bruised the enemy in the face, and having overpowered all resistance on the plain, began to force their way up the ascent of the hill in regular order of battle. Incited by their example, the other cohorts advanced with a spirit of emulation, and cut their way with terrible slaughter. Eager in pursuit of victory, they pressed forward with determined fury, leaving behind them numbers wounded, but not slain, and others not so much as hurt.

[1] These targets, in Latin *cetræ*, were made of osiers, or boards covered over with leather.

The Roman cavalry, in the meantime, was forced to give ground. The Caledonians, in their armed chariots, rushed at full speed into the thick of the battle, where the infantry were engaged. Their first impression struck a general terror, but their career was soon checked by the inequalities of the ground, and the close-embodied ranks of the Romans. Nothing could less resemble an engagement of the cavalry. Pent up in narrow places, the Barbarians crowded upon each other, and were driven or dragged along by their own horses. A scene of confusion followed. Chariots without a guide, and horses without a rider, broke from the ranks in wild disorder, and flying every way, as fear and consternation urged, they overwhelmed their own files, and trampled down all who came in their way.

XXXVII. Meanwhile, the Britons who had hitherto kept their post on the hills, looking down with contempt on the scanty numbers of the Roman army, began to quit their station. Descending slowly, they hoped, by wheeling round the field of battle, to attack the victors in the rear. To counteract their design, Agricola ordered four squadrons of horse, which he had kept as a body of reserve, to advance to the charge. The Britons poured down with impetuosity, and retired with equal precipitation. At the same time, the cavalry, by the directions of the general, wheeled round from the wings, and fell with great slaughter on the rear of the enemy, who now perceived that their own stratagem was turned against themselves.

The field presented a dreadful spectacle of carnage and destruction. The Britons fled; the Romans pursued; they wounded, gashed, and mangled the runaways; they seized their prisoners, and, to be ready for others, butchered them on the spot. Despair and horror appeared in various shapes: in one part of the field the Caledonians, sword in hand, fled in crowds from a handful of Romans; in other places, without a weapon left, they faced every danger and rushed on certain death. Swords and bucklers, mangled limbs and dead bodies, covered the plain. The field was red with blood. The vanquished Britons had their moments of returning courage, and gave proofs of virtue and of brave despair. They fled to the woods, and, rallying their scattered numbers, surrounded such of the Romans as pursued with too much eagerness.

Agricola was everywhere present. He saw the danger, and, if he had not in the instant taken due precaution, the victorious army would have had reason to repent of too much confidence in success. The light-armed cohorts had orders to invest the woods. Where the thickets were too close for the horse to enter, the men dismounted to explore the passes, and where the woods gave an opening, the rest of the cavalry rushed in and scoured the country. The Britons, seeing that the pursuit was conducted in compact and regular order, dispersed a second time, not in collected bodies, but in consternation, flying in different ways to remote lurking-places, solicitous only for their personal safety, and no longer willing to wait for their fellow-soldiers. Night coming on, the Romans, weary of slaughter, desisted from the pursuit. Ten thousand of the Caledonians fell in this engagement: on the part of the Romans, the number of slain did not exceed three hundred and forty, among whom was Aulus Atticus, the prefect of a cohort. His own youthful ardour, and the spirit of a high-mettled horse, carried him with too much impetuosity into the thickest of the enemy's ranks.

XXXVIII. The Roman army, elated with success, and enriched with plunder, passed the night in exultation. The Britons, on the other hand, wandered about, uncertain which way to turn, helpless and disconsolate. The mingled cries of men and women filled the air with lamentations. Some assisted to carry off the wounded; others called for the assistance of such as escaped unhurt; numbers abandoned their habitations, or, in their frenzy, set them on fire. They fled to obscure retreats, and, in the moment of choice, deserted them; they held consultations, and having inflamed their hopes, changed their minds in despair; they beheld the pledges of tender affection, and burst into tears; they viewed them again, and grew fierce with resentment. It is a fact well authenticated, that some laid violent hands upon their wives and children, determined with savage compassion to end their misery.

The following day displayed to view the nature and importance of the victory. A deep and melancholy silence all around; the hills deserted; houses at a distance involved in smoke and fire, and not a mortal discovered by the scouts; the whole a vast and dreary solitude. Agricola was at length informed by those who were sent out to explore the country, that no trace of the enemy was anywhere to be seen, and no attempt made in any quarter to muster their forces. Upon this intelligence, as the summer was far advanced, and to continue the war, or extend its operations in that season of the year, was impracticable, he resolved to close the campaign, and march his army into the country of the Horestians. That people submitted to the conqueror, and delivered hostages for their fidelity. Orders were now issued to the commander of the fleet to make a coasting voyage round the island. For this expedition a sufficient equipment was made, and the terror of the Roman name had already gone before them. Agricola, in the meantime, led his army into winter quarters, proceeding at the head of the cavalry and infantry by slow marches, with intent that, by seeming to linger in the enemy's country, he might impress with terror a people who had but lately submitted to his arms. The fleet, after a prosperous voyage, arrived at the Trutulensian harbour, and sailing thence along the eastern coast, returned with glory to its former station.

XXXIX. The account of these transactions, sent to Rome by Agricola, was plain and simple, without any decoration of language to heighten the narrative. Domitian received it in the true spirit of his character, with a smile on his countenance, and malignity at his heart. The mock-parade of his own German triumph, in which the slaves, whom he had purchased, walked with dishevelled hair, in the dress and manner of captives taken in war, came fresh into his mind. He felt the reproach and ridicule which that frolic occasioned, and the transition was painful to a real victory, attended with a total overthrow of the enemy, and the applause of all ranks of men. He now began to fear that the name of a private citizen might overshadow the imperial title. That reflection planted thorns in his breast. The eloquence of the forum was in vain suppressed; in vain the talents of men and every liberal art were put under an absolute prohibition, if a subject was to rob the prince of all military glory. Superior excellence in every other kind might be endured; but renown in arms belonged to the emperor, as a branch of his prerogative.

By these and suchlike reflections that restless spirit was distracted. He retired to brood in private over his discontent. His solitude was known to be dangerous. To be alone and innocent was no part of his character. Weary of his retreat and his own wounded spirit, he at last resolved to nourish resentment in sullen silence, till the tide of popularity, which attended the general, should ebb away, and the affection of the army had time to cool. Agricola was still in Britain, and had the command of the army and the province.

XL. Domitian, in the meantime, caused a decree to pass

the senate, by which triumphal ornaments,[1] the honour of a statue crowned with laurel, and all other marks of distinction, usually substituted in the place of a real triumph, were granted to Agricola. The language of compliment was freely lavished on this occasion. The emperor had also the art to circulate a report, that the province of Syria, at that time vacant by the death of Atilius Rufus, an officer of consular rank, was intended for Agricola, in order to do him honour by an appointment always given to men of the highest eminence. It is added as a fact, at that time currently believed, that a commission was actually made out, and sent by a favourite freedman, who was much in the emperor's confidence, to be delivered to Agricola, in case the messenger found him still possessed of his authority in Britain. But the freedman, we are told, met him on his passage in the narrow straits,[2] and without so much as an interview returned to Rome. For the truth of this anecdote I do not pretend to vouch: it was imagined perhaps as a stroke of character, that marked the genius of Domitian. However that may be, Agricola resigned the command, and delivered to his successor[3] a quiet and well-ordered government.

Lest his arrival at Rome should draw together too great a concourse, he concealed his approach from his friends, and entered the city privately in the dead of night. With the same secrecy, and in the night also, he went as commanded to present himself to the emperor. Domitian received him with a cold salute, and, without uttering a word, left the conqueror of Britain to mix with the servile creatures of the court.

The fame of a great military character is always sure to give umbrage to the lazy and inactive. But to soften prejudices, Agricola resolved to shade the lustre of his name in the mild retreat of humble virtues. With this view, he resigned himself to the calm enjoyments of a domestic life. Plain in his apparel, easy of access, and never attended by more than one or two friends, he was remarkable for nothing but the simplicity of his appearance; insomuch that they, who knew no criterion of merit but external show and grandeur, as often as they saw Agricola, were still to seek for the great and illustrious character. His modesty was art, which a few only could understand.

1 A real triumph, after the downfall of the republic, was reserved for the emperor only. The title of IMPERATOR was assumed by the prince.

2 The straits of *Dover*.

3 Agricola resigned the command A.D. 85.

XLI. After his recall from Britain, he was frequently accused before Domitian, and as often acquitted, unheard, and without his knowledge. The ground of those clandestine proceedings was neither a crime against the state, nor even an injury done to any individual. His danger rose from a different source; from the heart of a prince who felt an inward antipathy to every virtue; from the real glory of the man, and from the praises bestowed upon him by those worst of enemies, the dealers in panegyric.

The fact was, in the distress of public affairs, which soon after followed, the name of Agricola could not be suffered to remain in obscurity. By the rashness or inactivity of the commanders-in-chief, the armies of the empire were lost in Mæsia, Dacia, Germany, and Pannonia. Every day brought an account of some new misfortune; forts besieged and taken; garrisons stormed, and whole cohorts with their commanding officers made prisoners of war. Amidst these disasters the struggle was not to secure the banks of a river,[1] nor to defend the frontier: the very possession of the provinces, and the winter quarters of the legions, were fiercely disputed. In times like those, when calamity followed calamity, and every successive year was marked by the defeat and slaughter of armies, the voice of the people called aloud for Agricola to be employed in the public service. The vigour of his conduct, his firmness in danger, and his known experience, were the general topics, in opposition to the cowardice and insufficiency of other commanders. By remonstrances of the same tendency, it is certain that the ears of Domitian were often wounded. Amongst his freedmen, those who had the interest of their master at heart made a fair representation, while others urged the same arguments, not with honest motives, but with an insidious design to exasperate the mind of a tyrant fatally bent on mischief. In this manner Agricola, by his own talents, and the treacherous arts of pernicious men, was every day in danger of rising to the precipice of glory.

XLII. The year was now at hand, in which Agricola was to have by lot the proconsulship of Asia or of Africa; but the death of Civica, who had been lately murdered in his government, gave at once a warning to Agricola, and a precedent to Domitian. At this point of time, the spies of the court thought proper to pay their visits to Agricola. The design of those pretended friends was to discover, whether the government of

[1] The Rhine and the Danube were, at this time, the boundaries that divided Germany from the Roman empire.

a province would be acceptable. They contented themselves, in their first approaches, with suggesting to him the value of tranquillity in a private station, and then obligingly undertook, by their interest at court, to obtain permission for him to decline the office. At length the mask fell off: by adding menaces to their insidious advice, they gained their point, and hurried him away to the presence of the emperor. Domitian knew the part he had to act; with a concerted countenance, and an air of distant pride, he heard Agricola's apology, and complied with his request, conscious of his own treachery, yet receiving thanks for it without a blush. The proconsular salary, which had been usually granted in like cases, was withheld upon this occasion; perhaps, in resentment because it was not solicited, or the better reason might be, that the prince might not seem to gain by compromise, what he had a right to command.

To hate whom we have injured is a propensity of the human mind: in Domitian it was a rooted principle. Prone by nature to sudden acts of rage, if at any time he had the policy to disguise his anger, it was only smothered, to break out with fiercer rage. And yet that implacable temper was disarmed by the moderation and wisdom of Agricola, who was not in that class of patriots who conceive that by a contumacious spirit they show their zeal for liberty, and think they gain immortal glory, when by rashness they have provoked their fate. By his example the man of heroic fortitude may be informed, that even in the worst of times, and under the most despotic prince, it is possible to be great and good with moderation. He may further learn, that a well-managed submission, supported by talents and industry, may rise as high in the public esteem, as many of those who have courted danger, and, without any real advantage to their country, died the victims of pride and vain ambition.

XLIII. The death of Agricola was felt by his family with the deepest sorrow, by his friends with tender concern, and even by foreigners, and such as had no knowledge of his person, with universal regret. During his illness, the common people, and that class of men who care little about public events, were constantly at his door, with anxiety making their inquiries. In the forum, and all circular meetings, he was the subject of conversation. When he breathed his last, no man was so hardened as to rejoice at the news. He died lamented, and not soon forgotten. What added to the public affliction, was a report that so valuable a life was ended by a dose of poison. No proof of the fact appearing, I leave the story to shift for itself. Thus much is certain; during his illness, instead of formal messages, according to the usual practice of courts, the freedmen most in favour, and the principal physicians of the emperor, were assiduous in their visits. Was this the solicitude of friendship, or were these men the spies of state?

On the day that closed his life, while he was yet in the agony of death, the quickest intelligence of every symptom was conveyed to Domitian by messengers in waiting for the purpose. That so much industry was exerted to hasten news, which the emperor did not wish to hear, no man believed. As soon as the event was known, Domitian put on an air of sorrow, and even affected to be touched with real regret. The object of his hatred was now no more, and joy was a passion which he could more easily disguise than the fears that distracted him. The will of the deceased gave him entire satisfaction; he was named joint heir with Agricola's excellent wife, and his most dutiful daughter, and this the tyrant considered as a voluntary mark of the testator's love and esteem. A mind like his, debauched and blinded by continued flattery, could not perceive, that by a good father none but an evil prince is ever called to a share in the succession.

XLIV. Agricola was born on the ides of June, in the third consulship of Caligula; he died on the tenth before the calends of September, during the consulship of Collega and Priscus, in the fifty-sixth year of his age. As to his person, about which in future times there may be some curiosity, he was of that make and stature which may be said to be graceful, not majestic. His countenance had not that commanding air which strikes with awe: a sweetness of expression was the prevailing character. You would have been easily convinced that he was a good man, and you would have been willing to believe him a great one.

Though he was snatched away in the vigour of life, yet if we consider the space his glory filled in the eyes of mankind, he may be said to have died full of years. Possessing all the best enjoyments, that spring from virtue, and from virtue only; adorned with every dignity, which either the consular rank or triumphal honours could bestow; what further advantage could he derive from fortune? Immoderate riches he never desired, content with an honourable independence. His wife and daughter left in a state of security, his honours blooming round him, his fame unblemished, his relations flourishing, and every tie of friendship preserved to the last, he may be considered as supremely happy, that he did not live to see the tempestuous times that soon after followed. It is indeed true, that to have reached the present auspicious era, and to have seen Trajan in possession of the imperial dignity, would have been the happy consummation of his wishes. To that effect we have often heard him, with a kind of prophetic spirit, express his sentiments; but to counterbalance his untimely end, it is at least some consolation, that he escaped that black and horrible period, in which Domitian no longer broke out in sudden fits and starts of cruelty, but, throwing off all restraint, proceeded in one continued course of unrelenting fury, as if determined to crush the commonwealth at a blow.

XLV. Agricola did not live to see the senate-house [1] invested by an armed force; the members of that august assembly surrounded by the prætorian bands; men of consular rank destroyed in one promiscuous carnage, and a number of illustrious women condemned to exile, or obliged to fly their country. Carus Metius, that detested informer, had as yet gained but a single victory. The sanguinary voice of Messalinus was heard in the Albanian citadel only; and even Massa Bebius [2] was at that time labouring under a prosecution. In a short time after, with our own hands we dragged Helvidius [3] to a dungeon; our eyes beheld the distress and melancholy separation of Mauricus and Rusticus; [4] we were stained with the innocent blood of Senecio.[5] Even Nero had the grace to turn away his eyes from the horrors of his reign. He commanded deeds of cruelty, but never was a spectator of the scene. Under Domitian, it was

[1] In a short time after the death of Agricola, the rage of Domitian broke out with collected violence, and like a tempest swept away numbers of both sexes, all distinguished by their virtues no less than by their illustrious rank.

[2] Bæbius Massa took up the trade of an informer, and rose to eminence in guilt; but, at the time of Agricola's death, he was under a prosecution for rapine and extortion in the province of Bætica in Spain.

[3] The Helvidius mentioned in this place by Tacitus, was the son of the great and good man so often celebrated by Tacitus. See his character, *Hist.* iv. 5.

[4] Mauricus and Arulenus Rusticus were brothers, united not only by the ties of natural affection, but by their manners and congenial virtues. They were cruelly separated in the sight of the senate, when Rusticus was hurried away to execution, and Mauricus ordered into banishment.

[5] The senate, amidst all these tragic issues, sat without voice or sentiment, a timid and speechless assembly; as Pliny has it, *Curia timida et elinguis.* They submitted, with passive obedience, to the tyrant's will; and therefore Tacitus says that their hands were imbrued in the blood of Senecio.

our wretched lot to behold the tyrant, and to be seen by him; while he kept a register of our sighs and groans. With that fiery visage,[1] of a dye so red, that the blush of guilt could never colour his cheek, he marked the pale languid countenance of the unhappy victims, who shuddered at his frown.

With you, Agricola, we may now congratulate: you are blessed, not only because your life was a career of glory, but because you were released, when it was happiness to die. From those who attended your last moments, it is well known that you met your fate with calm serenity; willing, as far as it depended on the last act of your life, that the prince should appear to be innocent. To your daughter and myself you left a load of affliction. We have lost a parent, and, in our distress, it is now an addition to our heartfelt sorrows, that we had it not in our power to watch the bed of sickness, to soothe the languor of declining nature, to gaze upon you with earnest affection, to see the expiring glance, and receive your last embrace. Your dying words would have been ever dear to us; your commands we should have treasured up, and graved them on our hearts. This sad comfort we have lost, and the wound, for that reason, pierces deeper. Divided from you by a long absence, we had lost you four years before. Every tender office, we are well convinced, thou best of parents, was duly performed by a most affectionate wife; but fewer tears bedewed your cold remains, and, in the parting moment, your eyes looked up for other objects, but they looked in vain, and closed for ever.

XLVI. If in another world there is a pious mansion for the blessed; if, as the wisest men have thought, the soul is not extinguished with the body; may you enjoy a state of eternal felicity! From that station behold your disconsolate family; exalt our minds from fond regret and unavailing grief to the contemplation of your virtues. Those we must not lament; it were impiety to sully them with a tear. To cherish their memory, to embalm them with our praises, and, if our frail condition will permit, to emulate your bright example, will be the truest mark of our respect, the best tribute your family can offer. Your wife will thus preserve the memory of the best of husbands, and thus your daughter will prove her filial piety. By dwelling constantly on your words and actions, they will have an illustrious character before their

[1] Domitian's complexion was of so deep a red, that nothing could add to his natural colour, and he was therefore said by Pliny to be a man of unblushing arrogance.

eyes, and, not content with the bare image of your mortal frame, they will have, what is more valuable, the form and features of your mind. I do not mean by this to censure the custom of preserving in brass or marble the shape and stature of eminent men; but busts and statues, like their originals, are frail and perishable. The soul is formed of finer elements, and its inward form is not to be expressed by the hand of an artist with unconscious matter: our manners and our morals may in some degree trace the resemblance. All of Agricola, that gained our love, and raised our admiration, still subsists, and will ever subsist, preserved in the minds of men, the register of ages, and the records of fame. Others, who figured on the stage of life, and were the worthies of a former day, will sink, for want of a faithful historian, into the common lot of oblivion, inglorious and unremembered; whereas Agricola, delineated with truth, and fairly consigned to posterity, will survive himself, and triumph over the injuries of time.

INDEX

THE END

Printed by BALLANTYNE, HANSON & Co.
Edinburgh & London

EVERYMAN.
I·WILL·GO·WITH
·THEE.
&·BE·THY·GVIDE
IN·THY·MOST·NEED
TO·GO·BY·THY·SIDE